THE MASSACRE OF ST. BARTHOLOMEW

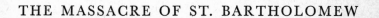

ARCHIVES INTERNATIONALES D'HISTOIRE DES IDEES

INTERNATIONAL ARCHIVES OF THE HISTORY OF IDEAS

75

ALFRED SOMAN

THE MASSACRE OF ST. BARTHOLOMEW

REAPPRAISALS AND DOCUMENTS

THE MASSACRE OF ST. BARTHOLOMEW
REAPPRAISALS AND DOCUMENTS

edited by

ALFRED SOMAN

MARTINUS NIJHOFF / THE HAGUE / 1974

ISBN 90 247 1652 7

TABLE OF CONTENTS

PREFACE

On 18 August 1572, Marguerite de Valois, sister of King Charles IX, was married in Paris to Henri de Navarre, "first prince of the blood" and a Protestant. This union, which was to cement the provisions of the Peace of St. Germain (1570) ending the third of the French wars of religion, was the occasion of an extraordinary influx of French Calvinists into the notoriously Catholic capital. Hundreds of Huguenots had journeyed to Paris to honor their titular leader and participate in the wedding celebrations. Tensions were already running high when the court made the fatal decision to take advantage of the situation and assassinate the admiral of France, Gaspard de Coligny, the recognized leader of the Huguenot armies which had helped plunge the country into ten years of intermittent civil war, and who now threatened to embroil the kingdom in a full-scale foreign war with Spain. On Friday the twenty-second, as he returned from the Louvre to his lodgings, Coligny paused in the street – some say to receive a letter, others to doff his hat to an acquaintance or to adjust his hose – and was fired on by a hired assassin hidden in a house known to belong to one of the ultra-Catholic Guise faction. The arquebus shot missed its mark and succeeded only in wounding the admiral in his hand and arm, whereupon he was carried by his followers to his bed. In the face of the outcry raised by the Huguenots who protested against this flagrant violation of solemn guarantees of personal safety, the king, the queen mother Catherine de Medici and their council disclaimed all responsibility for the deed, as if they were continuing their long-pursued policy of steering a middle course, playing Catholics and Protestants off against each other. Exactly when and how the crown had decided to abandon this policy, and what precisely happened in the frantic discussions in the royal council during the next thirty-six hours, are questions to which it seems we shall never have satisfactory answers. But sometime between

Friday noon and late Saturday evening, the court determined to rid itself once and for all of the menace of the admiral and a handful of obstreperous Huguenot aristocrats of his party. In the small hours of Sunday morning 24 August – a day dedicated to St. Bartholomew, the patron saint of the butchers, traditionally depicted holding his own flayed skin in his hand – armed bands broke into the houses of Coligny and other leading Protestant noblemen and murdered them. Before these assassinations had ended, the fanatically Catholic populace of Paris began to run riot. To what extent was this planned? Again, we shall probably never know for certain. The spark may have been struck by the municipal militia hastily assembled to give support to the assassins. In any case, given the dry tinder of religious hatred, the violence was soon out of control, as mobs sacked the houses of Huguenot merchants, artisans, lawyers and teachers, killing all suspected heretics on sight, mutilating and degrading the corpses, and looting their property. Estimates vary, but the number of victims of this massacre may well have been in the neighborhood of two thousand. It was several days before the royal government could restore order to the city, and as the news spread to the rest of France, the carnage was repeated in many of the provincial capitals: Lyons, Rouen, Orléans, Bourges and, after a lapse of some weeks, in Bordeaux and elsewhere.

This sequence of events – the abortive first attempt on Coligny's life, his assassination together with the murder of his principal adherents, and the mob violence (the "massacre" properly speaking) – have come collectively to be known as the Massacre of St. Bartholomew, a phrase which even to this day is capable of producing a thrill of horror and compassion among historians and the general public alike. The degree to which the Massacre has remained one of the most memorable events of European history is attested not only by its tenacious hold on the popular imagination but also by the steady accumulation of scholarly activity devoted to the circumstances of the Massacre, its causes and effects, and its persistence as one of the major historical "myths" throughout the course of subsequent centuries.

There is little to be added to the huge quantity of information which historians have by now succeeded in accumulating on the Massacre of St. Bartholomew; and the conclusions at which the best of them have arrived (if we discard the bias and religious prejudice which in past generations tended to dominate their works) have finally resulted in an agreement nearly unanimous among specialists on the subject. Whatever it is possible to discover about the event itself, about its antecedents, the circumstances which surrounded it, and its repercussions – these are already well known, and it is unlikely that additional documents will substantially modify what has now become the classic interpretation of the facts.[1]

There is much truth in these words of one distinguished historian, whose recent edition of the correspondence of the papal nuncio Salviati makes accessible an important heretofore unpublished body of documents bearing on the question. Still, scholars widening the horizons of their research find much to say about St. Bartholomew.

In 1972, on the occasion of its fourth centennial, a five-day colloquium was held in Paris, sponsored by the Société de l'histoire du protestantisme français; the proceedings have now appeared in a separate volume published by the Society.[2] In the United States, there were two conferences commemorating the event. On 22 April, the Folger Shakespeare Library in Washington, D.C., was host to a program organized by Dr. Philip Knachel, including a dramatization of excerpts from Christopher Marlowe's "The Massacre at Paris," and papers by Robert M. Kingdon, A. G. Dickens and Lewis W. Spitz. Professor Harry McSorley was chairman and general commentator. Two weeks later, on 5–6 May, the present editor presided over a series of meetings at The Newberry Library in Chicago, at which papers were offered by N. M. Sutherland, Natalie Z. Davis, Alain Dufour, John A. Tedeschi, Robert M. Kingdon, Donald R. Kelley and Elisabeth Labrousse. An informal panel of critics – H. G. Koenigsberger, Ralph E. Giesey, De Lamar Jensen, Theodore K. Rabb, Orest Ranum and Nancy L. Roelker – led the discussions which followed each of these contributions with their incisive remarks, some prepared and some impromptu.[3]

The volume now in hand brings together the principal papers read at the Folger and Newberry conferences, plus the texts of the two Italian documents described respectively by Dufour and Tedeschi.

---

[1] Pierre Hurtubise, O.M.I., "Comment Rome apprit la nouvelle du massacre de la Saint-Barthélemy: contribution à une histoire de l'information au XVIe siècle," *Archivum Historiae Pontificiae*, X (1972), 187–88.

[2] *Actes du colloque L'amiral de Coligny et son temps (Paris, 24–28 octobre 1972)* (Paris, 1974). See also in the *Revue d'histoire littéraire de la France*, LXXIII, the issue of Sept.–Oct. 1973, devoted to "La Saint-Barthélemy dans la littérature française," and containing the papers read at a symposium held at the Collège de France on 20 April 1972.

[3] In addition, Professor Philipp Fehl contributed to the Newberry meetings a stimulating, illustrated lecture on the Vasari frescoes in the Sala Regia of the Vatican, indicating some of the moral and technical problems confronted by an artist commissioned by an interested party to do a history painting of so controversial and bloodcurdling an event as the Massacre of St. Bartholomew. In his fresco of the Battle of Lepanto, Vasari had depicted the Turks dying with human dignity, but his Huguenots are portrayed with contempt, almost as devils. The text of this interesting paper unfortunately could not be included here. It will appear in a forthcoming issue of the *Gazette des Beaux Arts*.

Kingdon has welded his two separate offerings into a single unified essay. Since the authors in preparing their papers for publication took into account many of the points raised at the conferences, it would have been superfluous to include verbatim transcripts of the discussions themselves, especially as the substance of a number of other remarks is touched upon in the Introduction and Conclusion graciously contributed by Messrs. Koenigsberger and Rabb, each expanding upon his comments made in the course of the Newberry conference. In one case, however, portions of a letter by Pierre Hurtubise (who regretfully was unable to attend the Newberry meetings) seemed appropriate for inclusion as a final note to that part of Kingdon's essay which is concerned with the ramifications of St. Bartholomew in Rome. The contributions by Dufour, Labrousse and Hurtubise have been translated from the French by the editor.

As the reader will see, by a coincidence in itself reflective of trends of interest within the historical profession today, almost all the authors have chosen to concern themselves with reactions to the Massacre in France and abroad (Kingdon, Dickens, Spitz, Labrousse), with its implications for the development of political philosophy and politico-religious ideologies (Kingdon, Dufour), and with the problem of popular mentalities which underlay the actual unfolding of the event itself (Kelley, Davis). In his introduction to the text of Tomasso Sassetti's "Brieve Raccontamento," Tedeschi sheds additional light on the career of that curious literary figure, Giacomo Castelvetro. And the "Brieve Raccontamento," apart from its interest as one of the major unpublished contemporary accounts, reveals once again how many of the legends surrounding the Massacre reflect initial rumor, presupposition and misinformation – for example, the supposed poisoning of Jeanne d'Albret, the traditionally assumed ascendancy of Coligny over the impressionable young king Charles IX (convincingly refuted by Sutherland), and the early premeditation of the assassination of the admiral.[4] To cite but one of the many intriguing questions raised by these papers, the juxtaposition of the essays by Kelley and Labrousse provides a study in itself of the use and non-use of historical myths for

---

4 It is noteworthy that Gregory XIII, now generally remembered as one of the villains of the piece for his jubilant reception of the news of the Massacre, was described by the moderate and tolerant Montaigne eight years after the event in these terms: "d'une nature douce, peu se passionnant des affaires du monde, grand bastisseur; et en cela il lairra à Rome et ailleurs un singulier honneur à sa memoire; ... et à la vérité, a une vie et des moeurs auxquels il n'y a rien de fort extraordinere ny en l'une ny en l'autre part, toutefois inclinant beaucoup plus sur le bon" (*Journal de voyage en Italie*, 29 Dec. 1580 [ed. Pléiade], p. 1208).

polemical purposes under changing socio-political circumstances. It seems altogether fitting, therefore, that the proceedings of the Folger and Newberry conferences should appear in a series devoted to the history of ideas.

Two of the articles in this book have already appeared in print. The essay by Natalie Z. Davis was first published in *Past and Present* (No. 59 [May 1973] pp. 51–91) and is here reprinted with the kind permission of The Past and Present Society, which retains world copyright. Donald R. Kelley's article appeared in *The American Historical Review* (LXXVII [Dec. 1972], 1323–42) and is republished here by the author's permission. In both cases, minor changes in style have been made for the sake of the harmony of the volume as a whole.

The editor would like to take this opportunity to express his gratitude to the officers and staffs of the Newberry and Folger Shakespeare libraries for their coöperation, and to all the participants in the discussions, who made the two conferences the lively successes they were. And it is a pleasure to acknowledge the generosity of the National Endowment for the Humanities and of Mr. and Mrs. Manuel Weisbuch of Kings Point and New Lebanon, New York, for their financial assistance to the Folger and Newberry conferences respectively.

ALFRED SOMAN

INTRODUCTION

by

H. G. KOENIGSBERGER

"One of the great needs of the twentieth century is a scientific study of atrocity and of the moral issues involved." So wrote Herbert Butterfield, more than twenty years ago, with special reference to Catherine de Medici and the Massacre of St. Bartholomew.[1] Historians have only just begun systematically to fill this need; but the Massacre of St. Bartholomew at least has kept their interest, and this not only in the two symposia commemorating the quatercentenary of the event, of which this volume is the result. Such sustained interest is in itself curious. Our own century can compete with any other in the number and scale of massacres that men have inflicted on each other. Yet, at each new revolting instance, we tend to turn away with weary disgust, with a heart-sick feeling of *déjà vu*.

Is it that, in a world shrunk geographically, distance is no longer the safeguard it was, and that therefore we prefer to contemplate massacres safely removed in time? Perhaps. But this can hardly be the only reason; for not all the many bloodbaths of history have held our interest equally. St. Bartholomew still stands out. To nineteenth-century historians it was often still a matter of fighting old religious battles over again, as John Lingard and John Allen did, in order to apportion guilt or exonerate one's own side.[2] Even Lord Acton's sophisticated concern over the morality of his own church did not entirely escape from this tradition.[3] But the principal problem exercising the denominationally committed historians was solved in the nineteenth century: did Catherine de Medici and Charles IX plan the Massacre in advance, from the time of the Peace of St. Germain with the Huguenots, in 1570 – or even earlier, from the time of the con-

[1] H. Butterfield, *History and Human Relations* (London, 1951), p. 125.
[2] See Philip Hughes, "Lingard and St. Bartholomew," in C. H. Carter, ed., *From the Renaissance to the Counter-Reformation: Essays in Honor of Garrett Mattingly* (New York, 1965).
[3] See H. Butterfield, *Man on His Past* (Cambridge, 1955), chap. vi.

ference of Bayonne between Catherine and the duke of Alva, in 1565? No one any longer believes that there was such premeditation, even though Catherine herself claimed it, after the event, when it suited her to do so.

I think that perhaps the most important reason for the continued interest of historians in St. Bartholomew is the fascination of the psychological problems it presents. This fascination operates in a number of different areas. For western Europeans and Americans there is, in the first place, the disturbing fact that the Massacre was very close to home. Here was no Tamurlane butchering the inhabitants of Delhi, no Ivan the Terrible decimating the boyars, nor even a Cortés destroying the Aztecs of Tenochtitlan together with their bloodthirsty idols. This was Charles of France unleashing the Parisian mob to murder his own noble and respectable subjects. How could civilized Frenchmen have done such things to each other?

If this question represents a general puzzle of human behavior as evidenced by apparently civilized western Europeans, there is moreover the specific puzzle of the politics of the event. The Nazi extermination camps, the slaughter in Indonesia or Bangladesh, make one wonder about human nature; but they have left few problems or puzzles for the historian to solve. Even the crusade against the Albigensians and the Terror of the French Revolution are relatively transparent events. It is otherwise with the Massacre of St. Bartholomew; for, while its general outlines now seem clear enough, its details, and sometimes its most significant details, are far from being universally agreed on.

And finally, perhaps more important than any other reason for our continued interest in *la Saint-Barthélemy*, there are the almost classically dramatic qualities of the event and the spell cast over our imaginations by the personalities of the principal actors. For this was the *noces vermeilles*, the blood wedding, the marriage feast of Deidamia and Peirithous invaded by the centaurs. Here were the Huguenots, like the Nibelungs at King Etzel's court, breaking lances in games and jousts with players who would turn to kill them after nightfall. Here was Coligny, brave, wise, incorruptible – and doomed, with a doom that followed as inexorably on his hubris as the doom of Aeschylus' Agamemnon. But, above all, there was Catherine de Medici. How can the nameless bomber pilots of Guernica, the happily unremembered Pakistani generals in Bengal, how can the frighteningly ordinary Eichmanns, Himmlers and Berias, how even the vulgarly brutal

Hitlers and Stalins compare in fascination with the cultivated and aristocratic lady from Florence, the queen of France who could persuade her son the king to murder a member of his own council – to whom he had offered repeated guarantees of personal safety – and then take credit for the premeditation of a massacre that was, it seems, the result of a panic decision?

It is best, however, to start with the ordinary people, the thousands of Frenchmen who were killed and who did the killing. For the Huguenots, as Donald Kelley points out, there was no problem of understanding. They had suffered martyrdom for their belief in the true word of the gospel. Thus they had read their fate, even before St. Bartholomew, in the enormously popular martyrologies of Crespin and Foxe, of Rabe and Flaccius Illyricus. Their glories were no less than those of the early Christian martyrs; the iniquities of their executioners were as black as those of Nero and Diocletian. Yet, as the discussion which followed Kelley's paper emphasized,[4] while many Huguenots believed in the spiritual value of martyrdom and in the analogy of their own position with that of the early Christians, this analogy was not really very close, nor was the quest for martyrdom at all universal among the Huguenots. Unlike the early Christians, the Huguenots did not believe in the imminent end of the world. Martyrdom was, no doubt, splendid, but it was not the most important way of achieving their aims, of strengthening their numbers and their legal and political position in the nation, or perhaps even of converting the whole kingdom. For such ends, and of course for their survival as a religious group, they were willing to fight a succession of most unmartyrlike civil wars.

In consequence, what the Huguenots interpreted as an unprovoked massacre and a glorious martyrdom, appreared to their Catholic opponents as a "tumult" or a "disorder" raised by rebels. To a very considerable extent the Catholics saw themselves as the upholders of law and order against those who were willfully disturbing the peace. The government of Charles IX, aware of this feeling and anxious to exploit it, had consistently characterized Coligny as "giltie of traison,

---

[4] It will not always be possible to point specifically to the discussions following the papers, among other reasons because I was not present at the symposium in the Folger Shakespeare Library. I am, however, incorporating some of the more important points raised in the discussions in the Newberry Library in this Introduction.

distourber and breaker of peace, ennemy of repos, and tranquillitie of the commonwealth."[5]

But the psychology of massacre in the sixteenth century was a great deal more complex than the paradoxical but characteristic quest for law and order through manhunts and lynchings. Natalie Davis leaves us in no doubt as to the genuinely religious motivation of the massacres, both the St. Bartholomew Massacre and the many smaller, local ones of the period. There were different patterns to Protestant and Catholic religious riots. On the whole, the Protestants destroyed objects: images, crucifixes, even the consecrated host – all heathenish abominations offending the pure Word of God and likely to call down His wrath on those who permitted them. The Catholics would sometimes destroy Huguenot bibles, but mostly they went for persons, for the agents, the vessels and propagators of soul-destroying heresies and insults to their adored and long-proven saints. Often, no doubt, more mundane motives were mixed with religious emotions – class hatred, private revenge or sheer brutality. But time and again it was the religious element which predominated. "Religious riot," says Davis, "is likely to occur when it is believed that religious and/or political authorities are failing in their duties or need help in fulfilling them." In the Protestant riots and image breaking in the Netherlands in 1566, the rioters claimed (quite wrongly) that they were acting on the express authority of the count of Egmont and other great lords. So far from being primarily the result of class struggle, the religious riots of the sixteenth century were often motivated by the felt need of upholding the proper order of society when others were apparently breaking it down. Since it is notoriously difficult to accept opposing religious convictions as sincere, sixteenth-century explanations of the actions and beliefs of one's opponents are full of a kind of Marxist analysis which interpreted religious actions in terms of non-religious and often economic motivations. But this was not necessarily the truth, and certainly never the whole truth. The ritual aspect of many of the massacres, the very gruesomeness of some of the killings, show that more was involved than economic envy, class hatred and brutality, even if all these played their part. Uppermost in the killers' minds seems to have been the need to defend their most precious values against those who would tear them down. There was, as Davis points out, little correlation of the massacres with high food prices. Equally, they cannot be linked with any racial feelings. These were Frenchmen

[5] Cf. below, p. 195.

killing Frenchmen, respectable neighbors murdering respectable neighbors – a chilling thought, in view of the currently fashionable belief that the dehumanization of one's opponents and consequent atrocities always originate in racial or ethnic hatreds.

Davis concludes that the "rites of violence" of sixteenth-century France were less a matter of "deviants" than of the central values and traditions of French (or, indeed, European) society. This is an important conclusion and it has never before been documented so fully, nor stated so explicitly. But it is not sufficient in itself (nor do I imagine that Natalie Davis would think it was) to explain the phenomenon of the Massacre of Saint Bartholomew. There is a difference not only in scale but in kind between the habitual violence against the heterodox and even the small massacres of the period, and the slaughter of thousands, in Paris and the provinces, on 24 August 1572 and in the following weeks. The very fact that it did not occur in all cities and provinces where the Huguenots lived as a minority should warn us that we are here dealing with phenomena that depend not only on mass psychology but on the conscious and deliberate decisions of certain individuals. Contemporaries of the massacres understood this perfectly well; and when they speculated on the motives of Charles IX and his mother, of Guise and Coligny, they were not fooling themselves about the importance of these personages. These individuals were, to a varying degree, involved in the policy and decision making of the international relations of France. This fact has been recognized by historians for a long time; but the discussion which followed N. M. Sutherland's and Robert Kingdon's papers – in which divergent interpretations of the continuity of papal policy were aired – show that even in this relatively well-worked field the last word has not yet been said.

In the years following the Peace of Cateau-Cambrésis (1559), which put an end to the long series of Habsburg-Valois wars of the first half of the sixteenth century, the struggle between Calvinism and the Catholic Church was rapidly growing in intensity. I am doubtful whether, as Sutherland argues, it was this struggle which prevented an effective détente between France and Spain. It certainly did not make it easier; but Cateau-Cambrésis, for all its carefully arranged dynastic marriages, had done nothing to resolve the fundamental great-power rivalry between France and Spain. The succession problems of both England and Scotland were liable, at any moment, to involve the Continental powers and to upset the precarious equilibrium established by the treaty, and this quite regardless of the confessional issues involved. In Italy and the Mediterranean, where there were no such issues at all, the apparent Spanish predominance was just as precarious. France still had important friends, both in Italy and at the Porte, and the Turkish threat to Spain was becoming more formidable every year and was not even fully contained by the battle of Lepanto, ten months before the Massacre of St. Bartholomew. But for the Spanish empire it was always France itself, with its large compact territory, its rich natural resources and a population at least twice that of Spain, which remained the greatest potential threat, right into the seventeenth century.[6] Much more than has often been realized, the political preponderance of Spain in Europe between 1560 and 1630 depended on the unusual political and military weakness of France caused by her internal divisions. The governments of Madrid and Brussels were at least always sensitive to the potential threat of a united France. For all their detestation and fear of heresy, their attitude towards the French civil wars was always somewhat ambivalent, so much so, that in the 1580s Philip II actually made secret offers of support to Henri de Navarre.[7] It was inevitable that the religious problems and passions of the age should have become entangled with the great-power politics of the European monarchies and that, to the confusion of both contemporaries and of later historians, the political line-up would not necessarily follow tidily along confessional lines.

In the summer of 1572, the relations between France and Spain were rapidly moving towards crisis. The immediate reasons for this were the internal political developments in France and in the Netherlands. The role of the papacy, whatever it was – and there was some controversy about this, at the Newberry Library, following Kingdon's paper – was not, I think, crucial in the extraordinarily rapid movement of events to their climax on St. Bartholomew's eve. Sutherland has most admirably sketched the French side of these events. In those hot August days of 1572, time was running out in Paris for those who wanted to prevent Coligny from committing France to a war with Spain. But time was running out just as fast for the duke of Alva in Brussels. In April 1572, the Sea Beggars had captured Brill, and during

---

[6] This basic fact of Spanish foreign policy has recently been emphasized and documented from Spanish military expenditure by Geoffrey Parker, "Spain, Her Enemies and the Revolt of the Netherlands, 1559–1648," *Past and Present*, No. 49 (Nov. 1970), pp. 72–95.

[7] T. A. d'Aubigné, *Histoire universelle*, ed. A. de Ruble (10 vols.; Paris 1886–1909), VI, 286–88. Cf. also *Calendar of State Papers, Venetian*, VIII, 270.

the spring and summer, town after town in Holland and Zealand had fallen to the rebels. The governor-general had been unable to do anything about it. With hindsight, it is possible to argue that Alva made a great mistake in not marching north immediately. When he did finally turn north, it was too late and the Spaniards never reconquered Holland and Zealand. At the time, however, it seemed reasonable to Alva to suppose that the invasion which the prince of Orange was mounting in the South, and the actual capture of the fortress of Mons, near the French frontier, were much more dangerous than the exploits of the Sea Beggars. If a united France were to attack him now, the prospects for continued Spanish rule of the Netherlands would be bleak indeed.

For all that, it does not seem as if Alva attempted to intervene directly in the struggles going on in Paris for control of French foreign policy. There is, at least at present, no evidence that he masterminded the Massacre of St. Bartholomew in the way that, sixteen years later, Philip II and his ambassador, Bernardino de Mendoza, masterminded the "Day of the Barricades" in order to paralyze any possible French intervention against the Armada and the "Enterprise of England." Whatever contact the Catholic party in Charles IX's council had with the Spaniards in 1572 – and they almost certainly had some contact – the initiative remained with them.

This raises a problem which was discussed but not fully answered in Chicago. If, as is usually assumed, the king could not move without his council and the general support of the realm, and if Coligny's support of the intervention in the Netherlands was opposed by the rest of the council, why was it necessary to kill him? Guise had personal reasons for revenge, for he was convinced that Coligny had been implicated in the assassination of his father, François duc de Guise. But Catherine de Medici, while perfectly capable of revenge for personal reasons, did not usually allow such feelings to determine her policy. From her point of view, Coligny had always been a useful, even though distasteful and exasperating counterbalance to Guise. Why, in those fateful August days, could he not be simply overruled by an almost unanimous council?

From Dr. Sutherland's research it now appears virtually certain that we can no longer maintain the traditional view of Catherine fearing to lose her influence over her son to the charismatic personality of Coligny.[8] The admiral had been at court only since 6 June and his

[8] N. M. Sutherland, *The Massacre of St Bartholomew and the European Conflict 1559–1572* (London, 1973), *passim*.

access to the king was limited. Months before this date, Charles IX had half committed himself to Louis of Nassau and his brother, William of Orange, to help the cause of the "Beggars" in the Netherlands. Throughout, he had hoped to commit England to the same course, in return for a virtual partition of the Netherlands between France, England and the house of Orange. Coligny had been skeptical of this policy, and with good reason. Elizabeth played Charles along, was willing to give the "Beggars" some help, but quite determined not to break with Spain nor to see the French permanently established in Flanders. But when a small contingent of Huguenots marched into the Netherlands and was promptly annihilated by the duke of Alva's army (17 July 1572), Coligny seems to have swung round to the need for full-scale French intervention. In this way he seems to have hoped still to meet his own treaty obligations to Orange, to counteract the disastrous effect of Alva's victory on the position of the Huguenots in France, and perhaps to prevent a renewed civil war in France.

Catherine seems to have been equally anxious to avoid another civil war, but she was much more frightened than Coligny of open war with Spain. Nevertheless, it is not at all clear that it was Catherine who instigated the abortive attempt to assassinate Coligny on 22 August. It may equally have been the work of any of the admiral's personal enemies, the Guises, Anjou, Retz or even the duke of Savoy.[9] There is no doubt, however, that, following this attempt, Catherine and the court decided on the elimination of the heads of the Huguenot party, and that this decision resulted in the massacre of 24/25 August.

Catherine's volte face makes sense on two assumptions. The first is that the government was aware that it could not prevent the Huguenots from starting another civil war when, after the assassination attempt, they felt that the king could no longer protect them. To Catherine this danger seemed clear from the experience of the previous ten years, and it was emphasized by the threatening behavior of the Huguenots in Paris, following the wounding of Coligny. The second assumption is equally important and only apparently contradictory to the first. The king could not control the armed parties in France; but he did have the power of committing the kingdom to war with a foreign enemy, and he could do so single-handed and against the advice of his own council and of other important personages in the kingdom. Not only did he have this right in theory, in the opinion of the lawyers and as part of the royal prerogative, but he had it, quite

9 *Ibid.*, p. 312ff.

clearly, also in practice. Loyalty to the king in the matter of a war against the traditional enemy, Spain, was evidently so strong and so universal that Catherine and the Spanish party at court could not hope, or even dare, to oppose the king openly. If Coligny were to march to Orange's help – and there was every indication that he intended to do so, perhaps even during the very next week – Charles would find it both politically and emotionally difficult to disavow him and might even prefer to throw the whole weight of the kingdom behind the admiral. If he did this, he would have a full-scale war with Spain on his hands and, conceivably, a civil war with the extreme Catholics as well. If he did not, the Huguenots were likely to restart the civil war. If this argumentation is correct, it makes it clear why Catherine could not afford to await the outcome of either alternative. At all costs she must regain the initiative. There was only one way in which this could be done: by the total elimination of the Huguenot leadership. This, she seems to have hoped, would prevent both a war with Spain and a renewed civil war.[10]

If this analysis of Catherine's policy is correct – and it must remain conjectural because she did not confide her reasoning to paper – it would explain why she gave up her previous policy of balancing the parties against each other and of attempting to play down their mutual hostility, a policy which she had been pursuing sincerely and consistently. It also involved the apparently formidable task of turning Charles IX's mind round completely. How exactly Catherine did this, we shall probably never know. It looks as if she took a great chance.[11] But perhaps the risk was not so great as it now appears. Catherine, after all, knew her son and knew also that he was neither deaf to her political reasoning nor immune from the fears and hatreds which had infected so many of his subjects. Looked at in this way, the decision to initiate the Massacre looks entirely logical and not really a panic decision at all. When we realize how rapidly Catherine was able to make up her mind and how unemotionally she could, at a moment's notice, scuttle policies in which, for years, she had invested all her enormous energies,

[10] Very much the same considerations may have been in Catherine's mind for some time previously and could have led her to the planning of the assassination attempt on Coligny – a possibility which Dr. Sutherland's researches have made appear less likely than they used to be thought, but have not fully ruled out.

[11] In 1630, Marie de Medici found herself in the analogous situation of contending with a charismatic minister for the confidence of her son, Louis XIII, and with it the fateful decision of a French war against Spain. She lost, perhaps not least because she could not call on as clear a religious fear to overtop Richelieu's jingoistic reason of state as her cousin Catherine had been able to do in 1572.

we can no longer be surprised at the *sang froid* with which she happily produced quite contradictory justifications for her actions after the event. If Catherine's contemporaries thought of her as a disciple of Machiavelli, this was quite justified. Not, however, as they wrongly supposed, because she had for years been planning the event and had managed to deceive Coligny all that time; but for the precise opposite, and much more genuinely Machiavellian reason – that she had looked at politics steadily and unromantically in terms of pure power, and that she had known how to master *fortuna*.

If the extraordinary strength of the king's authority is understood, a number of other matters fall into place. Firstly, Coligny's policy of uniting France in a war with Spain makes good sense and, moreover, it was very nearly successful. Twenty-five years later, Henri IV pursued precisely this policy with great success. In the second place, it throws at least some light on a phenomenon which puzzled contemporaries and which has puzzled historians ever since. This was the ease with which the Huguenots allowed themselves to be slaughtered. It was so unexpected a pattern of behavior that the contemporary Italian author of the discourse presented in this volume by Alain Dufour was reduced to quoting the classical adage, that those whom the gods wish to destroy they first make mad. The Huguenot gentlemen who had come to Paris to attend Henri de Navarre's wedding to the daughter of Catherine de Medici, were not at all the natural martyrs they became in the Protestant martyrologies. They were tough, experienced soldiers. After Coligny was wounded in the first assassination attempt, they swaggered through the streets of Paris, breathing fire and revenge. From the history of earlier riots, such as the affair of the Cross of Gastine, we know how effectively even small companies of disciplined professional soldiers could deal with quite large mobs. A few hundred resolute men, encamped in and around the house where Coligny lay wounded, could have been a very tough proposition for the forces Guise had available on the first night of the Massacre. The only rational explanation for the Huguenots' complete failure to take even the most elementary military precautions seems to have been their complete trust in the king and their assessment of his absolute authority. For all the differences between the Huguenot leaders, in this trust and assessment they were all at one with Coligny. They were assuredly right about the latter, but could not have been more wrong about the former.

One of the unforeseen effects of the Reformation in the sixteenth century had been to involve "the common man" in politics to an extent hitherto unimagined. Those who considered themselves "the natural rulers" were not pleased with this development; but they did not find it easy to reverse it. A change in religion causes a change in the state, i.e., a revolution. So Catholic statesmen and political writers told each other and their aristocratic religious opponents over and over again. The Massacre of St. Bartholomew now demonstrated that the Counter Reformation, the defense of the established religion, could have a very similar and equally alarming effect. This seems to have come as a surprise to most people, and their reactions accordingly varied considerably.

Undoubtedly, the authority of the monarchy, the regard which people had for their prince, suffered a great deal. Not only did this happen where one would obviously expect it, among the French Huguenots. Kingdon shows convincingly that the monarchomach tradition of political thought, while partly a purely intellectual development of an older tradition, was also undoubtedly influenced by the political events of 1572 and the following years. But, as A. G. Dickens demonstrates, it also happened in England. The reason of state of Elizabeth I and of Burghley, the queen's long pursuit of a marriage with a member of the murderous house of Valois – these proved religiously and morally abhorrent to many of her subjects, and did much to tarnish the traditional mystique of kingship.

At the same time there was an opposite reaction, a growing abhorrence of religious strife in general and of popular violence in particular. Kingdon makes the important point that the Huguenot political writers were as anxious as everyone else to guard against mob rule. It was for this reason that they developed medieval resistance theory, the *ius resistendi*, into a constitutional theory of resistance to tyranny by the lower magistrates. For many Catholics, however, the reaction took the form of elevating the importance of political over religious issues. It was not perhaps immediately obvious that this would also mean support for the monarchy and, eventually, for royal absolutism. But in France, at least, the constitutional movement centering on the Estates General came to be compromised, first by its association with the Huguenots and, later and even more fatally, by its association with the ultra-Catholic, apparently anti-national, and certainly revolutionary movement of the *Ligue*. In the end it was, paradoxically, only a strong king who was held to be able to provide security against renewed massacres and civil wars. Even the Huguenots came to believe this, and this belief, as Elisabeth Labrousse shows in her contribution to this volume, is the key to the Huguenots' ultimate catastrophe in the reign of Louis XIV.

It is a pity that we do not have a paper on the effects of St. Bartholomew on the development of the *politique* party and the spread of reason of state in France. In the two centuries following 1572, these were, at least outside England and the Netherlands, perhaps even more important than the shock to royal authority. We do hear something about them, however. The Italians in France, as Dufour tells us, took a special, almost nationalistic pride in their loyalty to the French crown. Theirs was a curious mixture of "modern" reason of state and "medieval" loyalty to the person of the prince, regardless of their own national origins. The reaction of the Germans was more ambivalent. For them, as for the English, the shock of the Massacre was great; not least, perhaps, because they, again like the English, saw French refugees with their own eyes and heard at first hand their tales of horror. But, as Lewis Spitz tells us, for the German Protestant princes, just as for Elizabeth of England, reason of state arguments soon won out over religious and humanitarian outrage. If so, this may help to explain the subsequent tragedy of Germany in the Thirty Years' War.

The Massacre of Saint Bartholomew changed the immediate political situation in France. Of that there can be little doubt. Quite possibly it changed the political situation of western Europe. What the effects of a fully supported French invasion of the Netherlands would have been on the whole power-political situation of Spain and of the Counter Reformation must remain a matter for speculation. For the rest, the Massacre did not initiate anything new, either in action or in thought. But it did change the tempo of men's behavior and men's thinking. It accelerated them, as the narrow walls of a gorge accelerate the flow of a river, and it spread them in sharply divergent directions, as a prism spreads a ray of light. In these contrasting effects lies the perennial fascination of the events of August 1572.

PART I

ST. BARTHOLOMEW AND EUROPE

THE MASSACRE OF ST. BARTHOLOMEW
AND THE PROBLEM OF SPAIN*

by

N. M. SUTHERLAND

The meaning of the Massacre of St. Bartholomew has long exercised historians and bedeviled the history of sixteenth-century France. Why should it have been more significant than any other massacre, and what was it all about? It is important to understand, in the first place, that the "Massacre" comprised not one event, but three. The first of these was the abortive attack, in the streets of Paris, upon the admiral of France, Gaspard de Coligny, seigneur de Châtillon, on Friday morning 22 August 1572. The second was the further assault during the night of Saturday 23–24 August upon Coligny and his principal adherents – which was followed or accompanied by the massacre in the popular sense. This last was the only respect in which it might be called a religious outrage of Catholics against Protestants. It was not, therefore, primarily a religious incident, although Paris had long been fiercely Catholic and can hardly have forgotten the Protestants' siege of 1567.

In my book I have reached the conclusion – which is reasonably well-based, if not definitive – that the decision, apparently taken on the Saturday night, 23 August, to "eliminate" Coligny and the Protestant leaders, was a collective, pre-emptive act of war – civil war – on the part of the court, namely the royal family and some members of the council. This desperation reflected their great potential danger, on account of the furious Huguenot reaction to the assault upon the admiral the day before.

We are therefore back with the initial assault upon Coligny and the central problem of the Massacre: why did the admiral have to die, and why did he have to die then? There is no scholastically acceptable evidence to solve the mystery of the assault in its conspiratorial details.

* This paper derives from, though it is not a part of my book, *The Massacre of St. Bartholomew and the European Conflict 1559–1572* (London: Macmillan, 1973).

Apart from the satisfaction of curiosity, this is not very important, because the general answer emerges clearly enough: Coligny was an enemy of Spain, also of international Catholicism as an utterly ruthless, politico-religious movement which, in 1571–1572 at least, was more actively promoted from Rome than from Madrid. The reason why Coligny had to die just then, having contrived to evade or otherwise survive all previous attempts to dispatch him – and there had been many since 1562 – was because he had command of an impending invasion of the Netherlands. Indeed he actually had royal permission to depart in the week beginning 25 August, the day before the duke of Alva, Spanish governor of the Netherlands, left Brussels to march towards the French frontier to oppose a mixed force of French and Flemish exiles already occupying Mons. This permission clearly involved the king – who granted it – as distinct from the state of France, since his only support, in this respect, was that of the Huguenots themselves.

One way, therefore, of describing – describing, not explaining – the second and fortuitous stage of the Massacre episode would be the "elimination" of those who were about to invade Hainault in support of the revolt of the Netherlands, and therefore about to make war upon Spain. But although everyone involved – or who may have been involved, since the list varies slightly in different accounts – was opposed to foreign war, their opinions were too different, not to say disparate, to have acted together for this reason. The reason, as already stated, was a belief in their common danger at the hands of the enraged Huguenots. The more extreme were supporters of Spain and of political Catholicism in its aggressive, international sense; and the failure of the initial assault upon Coligny accommodated them by extending his liability to his principal followers. While this, in itself, was nothing new, upon that occasion the admiral alone had been singled out, possibly because of the perilous circumstances in crowded Paris. The more moderate opposed foreign war because they held the political circumstances to be inauspicious, and some went further, raising financial, military, and even patriotic objections. This disparity and confusion, exemplified in the circumstances of the Massacre, illustrates the predicament of the crown and the fragmentation of policy, which arose from the sectional divisions of the civil wars and lasted until 1598. Consequently, in relation to foreign affairs, one can never accurately refer to "France" as such, but only to particular French interests, which were conflicting and mutually exclusive.

Thus, whether one considers the Massacre as a domestic episode and turning point in the French civil wars, or as an international European incident – and it was both – the common element and central theme was Spain, and the admiral Coligny was the key figure. The Spanish and Catholic (both papal and French) pressures upon the internal affairs of France and the individuals concerned in them, in turn affected foreign relations and the fundamental, long-term Franco-Spanish rivalry, which was itself one aspect of the wider European struggle against the domination of Spain. Both internal and external affairs were immensely complicated after 1559 by the struggle for the survival of Protestantism – in different forms – hence the politico-religious conflict of the sixteenth century, of which the Massacre was symptomatic.

It is therefore necessary to examine more closely this "problem of Spain" and the several attitudes of those who desired or feared the war with Spain which, before 24 August, appeared inevitable, but which – *whatever else it may also have done* – the Massacre averted, with tragic consequences for all but the extremists involved in the "elimination" episode, for whom the renewal of civil war was not unwelcome.

After the division in 1555 of the empire of Charles V – Charles I of Spain – the traditional Franco-Habsburg rivalry, which had long found expression in the Italian wars, became the Franco-Spanish rivalry. Latterly these wars had also been pursued on the borders of the Netherlands, and in northern France, where Coligny, then *gouverneur* of Picardy, was captured at Saint-Quentin in 1557. It was during his imprisonment in Ghent that he became a Calvinist. After the treaty of Cateau-Cambrésis in 1559, the focus of political attention shifted from Italy to the Netherlands, whose troubled affairs rapidly began to affect Franco-Spanish relations – theoretically restored to amity by the treaty – on account of the growth of Calvinism, which, in Philip's explicit estimation, posed an alarming political threat to the stability of the Netherlands. Thus it was largely Calvinism in France (which before the death of Henri II the two monarchs had intended to extirpate) that frustrated the Franco-Spanish détente, primarily caused or permitted the interference of Spain in the internal affairs of France, and increasingly rendered those of the Netherlands the touchstone of Franco-Spanish relations. It was mainly to deflect Calvinist attentions from the Netherlands (where Coligny, for one, had distinguished relatives in count Horne and his brother Montigny) that Philip II persistently contested the inclusion of Calvinists – and not least of all the Châtillon brothers – in the council, was diversely instrumental in provoking civil war and, by adamantly opposing the treaties and edicts of pacification which terminated the first three civil wars, in thwarting the objectives of peace. But civil disturbance in France became less clearly advantageous to Philip II once the Netherlands were in combustion, and after the beginning of the assault by Alva (who arrived in August 1567), upon the nobility as a class – of which the execution of Egmont and Horne in June 1568 has long been regarded as symbolic. This assault upon the nobility necessarily connected the Netherlands' cause – no matter how different in domestic origin and ultimate aspiration – to that of the Huguenots, who were also threatened in their persons and property and, down through the ranks of society, suffered continual persecution from the agents of Rome and Madrid and other Catholics in France, in spite of the toleration clauses of the successive edicts of pacification which the crown was disastrously incapable of enforcing.

The nature and extent of the links between the cause of the Huguenots – whether that of the *noblesse* as a class, or the establishment of religious liberties – and the cause, or mingled causes of "rebels and heretics" as Philip II called them, in the Netherlands, is a very large subject. But their fusion, at least on the leadership level, is, for a start, sufficiently demonstrated by the formal treaty of mutual assistance concluded between William of Orange and the Huguenot leaders, Coligny and the prince de Condé, in August 1568, shortly after the execution of Egmont and Horne, among hundreds of others in the Netherlands, and immediately before the outbreak of the third civil war in France.[1] The timing of these events is significant. The third civil war began with an attempt by the cardinal of Lorraine – archpriest of Catholicism, dubbed by Sir Thomas Smith "the minister of mischief" – to "eliminate" certain Protestant leaders. Upon this occasion they all escaped, though Condé and d'Andelot (Coligny's brother) did not survive the war, and it was this same Catholic policy – papal, Spanish, and extreme political French Catholic – of "elimination" that was adopted and executed in Paris on 23 August 1572. Upon that dreadful occasion, however, others were forced to accede to the notorious long-term policy of the extremists, owing to the immediate danger of the court at the hands of the enraged Huguenots, following the assault upon the admiral.

---

[1] Groen van Prinsterer, *Archives ou correspondance inédites de la maison d'Orange-Nassau, série* I (8 vols.; Leiden, 1835–1896), III, 282–86.

In August 1568, Lorraine's abortive "elimination" coup averted an imminent Huguenot invasion of the Spanish Netherlands in support of the first attempt of William of Orange to raise rebellion; and the coup, together with the subsequent abrogation of the edict of pacification, resulted in the third civil war. The probability that further civil war – one way or another – was unavoidable, is a separate matter. When, four years later, in August 1572, the policy of "elimination" was at last successfully executed, it again averted an imminent invasion of the Netherlands, then intended to synchronize with William's second attempt to raise a general rebellion, and it precipitated the fourth civil war.

These two attempts to send help to the Netherlands may be related to the treaty of August 1568 between William of Orange and the Huguenots, which – though by no means the whole explanation – is sufficient to account for the idea that I have called "transference." This in fact meant slightly different things to different people, but in all cases involved some "French" – whether national or sectional – war in the Netherlands, preferably to avert or divert war in France. There was a fairly common conviction, based on past experience, that war, whether foreign or civil, could only temporarily be avoided. We have seen that war against Spain in the Netherlands had been one traditional expression of Franco-Habsburg rivalry. But after the treaty of Cateau-Cambrésis, and with the Calvinist reformation in France, such war had ceased to be either the policy of the king, or that of the French Catholic faction – this political cleavage having quickly followed the death of Henri II – since the Catholic faction leaders, so recently prominent in the Italian wars, forged stronger links with Spain than the dynastic alliance of the crown. But to their adversaries, the Huguenots, war in the Netherlands still remained a traditional concept, and was revived in the form of "transference" between the first and second civil wars. Indeed, the notion was explicitly embodied in the treaty between William of Orange and the Huguenots, which stipulated that if hostilities ceased in either country, they should be resumed in, or "transferred" to the other. Here is at least one reason why William and his brother, Louis of Nassau, both served in France in the third civil war. This in turn explains why the idea of "transference," this time back to the Netherlands, remained or became an important element among French attitudes to Spain during the two years between the treaty of Saint-Germain in August 1570 (at the end of the third civil war) and the Massacre in August 1572.

After 1570, however, the difference was that Charles IX, who developed an exploitable yearning for martial glory, was skillfully embroiled by those responsible for the Netherlands enterprise in this essentially sectional pursuit of "transference," though he did not, of course, see it that way, since he could neither conceive of fighting for Calvinism at home, nor for "rebels and heretics" abroad. This involvement of the king had at least two important results. By vastly increasing the attendant risk of open, general war with Spain, it implicated everyone who held some public policy or stake in the kingdom, and magnified the issue of "transference" into a national controversy which centered on proposals for an "enterprise of the Netherlands," as it was called. This was simultaneously strongly canvassed, deeply feared, and violently opposed by divers interests as it matured during 1571, and miscarried in 1572.

"Transference" or the enterprise of the Netherlands, was strongly canvassed by Louis of Nassau, who remained in France after the third civil war, and the Flemish exiles who clearly had the most to gain and little, if anything, to lose. If "transference" was also essentially a Huguenot policy, it is vitally important to understand that the party was deeply, albeit unequally, divided on the issue. It was some of the younger and perhaps more impetuous members, in particular Charles de Téligny (later Coligny's son-in-law), François de La Noue and Genlis, who combined with the Flemish to influence and enmesh the wayward king. Charles IX was then exceptionally exposed, since the court had been vacated by the leaders of both factions, which, if no longer engaged in fighting, could hardly be described as at peace. Coligny and others, including Nassau in the suite of Jeanne d'Albret, had opted for the relative security of La Rochelle; and Lorraine and the Guises were in disgrace.

The Netherlands enterprise was most deeply feared by Catherine de Medici and her moderate supporters, because the dread of war with Spain and the concomitant effort to maintain the amity of Cateau-Cambrésis was the lodestar of her political career. This alone makes continuous sense not necessarily of all she said, but of all she did. To her, war with Spain was the ultimate, because the most dangerous catastrophe, to be avoided at almost any cost – a conviction which was justified by future events and the near defeat of Henri IV in the 1590s.

The violent opposition to the Netherlands enterprise, however, did not come from Catherine, who could not afford to antagonize its supporters, but from all the ultramontane, pro-Spanish, extreme political

Catholics, led by the heir apparent and lieutenant-general, Henri duc d'Anjou, as their princely figurehead, and his mentor, the cardinal of Lorraine, whom Catherine had excluded from the council. Lorraine was not, however, ineffective from a distance. Besides, during these two years the court was mostly dispersed.

Here, therefore, are three distinct attitudes to the problem of Spain and the Netherlands, to which can be added no less than four others. Firstly there was the clear, personal attitude of Coligny, shared by a proportion of his followers, but not those who had been at court, since it took virtually no account of the king. There was also an apparently more conditional attitude on the part of Catherine, developed pragmatically in response to events and to the dilatory and ambivalent attitude of the king which cannot be clarified. Neither for Charles who had so recently received Spanish "help," nor for Catherine, who needed the Huguenots' support in other matters, was the Netherlands issue a straightforward one; nor were Charles and Catherine, in this respect, in agreement with each other. Finally, there was the more dispassionate view of a few serious councillors who propounded the absolute need of France for general peace, and emphasized her poverty and defenselessness.

The position of Coligny was different from that of either Charles or Catherine, and from that of Nassau and his own more extreme Huguenot supporters. It is true that Coligny was Spain's worst enemy among the French, and that he was bound by ties of treaty and kinship to the cause of the Netherlands, as the nobility conceived of it. Furthermore, he had always favored war in the Netherlands, and supported the idea of "transference"; but *not* unconditionally. In a petition of July 1569, during the third civil war, he had himself requested peace in France and proposed "transference." But he made it perfectly clear that it was a national war that he had in mind, categorically stating that the king should rather employ the two opposing armies together "pour ... le bien de vos affaires," which was in the Netherlands. But the national concept, then as always, was grotesquely unrealistic, since a principal consequence of civil strife was the disintegration of national policy.

After 1570, however, Coligny's personal conception of "transference" was as a sectional, Protestant war in and for the Netherlands, against Spain, with the full support and coöperation of England, separately and apart from the French crown, from which, in spite of the peace, he was still detached. This was a *simpliste* conception of the affairs of France, and still more of the disposition of Queen Elizabeth. In support of this, he favored the marriage, twice propounded in 1570 and 1571, of the Bourbon Henri de Navarre to Queen Elizabeth, as opposed to Henri's marriage to the king's sister, Marguerite de Valois. To be fair, however, it was not Coligny who pressed the idea of "transference" at all in 1571, when there were no hostilities in the Netherlands and he himself was preoccupied with the implementation of the Edict of Saint-Germain and personal and public problems of security. "Transference" with the "support" of the king would entail his own return to court, to which both he, and those who shared his opinions and feared for his person, were strongly opposed, since he could hardly be expected to trust either the motives or the efficacy of the king. Besides, Charles was not merely unstable; he was not a free agent; and even if his intentions were honorable, he could neither protect Coligny nor command any substantial – let alone national – support. We have already seen that he was in disagreement with Catherine de Medici; in some respects he was as strongly opposed as the Huguenots themselves by the Catholic extremists, and he had no money.

In the event – a story which cannot be retold here – by September 1571, in his absence at La Rochelle, and without his consent or approval, Coligny found himself and the party irretrievably committed by Nassau and his own belligerent extremists to *their* policy of "transference." This, albeit ill-defined, definitely involved invasion of the Netherlands in 1572 in what, to Coligny, was the worst possible combination of circumstances, namely without even the nominally assured support of England – upon which their preferred project of partition depended – and with only a personal and indeterminate commitment on the part of the king. Furthermore, there were grounds for believing that everything had been leaked to Spain. The ill-conceived, ill-planned and incompetently executed enterprise of the Netherlands, in its historic form, was not, therefore, despite the repetitions of historians, the policy of the admiral.

It was only then, after Coligny had been obliged, in his own estimation and that of his adherents, to brave the dire peril of the court, that he urged the king to declare war upon Spain. This was first reported in September 1571, but as he was only at court for five weeks and did not return again until the following June, his war policy primarily applies to the summer of 1572. Advocacy of war did not represent Coligny's conversion to Nassau's policy; it was rather a matter of tactics, a *pis aller* designed to bring the unhappy affair closer to his former conception of "transference" as a national undertaking. The obvious importance of doing so was to protect the Huguenots from the vacillations of the king, who might still be induced to abandon or turn against them, so long as he was publicly declaring his peaceful intentions; and thus deserted they would – after the entry of Nassau into the Netherlands in April 1572 – have been exposed to the awful vengeance of Alva. But Charles did not declare war upon Spain, and, although the dramatic denouement was unforeseeable, it would be difficult to argue that Coligny was wrong. So much for the traditional belief in the controlling influence of the admiral over the king.

Charles's attitude was much more elusive. He appears to have wanted war, some war, somewhere, in a romanticized way – perhaps as an alternative to hunting. By June 1572, when Coligny returned to court for the second time, Charles was deeply involved in the Netherlands enterprise, if not necessarily heavily committed. Nassau (whose assistance he had needed for the Bourbon marriage) had departed in April, followed in May by Genlis – from both of whom his vociferous disavowals failed to dissociate him. But the problem and paradox was that, unlike Coligny, he continued to recoil from a war with Spain. This was not *pure* perversity. Only in theory could Charles prosecute war upon his own authority despite the weighty opposition of Catherine, as well as that of the Catholic extremists – who might be expected to support Spain – and the entire council, in which the Huguenots had no influence.

Some of the council, in particular the duc de Nevers, the maréchal de Tavannes, and the *garde des sceaux* de Morvillier, were opposed to war for the patriotic reasons that France required peace, reconciliation and reform, and was in no position to sustain a war, which they envisaged as likely to be long. This indeed was the positive, constructive aspect of Catherine's policy. Coligny is said to have argued in June and July that Charles was already irreversibly committed, and that the choice was not between war or peace, but Spanish or civil war.

Apart from his crippling impotence in France, Charles was also prevaricating because he had not yet renounced the hope of an English declaration against Spain and her overt and sufficient support, for which he was striving with uncharacteristic application. Catherine, too, had long been and still was striving for English support, if not to facilitate the Netherlands enterprise, at least to protect France from Spain. English support would certainly have diminished the danger, and hence the opposition of all but pro-Spanish extremists. It was also the only thing which conceivably might, in this dreadful impasse, have brought Charles, Catherine and Coligny into a working agreement, which, if perceived, must have enjoined caution upon Philip II and Alva. But Queen Elizabeth was also exercised by the problem of Spain, whose attention and forces she wished to deflect from the shores of England. So her crucial reply to French entreaties was long and – since she intended to act but not to affirm – somewhat villainously delayed.

The reply was still anxiously awaited during the frenetic week of festivities which followed the marriage of Henri de Navarre and Marguerite de Valois on 18 August – the immediate reason for that unique, and uniquely dangerous assemblage in turbulent Paris. But, as Alva prepared to march south from Brussels, it was already the eleventh hour for the departure of Coligny to the support of his confederates in Mons, as well as the invasion of William of Orange. Coligny and his forces *must* go in a day or two, if they were ever to go at all. It was then, in that awful week of suspense, when his sole removal could still effect a dramatic alteration, that the assault upon Coligny occurred, followed by the "elimination" and the Massacre. Together these events frustrated the enterprise of the Netherlands, defeated the revolt as conceived in 1572, and averted war with Spain by deflecting the storm back into France, where the fourth civil war ensued.

REACTIONS TO THE ST. BARTHOLOMEW MASSACRES IN GENEVA AND ROME*

by

ROBERT M. KINGDON

The connections between high idealism and extreme violence which are such a sensational feature of the contemporary political scene can also be found in the past. One period in which they can be found in particularly striking forms is the age of the Reformation. This was a time which witnessed some of the greatest and most heroic accomplishments of the human spirit in the entire span of history. But it was also a time which witnessed some of the most appalling atrocities, made all the more appalling because they were committed in complete sincerity in order to advance the "true religion." Of the atrocities which disfigured the period of the Reformation, one of the most dramatic was the St. Bartholomew Massacre. This is a report on the two most extreme reactions to that event.

To make my report fully intelligible, however, I should first draw attention to one basic fact about the St. Bartholomew Massacre: it was actually a combination of two series of atrocities. This point deserves emphasis.[1] It has often been ignored by commentators yet it is very significant. Violence began with a series of political assassinations, almost all of which occurred during the early morning hours of 24 August. It then shifted to a succession of rather indiscriminate religious massacres by mobs of Catholic fanatics. This popular violence began in Paris but soon spread to other parts of France. In September and October about twelve cities witnessed massacres of Protestants by

* This article splices together two papers, one on Genevan reactions to the massacres, read at the Folger Library Conference, the other on Roman reactions, read at the Newberry Library Conference. In revising them for publication, I am indebted to many scholars who read or heard them in their original drafts. I am particularly grateful for the comments of Professor Derk Visser of Ursinus College on the Genevan paper, and of both Father Pierre Hurtubise of Saint Paul University in Ottawa and Professor A. Lynn Martin of the University of Adelaide on the Roman paper.

[1] It is one of the values of Janine Estèbe, *Tocsin pour un massacre: la saison des Saint-Barthélemy* (Paris, 1968), a popular but thoughtful study of the massacres, that this point is emphasized. I have followed her account for much of my general information on the massacres.

Catholic mobs that resembled those in Paris. These cities included some of the largest in the kingdom – Lyons, Rouen, Orléans. They were all cities which had had powerful Calvinist minorities living amidst a predominantly Catholic population. Some had even been controlled briefly in earlier years by Protestant city governments. In every case the massacre was the result of mob action, occasionally, as in Bordeaux, allegedly egged on by the preaching of a fanatic Catholic priest. In most cases governmental officials did little either to provoke or prevent the massacres.[2]

Now assassinations and massacres were not new to sixteenth-century Europe. They had become regrettably common in France, ever since the first war of religion had been touched off by a massacre of a Protestant congregation at Vassy in 1562, and ended with the assassination of a Catholic commander (François duc de Guise) in 1563. But violence so concentrated and on such a scale was unusual. And violence at this precise time was unexpected, given the truce just sealed by a royal marriage. News of these atrocities spread quickly all over Europe and provoked various reactions, some quite predictable, some rather unusual. It is upon these reactions that I have concentrated my research for several years. I believe they provide an unusually revealing index of sixteenth-century European society's fundamental ideas about the ways in which power should be used in human society. They are unusually revealing because the extent and unexpectedness of the massacres provoked unusually strong and spontaneous reactions.

The two most extreme reactions occurred in the city-states which served as international headquarters for the two versions of Christianity warring for the control of France. Rome, the headquarters of international Catholicism, was transported with delight. Geneva, the headquarters of international Calvinism, was plunged into despair. The best expressions of these two reactions took strikingly different forms. Thus Pope Gregory XIII, after attending several triumphal church services in celebration of the massacres, ordered the striking of a commemorative medal and instructed Giorgio Vasari to include graphic paintings of the massacres in a set of frescoes being prepared for the Sala Regia of the Vatican palace.[3] And thus Calvin's successor Theodore Beza, after presiding over a church service of prayer and supplication, turned to organizing the composition and publication

---

[2] Estèbe, chap. ix.
[3] Ludwig von Pastor, *The History of the Popes from the Close of the Middle Ages* (hereafter Pastor), XIX (London, 1930), 501–07.

of a barrage of pamphlets, denouncing the French government and urging Protestants to resist it with force. The reliance of these two ideological leaders on such different media is both significant and characteristic. The Catholic depended on the visual arts and turned to one of the greatest painters of the day. The Protestant depended on verbal communication and turned to the printing industry. This contrast should not be pressed too far, of course, since there were Catholic publications and Protestant woodcut pictures provoked by the massacres. But I think it contains an important kernel of truth.

I

To illustrate Genevan reactions to the massacres, I have analyzed one of the published treatises they provoked. This is a treatise which has interested me for several years and of which I have prepared a critical edition.[4] It is not one of the polemics printed immediately after the massacres, extolling Coligny as a martyr to his religion and attacking the king, the queen mother, and others responsible for the massacres as the blackest of villains. It is rather a work of political theory, published two years after the massacres, outlining a new political program for the Protestants and others who were radically dissatisfied with the royal government in France. It is one of a series of treatises, sometimes rather imprecisely labelled monarchomach, which is of some importance in the general development of political theory in the West. The title of this work is *Du droit des magistrats sur leurs sujets*, or *On the right of magistrates over their subjects*. It was printed anonymously, without any indication of author, publisher, or place of publication, purporting to be a reprint of a Lutheran political treatise drafted in Magdeburg back in 1550. I have identified ten separate printings of this treatise which appeared in French between 1574 and 1581. Many more printings of a Latin translation appeared in this period and beyond, well into the seventeenth century, sometimes published together with such other political classics of the period as Machiavelli's *Prince* and the *Vindiciae contra Tyrannos*.

Contemporaries suspected that the *Droit des magistrats* was written by Theodore Beza. Although he never published another work of political theory, he had been trained as a lawyer, had been extensively involved in Calvinist political intrigue, and had expressed ideas consonant with

---

[4] Théodore de Bèze, *Du droit des magistrats*, ed. Robert M. Kingdon ("Les classiques de la pensée politique," VII; Geneva, 1971), hereafter cited as Kingdon, *Bèze*.

those of the treatise in rudimentary form in some of his theological writings and in his published letters. That suspicion was proved decisively several decades ago, when scholars found entries in the registers of the Geneva city council, demonstrating that Beza applied as an author for permission to have the work printed in Geneva.[5] Permission was refused, however, at least twice. So the mystery of where the treatise was published remained. That mystery has been partially dispelled in recent years by an expert in sixteenth-century French type faces, Mlle E. Droz of Geneva. She has demonstrated that the first printing of the treatise appeared in Heidelberg, capital of the Palatinate of the Rhine, the most important Calvinist state in Germany. A second printing, deliberately designed to resemble the Heidelberg printing, was illegally published in Geneva. A third printing was published in La Rochelle, center for the most militant resistance to the Catholic government in the years immediately following the massacres.[6] Most of the remaining printings have still not been identified.

The basic argument of the *Droit des magistrats* is that there are times when constitutional resistance to legitimate government is justified, even necessary. This marks an important step forward in the development of political resistance theory in the West. For centuries it had been generally conceded that an illegitimate government, the government of an invader or of a usurper, could be resisted by any means at hand. For centuries it had also been conceded that resistance was possible even to a legitimate government if it had degenerated into a tyranny which was violating the basic purposes for which all government is created. Indeed there were medieval theorists who would even permit individuals to assassinate a legitimate ruler who had become a tyrant. What is new in the *Droit des magistrats*, and in certain other Calvinist political treatises published in the same decade, is that the power to resist a tyrant is located in certain specified political institutions. It is not granted to the community as a whole or to any individual member of the community. Rather it is limited to certain existing political institutions, with already-defined functions in the state. It is thus constitutional. The principal institution to which the *Droit des magistrats* grants a right of resistance is the Estates-General (or its equivalents in other countries – such as the English Parliament, the German Diet, the Spanish Cortes), the deliberative body made of

[5] Reprinted in Kingdon, *Bèze*, annexe 3.
[6] E. Droz, "Fausses adresses typographiques," *Bibliothèque d'Humanisme et Renaissance*, XXIII (1961), 380–86, 572–74; *L'imprimerie à La Rochelle*, vol. III: *La veuve Berton et Jean Portau, 1573–1589* (Geneva, 1960), pp. 42–43.

representatives of every influential class in the population of practically every state in Europe. These bodies were called regularly or irregularly by European governments, primarily to raise taxes but also for other purposes. Beza now insisted that the right to resist the central government was one of those vague other purposes.

Beza faced the obvious practical fact that in many circumstances an Estates-General would not be free to assemble or to act in resistance to a tyranny. In that case, he argued, the right to resist passes to the "inferior magistrates." These were the provincial governors, the elected municipal councils, and the other authorities who actually governed a country on the local level. In this latter form, Beza's argument was of particularly great use to French Huguenots. They did control a significant number of cities in France. A good number of provincial governors and other such authorities belonged to their party or sympathized with them.

In both forms, the theory is of considerable historical significance, particularly in the early modern period of European history. It could be used immediately by the Dutch, to justify the revolt of their Estates-General against the Spanish crown. It could be used a few decades later by the German Calvinist princes to justify their defiance of the imperial government. It could be used again by the Puritan Parliament in England to justify its revolts against the Stuart kings. In somewhat developed and modified forms it could be used in the eighteenth century by leaders of the American and French revolutions. All of these revolutions were constitutional, in that they assigned the power to resist the head of a government to a pre-existing institution or group of institutions which had a settled legal place in that government.

The theory, furthermore, seems to be new in the 1570s. While there are hints of it in a number of treatises and proclamations issued in the earlier course of the Reformation, both in Lutheran and Calvinist countries, it was never fully developed until after the St. Bartholomew massacres. Experts on this theory who know more about medieval thought than I do, also claim that there are no significant earlier precedents for it. There are, to be sure, analogies in the fifteenth-century conciliarists' arguments for resistance to the papacy led by ecumenical councils within the Church. But the analogies between ecclesiastical and temporal resistance do not seem to have been pressed.[7]

[7] Julian H. Franklin, tr. and ed., *Constitutionalism and Resistance in the Sixteenth Century: Three Treatises by Hotman, Beza and Mornay* (New York, 1969), pp. 11–15.

These reflections on the general development of resistance theory have led me quite far from the St. Bartholomew massacres. Perhaps they should. A number of recent experts on Calvinist resistance theory insist that it has very little to do with the massacres. They point to the fact that the important theoretical treatises, including the *Droit des magistrats*, never mention the massacres directly, indeed never say much about contemporary politics in any way. Instead these treatises construct a general theory of resistance, based on appeals to the timeless authorities which undergird most sixteenth-century thinking. These authorities include the Bible, to which Beza in fact appeals repeatedly in the course of his treatise. They include the Roman legal tradition, particularly as it was codified in the *Corpus Juris Civilis*. To this authority Beza appeals in many ways which have not been fully appreciated until quite recently,[8] partly because Beza's allusions to the law are often quite casual, covered by such vague formulae as "natural reason teaches us ...." These authorities include finally history, particularly political and constitutional history, beginning with examples drawn from ancient accounts of the Hebrews and Romans, moving on to a rather exotic and curious collection of examples drawn from medieval chroniclers' descriptions of medieval governments. Clearly Beza felt that the prescriptive power of time, as revealed in political traditions, significantly reinforces an argument based on revelation as recorded in the Bible and natural reason as recorded in law. Given this content to the *Droit des magistrats* and other treatises like it, several experts suggest that they are best studied as the logical fruition of a tradition in political thought, rather than as reactions to the pressure of political events.[9]

While I do see value in the approach to Calvinist resistance theory which places it in an intellectual tradition, I do not think it should exclude the approach which places this theory in a political context. It seems to me that political ideas often can and should be tied to political events before they can be fully understood. I would argue, furthermore, that this is particularly likely to be true of Beza's theory. For Beza was not a full-time thinker in an ivory tower. In addition to being a formidable theologian and Latinist, he was also an ecclesiastical

---

[8] A point emphasized by Ralph E. Giesey, "The Monarchomach Triumvirs: Hotman, Beza and Mornay," *Bibliothèque d'Humanisme et Renaissance*, XXXII (1970), 52–56.

[9] *Ibid.*, pp. 41–42. Cf. the detailed and persuasive application of this approach to another "monarchomach" treatise by Ralph E. Giesey and J. H. M. Salmon in the introduction to their critical edition and translation of François Hotman, *Francogallia* (Cambridge, 1972), esp. pp. 38–52.

statesman. He had been the founding Rector of the Academy of Geneva. He had succeeded Calvin in 1564 as Moderator of the Geneva Company of Pastors. He was in constant correspondence with theologians, ecclesiastical leaders, and leading political figures all over Europe. And he had been deeply involved in political intrigues, mostly in his native France, for more than a dozen years. In 1559, he had been consulted by young noblemen who were plotting to kidnap the king and dispose of his advisers. This abortive coup has come to be called the Conspiracy of Amboise, and it marks the first Protestant attempt to use violence to resolve the problems posed by persecution of the Reformation in France. In 1561, Beza had been invited to the royal court, at the suggestion of the great artistocrats who were assuming leadership of the Huguenot party. He was summoned in order to lead a delegation of Calvinist theologians in a public debate with the Catholic bishops of France, in hopes of working out a compromise that could head off further violence. When compromise failed and religious war began, Beza had joined the staff of the prince de Condé, supreme commander of the Protestant armies, serving him for a year as a speech-writer and negotiator. Since 1563, Beza had lived in Geneva and since 1564, had directed the international Calvinist movement from its headquarters. But he had not lost his interest in political intrigue, particularly in his native France. He had returned to France several times, for meetings of national synods of the French Reformed Church and for other purposes. And he had kept in close touch by correspondence with leaders of the Huguenot movement.[10] Clearly it would be really extraordinary if the St. Bartholomew massacres had not appealed to his taste for political activity.

In point of fact we can demonstrate that Beza was provoked to considerable activity by the massacres. This is revealed by his largely unpublished correspondence, records of the deliberations of Geneva's governing bodies, and a study of some of the pamphlets printed at the time. Beza's first reaction to the massacres was one of dismay and fear. In fact he came nearer to real despair in the first weeks after the grisly news reached Geneva than at any other time in his career. In letters to his good friend Henry Bullinger, leader of the Reformed church in Zurich, Beza says that he may never write another letter, that he thinks more of death than of life. He longs for the day so desired when the Lord will reunite him with the pious souls of his murdered friends. He claims to be so overwhelmed by mourning and tears that he can no

[10] On Beza's career, see Paul-F. Geisendorf, *Théodore de Bèze* (Geneva, 1949).

longer serve the church, that he can tolerate life itself only in the hope that it will soon end.[11] News of this sort must have come as a particularly severe blow to a man saturated in Calvinist theology – in the Calvinist conviction of the omnipotence of God, of the pervasiveness of divine Providence, of the ways in which God controls every event in this universe. These dreadful massacres may well have suggested to Beza the terrible possibility that God was not a Calvinist after all. This possibility did occur to at least one of the many Calvinist ministers who abandoned their faith and returned to Catholicism in the weeks following the massacres. He was Hugues Sureau du Rosier, and he published a lengthy explanation of his decision to switch, which turned out, incidentally, to be temporary. Sureau had been chafing under Calvinist discipline for several years, and thus had several reasons for abandoning the movement. But his sudden and overwhelming fear that the massacres revealed God's displeasure with the Calvinists seems to have been decisive.[12]

Beza, however, was made of stronger stuff than Sureau. And he was also soon pushed to action by the arrival in Geneva of hordes of refugees, fleeing for their lives from the cities in which massacres had occurred – above all from nearby Lyons – and pleading with him for support of every sort. Altogether there were several hundred refugees, including several dozen Calvinist pastors and a good number of noblemen. Faced with their overwhelming problems, Beza had no more time for reflection and despair.

The first formal step taken by Beza and the other ministers of Geneva was to wait upon the governing city Council. The ministers exhorted the Council to take courage, they assured it that the doctrine they announced was firm and certain, and they asked that a day be set aside for fasting and extraordinary prayers in order to protect the city from the wrath of God.[13] That request was granted, and the result was one of the first in a long series of public fasts proclaimed by the Geneva government in periods of crisis. In the nineteenth century the Genevan Fast became an annual event, celebrated in September, near to the anniversary of the day when news first arrived in the city of the St. Bartholomew massacres.[14] I have been in Geneva on this day several

---

[11] Qtd., *ibid.*, pp. 306–08.

[12] Robert M. Kingdon, *Geneva and the Consolidation of the French Protestant Movement, 1564–1572* (Geneva and Madison, 1967), p. 117.

[13] Henri Fazy, *La Saint-Barthélemy et Genève* ("Mémoires de l'Institut national genevois," XIV; Geneva, 1879), p. 7.

[14] Olivier Fatio, "Le jeûne genevois, réalité et mythe," *Bulletin de la Société d'histoire et d'archéologie de Genève*, XIV (1971), 391–435.

times, and I must say I find its current celebration a bit bizarre. For days ahead of time one finds advertisements in all the local newspapers in which the better local restaurants list the delicacies they propose to serve in the sumptuous meals which now mark the Genevan Fast.

The next steps taken by Beza are not as easy to follow. For he now plunged into secret and rather tortuous political intrigues. Records of them are extremely guarded, and it is sometimes difficult to find out just what they were about. But their cumulative purpose was clear. It was to revitalize and inspire the remnants of the French Calvinist movement to armed resistance against the entire French establishment.

For purposes of analysis, one can distinguish three parallel intrigues in which Beza was involved more or less directly.[15] A first was aimed at re-grouping French refugee noblemen for renewed war in France; a second was designed to influence the election of a new king of Poland; a third was mounted to protect the city of Geneva from attack by any neighboring Catholic power.

The first set of intrigues involved Beza in direct negotiations with the noblemen who had taken refuge in Geneva and in neighboring towns in Switzerland and in Germany. Beza was well fitted for intrigue of this sort. He was himself of a family of minor Burgundian noblemen, and thus acquainted from boyhood with the style of courtly life in France. And he had been involved in intrigues with French noblemen since 1559, as we have already noticed. It is not surprising, therefore, that one of the messengers who first brought word of the massacres to Geneva, a nobleman named Clermont d'Amboise, made a point of visiting Beza soon after his arrival in the city. The refugees' intrigues did not become serious, however, until it was clear that the massacres were over. At that point, the royal government, fearful of losing control of the population to the fanatic Catholics and the Guises, began to swing again to a mediating position. It proclaimed that it had sanctioned assassinations of Huguenot leaders only for political reasons, and was quite prepared to extend limited toleration again to Protestantism. This turn in policy made the refugee nobles hopeful that they could regain some of the power and status that they had lost in fleeing their homes. They decided to appeal to the French government for two things: (1) release of noble prisoners seized at the time of the massacres, several of whom had been converted to Catholicism, more or less forcibly; (2) return of their own landed property in France, or at least the right to sell that property so that their assets

[15] For what follows, see Kingdon, *Bèze*, p. xiv ff.

could be transferred abroad. These appeals were forwarded to the French ambassador in Switzerland. He was accredited to the Swiss cantons in order periodically to negotiate recruitment of the crack Swiss mercenary infantry which had become an important part of the French royal armies. The refugee nobles asked Beza to persuade his Swiss friends to put as much pressure as possible on the French ambassador to get him to secure a favorable response to their requests from the royal court. They even wanted Beza actually to go to the city in which the diet of the Swiss Confederation met, in order to put pressure directly on the ambassador. This suggestion was firmly vetoed by the Geneva city council, which noted that the Swiss Confederation was still half Catholic and met in a Catholic city, hardly a place Beza could prudently visit.

After several months of negotiations, the refugee noblemen received a cautiously favorable response from the royal ambassador. The king was disposed to allow the nobles to recover their property, provided they signed a loyalty oath. A text of a proposed oath was presented to them. It provided that each signatory swear loyalty to the king and affirm that he had left France only to escape mob violence. This proposal was examined in minute detail by a group of forty noblemen meeting in Beza's own house. They drafted a new substitute text of the oath they were to take. It provided that each signatory swear loyalty to the king and his laws and affirm that he had left France only to escape violence. The changes seem minor, but they in fact create significant loopholes. The revised oath left the refugees free to accuse the king, not just the mobs, of violence against their party. And it left them free to resist any action by the king not taken through normal channels of legislation. These changes are thus a tip-off that the refugees were plotting revenge. Beza in fact admitted as much, when he told an irritated city council that the meeting in his house had been kept secret so that the city government could not be accused of sanctioning a just war against the king of France.

The second set of intrigues involved Beza in indirect correspondence with the Calvinist nobles of Poland. The Polish Diet was at that time considering the election of a new king. One of the leading candidates was the duc d'Anjou, younger brother to King Charles IX of France. The French royal family wanted very badly to have Anjou win the Polish crown. A large French embassy, headed by a moderate Catholic bishop, had been sent to present the French case to the Polish Diet as forcefully and as eloquently as possible. An important faction of the

Diet was made up of Calvinists, however, and they wanted to make certain that any new king continued toleration of their form of religion. They had good reason to fear Anjou on this score, because of his deep involvement in the St. Bartholomew massacres. He had been an active member of the council which had decided on the assassinations of Coligny and his associates; he had personally supervised a group of assassins in the streets of Paris that bloody night; and at the time of his suit for the Polish crown he was commanding a royal army which was besieging the Protestant stronghold of La Rochelle, in desperate revolt against the royal government since the massacres. Not all of this was known immediately to the Poles. Beza quickly got in touch with them about Anjou's candidacy to their throne, arranging for several messages to be sent to Cracow by way of Zurich and Nuremberg. A special ambassador was even sent secretly from Geneva to Poland to reinforce personally these messages, but by the time he got there Anjou had already been elected king. I do not know the content of these messages, but it was reported in later years that Beza had worked vigorously to prevent Anjou's election. Very probably he sent to Poland as much damning information as he could collect about Anjou's role in persecuting French Protestants. While he did not succeed in preventing the election, he may well deserve some credit for some significant conditions attached to it. The French ambassador had to swear on Anjou's behalf that there would be no attempt to suppress Protestantism in Poland. He even had to swear that the French government would stop persecuting Protestants in France. This second promise went well beyond his instructions and angered the royal government back in Paris. Further negotiations between Polish ambassadors and the French government modified these agreements in some details before Anjou was finally permitted to ascend the Polish throne. While the French crown was extremely reluctant to grant much formal toleration, these negotiations did result in a perceptible relaxation of pressure on French Calvinists. For example the siege of La Rochelle was lifted.

The third set of intrigues did not involve Beza directly but they conditioned his ability to operate politically. They were between the government of Geneva and members of the Swiss Confederation and were aimed at establishing a multilateral alliance. The massacres had raised in the minds of the Genevan councilors the specter of an invasion by a neighboring Catholic power, most probably its traditional enemy, the duchy of Savoy. Geneva had been protected from earlier Savoyard attacks only by tight alliances with certain of the militarily powerful Swiss cantons, above all with Protestant Berne. The Genevans' immediate reaction on news of the St. Bartholomew massacres was that this probably was a first step in implementing a European-wide Catholic plot, involving the pope, Spain, France, and Savoy, and that Geneva would have to have even more extensive alliances for defense. They immediately set about tightening the Bernese alliance, and on Bernese advice approached the other Swiss cantons. But these Swiss cantons, as we have already noted, were allied to France. The Genevans had to take care, therefore, not to offend France in their negotiations for a Swiss alliance. And the French government was terribly irritated, as the ambassador to the Swiss kept pointing out, by the flood of inflammatory tracts pouring out of Geneva. In fact the ambassador specifically requested the suppression of a number of pamphlets printed in Geneva on grounds that they were insulting to the French royal family and subversive of the French government. Caught between ideology and self-interest, the Genevan government gave in, and agreed to censor all political tracts published in the city. Some of them were permitted to appear anonymously, without any indication of place of publication, but others were banned altogether. Beza and the other ministers complained bitterly about this infringement of a free press, but the government refused to budge.

It was at precisely this point, in July of 1573, nearly a year after the St. Bartholomew massacres, that Beza completed a draft of his *Droit des magistrats*. He presented it for publication permission to the Geneva city council and was turned down flatly. The councilors who read his draft found that it contained only the truth, but they still judged it scandalous and were afraid it would provoke troubles and emotions. They would not even permit its anonymous publication, since they feared that Beza's literary style was so distinctive that it would be easily recognized.[16] Beza then sent a Latin version of the treatise to his friends in Zurich. They liked it and explored the possibility of having it printed in some Swiss German city.[17] That also proved to be impossible, no doubt because of the importance to the Swiss of their alliance with France.

Meanwhile things were becoming hot in France. The Huguenots, having recovered from the shock of the St. Bartholomew massacres, were re-grouping, re-arming, and thinking again of war with the royal

---

16 *Ibid.*, annexe 3, p. 76.
17 *Ibid.*, annexe 4.

government. This would require, as it always did, a justification of their right to resist the royal government with armed force. Such a justification was needed to calm the consciences of loyal Frenchmen being asked to join a revolt against their king. It was also needed to reassure foreign governments, on whom the Huguenots depended for money and troops, that they were not opposed on principle to monarchical government.

Armed resistance had begun in France immediately upon spread of news of the massacres in 1572. It had begun in a few small cities which were already solidly controlled by Protestants and which were determined to protect their faith, above all in La Rochelle and Sancerre. La Rochelle was particularly defiant and refused to deal in any way with the royal government. It would not even accept an offer of a Protestant aristocrat as royal governor. When it was placed under siege by royal armies it grew yet more defiant. The Calvinist pastors in the city suggested the counter-massacre of Catholic prisoners in order to conserve scarce food supplies.[18] And the city hung on grimly until the royal armies finally abandoned the siege and withdrew.

Resistance next spread to the countryside, particularly in the South, above all in the province of Languedoc. There political assemblies of Protestant noblemen began meeting regularly to plot political and military action. More ominous still from the government's point of view, these assemblies occasionally were attended by Catholic noblemen who had become radically discontented with the royal government and persuaded of the futility of religious persecution. Even the royal governor for Languedoc, Henri de Montmorency-Damville, began negotiating with the Huguenot political assemblies and offering them his assistance.

Finally the prince de Condé, one of the two titular leaders of the Protestant party in France, escaped. Both he and his cousin, the king of Navarre, had been confined by the royal government on the night of the massacres. They had both agreed to convert to Catholicism under heavy pressure from the court in their first weeks of captivity, the king of Navarre rather lightheartedly, the prince de Condé with considerable reluctance. Once they escaped the court, both announced a return to Calvinist Protestantism and prepared to join the resistance. Condé escaped first and fled to Germany, to the still-German city of Strasbourg, then to Swiss Basel. There he got in touch with the

---

[18] According to contemporary Protestant reports qtd. by E. Droz, *L'imprimerie à La Rochelle*, vol. I: *Barthélemy Berton, 1563–1573* (Geneva, 1960), pp. 109–10.

French noblemen who had fled for refuge from the massacres to Germany and Switzerland. He approached the German princes and cities who had supported earlier Calvinist wars in France with troops and money. And he summoned Theodore Beza from Geneva to assist him in plotting a new war, just as Beza had assisted his father twelve years earlier.

Beza joined Condé in Strasbourg in August of 1574. He then went on to Heidelberg to negotiate with the Elector Palatine on the Huguenots' behalf. He evidently had brought with him a final draft of his *Droit des magistrats*. It was printed in that German Calvinist citadel by a French printer, a refugee from religious persecution in Lyons.[19] The printings in Geneva and in La Rochelle soon followed. Copies were forwarded to Languedoc and circulated among members of one of the political assemblies. A chronicler reports that while the representatives at that assembly were already inclined to fight, it was the reading of three pamphlets circulated among them which inspired them to make the final and fateful decision for war. One of these pamphlets was the *Droit des magistrats*. Thus it played a direct role in provoking the religious war which began in 1574, providing, of course, that the chronicler was accurate in his report. Even if he was not, however, there were other ways in which Beza's political ideas could have reached the delegates to the Languedoc political assemblies. We know that Beza and the other ministers in Geneva, both the local ministers and the refugees from France, were in touch with the political assemblies after November 1573.[20]

Taken all together, these intrigues explain better than ever before the form which Calvinist militancy took in the 1570s, particularly as it is expressed in such theoretical treatises as the *Droit des magistrats*. At least so it seems to me. They certainly explain many of the details of these publications. The *Droit des magistrats* was published anonymously and away from Geneva to avoid compromising that state in its continuing search for defensive alliances. It was published in 1574, because that was an opportune time to re-start religious war in France. The Polish negotiations had forced the royal government to back away from systematic persecution, and had given the Huguenots time to become re-grouped and revitalized. In addition, King Charles IX died in May of 1574, and Anjou had to return from Poland to succeed him as Henri III. This led to a period of transition and weakness in

[19] See above, p. 28.
[20] Kingdon, *Bèze*, pp. xxxv–xxxvi.

royal government and created an ideal opportunity for the Huguenots to attack. The treatise was first published in Heidelberg, because that was an important center of foreign diplomacy in support of a new Huguenot war effort, and was soon published in La Rochelle, because that was an important center of Huguenot resistance within France.

But these circumstances explain more than the details of this particular publication. They also explain the central argument of this and all the other Calvinist resistance treatises published in this decade, the argument for constitutional resistance to a legitimate government. Remember that the St. Bartholomew massacres consisted of two separate series of atrocities. They consisted of assassinations ordered by the royal government, and massacres carried out by fanatic mobs. Together they must have made it perfectly clear to Beza and the other Calvinist leaders in France that if the movement was to survive it would have to resist pressure from two fronts. On the one hand it had to resist frontally the legitimate royal government. Huguenots could no longer argue, as they had for more than a dozen years, that when they went to war they were not resisting the king himself but only such wicked advisers of the crown as the Guises. In 1572 the king had made it very clear that he took credit for personally ordering Coligny's death. But in turning to resistance against the government, the Huguenots could not claim to act in the name of all the people. They did not dare suggest that any group within the population was free to resist its government. That could easily open the gates for mobs, and mobs had slaughtered Huguenots. They thus limited the right of resistance to representative bodies like the Estates-General of the Netherlands and the political assembly licensed by the governor of Languedoc, or to inferior magistrates like the municipal government of La Rochelle and a prince of the blood royal like Condé. All of these authorities, but only such authorities, could resist a legitimate government which had become a tyranny. Armed with these convictions, the Huguenots continued to fight for toleration until they finally won a limited measure of it in France at the end of the century, with the Edict of Nantes. Armed with similar convictions, Calvinists in other countries also went to war for their beliefs, with consequences of considerable importance for the development of modern Europe.

II

The resulting wars of religion would not have been as ferocious as they did in fact become if a militancy parallel to that of the Calvinists had not been rising on the other side. This brings us to Roman reactions to the St. Bartholomew massacres. To illustrate these reactions, I have explored developments in papal diplomacy. I cannot connect them as directly to the massacres as the Huguenot treatises. But I believe there are connections which are significant. The St. Bartholomew massacres occurred, we should remember, at the beginning of the long thirteen-year pontificate of an exceptionally able and energetic man, Ugo Boncampagni, Gregory XIII. They occurred when his pontificate was still in its formative early months, before his policies and practices had had a chance to take definitive shape. Those policies and practices could thus have been influenced significantly by the massacres.

For purposes of analysis, I would like to distinguish two developments in papal diplomacy during this pontificate. One was a development in policy, the other a development in institutions. In policy, it seems to me that the papacy committed itself to greater militancy, to the use of really extreme tactics in meeting the Protestant menace. In the institutional arena, it seems to me that the papacy committed itself to greater professionalism, to the more systematic development of cadres of diplomats dedicated to careers of negotiating with foreign powers.

Looking first at policy developments, we discover that Gregory XIII announced his main policies at his very first consistory, on 30 May 1572. He committed himself to three primary objectives: (1) strengthening of the Holy League against the Turks; (2) resolute opposition to all forms of Protestantism; (3) full reception of the decrees of the Council of Trent.[21] It has been argued that of these three the campaign against the Turks took precedence.[22] A persuasive case can be made for this argument. At the time of the accession of Gregory, the wave of exultation provoked by the smashing victory a few months earlier over a Turkish fleet at Lepanto still had not spent itself. The pope's maneuvers in the first half of his pontificate to assist Spain in the Netherlands, in France, and in Britain, can be viewed as attempts to free Spain from distraction so that it could again assume leadership of a crusade. His maneuvers in the second half of his pontificate with the northern powers in Europe, can be viewed as attempts to persuade a new king of Poland to take leadership of the crusade now abandoned

---

[21] Pastor, XIX, 65. Also see Liisi Karttunen, *Grégoire XIII comme politicien et souverain*, in *Annales Academiae Scientiarum Fennicae*, ser. B. II, 2 (Helsinki, 1911), p. 1.
[22] By Karttunen.

by Spain. It may seem anachronistic to find a late-sixteenth-century pope still campaigning for a crusade, but no one who has studied papal diplomatic records of the period can doubt Rome's continuing commitment to war against the infidel.

Gregory never lost sight of his other objectives, however, and it is these which were significantly affected by the St. Bartholomew massacres. In particular the objective of opposing Protestantism won a higher priority and assumed a different shape after 24 August 1572. These changes can be followed in a number of ways. They can be demonstrated most convincingly by examining the instructions sent by the papal secretariat of state to its agents in France.

For evidence of papal policy before the massacres, I consulted the instructions prepared for Salviati, extraordinary nuncio to France late in 1571.[23] This was some months before the death of Pope Pius V, the predecessor of Gregory XIII. Salviati was instructed in the first place and in most detail to urge the French crown to join Spain, Venice, and the papacy in the Holy League against the Turks. He was to recall the glorious history of the French crown in supporting crusades and he was to try to shame the French from participation in lowly border skirmishes with other Catholic powers. Salviati was not limited to pleading for crusade, however. He was also instructed to complain about a number of developments within France, most of which followed from the peace treaty of St. Germain in 1570. He was to complain about mistreatment of Catholics in many specified parts of the kingdom. He was to complain about power given to Huguenots over Catholics in many areas, and in particular about the power being assumed at the royal court by Admiral Coligny. He was to reject French pleas for papal approval of the projected marriage alliance between the heretic Henri de Navarre and Marguerite de Valois. But he was not asked to seek persecution or suppression of the Huguenots. Their continuing existence is assumed in these instructions. The papacy sought only to deny them any power in the French government. This meant, to be sure, some moderation of Pius V's policy. He had earlier urged resolute military action against the Huguenots.[24]

[23] Archivio Segreto Vaticano (hereafter ASV), Pio 131, fols. 2–6, summarized in Pastor, XVIII (London, 1929), 138–39. This draft contains complaints about Protestant mistreatment of Catholics, added to the instructions proper, not noted by Pastor. The principal documents of Salviati's nunciature have recently been edited by Pierre Hurtubise (the 2d vol. in collaboration with Robert Toupin): *Correspondance du nonce en France Antonio Maria Salviati, 1572–1578* ("Acta Nuntiaturae Galliace," XII–XIII; Rome and Paris, 1974).

[24] Ch. Hirschauer, *La politique de St. Pie V en France (1566–1572)* ("Bibliothèque des Écoles françaises d'Athènes et de Rome," CXX; Paris, 1922), esp. chap. ii.

For evidence of papal policy after the massacres, I have examined the final instructions prepared for the legate Orsini in November of 1572.[25] Cardinal Orsini's mission had been organized well before the massacres, and in fact he received the cross and final commission for his trip in the same consistory at which news of the Massacre was reported.[26] Orsini was again sent to gain French support for the Holy League against the Turks, support which would require coöperation with the Spanish. He was to suggest a marriage alliance between the two royal houses to ensure this coöperation, specifically a marriage of Henri d'Anjou to one of the infantas of Spain. This part of his instructions continues to implement the policy line worked out in earlier years. But the rest of his instructions in this version are strikingly different. There is good reason to believe that they were added to the original instructions, after the papal curia had had time to collect some information on the massacres. These additions call for persecution of the bloodiest and most thorough sort, designed to eliminate all traces of Protestantism in France.[27] Orsini was to urge the French crown to use full military force to wipe out such pockets of Huguenot resistance as La Rochelle. He was to remind the king of a promise to the papal nuncio in Paris made shortly after the massacres that "in a few days there will not be one Huguenot in all his realm." He was to ask the king to require all bishops to return to their dioceses to supervise the abjuration and integration back into the Catholic Church of the thousands of Protestants who had abandoned their faith in the great shock which followed first news of the massacres. It was regarded as particularly important that bishops be on hand to prevent Protestants from returning "to [their] vomit at least in secret." The legate was to urge the creation of an inquisition within every diocese in France, on the Italian rather than the Spanish model. He was finally to urge formal reception and publication of the decrees of the Council of Trent as the ideal way to make definitive the suppression of Protestantism in France. In these final suggestions, we see an interesting merging of the second and third of Gregory XIII's general policy objectives.[28]

Not all of these suggestions are new. Earlier popes, for example, had recommended extension of the Inquisition in France. But it seems to

---

[25] ASV, Segreteria di Stato, Francia (hereafter S. S. Francia) 283, fols. 123–25.
[26] Como to Salviati, 8 Sept. 1572, ibid., fol. 52.
[27] Cf. the contribution to this volume by Alain Dufour.
[28] A point emphasized by Victor Martin, Le gallicanisme et la réforme catholique (Paris, 1919), pp. 109–12.

me that taken together they are more concerted and more extreme. They represent a new peak of militancy in the Counter-Reformation papacy. They reflect a heightened conviction in Rome that violence is an effective way to handle Protestant opposition, that war, massacre, and assassination are justifiable tools for advancing Christian truth. There are a number of reasons for this flare-up of militancy. A full decade of religious war in France, marked by a good deal of sacrilege, brutality and murder perpetrated by Protestants, had clearly angered and frustrated and alarmed the papacy. Additional experience with militant Protestant opposition in other countries had intensified these feelings. But it was the St. Bartholomew massacres that triggered this frighteningly savage reaction in Rome. Apparently the massacres persuaded the members of the Roman curia that God was truly on their side and that violence works. There is little evidence that anyone in Rome thought violence might be counter-productive. However it must be noted that curial animosity was directed mostly to the heretic leaders and to those who had seduced others. Ample provisions were made for reintegrating the seduced rank-and-file Christians into the Church of Rome.[29] Faculties were immediately granted to all the bishops in France to absolve heretics who were clearly aware of their errors and fully penitent.[30] In these provisions we see an example of the striking pastoral concern which also fills much of the diplomatic correspondence of Gregory XIII's pontificate.

Part of the savage excitement in Rome stemmed from a natural belief that the French government had fully committed itself to the eradication of heresy by force. It gradually became clear to Rome, however, that the French crown had made no such commitment. This must have first been suggested by the detailed and perceptive reports of the papal nuncio in France, Antonio Maria Salviati, who was clearly of the opinion that both the court-ordered assassinations which touched off the massacres and the court's post-massacre policy were motivated not by religious zeal but by complex intrigues among courtiers and other political considerations.[31] It must have become unmistakably clear when the Orsini mission failed completely. To

[29] This view is expressed very concisely in instructions to the cardinal-legate St. Sixtus for his negotiations with Henri III in 1574 (ASV, Misc., Armadio II, 130, fol. 129). He is instructed to tell Henri III to treat Huguenots like this: "Castigarli senza remissione, massime li capi, et quelli che seducono gli altri, perdonando sola a la plebe sedutta et mostreranno vero pentimento."
[30] The correspondence between Como and Salviati in the fall of 1572 (ASV, S. S. Francia 5 and 283) refers to these faculties several times.
[31] In ASV, S. S. Francia 5, fol. 133ff.

begin with, the French government refused for months to give Orsini permission even to enter the country. When he was finally permitted to visit the court, he found the king and queen mother completely inflexible. In his lengthy report back to Rome,[32] he indicates that he followed his instructions in formulating his proposals. Negotiations centered on the papal suggestions for a Franco-Spanish marriage alliance to prepare the way for a crusade against the Turks, but the proposals for eradicating Protestantism in France were also discussed. Orsini was rebuffed at every single point, sometimes in ways which seem derisive. His plea that all Huguenots be eliminated from the kingdom, for example, was referred to Damville, the governor of Languedoc and *politique* spokesman. But Damville had been in touch with the Huguenots for some time and was soon to join forces with them against the crown.

Frustration at this point did not lead Gregory XIII's curia to abandon militancy, however. The pope's own celebrated obstinacy and optimism may help to explain this. Instructions to later nuncios to France make it clear that whenever the French crown was considering a choice between peace and internal religious war, the official representative of the papacy was to urge war. Paragraphs containing this recommendation, in almost identical words, are to be found in the instructions prepared for Castelli in 1581,[33] and Ragazzoni in 1583.[34] Furthermore militancy can be observed in other areas of papal diplomacy. Thus the nuncios in Spain and France, along with papal diplomats in other areas, worked closely with English Catholics in plotting against the government of Elizabeth I, and Rome provided money and troops for an unsuccessful invasion of Ireland. Gregory XIII even indicated that he would approve the assassination of Elizabeth I, in response to an English query relayed to him through the nuncio in Spain.[35] Similarly the papal diplomats in Germany helped organize the army which successfully drove Gebhard Truchsess von Waldburg from the archbishopric of Cologne, when he had tried to turn Protestant and make of that archdiocese a hereditary principality.

---

[32] *Ibid.*, fols. 289–95 (7 Dec. 1572).

[33] Robert Toupin, ed., *Correspondance du nonce en France Giovanni Battista Castelli (1581–1583)* ("Acta Nuntiaturae Gallicae," VII; Rome and Paris, 1967), pp. 97–98.

[34] Pierre Blet, ed., *Girolamo Ragazzoni, évêque de Bergame, nonce en France: correspondance de sa nonciature (1583–1586)* ("Acta Nuntiaturae Gallicae," II; Rome and Paris, 1962), p. 137.

[35] Arnold Oskar Meyer, *England and the Catholic Church under Queen Elizabeth* (London, 1967; reprinting of a 1914 ed.), pp. 269–72.

Turning now to institutional changes, we discover that Gregory XIII endorsed professionalism in his very first appointments following his election as pope. He chose as his domestic secretary, with full power to receive and sign all diplomatic correspondence, Ptolomeo Gallio, the cardinal of Como. In doing this he broke with a powerful custom of appointing a cardinal-nephew to this key position. He turned instead to a thorough professional, with extensive experience in handling diplomacy for the papal curia. Gallio had worked intensively in the papal secretariat under Pius IV and had come to be the chief assistant of Carlo Borromeo, the cardinal-nephew who had general charge of all diplomacy in that pontificate. Toward the end of that reign, in fact, when Borromeo moved to Milan in order to begin directing personally the affairs of his diocese, Gallio seems to have taken over real direction of diplomacy. It was apparently on Borromeo's recommendation that Gregory XIII appointed Como to this key position.[36]

Once he had picked the man who was to serve in effect as his secretary of state, Gregory then began selecting the nuncios, who would serve as resident ambassadors to the major Catholic governments of Europe. He proceeded somewhat more slowly in this, avoiding the wholesale turnover one sees in the diplomatic appointments of certain popes of the century. Within a few months he had selected new nuncios for the most important posts in the papal service – Spain and France. The choice of nuncio for France was particularly shrewd. Antonio Maria Salviati was personally related to the queen mother Catherine de Medici. They were second cousins. His uncle, Bernardo Salviati, had earlier been close to Catherine, had even served as her personal chaplain. Antonio Maria, furthermore, already knew France well, having served as papal agent to the French court on several earlier occasions. In addition he was non-resident bishop of St. Papoul, a diocese in southern France which had been passed on from one member of the Salviati family to another.[37]

At this point the St. Bartholomew massacres intervene. Several months later, in 1573, the papacy began a major reorganization of its entire diplomatic apparatus. To understand this change we should

<hr>

[36] P. O. von Törne, *Ptolémée Gallio, cardinal de Côme: étude sur la cour de Rome, sur la secrétairerie pontificale, et sur la politique des papes au XVIe siècle* (Helsingfors and Paris, 1907), chaps. ii, iv; Pastor, XIX, 29.

[37] On the Salviati family relationships, see *Grosses vollständiges Universal-Lexicon aller Wissenschaften und Künste*, XXXIII (1742), cols. 1252, 1253, 1257, 1258. I am indebted to Father Hurtubise for further information on Antonio Maria. On his diplomatic career, see also Henri Biaudet, *Les nonciatures apostoliques permanentes jusqu'en 1648*, in *Annales Academiae Scientiarum Fennicae*, ser. B. II, 1 (Helsinki, 1910), p. 284 (hereafter Biaudet).

first take a look at the shape of that apparatus before the accession of
Gregory XIII. The modern papal diplomatic service, built around a
network of permanent resident embassies (known as nunciatures) is a
creation of the late fifteenth and early sixteenth centuries. First steps
toward it had been taken by a number of activist popes, notably
Alexander VI and Julius II, and it had been decisively expanded and
organized by the first two Medici popes, Leo X and Clement VII.[38]
Then there had been a pause in its development, as the great popes of
the Catholic Reformation busied themselves with the direction and
implementation of the work of the Council of Trent. Now Gregory
XIII was to expand and develop this service further, bringing it close
to its most highly developed form.

Gregory XIII began by shifting appointments at four of his nine
nunciatures.[39] He had, of course, already shifted his nuncios to Spain
and France. In some cases he simply switched an appointee of his
predecessor, Pius V, from one post to another. But in every position he
made a change. Further general changes occurred in 1577–1578, in
1580–1581, and in 1583–1584. Clearly the papacy was moving to a
system of frequent reassignments of ambassadors, probably modeled on
the Venetian system. This system had the advantage of training
diplomats who could take a broad view of the papacy's international
policies, rather than becoming narrowly specialized in its dealings with
only one nation.

Gregory XIII had already established a regular salary schedule for
all of the nuncios, graded according to the importance and expense of
their missions, but completely independent of the individual nuncio's
social position and other financial resources.[40] Until this pontificate
most nuncios had had to support themselves from family funds, from
the income of benefices they had accumulated, or from ecclesiastical
income assigned to them in the country to which they were accredited.
Now most nuncios received a precise and regular salary, based on
their work, not upon their needs. At the top of this diplomatic service
were the legates, ambassadors sent to a government for an important
special mission, like Orsini's to France in 1572. A legate had to be a
cardinal. He was paid 500 *scudi d'oro* a month. Next in rank came the
nuncios, ambassadors accredited to Catholic powers with whom the
papacy maintained permanent diplomatic relations. The two most

[38] Garrett Mattingly, *Renaissance Diplomacy* (London, 1955), pp. 154–55.
[39] Most of what follows is derived from Biaudet, p. 27 ff.
[40] Tabulated, *ibid.*, p. 78.

important nunciatures were those of Spain and France, and those
nuncios accordingly received the highest salaries, 300 *scudi* a month.
The nuncio to Spain's salary came from funds he gathered as a papal
collector in that kingdom. Then came other nunciatures which were
labeled first class, as were those of Spain and France. These first-class
nunciatures of the second rank were located in Poland, Venice, the
German Empire, and southern Germany. Each nuncio in these posts
received 200 *scudi* a month. The remaining second-class nunciatures
were located in Savoy, Florence, Graz (Austria), Cologne, and Switzerland. Each nuncio in these posts received 100 *scudi* a month, ex-
cepting the nuncio to Florence who received only fifty. A nuncio in
Portugal received a first-class salary derived from income as papal
collector. A nuncio in Naples received a percentage cut of income as
papal collector. Almost all of these nuncios were bishops. Most of
them were assigned small bishoprics in Italy. This would seem to be in
flagrant violation of the Tridentine requirement of residence of all
bishops, and is rather ironic in view of the fact that many of these
nuncios demanded repeatedly that bishops in the countries to which
they were accredited be required to reside in their dioceses. But the
papacy felt that prestige required use of men of episcopal rank. The
modern dodge of appointing a man bishop of a non-functioning diocese
in partibus infidelium was not as yet regularly used. At the lower ranks in
Gregory XIII's diplomatic service came a number of agents sent for
temporary negotiations of a less important or delicate sort than those
handled by legates. They were called extraordinary nuncios, inter-
nuncios, or apostolic delegates. At the lowest level came the secretaries
and cipher clerks who had to accompany every diplomat.

Taken all together these changes made of papal diplomatic service a
real professional career. Regular lines of advancement became clear.
A man could thus ascend in this diplomatic service from secretary, to
extraordinary nuncio, to nuncio, to cardinal legate. Antonio Maria
Salviati took just this route to power in the Church, and so did many
others. Some rose by this route all the way to the top, to election as pope.
That, in fact, is a route still open to leaders of the Catholic Church.

In addition, there was a significant extension in the geographic
coverage of the papal diplomatic service during the pontificate of
Gregory XIII. At his accession there were nine nunciatures. When he
died there were thirteen, an increase of almost 50%. Furthermore,
diplomatic relations of a more informal sort were opened with distant
governments which had heretofore had very little contact with Rome.

Thus Antonio Possevino was sent by Gregory XIII not only to Poland, but also to Protestant Sweden and Orthodox Muscovy.

Now to return to the St. Bartholomew massacres. Were there any connections between them and the growth of professionalism in the papal diplomatic service? I suspect there were, but they are not obvious. There are other possible explanations of this growth of professionalism. One explanation can be found in the background of the pope. Gregory XIII was a skilled lawyer. He had been a successful professor of law at Bologna before entering the service of the papacy, and he had worked for the Church as a lawyer, for example in drafting texts of some of the final decrees of the Council of Trent, and as a diplomat. One would expect from a pope of this background more interest in matters of organization than from popes trained in theology, such as his predecessor, Pius V, and his successor, Sixtus V. And changes toward professionalism in the papal service do begin before the massacres. Another explanation of this growth can be found in the papal campaign for a crusade against the Turks. Wholesale reassignments of nuncios follow both the withdrawal of Venice from the Holy League against the Turks in 1573, and the withdrawal of Spain in 1579.

But I think a full explanation requires attention to the perceptible rise in papal militancy which followed the St. Bartholomew massacres. This is best suggested by the rapid expansion of papal diplomacy in Germany, where the number of nunciatures was increased by Gregory XIII from one to four, accounting for most of the total increase in the papal diplomatic service during this pontificate. It seems quite clear that this German expansion was not merely a result of a commitment of the pope to professionalism, since there was no evident professional reason for concentrating expansion in one country. Nor can this expansion be explained as part of a move to meet the Turkish threat, since that threat was still felt primarily in the Mediterranean. Clearly the pressing problem faced by the Catholic Church in Germany remained the threat posed by Protestantism, for example in Cologne whose prince-archbishop, Gebhard Truchsess von Waldburg, attempted to convert his state to a Protestant secular principality during these years. The successful campaign of papal nuncios to organize a German army to depose Waldburg and substitute a committed Catholic in his place, is a prime example of the kind of assignment given to papal diplomats in Germany.

How could a policy of militancy have led the papacy to see a need for professionalism in diplomacy? To start with, such a policy required really reliable political information as its essential starting point. I believe the St. Bartholomew massacres gave the papacy dramatic new evidence that it could obtain reliable information only through its own professional diplomats. I am led to this conclusion by comparing the various reports Rome received of the massacres and their meaning. Clearly the papacy would have been misled, indeed it was somewhat misled at first, by the reports of the French in Rome. The reports of the French royal ambassadors to the papal court prove to be vague and tendentious and contradictory. They contain deliberate misstatements and were intended to deceive. The stories circulated in Rome by the cardinal of Lorraine and other prominent French ecclesiastics were extravagant and self-serving. They were also quite unreliable. In striking contrast stand the reports of the papal nuncio, Salviati. They are remarkably frequent, detailed, and perceptive, and include shrewd predictions of the future development of French royal policy. Reports of this type were elicited from Salviati by Como, who constantly badgered the nuncio for more information. For example Como scolded Salviati sharply for his failure to send Rome precise advance information on the plot to assassinate Coligny and the other Huguenot leaders, reminding the nuncio that he had been given a cipher to pass on information of just this kind.[41] The more reliable information supplied by Salviati thus made the papacy aware of just where it stood in France, of which policies were feasible and of which were not.[42]

In summary it seems to me that the St. Bartholomew massacres encouraged militancy on both sides of the ideological fence. Violence bred more violence as it so often has in history. Geneva encouraged the violent dismantling of existing governments into their constituent parts, in the hope that one or another of these parts could protect Protestantism from the persecution of a unified government. Rome used a more and more professional diplomatic service to mobilize and stimulate Catholic powers in attempts to crush Protestantism completely. Both developments reached a peak in the next century, early in the Thirty Years' War, then began slowly to fade away. The terrible intolerance which gave motive power to these institutional developments has by this time nearly disappeared in Geneva and Rome. Unfortunately it still lingers on in certain other parts of the world.

[41] ASV, S. S. Francia 283, fols. 53ᵛ–54, noted by Pastor, XIX, 498.
[42] Cf. Pierre Hurtubise, "Comment Rome apprit la nouvelle du massacre de la Saint-Barthélemy," *Archivum Historiae Pontificiae*, X (1972), 188–209, for an independent but somewhat similar conclusion.

COMMENT

by

PIERRE HURTUBISE, O. M. I.

There is no doubt that the Saint Bartholomew Massacre created the impression in Rome that violence paid, and that Protestants could be eliminated. But, as Professor Kingdon points out, this conviction was at various times tempered by diplomatic failures, like that of Orsini in the autumn of 1572; and throughout Gregory's pontificate the pendulum continued to swing between hope and despair in response to the changing prospects of a decisive action against the Protestants. Laureo, who came to Paris in the summer of 1573 as nuncio to the newly elected king of Poland (the duc d'Anjou), suggested to Catherine that she finish the good work started on 24 August 1572. In 1574 and 1575–1576, Frangipani was instructed by Rome to press for an all-out war against the Huguenots. In every case the hopes of the papacy were doomed to frustration, as the French court made concession after concession to the Protestants or settled for what the Vatican considered "humiliating" compromises.

There is much evidence, however, that this was already the situation under Pius V. Pius urged war against the Huguenots, whom he (and many others) considered to be traitors to the crown. He gave both financial and military support to the campaigns waged against the Protestants in 1567 and 1568–1569. He was convinced that the danger they constituted both for the crown and the Church had to be met by force, and at Moncontour he urged his soldiers to kill every one of them without mercy. Of course he too had been sorely disappointed, especially after the Peace of St. Germain in 1570. Nevertheless he remained convinced that the real answer to the Protestant threat was force. (See the work by Hirschauer, cited above by Kingdon).

Gregory XIII adopted a similar attitude, and we cannot disregard the statement he made at the beginning of his pontificate that he intended to tread in Pius V's footsteps. The Massacre of Saint Bartholomew certainly served to strengthen his resolve to use force, but we may ask: to what extent? I think it is rather difficult to say.

On the other hand, the many disillusionments experienced by both Pius V and Gregory XIII led these two popes to insist more and more on the necessity of spiritual and pastoral reform in France as a means of stemming the progress of Protestantism. This emphasis became increasingly apparent during Salviati's nunciature. And since France, always jealous of its "Gallican liberties," had not accepted – and never was to accept – the decrees of the Council of Trent together with its attendant institutions, especially the Holy Office, the functions normally assigned to inquisitors and other reformers directly dependent upon the papacy devolved (in accordance with the provisions of the Council) upon the nuncios and the local bishops. Thus there was an additional reason for the role of the nuncio in France to be gradually transformed to include spiritual matters which until then had been practically excluded from his mandate. To an ever greater extent, nuncios were invited to intervene in this area, and spiritual matters were one of Salviati's major preoccupations. I would like to suggest, therefore, that, when we consider the attitude of Rome toward the Protestants in sixteenth-century France, we remember that the belief in "violence pays" had a very important counterpart: "reform pays."

THE ELIZABETHANS AND ST. BARTHOLOMEW

by

A. G. DICKENS

Certain anecdotes of the Massacre of St. Bartholomew have long been enshrined in the established canon of the political history of the reign of Elizabeth. Readers of Froude will scarcely need to be reminded how Sir Francis Walsingham, then our man in Paris, heard from his house across the Seine the blood-chilling tumult around the Louvre. Another famous Englishman, Walsingham's young protégé Philip Sidney (who had recently been hobnobbing with Henri de Navarre), must somehow have repressed a heroic impulse to take on the population of Paris single-handed, and so stayed put in the embassy, or perhaps under the protection of the duc de Nevers.[1] Soon afterwards in England, Gloriana, dressed in mourning from head to foot, gave the cold shoulder to the embarrassed French ambassador La Mothe-Fénelon, a treatment which English ladies clad in the porcupine-costume of that day must have found so easy to accord, even to French gentlemen. From 1570 to 1582 Elizabeth was engaged in encouraging and repelling the advances of two French princes, first the duc d'Anjou, then François duc d'Alençon – who, if Burghley had had his way, might have terminated the aging queen's career in childbed, or else turned into an even more troublesome consort than Mary's Philip. As I shall show, that persistent specter, the French match, has acquired for social historians the utmost relevance.

But, since the narrative histories tell us all too little about the mental processes of the English people, I began my research for the present paper by passing to the other extreme, reached down my copy of the *Short-Title Catalogue* and started listing and counting Elizabethan books concerned with current affairs in France. Seized by a spirit of dull industry, I tried to quantify and classify in a manner which would

---

[1] On Sidney in Paris, see James M. Osborn, *Young Philip Sidney, 1572–1577* (New Haven and London, 1972), pp. 67–70.

almost have entitled me to a place in that justly famous team of historical statisticians working at Cambridge, England. At this point I started making two mild assumptions. In the first place, books and pamphlets about France should afford some rough indication of Elizabethan public interest in France. After all, these books were not subsidized by a Valois-Medici Foundation, any more than Luther's best-sellers had been subsidized by Godly Princes Incorporated. In both cases publication was stimulated and sustained by commercial profit, by the response to public taste and opinion of the men Luther had called "sordid mercenaries," the publishers. Again, I have assumed that Elizabethan reactions to St. Bartholomew can best be evaluated within the larger context of the long-term interest of the English in French civil war and politics running throughout the reign. I did also at this stage remember to re-examine John Salmon's valuable work,[2] which, though mainly concerned with the heavy debt of seventeenth-century Englishmen to earlier French political thinkers, contains a chapter on the initial Elizabethan reception of their work. So helpful is this chapter that I propose to say little or nothing about political thought in its more systematic and philosophical forms. Thinking about politics remains of course a very different matter, and with this we shall emphatically be concerned.

One should meanwhile be aware of the fact that publication in the English language does not delimit knowledge and opinion among the educated class. Writing of the last years of Henry VIII, Jusserand wishes that Du Bellay had translated Wyatt, and he continues:

That nobleman spoke French, all London spoke it; the king, the court, noblemen, ladies, everyone who was anybody at all; every traveller was struck by the general use of French in English society; Greek Nucius and Italian Jove [Paulus Jovius] concur in their testimony. "All the English almost," wrote Nucius, "use the French language."[3]

These witnesses and even Jusserand himself may err somewhat on the side of optimism; but since there were teachers of French even in provincial towns like York, and since a number of books in the French language were published in London, we must conclude that there existed a readership in the French language, one of somewhat uncertain size, but clearly extending below courtly circles.

Given this proviso, the list of books in English must still provide a useful guide to the tastes and reactions of the middle groups of society.

[2] J. H. M. Salmon, *The French Religious Wars in English Political Thought* (Oxford, 1959).
[3] J. J. Jusserand, *Shakespeare in France* (New York and London, 1899), pp. 30–31.

My own statistics amply confirm the impression of Matthias A.
Shaaber that the Elizabethans felt vastly more interest in France than
in any other foreign country, with the Netherlands running a rather
poor second, and the rest lagging far behind.[4] My own figures should
not indeed be accorded too much respect. They constitute an obvious
underestimate, in the sense that I decided to omit so-called "literary"
and theological works, some at least of which are in fact more than
marginally relevant to our present theme. Again, I included only books
immediately verifiable as of French interest, yet English works often
make unpredictable references to French problems and Anglo-French
relations. Without reading a high proportion of Elizabethan literature,
one could not possibly hope to locate these innumerable, and sometimes
significant passages. I omitted not only the hundred editions of Calvin,
but the fifty editions of works by Beza and the thirteen English editions
of Du Bartas published before 1603. I did supplement the *Short-Title
Catalogue* by reference to the Stationers' Registers. Yet considering the
large number of items extant in only one or two copies, one may
hardly doubt that other pertinent books have vanished without trace.

According to this highly selective count, 250 English works on
current French affairs are distributed over the Elizabethan decades as
follows:

1561–1570	31 titles
1571–1580	38 titles
1581–1590	117 titles
1591–1600	64 titles

Of the 117 issued during the third of these decades, no less than seventy
belong to the sensational years 1589–1590, the years of Arques and
Ivry; but in view of the omissions and the relatively small volume of
publication in England, the figures support the claim that the Elizabethans were following French affairs with considerable interest. All
the same it must be admitted that no really important work on the
French Wars of Religion originated in the mind of an Elizabethan.
Conditions militated against such original publication. Of this total
output, more than 85% represent straightforward translations from
French originals. It would seem that if a Frenchman had written a
thing first, an English publisher could anticipate a good chance of
avoiding trouble with the censor.

---

[4] Matthias A. Shaaber, *Some Forerunners of the Newspaper in England, 1476–1622* (Philadel-
phia and London, 1929), pp. 180–85.

Needless to add, there were limits to this principle. While Elizabeth ruled, the ardent monarchomachs did not attain English publication. There appeared no English texts of Hotman's *Francogallia* or of Beza's *Du droit des magistrats*. The *Vindiciæ contra Tyrannos* did have its famous fourth part Englished in 1588 under the deceptive title *A Short Apologie for Christian Soldiours*.[5] This part answered the question "whether neighbor princes or states may be, or are bound by law, to give succour to the subjects of other princes afflicted for the cause of true religion, or oppressed by manifest tyranny?" By 1588 this had presumably become an allowable question! To avoid misunderstanding it should be added that a French edition of the *Reveille-matin des Français* (1574) and two Latin editions of the *Vindiciæ* (1579, 1580) have the Edinburgh imprint,[6] but this is believed to be a subterfuge masking books published respectively at Geneva or Basel. It may be said with confidence that Scottish printers made no significant inroads upon English censorship.

Who translated works on French affairs? And exactly what sorts of books and pamphlets did it pay to translate and publish? Most of the translators seem to have been anonymous hacks, men in the game for wages rather than for literary fame, and doubtless very anxious to avoid imprisonment or mutilation by a sovereign who was notoriously ungrateful for advice on foreign affairs. Among the named translators, perhaps the most distinguished man of letters was the amazingly industrious Sir Geoffrey Fenton (ca. 1539–1603), who apart from doing Bandello and the back-breaking Guicciardini, contributed *A Discourse of the Civile Warres and late Troubles in Fraunce* (1570).[7] Another notable practitioner was Arthur Golding, well known as the translator of Ovid's *Metamorphoses*, who rendered Hotman's famous biography of Coligny: *The Lyfe of the most godly, valiant and noble Captaine ... Colignie Shatilion* (1576).[8] Yet another was the Suffolk parson Thomas Tymme, responsible for *The Three Partes of the Commentaries containing the whole and perfect Discourse of the Civill warres of Fraunce under the raignes of Henry the second, Frances the second, and of Charles the ninth* (1574).[9] This history

---

[5] *A Short-Title Catalogue of Books Printed in England, Scotland and Ireland*, ed. A. W. Pollard and G. R. Redgrave (London, 1926), No. 15207. This work is hereafter cited as *S.T.C.*, followed by the item number.
[6] *S.T.C.*, 1464, 15211–12. Cf. P. Chaix, A. Dufour and G. Moeckli, *Les livres imprimés à Genève de 1550 à 1560* (Geneva, 1966), p. 82.
[7] *S.T.C.*, 11271.
[8] *S.T.C.*, 22248.
[9] *S.T.C.*, 22242.

allegedly came from the Latin of that eminent victim of the Massacre, Peter Ramus, but was in fact by Jean de Serres.

During the late eighties and the nineties, when the public developed an unlimited appetite for newsletters, men like Edward Aggas and John Wolfe (the latter being the son of a Strasbourg printer) turned French news into an industry. Aggas personally translated a great number of these publications, no doubt conscious of the profit arising from swift reportage. Though the precise day or even month of an item is seldom ascertainable, it would appear that such pamphlets came out quite rapidly in England, most being dated in the same year, and many certainly appearing within a very short time of the events they described.

Classification into literary types must involve some subjective judgments; no two workers would emerge with the same figures, and we should do well to avoid the illusory precision of percentages. Having read in the British Library many of the items least clearly distinguishable by their titles, I would offer the following broad pattern. Less than a dozen of the 250 items could be called formal histories or historical biographies, though some of these will demand special attention. On the other hand a surprisingly high proportion – roughly one third of our total – takes the form of official documents in translation but without commentary. These are items to which the most authoritarian English government would have been unlikely to take exception:

> The King's Edict upon the Pacification of the Troubles (1568)
> The Protestation of the Duke of Allenson (1575)
> A Letter written by the King of Navarre (1585)
> The Letters Patents of the King's Declaration for referring the Generall Assemblie unto the 15 day of March (1590).

This list one could extend ad nauseam: the appetite of the Elizabethan reading public for recent French historical documents seems to have been almost boundless. About another quarter of the total is occupied by the newsletters, while yet another quarter offers serious discussion of the issues at stake in France, and could be labelled politico-religious treatises, letters or pamphlets.

Even so, the newsletters would seem to possess at least equal interest for historians of Elizabethan society. Very many are military reports originally by Frenchmen, but sometimes our own war correspondent managed to be, if not exactly on the spot, at least near enough to compile inaccurate statistics – for example, The Copy of a Letter sent *by an English Gentleman out of France to a friend of his in England, wherein is particularly expressed the names of sundry noble men, with the number of horsemen and footmen which were drowned, slaine, hurt and taken prisoners in the said battaile* (1590).[10] The strong impression arises that the English only wanted to hear good news; hence the immense multiplication of newsletters when Henri IV won his famous victories in 1589–1590. Indeed, from this stage it appears evident that Henri has become a folk-hero of the English, perhaps to such a degree that had Elizabeth enjoyed the benefit of public opinion polls, she might well have been disturbed. His *politique* conversion to Catholicism made little difference to his apparent popularity among the English, with their ineradicable taste for romance on horseback – and on the cheap! And while Henri de Navarre might be described without undue levity as one of the early cowboys in our fine Anglo-Saxon tradition, the Guises play the role of Indians, and singularly treacherous ones into the bargain. At all events, in English publications the king continued to figure as Henry the Great around the time of his assassination.

On the other hand, in only three or four items noticed by me does the *politique* attitude to the Wars obtain a fair hearing. The *Satire Ménippée* was licensed to J. Hardie by the Stationers' Company on 28 September 1594, the original French edition having been published only that summer. It duly appeared in 1595 as *A Pleasant Satyre or Poesie, wherein is discovered the Catholicon* [quack medicine] *of Spayne, and the chiefe Leaders of the League finely fecht over and laide open in their colours.*[11] The English rendering was uncouth, but more or less following the original, it paid due tribute on the accession of Henri IV:

> Unconquered prince, and of thine age the glorie eke alone,
> Even God himselfe doth set thee up upon thy grandsire's throne;
> And with a happy hand doth reach to thee two scepters brave,
> Which, taken from the Spanish foe, thou shalt uphold and have.

Thinking again of the *politique* outlook, we know that Bodin's great work attracted many English readers in the original (1576), and Gabriel Harvey remarks that Cambridge men were greatly admiring it about 1579.[12] Yet not until 1606 did it attain translation, as *The Six Bookes of a Commonweale, written by J. Bodin, a famous Lawyer ... out of the French and Latin Copies, done into English.*[13] It was in fact done by Richard Knolles, the admirable historian of the Turks. As for the Catholic

---

[10] *S.T.C.*, 10411.
[11] *S.T.C.*, 15489. Cf. Salmon, p. 20.
[12] Cited, *ibid.*, p. 24.
[13] *S.T.C.*, 3193.

standpoint, it came across in only two or three English pamphlets, presumably through the efforts of English émigrés. In other words, the output of Elizabethan printed material, insofar as it conveyed a partisan message, was overwhelmingly Protestant. It reflected the bias of a public which did not want to disturb the unity of the realm. yet had little sympathy with the fence-sitting so long practiced by Elizabeth in regard to the struggle in France and the Netherlands, People misunderstand the whole nature of the critical opposition by lumping it under the misleading and emotive term "Puritanism."

Meanwhile the most arresting feature of Elizabethan opinion is its hatred of the Guises. Students of the drama naturally tend to connect anti-Guise literature with the late plays: Marlowe's *The Massacre at Paris* (produced in 1593)[14] and even George Chapman's plays about Bussy d'Ambois (first edition 1607).[15] In fact, however, this hatred runs throughout the whole reign. It could hardly have been otherwise, with Mary Stuart – offspring, idol and instrument of Guise imperialism – fostering the murder plots from her English prisons. And even from Elizabeth's stuffy monarchist viewpoint, the Guises had no claim to be treated tenderly. Already in 1562, years before Mary Stuart became our national guest, we could read *The destruction and sacke cruelly committed by the Duke of Guyse, in the toune of Vassy*,[16] and before that year was out at least three further anti-Guise pamphlets. Thereafter the series steadily continues, culminating in accounts of the Guise share in the Massacre of St. Bartholomew, and the excesses of Mayenne and the Catholic League. If one accepted this standard of measurement, it would appear that English publishers and readers detested the Guises more than they detested King Philip himself, but Philip enjoyed protection by Elizabeth's censorship at least until the Armada. Then a tract of 1590 ventures to show that Philip was the real prolonger of France's agony.[17] All in all, the long-standing anti-Guise propaganda would seem to constitute the chief background against which

---

[14] See the edition by H. J. Oliver, *Dido, Queen of Carthage, and the Massacre at Paris* (1968); P. H. Kocher, "Contemporary Pamphlet Backgrounds for Marlowe's *The Massacre at Paris*," *Modern Language Quarterly*, VIII (1947), 151–73, 309–18. Cf. also Kocher's article, "Francis Hotman and Marlowe's *The Massacre at Paris*," *Publications of the Modern Language Association of America*, LVI (1941), 349–68.

[15] On Chapman's Bussy plays, see W. J. Lever, *The Tragedy of State* (London, 1971), chap. iii. For guidance on the drama I am deeply indebted to my fellow-worker at the Folger Shakespeare Library in the spring of 1972, Robert Adams, who also showed me relevant parts of his forthcoming work on the late Elizabethan tragic view of life.

[16] *S.T.C.*, 11312.

[17] *S.T.C.*, 684: *The coppie of the Anti-Spaniard made at Paris by a French man, a Catholique. Wherein is directly proved how the Spanish King is the onely cause of all the troubles in France.*

English reactions to the Massacre of St. Bartholomew should be evaluated.

If only to dispel the impression of philistinism I am doubtless conveying to lovers of Elizabethan literature, I wish I had more time and more expertise to talk about poetry and drama reflecting the French civil wars. Aesthetically, it looks to me undistinguished – even the contribution by Marlowe. Among the comic figures stands that inelegant Scotsman, Andrew Sempill, himself a fugitive from the Massacre, who published at St. Andrews a ballad disapproving of Guises and Italians, approving in general of Frenchmen, calling Charles IX "Charlie," and bidding Elizabeth take care that the papists should not repeat the Massacre in England.[18] That dark thought had of course already occurred to the English, who were then less dependent on the Scots to do their thinking. Like any good Scotsman, Sempill was also not averse to flaunting his erudition, comparing the Massacre with the deeds of Solyman, Tamburlaine, Pharaoh, Nero, Turks and infidels generally. To balance Andrew Sempill's ballad, I should also mention a more refined but possibly more obtuse scholar of Oxford, who published there a Latin poem, *De caede Gallorum regis*, to mark the widely unregretted death of Henri III.[19] A third poem is the long narrative in Alexandrines by Anne Dowriche, wife of a rector of Honiton, published in 1589.[20] With far more piety than inspiration the poetess covers three episodes in the French struggle, ending with the Massacre of St. Bartholomew.

While I mention this thin stock of poetry, I should not wholly neglect that more significant theme: the impact of the Massacre upon the English drama. Was it not one of that series of somber influences and events which brushed aside comfortable Tudor beliefs in "legitimate" monarchy and providential history; influences which around 1600 caused so many dramatists – Chapman, Jonson, Webster, Fulke Greville and the mature Shakespeare – to explore the profoundly disquieting implications of power and tyranny as they existed in a real world? Thus to accept the universe of Machiavelli as a tragic statement of reality was a very different thing from the former practice of wrapping up evil as abnormal or "Machiavellian" and pushing it under the carpet. Such a frank attitude obviously had sinister implications, not only for those who dared to adopt it, but for the whole

---

[18] Reprinted in Henry Huth, *Ancient Ballads and Broadsides* (London, 1867), pp. 54–60.
[19] *S.T.C.*, 13099.
[20] *S.T.C.*, 7159; *D.N.B.*, XV, 405–06.

future of Tudor-type monarchy. The theme will be highly familiar to those who have read W. J. Lever's suggestive lectures, *The Tragedy of State* (1971). But if in this context we try to assign importance to the Massacre as an inspirer of dramatists, it must clearly be as one of a number of overt influences: Senecanism, which incidentally had also influenced Machiavelli; Greek and Roman tyrannicide, the study of which was to be blamed by Hobbes as provoking the restive spirit leading to the Civil War;[21] and again, those countless lurid tales of faction, feud, bloodshed, lust and power-mania drawn from the history of Italian states and cities.

A further significant feature in the literary field is the series of translations by various hands from Du Bartas, for so long regarded in Protestant countries as the modern epic poet who outstripped us all – and the Ancients too. Between 1584 and 1603 there appeared no less than thirteen *English* editions of his works, to be followed by innumerable others as the seventeenth century advanced.[22] When one considers the theme of *Judith*, or the song of victory after Ivry, it is clear that I could legitimately have included some of these in any list of Elizabethan literature having topical reference to the grandeurs and miseries of France.

I now propose to push the camera closer and look merely at the three or four years following the Massacre. The horror did not, as might be expected, result in an explosion of pamphlets by godly and indignant Englishmen. No doubt the English government saw to that, since, in view of its bad relations with Spain, it had pressing reasons to allow only a controlled disapproval, followed by a speedy resumption of more or less friendly relations with the French court. As early as January 1573 the earl of Worcester was sent by Elizabeth to act as godfather to the infant daughter of Charles IX. So far as I can observe, not more than two or three important publications on French affairs fall within the years 1573–1574. One of them was Hotman's famous *De Furoribus Gallicis*, which came in 1573 in three Latin editions[23] and an English version: *A true and plaine report of the furious outrages of Fraunce*.[24] The following year there appeared the work we have already mentioned – *The Three Partes of the Commentaries* by Jean de Serres,

    [21] T. Hobbes, *Behemoth* (ca. 1668), cited by J. Hurstfield and A. G. R. Smith, *Elizabethan People: State and Society* (London, 1972), pp. 82–83.
    [22] *S.T.C.*, 21649–21673: cf. Anne Lake Prescott, "The Reception of Du Bartas in England," *Studies in the Renaissance*, XV (1968), 144–73.
    [23] *S.T.C.*, 13844–46.
    [24] *S.T.C.*, 13847.

translated by Thomas Tymme. This soon became popular, especially its tenth book, later used by Marlowe as the major source for the first six scenes and part of the eighth scene of *The Massacre at Paris*.[25] However, this tenth book is not in fact by de Serres; it is merely a reprint of Hotman's *True and plaine report* (*i.e.*, the *De Furoribus Gallicis*).

During 1575–1576 these items gained reinforcement from two readable and more outspoken books. One was the biography commonly attributed to Henri Estienne – *A mervaylous discourse upon the lyfe, deedes and behaviours of Katherine de Medicis, Queene Mother* – a volume falsely located at Heidelberg, and then in a later edition at Cracow.[26] Beginning with the ignoble origins of the Medici family and the evil prognostications of the stars at Catherine's birth, the author occupies the rest of nearly two hundred pages with specific accusations of poisoning, bawdry, prodigality, mass-slaughter and a variety of other crimes. "This is such a practise as she hath perfectly learned of her Machiavellistes."[27] Similar attributions of the Massacre to "Machiavellism" came from many writers, both Continental and English. The impression naturally derived support from the *Anti-Machiavel* of the Huguenot lawyer Innocent Gentillet, widely read in England from its publication at Geneva in 1576, translated in 1577 by Simon Patrick, a Cambridge student travelling in France, but not published in English until a quarter of a century later.[28] Meanwhile the antithesis, the Protestant hero in shining armor, appeared in 1576 with the 115-page English version of Jean de Serres' *The lyfe of the most godly, valeant and noble capteine and maintener of the trew Christian religion in Fraunce, Iasper Colignie Shatilion, sometyme greate Admirall of Fraunce*.[29]

Thus without producing an instant outburst of indignation, the presses gradually but efficiently over a period of four years clothed the participants in deep black and dazzling white. Then from this point new editions of the universally-read *Acts and Monuments* of John Foxe stamped the contrast between godliness and Machiavellism upon the English mind. In his 1576 edition Foxe briefly alludes to the Massacre as a matter of common knowledge and dwells on the image of

---

[25] Oliver, p. lxi.
[26] *S.T.C.*, 10550–51; the former comprises some 196 pages. See Chaix, Dufour and Moeckli, p. 84.
[27] *S.T.C.*, 10550, p. 114.
[28] *S.T.C.*, 11743: *A discourse upon the meanes of wel governing against N. Machiavelli* (1602). Gentillet's *An apology or defence for the Christians of France*, tr. Sir Jerome Bowes, had been published in 1579 (*S.T.C.*, 11742).
[29] *S.T.C.*, 22248.

Guise as "the great Archenemie of God and his Gospell."[30] Then in the version of 1583, the last of his lifetime, he narrates the Massacre in three pages.[31] "But because the true narration of this lamentable story is set forth in English at large, in a book by itself, and extant in print already, it shall be the lesse neede nowe to discourse of that matter with any new repetition: only a briefe touch of summary notes for remembraunce may suffice."

We may now leave the books and take a glance at the instant reactions to be found in private letters. Most of the interesting ones happen to have been printed in full by Strype or Wright, and though these survivors inevitably come from well-known people, several yield incidental information concerning opinion lower down the social scale. For example, Edwin Sandys (signing himself "Ed. London") writes on 5 September 1572 that "the citizens of London in these dangerous daies had need prudentlie to be dealt with all; the preachers appoynted for the crosse [Paul's Cross] in this vacation are but yonge men, unskilfull in matters politicall, yet so carried with zeale, that they will enter into them and poure forth their opinions" against the French alliance. The bishop then assures Burghley, "I will not faile to direct them so well as I can," but he then submits a list of nine points "for the safetie of our Queene and Realme, if God will" – papists to be gaoled, the queen surrounded by Protestant guards, leagues made with all Protestant princes, the Gospel earnestly promoted and the Church "not burdened with unnecessary ceremonies." But first of all he makes the obvious suggestion with cold ferocity – "Forthwithe to cutte of the Scottishe Queen's heade: *ipsa est nostri fundi calamitas.*"[32]

Many of the writers seem equally sure that catastrophe is lurking around the corner in a plot-riddled England, headed by a queen oblivious to her peril. On 19 September, Arthur Lord Grey of Wilton writes to Burghley, "This morning I receaved your letter, wherin your Lordship doth moste truly guess of th'encrease of my grief by the late horrible and tirannicall deelings in France, and with your Lordship I do pray to God that her Majestie maye have the wisdome to follow, and magnitude to execute, the things that may divert the same from hence."[33] An anonymous correspondent of Leicester discloses in six closely written and eloquent pages "the common voice, lamentation, and fear of good subjects." Let her Highness be prayed to remember

---

[30] Ed. 1576, p. 2001.
[31] Ed. 1583, pp. 2152–54.
[32] Thomas Wright, ed., *Queen Elizabeth and Her Times* (London, 1838), I, 438–39.
[33] *Ibid.*, pp. 443–44.

conscience and eternity, let her not bring on England murders, rapes, robberies and violence and barbarous slaughters and the damnation of so many seduced souls by the advancement of papistry

... and all for piteous pity and miserable mercy in sparing one horrible woman, who carries God's wrath where she goes.... Shall we not trust that her Majesty, our mother, will not stick to command to kill a toad, a snake, or a mad dog whom she finds poisoning her, gnawing the throats of her infants, and presently threatening the same on herself.[34]

Another discourse on the Massacre comes from Robert Beal, clerk of the Council, who envisaged a vast international conspiracy to eradicate Protestantism. "By these late horrible accidents in France, the conjuration of the Council of Trent to root out all such as, contrary to the Pope's traditions, make profession of Christ's Gospel ... which was so long hid, and never could hitherto be believed of Princes Protestant so manifestly now appeareth, as I think it cannot be denied."[35] He then gives alleged evidence of a conspiracy afoot in England to poison the queen.

Sir Thomas Smith had recently revisited Paris in order to negotiate concerning the match between Elizabeth and Alençon; on his return in the July he had been reappointed secretary of state, and from 12 September was writing letters entirely befitting so eminent a humanist. Full of boring and resonant antitheses, they sound as if translated straight out of Latin, yet they do show how well Smith knew his way around the court of the Valois. He congratulates Walsingham and the young men in his charge on their escape. "How fearful and careful the mothers and parents be here of such young gentlemen as there be there, you may easily guess by my Lady Lane, who prayeth very earnestly that her son may be sent home with as much speed as may be." More interestingly, Smith accords a few sentences to the lower classes.

Our merchants be afraid now to go into France, and who can blame them? Who would, where such a liberty is given to soldiers, and where *nec pietas nec justitia* doth refrain and keep back the unruly malice and sword of the raging popular. Nevertheless, to that prince or country, who have so openly and injuriously done against Christ ... nothing can be too sharply or severely answered; yet princes, as you know, are acquainted with nothing but *douceur*, so must be handled with *douceur*, especially among and between princes ... not that they [should] think the Queen's Majesty and her Council such fools, as [if] we know not what is to be done; and yet that we

---

[34] Cited by J. E. Neale, *Queen Elizabeth I* (Pelican ed., 1960), p. 229.
[35] Qtd. in J. Strype, *The Life and Acts of Matthew Parker* (3 vols.; Oxford, 1821), II, 129–30.

should not appear so rude and barbarous, as to provoke, where no profit is to any man.

Subsequently Smith notices how the Massacre had driven the young Scots king and his Protestant ministers into closer friendship with England, thus playing into Elizabeth's hands.[36]

While the queen's cool diplomacy infuriated her Protestant subjects, she did at least allow Archbishop Parker to set forth on 27 October a special form of prayer in regard to the Massacre. In the mellifluous phraseology of the Anglican tradition, it gives thanks for the miraculous safety of the queen and realm. It calls for divine mercy upon persecuted Christians, "who are as sheep appointed to the slaughter"; it even prays for the persecutors themselves.

And for that O Lord, Thou has commanded us to pray for our enemies, we do beseech thee, not only to abate their pride, and to stay the cruelty and fury of such, as either of malice or ignorance do persecute them which put their trust in thee, and hate us, but also to mollify their hard hearts, to open their blind eyes, and to enlighten their ignorant minds, that they may see and understand, and truly turn unto thee, and embrace that holy word, and unfeignedly be converted unto thy Son Jesus Christ, the only Saviour of the world, and believe and love his Gospel, and so eternally be saved.[37]

That Parker was not at this moment luxuriating solely in such beautiful sentiments we can see from two anguished but undated and unsigned letters he sent to Burghley just after the Massacre.[38] In one of these he so far forgot himself as to call the queen's government "this neutral government" and "this Machiavel government," which "brought forth strange fruits,"

when the true subject is not regarded but overthwarted: when the rebel is borne with ... when the faithful subject and officer hath spent his wits to search to find, to indite, to arraign, and to condemn; yet must they [the plotters, in particular Queen Mary] be kept still for a fair day, to cut our own throats. ... Is this the way to rule English people? O cruelty, to spare a professed enemy, and to drive to the slaughter herself and her best friends.

And Parker even goes on to remark that, if he himself had not been bound to Anne Boleyn (whose chaplain he had been back in 1535) he would not so readily have agreed to serve her daughter Elizabeth, for bishops were nowadays powerless and had a thankless task. Soon afterwards the archbishop may have begun to fear the consequences should the queen ever see this bitter effusion. At all events, some time

---

[36] J. Strype, *The Life of the Learned Sir Thomas Smith* (Oxford, 1820), pp. 119–23.
[37] Qtd. in Strype, *Parker*, II, 131.
[38] *Ibid.*, II, 119–20, 126.

during that month of October he wrote to Burghley again, apologizing for it and explaining he had written *in amaritudine animae et in insipientia sua* .... "And before Almighty God I speak it, no creature in earth knoweth of this my particular writing to you." The other letter of September had been rather less outspoken, but here he moaned that the queen seemed to be "void of fear of any harm from papists," and protested that there were "many worldlings, many counterfeits, many ambidexters, many neutrals, concealing themselves and all their doings." "God's will be done: and I beseech God send to the Queen's Majesty *aures ut audiat; cor docile et benignum ut intelligat;* and to be advised by the trustiest of her Council, to provide in time ...." Thus it was not John Stubbs or the Puritans or the dramatists who first saw that they were dealing with a ruler subject to a maddening sang-froid, indeed to Machiavellian rather than to godly impulses; it was the mild and scholarly archbishop Parker himself who made one of the strongest protests along these lines.

Meanwhile the horrors of St. Bartholomew were brought home to lesser Englishmen by the thousands of refugees who poured over the Channel to escape the Guises and the even more pitiless mobs in Paris, Rouen and other provincial cities. The refugees began to come in from Dieppe to Rye on 27 August, and La Mothe-Fénelon wrote, "Il n'est pas à croire combien cette nouvelle émeut grandement tout ce royaume." When Charles IX asked that they be sent back, Elizabeth did at least reply that amid the slaughter it was only natural for people to flee in self-defense; yet she assured him that she would favor and help only Frenchmen who continued loyal to their own king.[39] One would like to think that universal kindness was shown to the refugees, but obviously there were exceptions amid the still notorious xenophobia of the London working class. They were not yet inspired by that exalted liberal spirit which in 1850 prompted Barclay and Perkins' draymen to beat up the notorious Austrian general Haynau. Yet there obviously existed in England that familiar tension between an empirical foreign office and a more ideological, even idealistic public opinion. In the remoter provinces the impact of the Massacre seems likely to have been smaller. On 18 September Sir Thomas Gargrave, vice-president of the Council in the North, wrote to Burghley from Nostel in Yorkshire:

[39] J. Strype, *Annals of the Reformation* (4 vols.; Oxford, 1820–1840), II, Pt. I, 249–50.

The people here are, as I think, like others in other parts of the realm; one sort is pleased with the late affront in France; another sort lament, and are appalled at it. Others would seem indifferent, and those be the greatest number; they are dissemblers, and yet many of them obedient subjects, and to be led by authority, and by their landlords and officers.[40]

Gargrave, it may be recalled, was a keen Protestant and his disapproval of the not inconsiderable group of northern Catholic or half-Catholic gentry may well have colored this report. Even so, the element of indifference can be sensed around this time in many areas of northern and western England, where the old religion had not yet been resuscitated, while the new was making but slow progress. In the South at least educated Elizabethans proved strikingly liberal to refugees who shared their faith. Matthew Parker declared it a cardinal point of piety to befriend "these gentle and profitable strangers." In his *Perambulation of Kent* (1576) William Lambarde urges "that now at the last, having the light of the Gospel before our eyes, and the persecuted parts of the afflicted church as guests and strangers in our country, we so behave ourselves towards them, as we may both utterly rub out the old blemish and from henceforth stay the heavy hand of just *Jupiter hospitalis*. Which otherwise must needs light upon such stubborn and uncharitable churlishness."[41] The matter is further elucidated in a sermon by the future archbishop Dr. George Abbot, whose brother Robert was to defend the legality of the Huguenot position in a much later tract, *Antichristi Demonstratio* (1609).[42] George Abbot's sermon makes it clear that the uncharitable behavior had come from exactly where one would expect – members of the London rabble, who after "their last great massacre ... used to term them no better than French dogs."

But those ... that were wise and godly, used these aliens as brethren: considering their distresses with a lively fellow-feeling, holding it an unspeakable blessedness that this little island of ours should not only be a temple to serve God in for ourselves, but an harbour for the weatherbeaten, a sanctuary to the stranger, wherein he might truly honour the Lord ... because the time once was, when themselves were strangers in that cruel land of Egypt: and not forgetting, that other nations, to their immortal praise, were a refuge to the English in their last bloody persecution in Queen Mary's days: and in brief, recounting, that by a mutual vicissitude of God's chastisements, their case might be our case.[43]

40 *Cal. State Papers Domestic, Addenda, 1566–1579*, p. 425.
41 Strype, *Annals*, II, Pt. I, 253.
42 *S.T.C.*, 43; cf. Salmon, pp. 33–34.
43 Strype, *Annals*, II, Pt. I, 252.

The same problem persisted until the end of the reign; for example in 1593, when the Commons debated a bill prohibiting aliens from retailing foreign commodities. Speaking for the government, Robert Cecil valiantly resisted the proposed restriction. He asserted that the relief afforded by England to strangers "hath brought great honour to our kingdom; for it is accounted a refuge for distressed nations, for our arms have been opened unto them to cast themselves into our bosoms."[44] The divergence of the social classes on this issue should not be linked too exclusively with ancient traditions of proletarian chauvinism and with fierce economic competition against foreigners. True, we may suitably enough recall "Evil Mayday," 1517, and the several foreign witnesses to the chauvinism of Tudor Londoners. Yet it might be just as realistic to recall that the upper-class Protestants, who most clearly set the tone of Elizabethan England, had themselves been the well-treated refugees in the days of the Marian persecution. In contrast, their social inferiors had been obliged to stay in London facing not simply religious persecution but the offensive presence of King Philip's great entourage of Spaniards.

If one sought to describe the most obvious and immediate effects of St. Bartholomew on the mass of Elizabethans, one would doubtless have to say that it confirmed to the hilt the ugly conclusions they were drawing from the latest exploits of the political Counter Reformation – from Pius V's "roaring Bull" deposing the queen, from the northern rising of 1569, from the presence of a French garrison in Edinburgh Castle, from the savagery of Alva in the Netherlands, from the Ridolfi Plot and the endless conspiracy turning around Mary Stuart *alias* Guise. And should any have thought that the Massacre could not recur in England, John Foxe stood ever at hand to remind them in lurid detail of the fires lit by Mary Tudor, and extinguished only fourteen years earlier. It requires no lengthy research to show that the Massacre nourished their fear and hatred of Catholic rulers and politicians; that they did not merely believe in an immense international conspiracy but mistakenly supposed it to be a well-integrated plan organized from Rome, whence the *Te deums* soon resounded to celebrate the slaughter.

But having acknowledged the truth in this obvious truism, I shall venture to suggest that the Massacre also did something to promote a more creative and far-reaching attitude within the nation itself – a disillusion with authoritarian monarchy in general, a disillusion which

[44] British Museum, Cotton MSS, Titus F ii, fol. 74.

started to rub off on the shining surface of Tudor monarchy. Here was a reaction which can be shown to have contributed not merely to the drama but to the origins of free speech. Alongside all its shortcomings, misconceptions, arrogant dogmatism and other historical disadvantages, the Reformed phase of the Protestant Reformation fostered the critical adulthood, the civil courage of Europeans. It gave so many men a capacity to commit themselves to an international creed, quite irrespective of their local rulers. We have only to read the martyrologists – Foxe, Crespin or Haemstede – to see how it bestowed this strength upon the middle and lower orders of society. Begun in the religious sphere, the defiant spirit swiftly spread to fields which nowadays we should regard as predominantly political. In England at least, the Catholic Reformation was able to achieve a similar feat, albeit for a small minority.

Was this capacity to oppose heavy-handed paternalism linked in some perceptible degree with the Massacre of St. Bartholomew? I believe that this was the case – that it should be accepted as one of those events which promoted early politico-religious dissent and opposition in England. Its obvious predecessor seemed the resistance to the Marian persecution. In the popular mind it linked back to that dark episode not only in the manner noticed by George Abbot, but by another common factor: the marriage of an English queen to a foreigner, a Catholic and absolutist prince. Here revived a prospect most fearful to the majority of Englishmen, a prospect which seemingly united within their minds religious partisanship and the preservation of their national identity, customs and independence. It was Elizabeth's misguided persistence in the Alençon match which gave the Massacre far more domestic significance than it could otherwise have acquired. The most striking piece of evidence lies in that greatest of Elizabethan opposition-pamphlets, *The Discovery of a Gaping Gulf* (1579) by John Stubbs.[45] Despite the Folger Shakespeare Library edition by Lloyd Berry, this remarkable work has not yet attracted the attention it deserves. Though a Protestant bigot of his day, Stubbs cannot be dismissed as the fanatic of the textbook. He was an able lawyer, an eloquent writer, a patriotic and critical commentator on the contemporary world. He gave his right hand for freedom of speech, and in later years he died in Normandy as a member of Lord Willoughby's ill-fated expedition to aid Henri IV. In 1579 he dared to say with complete frankness what almost everyone thought about the

45 Ed. Lloyd E. Berry (Charlottesville, 1968).

Alençon match. The *Gaping Gulf* remains in effect a commentary on St. Bartholomew and its infamous perpetrators. Had the work not contained this emotive element, its tough political and historical argumentation would not have appealed so strongly, and perhaps it would not have aroused so cruel a riposte from the queen. The language is indeed pungent, almost choking with emotion: "Whereby it appears that whoso matcheth with any wicked race do make themselves and their seed partakers of the sins and plagues of that race and their ancestors." "The match of France with the Italian Athaliah and her furies in that land, especially at the marriage of her daughter Margaret," had resulted in the Massacre.

And when I remember the poor orphaned churches in France, I must needs give the prize of godless impudency to those which will needs forsooth maintain this marriage [of Elizabeth and Alençon] as a mean to assure religion in France and to preserve the professors there from more massacres. ... The last act was very lamentable. A King falsified his sworn word, the marriage of a King's sister imbrued with blood; a King murdered his subjects; many noble and honourable gentlemen shamefully used; valiant men surprised by cowards in their beds; innocents put to death; women and children without pity tossed upon halberds and thrown down [from] windows and into rivers; learned men killed by barbarous soldiers; the saints of God led to the shambles all the day long and all that week by vile *crocheteurs* or porters, the Church of Christ razed, ... and, that which was worst, those that lived were compelled to forswear their God.[46]

Here and in other passages the Massacre is made the driving force of the indictment; and once more the sinister term "Machiavellian" makes its inevitable entrance. Stubbs did not only express the views of politicians like Leicester and Walsingham. His view was shared by nobler minds. Philip Sidney incurred the queen's deep displeasure by cautioning her privately and doubtless in language more restrained. Edmund Spenser thinly disguised similar thoughts in the *Shephearde's Calendar* and in *Mother Hubbard's Tale*. Indeed, how few people can have wanted to see the blood-boltered Valois on the throne of England, apart from Burghley and a few aristocratic conservatives like Oxford and Northampton? So the Massacre and the match not only damaged the credit of French monarchy but began the erosion of English monarchy. Of course, the process would be retarded so long as the precious life of Elizabeth held at bay forces vastly more terrifying than the least acceptable elements of her rule.

Even so, we do not need to wait for the final years of the reign to

[46] *Ibid.*, p. 25.

observe signs of this erosion. Illegally, according to some professional opinions, Stubbs and his publisher were convicted under a Marian statute and had their right hands hacked off in the market place at Westminster. Prudently, the government did not stage this unfamiliar punishment within the city of London! The eyewitness William Camden relates the familiar story, how Stubbs raised his hat with his left hand, and before he fainted cried out in a loud voice "God save the Queen," thus consistently linking freedom of speech with loyalty to the crown. Then comes the overlooked but most interesting passage. Camden, himself an ardent admirer of Elizabeth, thus concludes: ". . . the multitude standing about was altogether silent, either out of horror of this new and unwonted punishment, or else out of pitty toward the man, being of most honest and unblameable report, or else out of hatred of the [French] marriage, which most men presaged would be the overthrow of religion."[47]

Looking back from our own age, we cannot but see the staunch gentleman from Norfolk, Cambridge and Lincoln's Inn as a true predecessor of Peter Wentworth, of Prynne, Hampden, Pym, Milton and Cromwell. In the silence of that crowd, did not the Tudor myth begin to sicken, even though it was to be given many a blood transfusion by the Whitgifts, the Hookers, Bancrofts and Lauds? With a truly splendid irony, Stubbs and his publisher lost their right hands but a few yards from the spot where seventy years later their cause was to exact a greater trophy: the head of a king.

[47] W. Camden, *Annals* (1635), pp. 238–39.

IMPERIALISM, PARTICULARISM AND TOLERATION IN THE HOLY ROMAN EMPIRE*

by

LEWIS W. SPITZ

In considering the "blood wedding" in Paris and its significance for the Holy Roman Empire, we shall treat first the political and religious situation in the Empire between the Peace of Augsburg and the outbreak of the Thirty Years' War, next the impact of the St. Bartholomew's Day Massacre, and finally the importance of the event and political developments for toleration.

I. PARTICULARISM AND RELIGIOUS PEACE

"Every German prince," wrote Bismarck in his *Gedanken und Erinnerungen*, "before the Thirty Years' War who opposed the emperor annoyed me; although from the Great Elector on I was partisan enough to decide against the emperor and naturally to find that the Seven Years' War was brewing." The geographical problem of the Empire – located in the very center of Europe with the French on one side and the Turks on the other –, the particularism of the princes, and the effect of political events on religious toleration made the German situation even more complicated than that in France or England. While major states of western Europe were developing greater national cohesion at home and expanding their empires abroad, the Holy Roman Empire of the German Nation stagnated politically and then paid the price of weakness in a hard world on the terrible rack of a war stretched over thirty years. The Germanies, to be sure, enjoyed sixty-three years of peace between the Peace of Augsburg (1555) and the outbreak of the Thirty Years' War (1618) while wars raged in the neighboring states. But the pursuit of selfish particularist interests by the German states kept the Empire divided into power blocks and

* Research for this paper was completed with the help of a fellowship awarded by the American Council of Learned Societies.

political configurations which were potentially extremely incendiary. The conflagration began by spontaneous internal combustion and eventually drew many nations of Europe into its flaming vortex.

Duke Christoph of Württemberg while riding along the Rhine reading the provisions of the Peace of Augsburg felt upset by the small gains and the large concessions which the Lutherans had made, even, he believed, in matters of conscience. He wondered whether a Christian could agree to such terms and observed: "If the Protestants do not consider Christ and his Word with greater earnestness and zeal, they will not long go unpunished."[1] He felt that greater unity on the part of the Protestants would have achieved more decisive concessions and considered a plan for reassembling the Protestant princes after the Diet to repair the damage. Most of the Lutheran princes, however, were more conservative and were quite satisfied with achieving the right of equal coexistence with Catholic territories within the Empire. The medieval *corpus christianum* construct of one empire and one religion was now legally broken. Although the legist Joachim Stephani in his *De Iurisdictione* (1582) first used the term *cuius regio, eius religio*, the principle was imbedded in the Peace of Augsburg and was assured to Catholic and Lutheran states, though not to Calvinist or any other. When Sir Philip Sidney (1554–1586), the Elizabethan diplomat and author, declared it to be a sign of true statesmanship never to separate religion from politics he was expressing the common view of the age.[2] Certainly it was a basic principle of the Peace of Augsburg, and despite the misgivings of a Christoph, the people rang the church bells and celebrated the peace as a great victory.

During the two decades following the Peace, Lutheranism continued in its ascendancy. In north Germany only three secular princes, Cleves, Grubenhagen, and Brunswick-Wolfenbüttel remained Catholic, plus the imperial coronation city of Aachen. Lutheranism penetrated the South to the extent that some local diets in Bavaria, Bohemia, Austria and Hungary were given the right to celebrate communion in both kinds with married clergy officiating. Four of the seven electors remained Catholic, the "bishop's alley" along the Rhine – Mainz, Trier and Cologne – holding out, although Cologne was returned to the fold by Bavarian troops when the archbishop defected and received

[1] Viktor Ernst, *Briefwechsel des Herzogs Christoph von Wirtemberg*, III (Stuttgart, 1900), No. 175, pp. 340–41. Gerhard Ritter (*Die Neugestaltung Europas im 16. Jahrhundert* [Frankfurt a.M., 1967], pp. 377–88) characterizes the princes who came to power around mid-century; see pp. 380–81 on Christoph.
[2] Fulke Greville, *Life of Sir Philip Sidney* (London, 1907), p. 35.

no aid from the Protestants. It has been estimated that in 1570 about seven-tenths of all the people in the Empire were Protestant. The Lutherans actually had a preponderance of influence in the Diet.

The Habsburg emperors themselves showed a tempered attitude toward Lutherans. With the resignation of Charles V the era of the grand design to fit the Empire into a universal dynastic monarchy was ended. The half century which followed saw the Empire turn toward a preoccupation with its internal problems, disturbed occasionally by the Turkish threat or other outside interference. Matters such as the Grumbach affair loom large in the annals of the time.[3] Emperor Ferdinand I (1558–1564), Charles V's brother, was thoroughly Catholic, but with an Erasmian caste, quite prepared to make concessions to the Protestants. Pope Paul IV rebuked him for the Peace of Augsburg and for allowing a "heretical education" for his son. He assaulted young prince Maximilian as a "wicked heretic" who owned a library of Lutheran books, had a Lutheran preacher, and sided with the Lutheran princes. The Spanish ambassador tried in vain to get Maximilian's wife Mary to leave her heretical husband. Ferdinand finally yielded to papal pressure and delivered an ultimatum to Maximilian, giving him a choice between submission or disinheritance. When Maximilian turned for help to the Lutheran princes – and as a young man he had corresponded over a long period with Christoph of Württemberg – they let him down, for they were not ready to oppose the emperor and saw no prospect of Protestantizing the Empire. In February 1562, in Prague, Maximilian submitted, placing his hands in his father's and promising to keep the faith. Unlike Henri IV, who after his final conversion in 1593, seems to have been a sincere Catholic, Maximilian (1564–1576) continued to harbor secret Protestant convictions. To the papal legate Hosius he had declared, "I am neither Catholic nor Protestant but a Christian." He took as his motto "Da pacem patriae."[4] When in 1568 the Austrian estates urgently requested that they be permitted to adopt the Augsburg Confession, Maximilian set up consultations with Christoph von Carlowitz, emissary of Elector August of Saxony and Joachim Camer-

[3] See M. Koch, *Quellen zur Geschichte des Kaisers Maximilian II. in Archiven gesammelt und erläutert* (Leipzig, 1857), pp. 8–85; Moriz Ritter, *Deutsche Geschichte im Zeitalter der Gegenreformation und des dreissigjährigen Krieges (1555–1648)*, I (Darmstadt, 1962), 431–34. Grumbach, a Franconian knight, allegedly plotted against Elector August; the bishop of Würzburg attacked Grumbach for breaking the peace – an example of interconfessional princely coöperation against a knight errant in error.

[4] See the spirited account of Friedrich Heer, *The Holy Roman Empire* (New York, 1968), pp. 176–96: "The Madrid-Vienna Axis."

arius, a philosopher theologian at the University of Leipzig. When the full Saxon delegation arrived and discussions proceeded, the Lutheran members of the Austrian estates discerned Calvinist taints in the Wittenberg theologians, which aspersions enfuriated Elector August.[5] Under the mild good-natured Maximilian the evangelical cause made astonishing progress in Habsburg lands, as Linz, Freistadt, and Steyr in Upper Austria as well as Enns, Gmunden, Vöcklabruck and Wels adopted the Augsburg Confession. It penetrated even into the Burgenland.[6] When Maximilian died he was widely mourned by Protestants and Catholics alike. Rudolf II (1576–1612) gave the forces of the Counter Reformation virtually a free hand in Austrian lands.

The evangelical faith came very close to becoming the universal creed of Germany. Had it become just that, the religious ideological ground for conflict within the Empire would have been removed. But three developments prevented such an easy solution – internal dissension within Lutheranism, the expansion of a militant Calvinism, and the success of the Counter Reformation within the Empire.

A. Lutheran Dissension

During the decades which followed Luther's death Lutheranism was plagued by internal dissension and dogmatic quarrels that prevented a united front against the old foes or the new. The problem of religious authority was the Achilles' heel of Protestantism. Political rivalries played an important role as well. As a result of the Schmalkaldic War, Ernestine Saxony lost the electoral dignity to Albertine Saxony. There was constant rivalry between both Saxonies and Hesse for the leadership of the Protestants. Moreover, the emphasis upon dogmatic correctness, pedantic criticism, bellicosity and factionalism produced intolerance and an intolerable situation which threatened to render Lutheranism impotent. The University of Wittenberg, now in the territory of Albertine electoral Saxony, was Philippist, accepting Philipp Melanchthon's mediating positions. Ernestine Saxony, decisively gnesio-Lutheran in outlook, established the University of Jena, begun in 1548 and ceremoniously inaugurated in 1558 as a citadel of orthodoxy. The dogmatic war with the "Crypto-Calvinists" and Philippists was on! The adiaphoristic controversy (1548–1552), the Osiandrian controversy (1549–1566), the Majoristic controversy

---

[5] Friedrich Albert von Langenn, *Christoph von Carlowitz. Eine Darstellung aus dem XVI. Jahrhundert* (Leipzig, 1854), pp. 319–20.
[6] Grete Mecenseffy, *Geschichte des Protestantismus in Österreich* (Graz and Cologne, 1956), pp. 50–70: "Die hohe Zeit des österreichischen Protestantismus."

(1552–1558), and, the most devastating of all, the Synergistic controversy (1556–1560) kept Lutheranism in a constant boil. Melanchthon was mercifully delivered by death on 19 April 1560 from the scene of battles so alien to his mild nature and ecumenical disposition. In 1561 Duke John Frederick dismissed Flacius Illyricus, watchdog of orthodoxy, and some forty other clergymen for "doctrinal tyranny." In 1574 Elector August had Melanchthon's son-in-law and several others imprisoned for Crypto-Calvinism.

Fortunately a new irenic spirit emerged as Jakob Andreae, chancellor of the University of Tübingen, initiated a move toward Lutheran unity. Supported by moderate Lutheran theologians, notably Martin Chemnitz, and various princes such as Christoph of Württemberg and Julius of Brunswick, Andreae worked toward a doctrinal formula to which all Lutheran estates might agree. The result of protracted meetings and near endless negotiations was the Formula of Concord of 1577, which became the definitive confession of a large majority of the Lutheran principalities and kingdoms. On 25 June 1580, precisely fifty years after the presentation of the Augsburg Confession to the Diet of the Empire, the *Book of Concord* was published containing the three ecumenical creeds and the specifically Lutheran confessions.

A key and in many ways a representative Lutheran prince during this entire period was the elector August of Saxony (1553–1586). At the Diet of Augsburg in 1555 he had one objective in mind, achieving "peace of eternal duration."[7] Rather than adopt an aggressive Protestant policy in the decades which followed, he continued to seek a balance between Catholics and Protestants which would enable him to develop his territorial power in all possible peace and security.[8]

B. Calvinism Gains

The Peace of Augsburg provided for a mutual toleration of Catholics and Lutherans, but deliberately excluded concessions to Calvinism. Calvinism would not allow itself to be so blithely ignored, penetrating into Württemberg, lying close to Switzerland, and especially into the Palatinate. In the Palatinate the elector Frederick III (1559–1576) adopted Calvin's sacramental doctrine. He appointed Calvinist theologians educated in Geneva to professorships at Heidelberg. In 1563 his theologians wrote the famed Heidelberg catechism which was

---

[7] Lewis W. Spitz, "Particularism and Peace: Augsburg – 1555," *Church History*, XXV (1956), 9.
[8] Friedrich von Bezold, *Kaiser Rudolf II und die heilige Liga* ("Abhandlungen der Akademie der Wissenschaften," No. 17 [Munich, 1868]), p. 349.

used not only for instruction but also as a confessional statement for the
Calvinist churches in the Germanies and the Netherlands. The name
"Reformed" was, in fact, first used in order to distinguish Calvinist
congregations from the Lutheran communions. His eldest son, John
Casimir, fought several campaigns alongside the Huguenots in France,
and his youngest son Christoph died on the battlefield of Moorwyck
with the brothers of William the Silent in 1574. Elector August of
Saxony considered Frederick III to be a black sheep and a defector.
Religious and political sentiments were so closely interwoven that the
opposition between electoral Saxony and electoral Palatinate domi-
nated Protestant politics into the first decades of the seventeenth
century.[9] In 1613 Elector John Sigismund of electoral Brandenburg
turned Calvinist, intending like Frederick III to bring about the
conversion of his people. But there was so much opposition that in 1615
he had to guarantee the Lutheran confession.

C. Catholic Resurgence

The term "Counter Reformation" was first used by the Göttingen
jurist Johann Stephan Pütter in 1776, replacing the traditional
"Catholic Reformation," now once again in vogue, but the reality of a
counter-thrust was felt by mid-sixteenth century already.[10] As the
century wore on, the Counter Reformation gathered momentum in
the Empire. Even in the 1540s individual Jesuits were at work. Peter
Canisius (1511–1597) wrote the widely adopted catechism as an answer
to Luther's, edited the works of Johannes Tauler, and established
schools. From 1549 on, the Jesuits were at work in the Habsburg lands,
in Bavaria, and in the archepiscopacies along the Rhine. Their piety,
ceremonies, processions, pilgrimages, and in due course their archi-
tecture impressed the common people. Their excellent schools for
children of the nobility and their service as counselors to princes made
them politically very effective. At the Collegium Germanicum in

---

[9] In a recent monograph, Lothar Paul explores an instance of Calvinist political activism
in the Empire, describing the attempt to continue an alliance on the pattern of the Schmal-
kald League, following the examples of Philip of Hesse and Zwingli (*Nassauische Unionspläne.
Untersuchungen zum politischen Program des deutschen Kalvinismus im Zeitalter der Gegenreformation*
[Münster, 1966]). The Lutherans in general seemed to prefer Catholics to Calvinists, and
the theologian Polycarp Leiser even wrote a treatise "Ob, wie und warum man lieber mit
den Papisten Gemeinschaft haben und gleichsam mehr Vertrauen zu ihnen tragen sollte
denn mit und zu den Calvinisten." Well into the 17th century the evangelical subscribers
to the Augsburg Confession continued to view themselves as the true adherents of the
Catholic Church, and the Lutheran dogmatician Johann Gerhard named one of his major
works *Confessio Catholica* (4 vols., 1634–1637).
[10] Albert Elkan, "Entstehung und Entwicklung des Begriffs 'Gegenreformation,'"
Historische Zeitschrift, CXII (1914), 473–93.

Rome the Jesuits trained German priests and imbued them with an ultramontane spirit.

The Catholic counter-thrust gained power after the death of Melanchthon (1560) and the final session of the Council of Trent (1563). Pope Gregory XIII (1572–1585), remembered for his medal celebrating the Saint Bartholomew Massacre, was extremely energetic in his efforts to bring the Germanies back into the fold. He appointed very able nuncios to the Empire, skilled both in observation and manipulation.[11] He established the *Congregatio Germanica*, a permanent committee of cardinals to handle the "German Question."

The results of these efforts were quite astonishing and, to the Protestants, very alarming. Within a single generation one third of the Empire was once again safely Catholic. By 1600 Styria, Carinthia, Carmola, Baden-Baden and Bavaria had returned to the Catholic fold. Salzburg, Bamberg, and Würzburg, which had a large number of evangelicals, were Catholic again. In the North several strategic ecclesiastical territories were brought home to the Church – Fulda, Eichsfeld, Paderborn, Münster, and Cologne. As the key to Westphalia and the Rhineland, and as one of the electoral territories, Cologne was of critical importance. An earlier archbishop, Hermann von Wied, had nearly succeeded in secularizing the archdiocese of Cologne. Between 1580 and 1583 the struggle broke out again when Archbishop Gebhard Truchsess von Waldburg became Protestant in order to marry his lover the Canoness Countess Agnes von Mansfeld. Despite the ecclesiastical reservation required under the terms of the Peace of Augsburg, Archbishop Gebhard tried to maintain his control of the territory of the archdiocese, guaranteeing religious liberty to all his subjects. But the opposition of the city, the canons, and Bavarian intervention were so determined that Gebhard, aided hardly at all by the Protestant princes, lost the struggle.[12] As Catholicism gained in power the threat of a religious war between fairly evenly balanced sides became increasingly ominous. These were the decades which

[11] Cf. Robert M. Kingdon's contribution to the present volume. Walter Goetz ("Die Gegenreformation in Deutschland," *Das Zeitalter der religiösen Umwälzung Reformation und Gegenreformation 1500–1600* [Berlin, 1930], pp. 354–55) refers to the effectiveness of Gregory's nuncios. See also Moriz Ritter, I, 451–52, on Gregory XIII and Germany. Of interest also is Ludwig von Pastor's picture of Gregory XIII's relation to the Massacre, exculpating him from any guilt in planning it, quite correctly, and describing his role in the German effort (*The History of the Popes*, XIX [London, 1930], 482–518; XX [London, 1930], 25 ff.). Invaluable as sources are the *Nuntiaturberichte aus Deutschland 1572–1585*, ed. Joseph Hansen *et al.* (5 vols.; Berlin, 1892–1909).

[12] For a nice general account see Hajo Holborn, *A History of Modern Germany: The Reformation* (New York, 1959), pp. 266–83, 290–93.

Heinrich von Treitschke called "die häszlichsten Zeiten der deutschen Geschichte!"[13]

2. THE IMPACT OF THE BLUTHOCHZEIT ZU PARIS
ON THE EMPIRE

In "The Massacre at Paris" Christopher Marlowe has the king say to the queen mother:

> Madam, it wilbe noted through the world,
> An action bloudy and tirannicall:
> Cheefely since under safetie of our word,
> They iustly challenge their protection:
> Besides my heart relentes that noble men,
> Onely corrupted in religion,
> Ladies of honor, Knightes and Gentlemen,
> Should for their conscience taste such rutheless ends.[14]

The action was indeed noted throughout the world, with jubilation in such Catholic capitals as Rome, Madrid, Brussels and Venice, with horror by a large part of the English public.[15] The reaction to the news in the Empire and in Protestant Switzerland, still theoretically part of the Empire, was anything but enthusiastic. Emperor Maximilian II decried the "unspeakable deed," the "shameful bloodbath," and regretted that this "murderous gang" were among his kinsmen. "The course of the world runs contrary to all reason," he remarked to Micheli, the Venetian ambassador. In order to draw the house of Austria closer to Spain and France he had married his daughter Anna to Philip II and his daughter Elisabeth to Charles IX. In a letter to Elector August of Saxony in his own hand, dated 13 December 1572, he spoke of the Massacre as an infamy which the French would have bitter cause to regret. He passed this verdict on his son-in-law: "I know that it is not my son-in-law who governs. But that is not enough

---

[13] Heinrich von Treitschke, *Deutsche Geschichte im 19. Jahrhundert* (Leipzig, 1886), Pt. I, p. 4.

[14] Christopher Marlowe, "The Massacre at Paris; With the Death of the Duke of Guise," *The Works of Christopher Marlowe* (Oxford, 1910), p. 451, lines 211–18.

[15] See the articles by R. M. Kingdon and A. G. Dickens immediately preceding this essay. O. Hartwig discusses a rare brochure found in the Bodleian describing the Venetian celebration: *Ordine della solennissima processione fatta dal sommo pontifice nell'alma città di Roma per la felicissima nova della destructione della città Ugonotaria* (Rome, 1572), *Deutsche Zeitschrift für Geschichtswissenschaft*, VII (1892), 341.

to pardon him. Had he asked my advice, he would not now be soiled by a stain he will never be able to wipe away."[16]

When word of the Massacre reached him in September, one German prince declared that as long as the world stands the Rhine will not be able to wash away this bloodbath from the French royal house.[17] The stain on the Valois escutcheon has indeed remained in the popular mind to the present day. There seemed to be something to the accusation which the old cardinal de Bourbon threw into the face of the dying queen mother, Catherine de Medici, after the murder of the Guise brothers in 1588 – that she could not rest until she had led all to the slaughter bench. The French envoy to the Swiss cantons, Gantrie, wrote to Catherine that he "would never dare to report what he had heard about her and her son." Jean de Montluc and Jean Choisnin, who were urging the cause of the duke of Anjou for the throne of Poland in the Empire, initially found a favorable response. But that favor lasted only twenty-four hours, for "forthwith someone came bearing news of St. Bartholomew's day," Choisnin related in his *Mémoires*, "enriched with so many recollections and particulars that in a few hours most people despised the name France."[18] In Brandenburg the people believed that an earthquake in August was a sign of the catastrophe in France and when a new star appeared in the constellation Cassiopeia they believed it to be the soul of the admiral.

As the refugees poured out into various parts of Germany and Switzerland telling their story of the murders and plundering, the common people also felt a surge of revulsion. According to the Italian historian Davila, Huguenots from "Champagne and Burgundy were gotten into the cities of Germany and there endeavored to make the actions of the King of France to be suspected and ill-tempered by the Hanse towns and Protestant princes."[19] Eyewitness accounts reached

---

[16] Henry Noguères, *The Massacre of Saint Bartholomew*, tr. Claire Eliane Engel (New York, 1962), p. 152. Charles IX's widow in later life washed the stain of guilt away. She moved to Prague where she built the All Soul's Chapel in the Hradčany Palace. To compensate for the *Bluthochzeit* in Paris she founded a house of Dorothean nuns on what is now the Dorotheergasse in the heart of Vienna. Joseph II, in an enlightened mood, gave the great church and convent buildings to the Lutherans, and they still serve as the center of the evangelical church in Austria with a congregation of some 18,000 members.

[17] Walter Platzhoff, "Die Bartholomäusnacht," *Preuszische Jahrbücher*, CL (1912), 52.

[18] *Mémoires de Jean Choisnin, Livre deuxième*, ed. Michaud and Poujoulat ("Nouvelle collection des mémoires pour servir à l'histoire de France"; Paris, 1838), p. 398. See also the marginal note by Giacomo Castelvetro to the account of the Massacre by Tomasso Sassetti, below, p. 146.

[19] H. C. Davila, *The Historie of the Civill Warres of France* (London, 1647), p. 380. Another near-contemporary account describes the generous reception accorded the refugees in England, Germany, esp. by Elector Frederick III of the Palatinate, and by Berne, Zurich and Geneva in Switzerland (*Ioan. Sleidani veri et ad nostra tempora usque continuati, Das ist*

many parts of the Empire. A German law student at Orléans, Johann Wilhelm Botzheim, wrote a sixty-one page report on the massacre there. He himself barely escaped death some twenty times, and many of his comrades and compatriots shared the fate of the Huguenots. He described the violence and cruelty of the pillaging papists who robbed, sacked houses, forced people to show where their treasures were hid on threat of death, and then killed them anyway. They threw some into latrines to drown. They killed one publisher, dragged his body into the streets and then plundered his house and wine cellars. Even professors enriched their libraries with books taken from the Protestants. Laurent Godefroid, professor of the Pandects, acquired the books of George Obrecht and some of Botzheim's books which he had lent to Obrecht. Dr. Beaupied, professor of canon law, took the books of Botzheim's brother Bernhard as well as his garderobe and coats, following the pillaging of the house of Saint-Thomas, his hostel. Botzheim, who later became a judge in Speyer and an imperial councilor in the Palatinate, estimated that 1500 to 2000 were killed in Orléans alone and compared the massacre with the persecutions by Nero.[20]

A citizen of Strasbourg gave an eyewitness account of events in Paris, the vindictiveness with which the body of Coligny was mutilated, and how the Massacre spread to Chalons, Orléans, Vassy and other cities.[21] The rector of the Strasbourg gymnasium, Johannes Sturm, thought the Massacre to be more gruesome than the meal of Pelops, whose father killed him to be eaten by the gods.

Reports came to Germany from widely spread sources. An agent of the Fuggers reported to Augsburg from Amsterdam as early as 30

Warhafftige Beschreibung allerley fürnemmer Händel und Geschichten so sich in Glaubens und andern Weltlichen Sachen bey Regierung der Groszmächtigsten und unüberwindlichsten Keyseren [Strasbourg, 1625], cols. 247–48). This continuation of Sleidan's history is by Osea Schadaeus. Unfortunately the valuable work by C. Weiss, *Histoire des réfugiés protestants de France* (2 vols.; Paris, 1853), begins the story at the end of the 16th century and concentrates on the refugees from Louis XIV's regime.

[20] Frederick W. Ebeling, ed., "La Saint-Barthélemy à Orléans racontée par Joh.-Wilh. de Botzheim, étudiant allemand témoin oculaire, 1572," *Bulletin de la Société de l'histoire du protestantisme français*, XXI (1872), 345–92, esp. pp. 350, 359. The manuscript is now preserved in the Saxon archives. Karl Schottenloher (*Bibliographie zur deutschen Geschichte im Zeitalter der Glaubensspaltung 1517–1585*, IV [2d. ed.; Stuttgart, 1957], 49) lists contemporary German tracts describing the *Bluthochzeit* and distributed in Germany at that time.

[21] Rod Reuss, "Un nouveau récit de la Saint-Barthélemy par un bourgeois de Strasbourg," *Bulletin de la Société de l'histoire du protestantisme français*, XXII (1873), 374–81. The account was notarized at Heidelberg, 7 Sept. 1572. Alkuin Hollaender ("Hubertus Languetus in Strassburg," *Zeitschrift für die Geschichte des Oberrheins*, XLIX [1895], 42–56, esp. pp. 50–56) gives the text of the first report to reach Strasbourg officials on 29 August and Hubert Languet's report on the Massacre to a representative of the city council, Theodosius Gerbel, during Languet's stay in the city in September.

August 1572. He compared the Massacre with the Sicilian Vespers and chortled that the Huguenots and the Guises alike had had their wings clipped. He suspected that there were more people involved than appeared on the surface.[22]

On 10 September 1572 Theodore Beza wrote to Thomas Tilius (Du Tillet?) in Heidelberg describing the Massacre and the plight of the refugees pouring into Geneva:

We are in mourning and lamentations. May God take pity on us! Never has anyone seen such perfidy, so great an atrocity. . . . Our city where the plague and fever reign is filled with the most unfortunate people on earth. They have escaped thanks only to the cupidity of their enemies. For otherwise no one would have been spared, neither by reason of rank, age, or sex. From the beginning the king put the Guises in charge; now he writes that all was done on his orders and that those men whom he assassinated in their beds in Paris, those men "of whom the world is not worthy," he dares to accuse them of conspiracy![23]

Beza tells of the nonresisting Huguenots in Lyons, slaughtered like lambs. In a letter of 3 December he reports his anguish at the unbelievable number of defections, but that even defection will not save many, for the ferocious beasts have resolved to kill all who had apostasized together with their families. Among the French refugees in Basel who registered at the university, including authors and lawyers, there was one, a certain Professor Petrus Carpentarius Tolosas, who turned out to be a spy in the hire of the French ambassador. When exposed he published a letter on 15 September 1572, pleading extenuating circumstances for the Massacre.[24]

That the role of the émigrés could have a long-term influence in German states is best illustrated by the career of Daniel Toussain, the great Huguenot preacher of Orléans who served ten years in France, but thirty in Germany. When the third religious war scattered his flock in Orléans he became a refugee in Montargis, and then he aided his aged father in Montbéliard, a dependency of Württemberg, and superintendent of the churches there. But the Lutheran officials (cyclopses with their doctrine of manducation, said Toussain) became

<hr />

[22] Victor Klarwill, ed., *Fugger-Zeitungen. Ungedruckte Briefe an das Haus Fugger aus den Jahren 1568–1605* (Vienna, 1923), pp. 17–18, No. 15: "Die Bartholomäusnacht."

[23] A. Müntz, ed., "Deux lettres de Théodore de Bèze sur la Saint-Barthélemy, 1572," *Bulletin de la Société de l'histoire du protestantisme français*, VII (1858), 16–17.

[24] "Documents: Quelques réfugiés de la Saint-Barthélemy à Bâle. Extrait de la matricule du recteur de l'Université de Bâle 1572–1573," *Bulletin de la Société de l'histoire du protestantisme français*, XLI (1892), 408–10. See also L. A. Burckhardt, "Die französischen Religionsflüchtlinge in Basel," *Beiträge zur vaterländischen Geschichte*, VII (Basel, 1860), 301–33; Th. von Liebenau, "Luzernische Berichte über die Bartholomäusnacht," *Anzeiger für schweizerische Geschichte*, N.F., II (1874–1877), 249–60.

increasingly intolerant and he accepted a call back to Orléans and, in October 1571, began to preach in the chateau of Jerome Groslot outside the city. "On that black, dreadful and bloody day, 24 August 1572," said Toussain, "I preached the last sermon heard on the Place de l'Isle; there followed a deluge of Christian blood throughout all France." The fact that he was living outside the city was his salvation, for the gates were closed during the massacre. Saved "from the very jaws of the lions," as he put it, he brought his wife and four children to Montargis, where the duchess Renée of Ferrara hid them. On 3 November he reached Montbéliard where the authorities bowed to a demand of the French king that they were not to harbor refugees. After a few weeks he moved in to become a pastor to the refugees in Basel. But the elector Frederick III ("the Pious") of the Palatinate, on Beza's prompting, took Toussain as his councilor, for the Reformed Church had been torn by the Erastian controversy over ecclesiastical organization and by defections to unitarianism. For thirty years Toussain exercised a powerful influence in the Palatinate as councilor and court preacher. During the rule of the Lutheran Ludwig VI (1576–1583), Toussain stayed with Count John Casimir, who then served as regent for young Frederick IV. Toussain directed the Reformed churches of the Palatinate, served as court preacher, superintendent of schools, member of the ecclesiastical councils, and as professor of theology at Heidelberg until his death on 10 January 1602.[25] The pivotal importance of the Palatinate in the political constellation within the Empire, to say nothing of its role in precipitating the Thirty Years' War, suggests the historical significance of Toussain's career in strengthening the Reformed Church in the electorate.

The celebrations of the Massacre by the Catholic powers convinced the Protestants further that the crime had long been premeditated and that there was a secret alliance among the papal powers to unite in crushing the Reformed in France, the Netherlands, and then perhaps in the Empire. Within two months of the event a certain Capilupi published a work in Rome which fixed this theory in the literature – *Lo stratagemma di Carlo IX. contra gli Ugonotti ribelli di Dio*. In this work he praised the behavior of the king during the preceding years, the Peace of St. Germain, the greater closeness to the Huguenots, and the

---

[25] A. Bernus, "Trois pasteurs échappés aux massacres de la Saint-Barthélemy," *Bulletin de la Société de l'histoire du protestantisme français*, XLI (1892), 393–414. The other two refugee pastors are Merlin, Coligny's chaplain, who fled to Geneva and settled in Berne, and L'Espine, who fled to Renée of Ferrara and then to Geneva, where he was admitted to the Venerable Company.

support of their politics, all as a cleverly designed trap for the rebellious heretics. Capilupi's distortions are made clear in the most recent scholarly study of the Massacre by N. M. Sutherland, where it is argued that the repeatedly revived policy of "eliminating" the Huguenot leaders was the work of the cardinal of Lorraine and other Catholic extremists, for the purpose of widening the split between the French throne and Protestantism, and to force Catherine into the toils of Guise politics. But this was not generally perceived at the time, and, after the event, the French government was caught in a real dilemma, for the more zealously it cultivated the picture at Catholic courts of its hostility to the Huguenots, the more necessary it was to deny the religious character of the act and any premeditation when dealing with Protestant courts.[26] To the Protestants they defended their action on the basis of *raison d'État*, a step necessary to frustrate the high treason and conspiracy of Coligny and his followers. Even the papal nuncio in Paris reported to Rome that the king's claim of a conspiracy made to the parlement three days after the Massacre was false. The idea of premeditation and a secret alliance of the Catholic powers could not be rooted out. In Protestant Switzerland there was a widespread and deep suspicion that there was a conspiracy between the pope, the emperor, the French and Spanish kings, and the duke of Savoy to eradicate the new faith.[27]

[26] N. M. Sutherland, *The Massacre of St Bartholomew and the European Conflict 1559–1572* (London, 1973); Walter Platzhoff, "Die Bartholomäusnacht im Lichte der Jahrhunderte," *Vergangenheit und Gegenwart*, II (1912), 49–57, esp. p. 50. It seems ironically to have been German scholarship in the 19th century which first established the now generally accepted view that the Massacre was planned only after the attempt on Coligny had failed and that Charles IX was convinced only at the last minute by Catherine and confidants. This view was first presented by Ludwig Wachler in *Die Pariser Bluthochzeit* (2d. ed.; Leipzig, 1828), further developed by Wilhelm Gottlieb Soldan ("Frankreich und die Bartholomäusnacht," *Historisches Taschenbuch*, 3d. series, V [1854], 75–241, esp. p. 83), and was adopted by Leopold von Ranke, who, however, found that Catherine had felt murderous impulses earlier and ascribed much to the "true duplicity" imbedded in her psychology ("Gegensatz Colignys und der Königin-Mutter – Bartholomäusnacht," *Französische Geschichte vornehmlich im sechzehnten und siebzehnten Jahrhundert*, I [Munich and Leipzig, 1924], 242–71). Hermann Baumgarten (*Vor der Bartholomäusnacht* [Strasbourg, 1882]) tried to explain the motive in the light of preceding events. Alfred Stern ("Der Ursprung der Bartholomäusnacht nach den neuesten Untersuchungen," *Westermanns Illustrierte deutsche Monatshefte*, LIV [1883], 571–84) praises Baumgarten and other scholars for discrediting the long-premeditated plot theory.

[27] Th. Müller-Wolfer, "Der Staatsmann Ludwig Pfyffer und die Hugenottenkriege," *Zeitschrift für schweizerische Geschichte*, VIII (1928), 1–63, 241–320, esp. p. 39. Pfyffer (1524–1595) led Charles IX's Swiss regiments against the Huguenots from 1562 on, and after 1571 was mayor of Lucerne and very influential in the Catholic cantons. On 7 December 1572, Charles IX sent a special emissary to Baden to convince the *Eidgenossenschaft* that the king might have lost his kingdom due to Coligny's conspiracy and had to act as he did (H. V. Sauerland, "Zur Geschichte der Bartholomäusnacht," *Mittheilungen des Instituts für österreichische Geschichtsforschung*, XIII [1892], 330–33).

If the German princes were shocked and the people horrified at the *Bluthochzeit*, the historian might confidently assume that relations with the French king would be terminated and a rapprochement with the mild and beloved emperor would be broached.[28] But such an assumption would be quite mistaken, for after an initial chilling emotional reaction the princes proceeded as true *politiques* to pursue policy in accord with their particularist interests. The most efficient way of checking out their immediate reaction and subsequent action is to examine their response to the blandishments of Gaspard de Schomberg, the most important of Charles IX's emissaries who swarmed into the Empire to represent French policy. The proposals with which the French emissaries approached the Protestant princes from September 1572 through the spring of 1574 were much the same as before St. Bartholomew, as though it had been no more than a brief civil disorder and as if nothing had changed. They urged common support for the Netherlands against Spain, a defensive alliance between France and the Protestant princes, the bestowing of the crown of the Holy Roman Empire on Anjou, King Charles IX's brother, and support for Anjou to receive the throne of Poland, which had fallen vacant on 7 July 1572. When Anjou did in fact, on 9 May 1573, receive the crown of Poland, they urged that the same treaties made by the princes with France be made also with Poland.

Gaspard de Schomberg (Caspar von Schönberg) (1540–1599) was a Saxon who studied at Strasbourg, then at Angers to perfect his French, and fought for the Huguenots for a brief time after 1562. He entered the service of the government, recruited troops in Hesse for the French king, and eventually became a favorite of Charles IX, who sent him as his highest ambassador to handle diplomatic affairs at the most important princely courts.[29] At the time of the Massacre Schomberg was in the Empire trying to win support for Anjou's candidacy for the Polish throne. The news hit like a bombshell. The ambassador was in Kassel when word of St. Bartholomew arrived. He needed all the manliness and strength of his own good conscience to stand the storm of accusations heaped on him. When in excusing the deed he cast aspersions on the admiral, the Landgrave Wilhelm of Hesse, who was

---

[28] This *a priori* assumption is not infrequently made by authors not familiar with the German scene. See, e.g., Henry White, *The Massacre of St. Bartholomew* (New York, 1868), p. 471: "The German Protestant powers were alienated, and the English nation shrank in horror from the French alliance."

[29] Schomberg's friend de Thou reports on Schomberg's position and diplomatic missions in his history, *Jac. Augusti Thuani Historiarum Sui Temporis* (London, 1733), esp. books 29, 30, 40 and 41.

otherwise favorably disposed toward the French king, reminded him that he was a German and that Coligny had raised him up in France. Nevertheless in his written response to the king, the Landgrave expressed his sympathy and aversion in such a mild way as to justify Schomberg's later assertion that "the fleur-de-lys is buried deep in the heart of the Hessian." Although the people were incensed, the prince very quickly found grounds for reconciliation in the political situation and gave the plans of the Valois a new powerful boost.[30]

Things were more difficult in the case of Elector August of Saxony. When word of the Massacre arrived on 7 September, Elector August would not receive M. de St.-Colombe, even though he had brought him hunting hounds and mules as a present, and travelled immediately to his brother-in-law Frederick II in Denmark. Schomberg travelled to north Germany and there he received a letter from King Charles IX on 13 September making stronger accusations against the admiral, as though he had had designs on the king's throne and very life. But he added that he had ordered all provincial officials to spare the Huguenots and for a time to allow them preaching and assembly. Schomberg should also remind the princes of the true friendship of Charles's grandfather François I and assure them that he wished actively to continue the same. François I had punished Lutherans, he wrote, but did not cease to be on good terms of friendship with the Protestant princes. Catherine and the Guises were so deceptive they did not even tell the truth to their own ambassadors, informing them, for example that La Rochelle had fallen, in order to urge them on to speak more effectively.[31] At one point Catherine wrote to Schomberg: "Do not think that what has been done to the Admiral and his accomplices was done out of hatred for the new religion, or to eradicate it, but merely to punish the dastardly conspiracy they had made."[32] Schomberg waited patiently in Rostock until Elector August returned from Denmark on 4 October.

At this juncture (9 October) Schomberg wrote a fascinating letter to Charles IX, which revealed the difficulties of the situation. The elector is cold, will communicate with him only through Dr. Crato (Krakow), claiming exhaustion from the trip, pressing business, and the inconvenience of the place. The said doctor has given him a written response,

[30] Friedrich Wilhelm Barthold, "Kaspar von Schönberg, der Sachse ein Wohlthäter des französischen Reichs und Volks," *Historisches Taschenbuch*, N.F., X (1849), 165-362, esp. p. 219.
[31] *Ibid.*, pp. 219-21.
[32] Qtd. by H. Noguères, p. 151.

however, in which the elector assures the king of his good and loyal friendship and wishes to maintain the same relations with France as his ancestors. But in view of what has happened the elector does not wish to make a closer alliance with the king; for in response to Schomberg's remonstrances that he must not take offense and that he needs the help of a strong friend, the elector replies that he has heard of the shedding of blood in Paris, Orléans, Rouen, Lyons, that it continues daily in other cities, that the king of Navarre and prince de Condé have been forced to go to mass, that Huguenots' children are rebaptized Catholic, and that the watchword of all France is "To mass or to the river!" The king must protect the Huguenots, suspend dealings with Spain and Alva and give the lie to the slanders spoken against him. The elector writes that for the present he can change nothing which he has written, which causes Schomberg to hope that time will heal all. The enemies of France have sent letters throughout all Germany saying that the elector would have Schomberg imprisoned, intending to behead him for telling him lies. Schomberg is now leaving for the Leipzig fair, where many of the nobility will be gathered, in order to exert his influence in behalf of the truth regarding the events in Paris as his Majesty has reported the truth in his dispatch of 25 August and in order to counteract the slanders against his Majesty's so virtuous and royal reputation throughout all Germany. If he had one hundred thousand lives he would hazard them all and dedicate them all as a loyal servant to his master. "Time is able to do much in such maladies which proceed only from a passion founded on unhappy slanders and vain and frivolous suspicions, and in waiting I will pray the Creator, Sire, if it pleases Him, to grant to you victory against all your enemies and a very happy and a very long reign."[33] The following day Schomberg wrote a letter to Sébastien de l'Aubespine, bishop of Limoges, one of Charles IX's leading councilors, telling him of the feeling against the king and advising that the king must be gracious to the Huguenots, show that he does not intend to exterminate their religion, avoid all secret intelligence with Spain and her adherents, and must take every step possible to keep the German princes from throwing themselves in despair into the traps of the criminal enemies of the crown of France.[34]

The elector was getting heated reports from his ambassador at the

---

[33] "Documents inédits et originaux: La diplomatie française et la Saint-Barthélemy. Deux lettres de M. de Schomberg, ambassadeur de France en Allemagne (9 et 10 octobre 1572)," *Bulletin de la Société de l'histoire du protestantisme français*, XVI (1867), 546–50.

[34] *Ibid.*, pp. 550–51.

French court from 1573 to 1577, Hubert Languet (1519–1581), a Huguenot author and diplomat who barely escaped death in the Massacre himself. He returned in November to Dresden, filled with hatred of tyranny.[35] On 31 December he wrote the elector that the French court was not only concealing the truth from Schomberg but was sending him pure fabrications, such as the report of the submission of La Rochelle. But for all that, the elector August eventually came around and backed Anjou for the crown of Poland.

Strangely enough Schomberg's success was the greatest in the Palatinate, where the Reformed prince was religiously closest to the Huguenots. Schomberg seems to have convinced even John Casimir (the "Knight St. George of the Huguenots") of France's honorable intentions.[36] In fact, the court of Frederick III showed itself ready for an alliance with France, supported the French candidacy in the Imperial election, and contributed in addition to France's 100,000 crowns a loan of 50,000 gulden to the House of Orange.[37] The very Calvinist state which under Toussain's leadership was organizing an efficient and zealous Reformed Church, and which had supplied troops for the Huguenots led by the elector's son, now took the lead in a pro-French policy. John Casimir even wrote his father that if the French alliance had been consummated earlier, perhaps the catastrophe of St. Bartholomew would not have occurred. Still, the Palatinate did make more comprehensive religious freedom for the Huguenots a precondition of an alliance of the German princes with the French king, while the French king tried his best to cut off the Huguenots from their German sympathizers.[38]

This entire scene, including the broad political and religious picture in the Empire as well as the specific nexus of events related to the *Bluthochzeit* in Paris, reveals historical developments at work pregnant with implications for the problem of religious toleration. First, it is evident that the German princes were pursuing their own particularist interests with even greater consistency and determination than they had shown up to the time of the Peace of Augsburg. Whatever "nation-

---

[35] Languet has often been mentioned, together with Mornay, as possibly the author of the *Vindiciae contra Tyrannos* (1579), although the most recent theory proposes the authorship of Johan Junius de Jonge (1525–1593). See Derk Visser, "Junius: The Author of the *Vindiciae contra Tyrannos?*," *Tijdschrift voor Geschiedenis*, LXXXIV (1971), 510–25.

[36] Barthold, pp. 222–23.

[37] Ritter, p. 441.

[38] Janine Estèbe, *Tocsin pour un massacre: La saison des Saint-Barthélemy* (Paris, 1968), p. 172: "Les princes protestants allemands sont également indignés du massacre des huguenots; mais leur attitude est, comme celle d'Elisabeth, entachée de politique."

al consciousness" or "Empire patriotism" the territorial princes may
have developed at the time of Maximilian I or still had under Charles
V, there is little evidence that it was operative in these decades when,
despite the Massacre of St. Bartholomew, they preferred a French to an
Austrian tie.[39] Geoffrey Barraclough has maintained that Germany's
history was determined during the Investiture Controversy which
prevented unity in the Empire. The particularism of the Protestant
princes does indeed suggest that Gregory VII was a more powerful
determiner of German fortunes than was Gregory XIII.

Secondly, within each territorial state the struggle of the princes
with the estates took on a religious cast, especially in the Catholic
states. This was a general European phenomenon, of course, in evidence
in France, Scotland, the Netherlands, and Poland, for example. But
within the Empire the close interweaving of the political interests of
the estates with a religious cause was particularly acute as the forces of
the Counter Reformation gained momentum under Rudolf II (1576–
1616), and the pressure for the complete re-Catholicization of the
Habsburg lands increased.[40] The same phenomena occurred in Bavaria
under Albert V (1550–1579), in the now not-so-free imperial cities, in
the episcopal princedoms, and in myriad lesser states.

Thirdly, it seems evident that "pure religion" was becoming ever
less significant as a factor determining policy. During the first phase of
the Reformation (1521–1555) princes not infrequently risked all, even
their lives for the sake of their evangelical or Catholic convictions. By
the time of the Peace of Augsburg particularist interests definitely
weighed more heavily than confessional concern with all but a few
princes such as Hans von Küstrin[41] and Christoph of Württemberg.

---

[39] A recent study of this problem focussing on a date a few decades later is Adam Wand-
ruszka, *Reichspatriotismus und Reichspolitik zur Zeit des Prager Friedens von 1635. Eine Studie zur
Geschichte des deutschen Nationalbewusztseins* (Graz and Cologne, 1955).

[40] Hans Sturmberger (*Georg Erasmus Tschernembl. Religion, Libertät und Widerstand* [Graz,
1953]) provides an intimate insight into this struggle through the life of Tschernembl
(1567–1626), the most important personality of the Protestant estates in Austria (ob der
Enns) in the fight against absolutism and Counter Reformation. On the general place of the
Landtags and estates in the Empire, see F. L. Carsten, *Princes and Parliaments in Germany*
(Oxford, 1959), and Dietrich Gerhard, "Ständische Vertretungen und Land," *Festschrift für
Hermann Heimpel* (Göttingen, 1971), pp. 447–72, esp. p. 455: "Intensiver waren die Be-
mühungen der Habsburger zum Zusammenschlusz ihrer Stände in den österreichischen und,
im Verfolg der Politik ihrer Vorgänger, in den burgundischen Ländern. In beiden Fällen
mündeten sie ein in einen Religionskonflikt, der zugleich zum Kampf um die politische Verfassung dieser Gebiete wurde." The recently published study by R. J. W. Evans (*Rudolf II
and His World: A Study of Intellectual History, 1576–1612* [Oxford, 1973]) provides a brilliant
analysis of Rudolf's thought world, his religious complexities and politics. He emphasizes
(p. 86) the atmosphere of anxiety and fear produced in Germany and Bohemia as an aftermath of the St. Bartholomew's Day Massacre.

During the second phase (1555–1618) it seems evident that particularist interests were predominant in determining princely policy, even when religion was used to cloak action or non-involvement. A typical instance was the case of Cologne in 1582 when the Wittelsbachs used Bavarian arms to establish Ernest of Bavaria, an immoral pluralist, as the Catholic archbishop. The Lutheran elector Ludwig of the Palatinate could not persuade Brandenburg and electoral Saxony to defend the Protestant Gebhard Truchsess von Waldburg, deposed by the pope, against Ernest. "One must leave it to Almighty God," said Elector August, "as to how He wishes to preserve His wholesome Word against the onslaught of the pope and the devil." During the third phase (1618–1648), the thirty years of war, with international power-political forces at work, religious motivations faded further away. At the congress which led to the Peace of Westphalia, the outstanding differences between Catholics and Protestants which for more than a century had been dealt with by military and diplomatic means stood for the last time at the head of the agenda for an imperial assembly. For the last time both parties sought to achieve confessional ends by political means. But it was little Ernestine Saxony and the smaller ecclesiastical princes who were most articulate and determined in this. The larger states were relatively cool, and as negotiations proceeded the voices of foreign powers and the exigencies of *raison d'État* became increasingly decisive. The representative of Saxony-Altenburg, von Thumshirn, in a letter to the privy councilor of Altenburg, von Brandt, wrote: "*Ratio status* is a wonderful animal; it drives away all other *rationes!*"[42]

Fourthly, the longest-range effects of the *Bluthochzeit* on German history almost elude our grasp. Though such an outrage heightened confessional mistrust and hostility, it did not result in more than a temporary alienation between the Protestant princes and the French king. When war came to the Empire it was precipitated by Frederick V of the Palatinate's acceptance of the Bohemian throne offered by the Protestant Bohemian estates without really appreciating all the implications, such as almost certain war with the Habsburgs. Deep down, on the popular level, the Massacre may well have increased

---

[41] Willy Hoppe, "Drei lutherische Landesfürsten in Brandenburg. Kurfürst Joachim II. Markgraf Hans von Küstrin. Kurfürst Johann Georg," *Forschungen zu Staat und Verfassung. Festgabe für Fritz Hartung* (Berlin, 1958), pp. 91–112.

[42] Gerhard Schmid, "Konfessionspolitik und Staatsräson bei den Verhandlungen des westfälischen Friedenskongresses über die Gravamina Ecclesiastica," *Archiv für Reformationsgeschichte*, XLIV (1953), 203–23, quotation on p. 223.

hatred for Catholics in a lasting way, but historians can do no more than point to such a possibility, since there is no instrument by which to measure its reality. Just as there were irrational socio-pathological forces at work in the pogrom in Paris, involving elements of class and ritual crime, such forces also played a part in the horrors of the long war in the Empire.

3. TOLERATION

In his *De hæreticis an sint persequendis*, Castellio pointed to Luther as his chief witness for the advancement of toleration and religious freedom, followed by the Lutheran Johannes Brenz,[43] and then the humanist Erasmus and the spiritualist Sebastian Franck. Castellio was quite perceptive in laying out this order of priority, for with the Reformation the hour of religious liberty had come. From a legal point of view the provision of the Peace of Augsburg for the equal coexistence of two forms of Christian church structure and teaching not only recognized the reality of religious pluralism but formally acknowledged the end of an era of unity between *sacerdotium* and *imperium* that dated from the times of Constantine, Galerius, and Theodosius.[44] The story of toleration and the theoretical limitations on toleration in the evangelical and Catholic reformers alike has often been told. Nor would it serve any useful purpose to rehearse even with the intent to correct and refine the brilliant, if somewhat partisan account of Joseph Lecler, S.J., on "the problem of religious freedom in the Empire."[45] The special contributions of Mino Celsi, Ochino, Acontius, Sebastian Franck, Schwenkfeld, Cornheert, Postel, Bodin and other minority spokesmen have also been adequately assessed. It will be more profitable to remain within the political and religious framework developed

[43] Martin Brecht, *Die frühe Theologie des Johannes Brenz* (Tübingen, 1966), pp. 302–08: "Die Obrigkeit und die Wiedertäufer." See p. 303: "Darum ist es der beste Weg, allein das Evangelium und die Schrift wider die Ketzer fechten zu lassen, die auch ihren guten Schein zu entlarven vermögen. ... Die Ketzer aber werden gestraft durch das Evangelium und durch Gott in der andern Welt. Würde man sie töten, so könnten sie nicht mehr umkehren."

[44] Martin Heckel, "Autonomia und Pacis Compositio. Der Augsburger Religionsfriede in der Deutung der Gegenreformation," *Zeitschrift der Savigny-Stiftung für Rechtsgeschichte, Kanonistische Abteilung*, XLV (1959), 142. Heckel argues that legally the Peace of Augsburg marks for the Empire the decisive turn from the Middle Ages to modern times.

[45] Joseph Lecler, S.J., *Toleration and the Reformation*, tr. T. L. Westow (2 vols.; New York, 1960), I, 147–304. Another general account is Karl Völker, *Toleranz und Intoleranz im Zeitalter der Reformation* (Leipzig, 1912), from the Protestant point of view. Nikolaus Paulus (*Protestantismus und Toleranz im 16. Jahrhundert* [Freiburg i.B., 1911]) discusses the theological

above in order to explore the fortune of religious toleration not as an abstract ideal, but as an operative concept in the real political world. "Ideas lie closely together," wrote Goethe, "but matter jostles itself in space."

Ecclesiastical and political official policy in the sixteenth century was definitely set against toleration. Pope Clement VIII (1592–1605) once spoke of the "phantoms of freedom of conscience." Philip II declared that he would sooner lose all his kingdoms than grant religious freedom. Queen Elizabeth and other Protestant leaders were very much of the same mind, even though less rigorous and efficient in applying such a policy. Given this fact of life, the breakthrough of the Peace of Augsburg seems all the more remarkable. There was very little imperial virtue invested in this concession to the Lutherans, for the emperor agreed to it only because he saw himself on the very verge of catastrophe, thanks to the duplicity and surprise attack of Maurice of Saxony. What exactly did the document say? The famous third article declares that religious controversies should be settled "in no other way than by Christian, friendly, peaceful means and ways." No one should "because of their teaching, religion and faith with any kind of act of force overrun, harm, or violate the Evangelicals, or force them in any other way against their conscience, scruples and will away from this Augsburg confession, religion, faith, church practices, orders and ceremonies and enjoy their property and goods, and leave in quiet and peace their land, people, estates, authorities, excellences, and rights."[46] Article Four made the same guarantee to the Catholic princes. In effect this meant that the princes of the Empire (except the ecclesiastical princes) mutually guaranteed to themselves and to their territories the freedom to choose between Lutheranism and Catholicism. No provision was made for both confessions in the same state, except for Article Fourteen, which allowed for parity in the imperial cities, an important concession.[47] Conciliatory Ferdinand issued a proclamation, the *Declaratio Ferdinandea* on 24 September 1555, assuring the knights, cities and congregations which had held to the Augsburg Confession for a long time that they would not be disturbed in their religious practice until a religious agreement had been

---

questions of Reformation and toleration from a Catholic point of view.

[46] Carl Mirbt, *Quellen zur Geschichte des Papsttums* (5th ed.; Tübingen, 1934), p. 286.

[47] On the importance of the cities for the progress of the Reformation in the early decades, see Hans Baron, "Religion and Politics in the German Imperial Cities during the Reformation," *The English Historical Review*, LII (1937), 405–27, 614–33.

achieved. But it was merely a proclamation which had only slim prospects of being realized.[48]

The Peace of Augsburg deliberately excluded Calvinism, as well as the smaller sectarian groups. Nevertheless, when Frederick III the Pious of the Palatinate, who had initially become evangelical Lutheran under his wife's influence, turned Calvinist, announcing to the princes' meeting at Naumburg in 1561 that he believed Article Ten of the Augsburg Confession to represent papist teaching on the Sacrament, he was able to assert the *cuius regio, eius religio* principle in his domain. He pressed for uniformity and in 1572 beheaded the unitarian Johann Sylvanus for blasphemy. He knew his son and successor Ludwig VI (1576–1583) would be a strong Lutheran, but he believed that he "would not be a great persecutor since he is by nature pious and good-natured."[49] It was only his grandson Frederick IV (1583–1610) who granted religious freedom to the Lutherans and Catholics, though he gave the Calvinist synod official standing and many privileges. This concession made it possible for the upper Palatinate to remain Lutheran.

There seems to have been one major breakthrough of special importance for religious toleration in this period. When Elector Johann Sigismund of Brandenburg in 1614 published his confession of faith, he wrote that he did not wish to force any of his subjects to do the same. In a festive proclamation on 5 February 1615, he told the estates west of the Oder that "no one should be put upon with either force or pressure," for he did not arrogate to himself the rule over their consciences. While this has been hailed by some historians as the first "toleration proclamation," the fact is that, had he been able to do so, he probably would have required the whole of Brandenburg to turn Calvinist with him. For beginning with his wife he ran into such determined Lutheran resistance that he had no alternative but to tolerate them.[50]

---

[48] Kurt Aland, "Toleranz und Glaubensfreiheit im 16. Jahrhundert," *Reformation und Humanismus*, ed. Martin Greschat and J. F. G. Goeters (Witten, 1969), pp. 67–90, esp. 73. Ernst Wolf (*Peregrinatio* II: *Studien zur reformatorischen Theologie, zum Kirchenrecht und zur Sozialethik* [Munich, 1965], 284–99) discusses Luther's theological conceptions of conscience and freedom of religious belief in contrast to the modern secular notion of the autonomous conscience and secularized beliefs. Heinrich Hoffmann ("Reformation und Gewissensfreiheit," *Archiv für Reformationsgeschichte*, XXXVII [1940], 170–88) explores the question of the extent to which freedom of conscience had roots in the Reformation.

[49] Aland, p. 74. For a minor case study of inter-confessional relations, see Heinrich Franz Röttsches, *Luthertum und Calvinismus in Nassau-Dillenburg. Beiträge zur Kirchenpolitik in Nassau-Dillenburg unter Wilhelm dem Alten und Johann dem Alten* (Herne, 1954).

[50] Aland, p. 75.

On the Catholic side, mild Maximilian II moved to allow civil tolerance for the upper-class adherents of the Augsburg Confession in his own lands. The irenic Lutheran theologian David Chytraeus of Rostock helped to draft a church order for the evangelicals. In 1571 the emperor issued an edict, the *Assecuratio*, granting civil tolerance in his own lands. Maximilian's decree, the first such decree in the Empire, derived from his mediating religious position which happened to coincide with the pragmatic need to accommodate the evangelical-minded estates. Of a somewhat less virtuous order was Rudolf II's *Majestat* or *Letter of Majesty* (1609) for the kingdom of Bohemia. There the Catholics were in a minority and the rest of the population consisted of Lutherans, Calvinists, Utraquists, and Moravian Brethren. The *Majestat* confirmed the mutual agreements of the Catholic and Protestant diets to allow complete freedom of worship and independence in managing ecclesiastical properties and affairs.[51]

During this period the most prominent of the German statesmen to give theoretical expression to the desirability and need for religious toleration and liberty was Lazarus von Schwendi (1522–1584), imperial commissioner, councilor, field marshal, and baron of Hohenlandsberg. It is evident from his last will and testament that he considered himself to be a good Catholic. Yet he could write like an evangelical about how the pure gospel had been buried by abuses, false religious practices and superstitions. He was deeply involved in the mediating policies of Maximilian II. He wrote practical pieces on the art of war, but of greater interest are his memorials on the religious situation. In 1570 he wrote a *Discourse and Reflection on the Present Situation and Condition of the Holy Empire, Our Beloved Fatherland*, and in 1574 he wrote a *Deliberation on the Government of the Roman Empire and the Setting Free of Religion*. In this discourse of 1574 he proved to be the most forceful and leading advocate of the toleration movement in the Empire, urging very unambiguously freedom of conscience, freedom of worship and religious practice for evangelicals and Catholics. His program called for action in three stages: first, in the imperial hereditary lands; second, the general extension as widely as possible throughout the Empire; and third, a time of waiting during which tensions would be relieved and domestic quiet achieved, followed by the calling of a national council to move beyond the provisions of the Peace of Augsburg.

Schwendi felt the situation to be extremely urgent, for he saw

51 Lecler, I, 268, 285–86.

France torn apart by religious wars. He was greatly shocked by the St. Bartholomew's Massacre and felt the need to direct the Empire on a saner course than that taken by France. But two years later, by the time of the Diet of Regensburg and the election of Rudolf II, he had run into such harsh political realities in the Empire that he now merely urged liberty of conscience and not freedom of public worship throughout the Empire (*Discourse and Reflection on Permitting or Forbidding Freedom of Conscience, presented at Regensburg anno 1576*).[52] He was very apprehensive about the future of the Empire, for he foresaw increasing intervention by foreign powers in imperial affairs and predicted a catastrophe such as that which actually befell the Empire in the Thirty Years' War.

One force quietly at work in favor of toleration was that of the Erasmian chancellors and jurists present here and there throughout the Empire.[53] The importance of the jurists in determining the relations of church and state in a concrete context in the sixteenth and seventeenth centuries has of late been given greater recognition.[54] By the time of the Peace of Westphalia a jurist, Jacobus Lampadius, taught freedom of conscience, that neither the teaching office nor freedom of faith could be subjected to the political powers.[55] In saying this he was close to Luther's position in his *On Secular Authority* of 1523.

In general, it would seem from the behavior of men at the time that when a minority gained control of governmental power or became a majority it proved to be quite intolerant in turn. Persecution and

[52] Eugen Dollmann, *Die Probleme der Reichspolitik in den Zeiten der Gegenreformation und die politischen Denkschriften des Lazarus von Schwendi* (Ansbach, 1927), pp. 104–37. On Schwendi at Regensburg, see Hugo Moritz, *Die Wahl Rudolfs II., Der Reichstag zu Regensburg (1576) und die Freistellungsbewegung* (Marburg, 1895), p. 91, n. 1. The way in which Schwendi applied the lessons of the French wars of religion and the Massacre to the German situation is similar to the way in which the English made use of the French experience and political tracts a century later. See J. H. M. Salmon, *The French Religious Wars in English Political Thought* (Oxford, 1959). On resistance theories – such a vital part of the French political dialogue at the time – the old work by Ludwig Cardauns (*Die Lehre vom Widerstandsrecht des Volks gegen die rechtmässige Obrigkeit im Luthertum und im Calvinismus des 16. Jahrhunderts* [Bonn, 1903]) is now superseded by a number of important studies by Julian H. Franklin, Ralph E. Giesey, and Donald R. Kelley.

[53] This factor is discussed by Robert Stupperich in *Der Humanismus und die Wiedervereinigung der Konfessionen* (Leipzig, 1936).

[54] See, e.g., Martin Heckel, "Staat und Kirche nach den Lehren der evangelischen Juristen Deutschlands in der ersten Hälfte des 17. Jahrhunderts," *Zeitschrift der Savigny-Stiftung für Rechtsgeschichte, Kanonistische Abteilung,* XLII (1956), 117–247; XLIII (1957), 202–308. More attention has been focussed of late on the legal aspects involved in the Reformation movement. See, e.g., Wilhelm Borth, *Die Luthersache (Causa Lutheri) 1517–1524. Die Anfänge der Reformation als Frage von Politik und Recht* (Lübeck and Hamburg, 1970).

[55] Richard Dietrich, "Landeskirchenrecht und Gewissensfreiheit in den Verhandlungen des westfälischen Friedenskongresses," *Historische Zeitschrift,* CXCVI (1963), 563–83, esp. pp. 564–76.

repression seem to have been more severe when directed against more radical or active groups to the left. The spectrum of those included in toleration was broadened only under duress. Moderates politically seeking a middle way experienced the greatest difficulties. The maxims of theologians or intellectuals in favor of toleration were of less importance, so far as one can tell, than the political realities of the concrete situation.[56] One is forced to agree with Plato's *Chalepa Ta Chala* – the good is always difficult. As an old man, the statesman Oxenstierna, reflecting on the disastrous Thirty Years' War, exclaimed, "My son, my son, if you knew with what little wisdom the world is ruled!" Two hundred years earlier a pope in Rome had in nearly the same words said the same thing. The confession of a secular statesman suggested that perhaps worldly rulers might not succeed any more gloriously than had the ecclesiastical powers in establishing the right order of things among men.

[56] A. A. Van Schelven ("De opkomst van de idee der politieke tolerantie in de 16e-eeuwsche Nederlanden," *Uit den Strijd der Geesten* [Amsterdam, 1944], pp. 9–71) argues that the development of religious toleration should be traced not to Castellio or Erasmianism but to the political situation in France and the writings of DuPlessis-Mornay which derived from that situation. In France toleration was possible and necessary and not detrimental to the crown. When a similar situation developed in the Netherlands, William of Orange became the center of the demand for toleration. By 1581 toleration as a political expedient was established, but its potentially greatest benefit to the country, the uniting of Catholics and Reformed, was not realized. Gerhard Güldner (*Das Toleranz-Problem in den Niederlanden im Ausgang des 16. Jahrhunderts* [Lübeck and Hamburg, 1968], pp. 41–64) discusses tolerance and politics, as well as the contributions in subsequent decades of Coornhert and Lipsius. Erich Hassinger takes into account economic or business motivations in promoting toleration in two studies: "Wirtschaftliche Motive und Argumente für religiöse Duldsamkeit im 16. und 17. Jahrhundert," *Archiv für Reformationsgeschichte*, XLIX (1958), 226–45; "Religiöse Toleranz im 16. Jahrhundert. Motive – Argumente – Formen der Verwirklichung," *Vorträge der Aeneas-Silvius-Stiftung an der Universität Basel*, VI (Basel and Stuttgart, 1966).

PART II

TWO UNPUBLISHED DOCUMENTS

TOMASSO SASSETTI'S ACCOUNT OF THE ST. BARTHOLOMEW'S DAY MASSACRE

by

JOHN TEDESCHI

Dudley Carleton had been England's ambassador to Venice for almost a year when he was suddenly faced, early in September 1611, with his first serious crisis. The Inquisition of that city had arrested Giacomo Castelvetro, an ailing and elderly gentleman, who many years before had served as Italian master to King James and who was then employed by the English embassy in Venice. Carleton immediately remonstrated before the Council of Ten for what he considered a breach of diplomatic privilege. At the same time, he sent servants on a mission of reconnaissance to Castelvetro's residence. "It was my good fortune," Carleton wrote later to the earl of Salisbury, "to recover his books and papers a little before the officers of the Inquisition went to his lodgings to seize them, for I caused them to be brought unto me upon the first news of his apprehension, under cover of some writings of mine which he had in his hands. And this indeed was the poor man's safetie, for if they had made themselves masters of that Magazine, wherein was store and provision of all sorts of pasquins, libels, relations, layde up for many years together against their Master the pope, nothing could have saved him."[1] And we, in turn, might have been deprived of Tomasso Sassetti's account of the St. Bartholomew's Day Massacre, and the brief accompanying anonymous opinion upon it. There is a strong likelihood that the nine volumes of Castelvetro's manuscripts, one of which contains the Massacre account, acquired by

---

[1] Qtd. in K. T. Butler, "Giacomo Castelvetro, 1546–1616," *Italian Studies*, V (1950), 28. This article (pp. 1–42) is the best general study of Castelvetro; for additional bibliography, see notes below. English diplomatic efforts for Castelvetro are recorded in H. F. Brown, ed., *Calendar of State Papers, Venice, 1610–1613* (London, 1905), *passim*. There is an inconsistency in Miss Butler's account. She dates Castelvetro's arrest 4 September (p. 26) and Carleton's first letter to Cecil informing him of this event 30 August (perhaps old style?). The documents published in *C.S.P. Venice* confirm that the arrest took place on 4 Sept. Castelvetro's imprisonment was of short duration. On 9 October, James I personally wrote to the doge expressing thanks for his release (*ibid.*, p. 222).

The Newberry Library in 1963, were a part of the store of documents saved from probable destruction by the quick-witted ambassador.[2] At any rate, our manuscripts resemble to a degree his description of the papers that he saved from the Inquisition. The Castelvetro collection in the Newberry contains copies of extremely interesting official and diplomatic documents, reports of ambassadors dealing with court and state affairs (many are copies of the famous Venetian *relazioni*) and contemporary, frequently anonymous private accounts of the political and religious situations in a number of European countries, almost all from the second half of the sixteenth century – the majority of these seemingly unpublished and unstudied.[3] The marginal comments added by Castelvetro in his own hand, comments that convey with passion his hatred of the Roman Church, justify Carleton's fear for his safety had they fallen into the possession of the Inquisition.

Giacomo Castelvetro, a Modenese of patrician birth, had abandoned Italy in 1564 at the age of eighteen to rejoin his uncle Lodovico Castelvetro, the celebrated literary critic who had been compelled because of his Italian translations of Melanchthon and other alleged manifestations of Protestant sympathies to flee his homeland in 1561.[4] After eight years of turbulent wandering together, the uncle died at Chiavenna in 1571. Giacomo settled in England where he embarked on a rich and varied literary career. In fact, with his noisy and more flamboyant contemporary John Florio, he may be ranked as a leading champion of Italian culture in Elizabethan and Jacobean England. Castelvetro served as tutor to James VI of Scotland (later James I of

---

[2] The collection is catalogued Case MS. J 93.154. Sassetti's account, the "Brieve Raccontamento," is contained in Codex 78/2. It is followed immediately by an anonymous opinion upon it entitled "Parer di N. sopra il Raccontamento del Grande, e Crudele e Biasimevol Macello di Parigi, et di tutta la misera Francia" (fols. 31ᵛ–32ᵛ). My guess is that the commentator is Castelvetro himself. The bulk of his papers, ranging from a dietary treatise to press-ready copies of then still-unpublished writings by Tommaso Campanella, are divided between the libraries of Cambridge University and the British Museum (Butler, p. 3).

[3] In 1929 when they were examined by Hugo Triesel, the manuscripts were in the Dietrichstein Family Library at Mikulov (Nikolsburg), Czechoslovakia. It is unknown at what date they entered that library, but we know that a notable collection was already in existence during the lifetime of Franz Dietrichstein (1570–1636), cardinal-bishop of Olmutz. The Castelvetro MSS may have been removed from the library during the German occupation of Czechoslovakia in World War II. The collection originally consisted of eleven volumes, but only nine reached the Newberry. A cursory description is in Hugo Triesel, "Die Handschriften des Giacopo Castelvetro in der Dietrichstein'schen Fideikommiss-Bibliothek zu Nikolsburg," *Zeitschrift des deutschen Vereins für die Geschichte Mährens und Schlesiens*, XXXI (1929), 129–64.

[4] The only reasonably comprehensive studies of his life remain T. Sandonnini, *Lodovico Castelvetro e la sua famiglia* (Bologna, 1882) and G. Cavazzuti, *Lodovico Castelvetro* (Modena, 1903).

England) and to the noblest families of the realm;[5] he wrote a treatise in which he urged the English to introduce fruits and vegetables into their heavily meat-centered diets; and through his association with the London printer, John Wolf, he edited and subsidized the publication for the first time in England of the finest pastoral dramas which Renaissance Italy had produced, Tasso's *Aminta* and Giovanni Battista Guarini's *Il Pastor Fido*, both published together at London in one volume in 1591.[6] Further research may ultimately determine that he also had a hand in the Machiavellis published by Wolf in 1584 and 1588 with the false imprints of Rome and Palermo. Castelvetro's marginalia in the Newberry manuscripts (including those to the Sassetti account of the Massacre) reveal him to have been a fervent admirer of the Florentine secretary.

Castelvetro was himself directly involved in questions of statecraft. In 1587 he married the widow of the Basel physician Thomas Lüber (known to posterity as Erastus), and her dowry included a desk filled with her deceased husband's unpublished writings. Two years later Castelvetro issued, again through John Wolf, Erastus' *Explicatio Gravissimae Quaestionis*, an attack on excommunication and the coercion of consciences; and Erastianism, which has come to be understood as a theory of state supremacy over the church, unwittingly was born.[7]

Castelvetro's interest in political matters was not purely academic and theoretical. As early as 1586, when his name first appears in the *Calendar of State Papers* as a bearer of official dispatches to the Continent, he was an occasional member of the English diplomatic service.[8] In January 1598 Sir Robert Cecil drew up a list of active intelligence agents. One of the entries reads: "In Swedlande, Castelvetro

---

[5] Butler, "Giacomo Castelvetro," p. 14ff. Castelvetro was in Edinburgh at the court of James 1592–1594.

[6] See K. T. Butler, "An Italian's Message to England in 1614: 'Eat More Fruit and Vegetables,'" *Italian Studies*, II (1938), 1–18. This extremely interesting treatise filled with biographical and historical information remains unpublished. It has survived in several copies. For the full range of Castelvetro's editorial activity, see Butler, "Giacomo Castelvetro," p. 9ff.; Eleanor Rosenberg, "Giacopo Castelvetro, Italian Publisher in Elizabethan London and His Patrons," *The Huntington Library Quarterly*, VI (1943), 119–48; Sheila E. Dimsey, "Giacopo Castelvetro," *Modern Language Review*, XXIII (1928), 424–31.

[7] Castelvetro also published Erastus' *Varia Opuscula Medica* (Frankfort, 1590). In the preface to this work Castelvetro refers to his marriage and to the inheritance of Erastus' papers. Ruth Wesel-Roth (*Thomas Erastus. Ein Beitrag zur Geschichte der reformierten Kirche und zur Lehre von der Staatsouveränität* [Lahr/Baden, 1954], p. 149) is not helpful in this regard: "Uber die Persönlichkeit [Castelvetro's] ist nichts in Erfahrung zu bringen." Cf. Butler, "Giacomo Castelvetro," pp. 11–12.

[8] Castelvetro is mentioned as a diplomatic courier in two letters from Horatio Palavicino to Francis Walsingham, dated at Frankfort, 4 and 11 September 1586 (*Calendar of State Papers, Foreign, Elizabeth, June 1586–June 1588* [London, 1927], pp. 81, 87).

who is well known here in England, a long dweller, and now in house with Duke Charles."[9] Before entering the service of the future Charles IX of Sweden, Castelvetro had spent two years in Copenhagen. It was during his Danish sojourn, from late in 1594 through 1596, that Castelvetro assembled under extremely mysterious circumstances the fascinating collection of historical documents which is in The Newberry Library.

The nine volumes that comprise it contain, as I have mentioned, accounts of the political, religious and economic situations in various European states. There is a volume devoted to each of the following: the court of Rome; Venice and her relations with the Ottoman Empire; the minor Italian states (Urbino, Ferrara, Tuscany and Genoa); Britain; Spain and Portugal; and, of course, France. There are two volumes of a miscellaneous nature and one devoted to fifteenth- and sixteenth-century papal elections. The latter codex, which includes an independent recension of Aeneas Sylvius Piccolomini's colorful description of the conclave from which he emerged as Pius II, has been studied in an interesting article which remains, to the best of my knowledge, the first and only instance of critical research conducted in this collection[10] – a collection that has escaped the notice of all Castelvetro's biographers.

Codex 78/2 contains twelve items connected with sixteenth-century France, all presumably unpublished with the exception of the *relazione* read before the Senate of Venice by Marino Cavalli, returning from his embassy to France in 1546.[11] The most substantial and possibly the most interesting of these, aside from the Massacre account, appear to be a long "discorso" and a vivid eye-witness report of the siege of Paris in 1590.[12] The "discorso," dated 1589, which today might be called a position paper, assessed negatively the advisability of papal recognition of Henri IV as king of France.

[9] Qtd. in Hugh G. Dick, "A Renaissance Expatriate: Giacomo Castelvetro the Elder," *Italian Quarterly*, VII (1963), 12.

[10] Aldo Scaglione, "Giacomo Castelvetro e i conclavi dei papi del Rinascimento," *Bibliothèque d'Humanisme et Renaissance*, XXVIII (1966), 141–49.

[11] The codex is entitled "Diverse belle scritture et relationi intorno il nobil reame della Francia. Come meglio apparirà dalla contenza posta nella seguente carta. Di Giacopo Castelvetri ... In Hafnia l'anno MDVC." Cavalli's report is published in E. Albèri, *Le Relazioni degli ambasciatori veneti al Senato*, ser. I, vol. I (Florence, 1839), pp. 217–88. In the Castelvetro codex it appears at fols. 151^r–220^r.

[12] Codex 78/2, fols. 68^r–104^r: "Discorso se sia bene per il Pontefice & altri principi italiani consentire la corona di Francia al Re di Navarra" (dated September 1589); *ibid.*, fols. 104^v–128^r: "Relatione dell' Assedio di Parigi, della liberatione d'esso & di tutti i particolari degni di consideratione, seguiti fin dal tempo della rotta data all'essercito della Lega di Marzo del MDLXXXX."

The most baffling question raised by these documents is that of provenance. We have Castelvetro's own testimony not only that the copying was executed in Copenhagen, or during his occasional brief visits outside the city, either by himself or by Danish scribes employed for the purpose, but also that the copies of many of them – and this is the really curious thing – were made from originals supplied to him there by a certain Michele. On the inside covers of each volume Castelvetro has meticulously recorded the sum in Danish currency expended to obtain the originals and to have them copied and bound.[13] A few of the reports, however, had passed into Castelvetro's hands well before his Danish sojourn. The colophon of the Massacre account explicitly declares that the original had been turned over to him for copying by its author, Captain Tomasso Sassetti, in London on the 20th of June 1583, eleven years before Castelvetro put into play the idea of assembling his curious library of sixteenth-century political texts.[14]

There is no need to speculate how Castelvetro and Sassetti might have met – after all, the Italian colony in London was tiny. In 1568, for example, it numbered only eighty-four according to the "Returns of Aliens." At one time or another, moreover, they both served as agents for Francis Walsingham, Elizabeth's first secretary and her chief of intelligence.[15] In contrast to the anonymity which conceals the author of the "Discourse" dedicated to Count Guido San Giorgio Aldobrandini (discussed and excerpted elsewhere in this volume), we are reasonably well informed on the career of Captain Tomasso Sassetti. A Florentine of good birth (he was related to the Strozzi and

[13] See, e.g., the note on the inside back cover of the French codex: "1595. Contiene questo libro 232 carte scritte, la cui scrittura mi costa, oltre a quello c'ho donato a Michele per darmi questi scritti gli originali un talero e [illegible symbol] 14." There are curious biographical appendages to some of the colophons. See, e.g., Castelvetro's jottings at the conclusion of Giacopo Soranzo's *relazione* (Codex 79/2, fol. 65ʳ): "Compiuto di riscrivere ... a xxix di Novembre 1594 in Copenhagen. Nota come è la sera del venerdì 29mo predetto, e come nella passata notte mi son sognato haver perduto l'un de' migliori denti che in bocca vi havessi, di che ne sentì dispiacere non picciolo."

[14] On the pre- or non-Danish provenance of some of the other documents in the collection, see Scaglione, p. 143. He noticed that the probable origin of at least a part of this material is indicated in Codex 73/2 in two lists contained at fols. 66ʳ–67ᵛ and fols. 68ʳ–79ʳ: "Memoriale d'alcune scritture politiche che furon donate alla Reina Maria Stuarda prigioniera in Inghilterra l'anno di salute 1583 dal Sre di Cherelles," and "Registro di tutte le scritture politiche del Sr Christiano Bernicò." (A few of the documents enumerated here are also a part of the Newberry collection.) There are suggestions in Castelvetro's marginalia that the documents were not in a final form or order. See, e.g., his comment at fol. 269ʳ of Codex 79/2: "Questo raccontamento si doverà porre di dietro la relatione di Cipri." His ulterior plans may well have included their publication. In this regard, see Scaglione, p. 144.

[15] On the Italian colony in London, see Luigi Firpo, "La chiesa italiana di Londra nel cinquecento," *Ginevra e l'Italia* (Florence, 1959), p. 336n. For Castelvetro's connection with Walsingham, see above, n. 8. For Sassetti's, see the discussion below.

the Valori), a soldier by trade and adventurer, he was a man for all seasons who could have served as a model of the Italian *bravo* who swaggers across the landscape of Walter Scott's *Kenilworth*.[16] For a time, in fact, Sassetti was one of the creatures of Robert Dudley, earl of Leicester, bound to him by a firm debt of gratitude. In 1569 Sassetti had been declared guilty of the murder of Richard Foden, a yeoman, and escaped the gallows only through Leicester's intercession.[17] A contemporary letter to Queen Elizabeth, preserved among the Salisbury manuscripts in Hatfield House, from an Italian merchant who had a certain experience with English life, attempts to explain why Leicester in his various intrigues and plots relied more on foreigners than on his own countrymen. "They [the former] are poor and therefore daring, and resigned to every danger; because they have no earthly goods and have nothing to lose, they are more ready to risk everything."[18] Sassetti had been soldiering in Ireland when the earl called him to his service.

For fifteen years, roughly from 1570 into the mid-1580s, Sassetti served intermittently as an agent of English intelligence in France and the Low Countries. The *Calendar of State Papers* contains many entries for these years in which he is named as a courier between Walsingham and the English embassy in Paris, while other entries are his own reports directly to Walsingham or to one of his lieutenants, transmitting information concerning the south of Europe, usually gleaned from new

---

[16] Firpo ("La chiesa italiana," p. 373) suggests 1523 as his date of birth. The Sassetti, a wealthy and prominent mercantile family in the 15th century, had fallen on hard times. Tomasso was related to the celebrated traveler and literary figure Filippo Sassetti. See "Notizie dell'origine e nobiltà della famiglia de' Sassetti raccolte da Francesco di Giambatista Sassetti. MDC," in E. Marcucci, *Lettere edite e inedite di Filippo Sassetti* (Florence, 1855), pp. xv–xlvii. On Tomasso, see p. xxxiv. His two brothers, also soldiers, died in 1565 in events connected with the siege of Malta. Despite Sassetti's long employment by the English, there is evidence that he also served Catherine de Medici (see below, n. 21); and although his name appears as an occasional member of the Italian evangelical exile church in London, the anonymous author of the "Parere" which immediately follows the "Brieve Raccontamento" refers to Sassetti as "veramente catolico papesco."

[17] A record of these proceedings can be found under the date of 5 Oct. 1569 in the *Calendar of the Patent Rolls, Elizabeth I, 1566–1569* (London, 1964), p. 337.

[18] The letter from a Battista di Trento to Elizabeth (1577) also names the protagonists in an alleged plot headed by Leicester to deprive her of the throne: "... et [Leicester] ha fatto venire di oltre mare un certo capitan Sassetti italiano, quale militava altre volte in Hirlanda per V.M., et era Capitano in quelli paesi, ma per un homicidio che fece in Londra fu condenato alla forca, et il conte de Lesiter li fece havere la gratia de V.M. Hora et [*sic*] venuto ad aiutare il conte di Lesiter, perchè li è tanto obligato contra V.M. che li fece la gratia della vita, è homo di guerra ..." (*Historical Manuscripts Commission. Calendar of the Manuscripts of the ... Marquis of Salisbury preserved at Hatfield House*, II [London, 1888], p. 169). In Giordano Bruno's *La Cena de le Ceneri* published in London in 1584, Sassetti is described as one of the "false et onorate reliquie di Firenze in questa patria" (qtd. from G. Aquilechia's edition [Turin, 1955], p. 86).

arrivals in the French capital – that Savoy was levying troops for the enterprise against Montferrat; that the five year old heir to the Grand Duchy of Tuscany had died leaving the duke without legitimate sons; that Spain was constructing fifty heavy ships along the Bay of Biscay, and so on.[19] Occasionally his assignments were of a personal nature. In January 1573 he accepted Walsingham's commission to find a rider "who is both skilful and honest" from among his Italian acquaintances to serve under his old master the earl of Leicester in England.[20] There is unconfirmed evidence that Sassetti was also at an unspecified time in the employ of the queen mother Catherine de Medici.[21]

Sassetti was not in Paris on that fateful 24th day of August 1572. He tells us towards the end of the "Brieve Raccontamento" that, shortly before, he had set out for Lyons with Ludovico da Diaceto, a Florentine banker who had attained great wealth and influence at the French court.[22] They passed the tedious hours of travel in conversation. Sassetti remarked to his companion that Coligny and his followers should read Machiavelli carefully. They would discover his precept that the great and the powerful of this earth never forget the injuries they have received. Even if for a time they give the impression

---

[19] *C.S.P. Foreign, Elizabeth, 1572–1574* (London, 1876), p. 538; *C.S.P. Domestic, Edward VI, Mary, Elizabeth, 1547–1580* (London, 1856), p. 689; *C.S.P. For., Eliz.* for the years 1581–1588, *passim* (see indexes). Further references in C. T. Martin, ed., "Journal of Sir Francis Walsingham, from Dec. 1570 to April 1583," *Camden Miscellany*, VI (1870–1871), 9, 13. Walsingham considered Sassetti an expert on the Low Countries. Cf. Conyers Read, *Mr. Secretary Walsingham and the Policy of Queen Elizabeth* (3 vols.; Cambridge, 1925), I, 263. It is interesting that Lodovico Guicciardini, author of a famous history of Belgium, described Sassetti (in a letter to Walsingham dated 30 June 1584) as "my dear friend" (*C.S.P. For., Eliz., July 1583–July 1584* (London, 1914), p. 560.

[20] The exchange of correspondence between Walsingham and Leicester is in Dudley Digges, *The Compleat Ambassador* (London, 1655), pp. 270, 345. Despite their willingness to use him, Sassetti did not enjoy the full confidence of his superiors. See Walsingham's letter to Leicester dated 8 Oct. 1572: "... his [Sassetti's] imperfections I know well enough, notwithstanding his service may be profitable; and if it be to no other end, yet were the entertainment of him necessary in respect of the harm he may do. At all times when any danger did seem to grow towards her Majesty, he hath requested me to present to her his service: though that Nation be very much inclined to treason, yet surely I think him in that point to stand much upon his honor" (Digges, pp. 270–71).

[21] At fol. 2ᵛ of the "Brieve Raccontamento" where Sassetti described Catherine as a "prudente Prencipessa," Castelvetro remarked in a marginal comment: "Era lo scrittore di questa opera fiorentino, et da lei salariato." But I have not encountered Sassetti's name in Catherine's collected correspondence or in monographs devoted to her court and to her career.

[22] Diaceto is depicted in the company of another favorite of Catherine's, Alberto Gondi, comte de Retz, in a painting that hangs in a hall of the Uffizi established to immortalize Florentines who had acquired fame abroad (M. J. de Pommerol, *Albert de Gondi, maréchal de Retz* [Geneva, 1953], p. 159). See also Scipione Ammirato, *Delle famiglie nobili fiorentine* (Florence, 1615), pp. 5–20; Charpin-Feugerolles, *Les Florentins à Lyon* (Lyons, 1894), p. 196; Abel Desjardins, *Négociations diplomatiques de la France avec la Toscane*, IV (Paris, 1872), *passim; Lettres de Catherine de Médicis* (11 vols.; Paris, 1880–1943), V, 305; VII, 166n., 169n.; VIII, 235n.

of having done so, there are always minor officials in their entourage
who will remind them.[23] And the queen mother, it was worth remem-
bering, was a woman of enormous spirit and pride. Ludovico scoffed
at these premonitions. "What you are suggesting is impossible. The
Huguenots are powerful and such retribution against them would be
too difficult to carry out." Not long after their arrival in Lyons the
Massacre in Paris was an accomplished fact. On the last day of
August, according to Sassetti's reckoning, the violence struck Lyons
itself. He lingered on for another day to witness the fury of the printers
and silk workers – carrying on their butchery, he thought, with the
approval of the governor, Mandelot. The role which Sassetti assigns
in the Massacre to these two groups is not supported by other contemporary accounts.[24]

On the ninth of September Sassetti re-entered Paris where he began
to try to piece together the tragic events which had transpired during
his absence. He must have worked feverishly. By the thirteenth of the
month he had completed his "Brieve Raccontamento," which now
occupies the first sixty-four pages of Codex 78/2, the French volume in
the Castelvetro collection.[25] Sassetti's account is addressed "Molto
Magnifico Signor Mio Osservandissimo." This anonymous addressee
cannot have been Walsingham (England's ambassador in Paris at this
time) who is referred to in the account as "Valsingame, di sopra
mentionato" (fol. 28^r). But the naming of a "Maestro Rinieri Melanese
vostro" (fol. 31^r) who had achieved notoriety during the Massacre
may be a clue that the addressee was an Italian.

Sassetti's motive in writing was to determine how the assassination
attempt on Coligny on 22 August, and the Massacre two days later
had come to pass. He also questioned more specifically whether these
events had been long premeditated or had been sudden decisions – the
same queries that have preoccupied historians for the last four hundred
years. At the beginning of his account, he described his informants as

[23] I have not succeeded in locating this teaching either in *The Prince* or *Discourses*. The
consolidation of power by the new prince and the swift and efficient destruction of disaf-
fected elements of the population is, of course, a constant refrain in the writings of Machiavelli. See, e.g., *The Prince*, chaps. vii and viii.

[24] Cf. Natalie Z. Davis, "The Rites of Violence," n. 110, elsewhere in this volume. The
passage near the end of the "Brieve Raccontamento" discussing the violence in Lyons is in a
chaotic state, with several words erased and transposed.

[25] It is obvious that the original version completed on 13 September was later revised,
perhaps by Sassetti, but more probably by Sassetti and Castelvetro in turn. At fol. 5^v, e.g.,
there is a reference to Renato di Birago as a cardinal. Birago was not elevated to the cardinalate until 1578. Originally the "Brieve Raccontamento" was numbered fols. 69–100. At
the time of binding the leaves were renumbered and placed at the front of the codex.

"persons who had been eyewitnesses and others at court who, even if they are Catholics, make it their occupation to displease neither one side nor the other." It is probably safe to assume that among them were his Florentine acquaintances attached to Catherine's household.[26]

Sassetti began his assessment of recent events with a long backward glance. He traced the origin of the disorders to the death of Henri II, father of the reigning king, who left France denuded of justice, funds and valorous captains. There ensued a three-way struggle for control of the young Charles IX. The contenders were the queen mother, the Bourbon princes of the blood and the foreign house of Lorraine. In August 1570 the Peace of St. Germain was concluded between the crown and the Huguenots. The latter were restored to their civil rights and to their offices. Sentences which had been pronounced against them were annulled. And all over France those macabre effigies of Protestants who had been tried and condemned to death *in absentia* were lowered from the gallows where they had hung.

At this point in the "Raccontamento" Sassetti turned to analyze the train of events which had led, gradually but inexorably, to the Massacre. Above all, he emphasized the critical results of the reconciliation between the court and the Protestants. Among these results, the first was the irritation of Catholics and those who had served the crown faithfully, and who took offense at the favor now bestowed on former enemies. Coligny, moreover, not satisfied with the great concessions already obtained by his faction, gave affront by going to court and flaunting his influence in the highest councils of government. Sassetti found an instance of this alleged arrogance in Coligny's insistence that the king should tear down an "obelisk with a cross" bearing an inscription defaming Protestants. It had been erected on the site of a Huguenot house in Paris which had been leveled by a mob. Sassetti attributed great importance to this affair, clearly referring to the famous Gastine cross, the pyramid of which bore an inscription offensive to Protestants, and which the government had erected on the location of the home of Philippe de Gastines, a Huguenot merchant executed in 1569. The Treaty of St. Germain had ordered the destruction of this monument, along with other symbols of opprobrium and mutual contumely. The king granted the admiral his wish, but to the great scandal of the people, who came to the brink of rebellion. They looted homes and shops and attacked suspected Huguenots on the

---

[26] Several are named in the course of the narrative. Sassetti may have had some official contact with Catherine at this time, as I have noted above (n. 21).

streets. The affair helps to shed light on the mood of the Parisian populace on the eve of its great August rampage.[27]

Another major cause of Catholic grievance resulting from the St. Germain reconciliation, emphasized by Sassetti, was the marriage contract concluded by the Huguenot Henri de Navarre with Marguerite de Valois, sister of Charles IX – a treaty containing articles considered extremely dishonorable to the Catholic cause. And with each passing day, according to our narrator, hate and ill feeling grew against the admiral and his followers.

Ultimately, the queen mother herself turned against Coligny. She could not tolerate the ascendancy that he was gaining over her impressionable son, especially when his influence was bent towards involving France in a war against Spain – a conflict which she desperately wanted to avoid.[28] Sassetti was convinced that Catherine and her councilors had discussed and deliberated the assassination of Coligny on diverse occasions. Thus the favor that the Huguenot leader received at court in the last few weeks of his life must have been merely a ruse to disarm him. To Sassetti, the behavior of the court was explainable in terms of the old Italian proverb, "Chi ti fa più carezze che non suole, o che t'ha ingannato, o che ingannar ti vuole" (roughly equivalent to "Beware the Greeks bearing gifts"). In the "Brieve Raccontamento" it is Catherine who holds the center of the stage. Sassetti hardly mentions the Guise faction, giving it only a minor role, although he acknowledges that the first popular reaction attributed the assassination attempt to it.

After the Massacre Sassetti met an old acquaintance, Giovanni Galeazzo Fregoso, the *lupo bigio*, or gray wolf, a Medici agent who figured prominently in the diplomatic intrigues of the day.[29] This encounter may have occurred during Sassetti's return journey to

---

[27] See N. M. Sutherland, *The Massacre of St Bartholomew and the European Conflict 1559–1572* (London, 1973), pp. 185–86, 208, 340–41.

[28] See the essay by N. M. Sutherland in this volume.

[29] During 1571 Fregoso attempted to persuade Cosimo I to join France and the Netherlands in a proposed anti-Spanish alliance. Immediately after the Massacre he was sent to Germany to convey the French court's version of the tragedy. Fregoso's long career ended when Henri III (who suspected him of clandestine activity in the service of Spain) ordered him to be strangled in April 1581. There are references to Fregoso scattered in many collections of contemporary diplomatic correspondence. See, among others, E. Palandri, *Les négociations politiques et religieuses entre la Toscane et la France* (Paris, 1908), *passim; Mémoires inédits de Michel de La Huguerye* (3 vols.; Paris, 1877–1880), *passim;* Desjardins, *Négociations*, III, 438–39; A. Kluckhohn, *Briefe Friedrich des Frommen, Kurfürsten von der Pfalz* (2 vols.; Braunschweig, 1868–1872), *passim;* Ivan Cloulas, ed., *Correspondance du nonce en France Anselmo Dandino (1578–1581)* (Rome and Paris, 1970), pp. 56, 817, 818; Catherine de Medici, *Lettres*, III, 290; IV, 76, 196, 232; V, 311; X, 315n.

Paris from Lyons.[30] It was known that Catherine had sent Fregoso to comfort and reassure Coligny after the first abortive attempt on his life, and that the Italian was at the admiral's bedside a few hours before his murder, thereby running the risk of sharing his fate. Sassetti confronted him squarely: "Signor Fregoso, I do not doubt for one moment that you are familiar with every detail of what happened ..."[31] The other shrugged in reply that he was a loyal retainer of their Majesties. As long as the admiral had walked an honorable path in the service of the king, he had been his friend and servant. But when Coligny strayed from it and plotted against the crown, then he took all those measures that any gentleman in his position would have considered proper in the service of his master. For he had seen and discovered matters which were diametrically opposed to his sovereigns.

Everything learned by Sassetti helped to persuade him that the assassination of Coligny was a premeditated affair, planned and masterminded by the queen mother. But he did not hold the same to be true of the Massacre, a view which sets him in disagreement with two other important contemporary Italian accounts, Camillo Capilupi's *Stratagemma*[32] and the *relazione* read to the Venetian Senate two months later, on 11 November 1572, by Giovanni Michiel, returning from a special embassy to France.[33] Capilupi and Michiel believed that the Massacre had been preceded by a lengthy preparation. In Sassetti's opinion the plot originated during the two days after the abortive assassination attempt, and as a reaction to the threats of

[30] Sassetti did not return to Paris until 9 September, and Fregoso had left the capital on his mission to the German princes (see n. 29 above) on the first of the month. The date of his departure is provided in a letter written by the Florentine ambassador in Paris, Giovanni Maria Petrucci, to Francesco de Medici on 2 September: "Il Fregoso partì ieri" (Desjardins, *Négociations*, III, 835). It is also possible, of course, that this part of Sassetti's account is a late addition. There is evidence of additions and revisions scattered throughout the "Brieve Raccontamento."

[31] See below, p. 148.

[32] *Stratagemma di Carlo Nono Re di Francia contro i ribelli di Dio et suoi l'anno MDLXXII, descritto da Camillo Capilupi*, dated 22 October 1572 but not printed until 1574. Capilupi was in Rome at the time of the Massacre. His sources were the dispatches of the nuncio Salviati (Capilupi was a papal secretary); and he also would have had access to information sent to the cardinal of Lorraine, then in Rome, from Paris. See G. B. Intra, "Di Ippolito Capilupi e del suo tempo," *Archivio storico lombardo*, XX (1893), 76–142; *id.*, "Di Camillo Capilupi e de' suoi scritti," *ibid.*, pp. 693–735; Pierre Hurtubise, "Comment Rome apprit la nouvelle du massacre de la Saint-Barthélemy," *Archivum Historiae Pontificiae*, X (1972), 187–209.

[33] Published in Albèri, *Relazioni*, ser. I, vol. IV, 274–310. Michiel ascribed full responsibility for the Massacre to the queen mother and the duc d'Anjou. He interpreted the wedding between Navarre and Marguerite de Valois as a ruse to trap Coligny and his followers in Paris. Cf. G. Soranzo, "Come fu data e come fu accolta a Venezia la notizia della S.te Barthélemy," *Miscellanea in onore di Roberto Cessi*, II (Rome, 1958), pp. 129–44.

Coligny's enraged followers that the streets of Paris would flow with blood if justice was not done.[34] The extent of the Massacre, moreover, was intended to be the liquidation of the Huguenot leaders, and not the widespread killing and looting that actually occurred.

One of Sassetti's chief arguments against the premeditation of the Massacre was the confusion that accompanied it – the same argument used by another Venetian ambassador in Paris at this time, Sigismondo Cavalli, whose belated account of the event was read to the Senate in 1574.[35] How could the attack on the Huguenots be considered a lengthily planned affair, Sassetti asked, if on the very eve of St. Bartholomew, Guise, Anjou and others who would lead the dawn raids were still without either defensive or offensive weapons, and that same night had to send for them hurriedly from the armorers of the city and other places?[36]

The Protestants, on the other hand, had arms and horses. If they had stood together they might have been saved, but not a man among them effectively defended himself. Sassetti had heard only of a solitary magistrate who made his assailants pay dearly for his life. The others, he noted ruefully, were seized in their beds, pulled down from chimney flues, dragged from rooftops or out of stables where they had hoped to find safety in the costumes of their grooms – all forlorn attempts to save that life which to each was so precious.[37] And what of the survivors? They were, Catholic and Huguenot alike, swept up in the delirium of religious fervor that gripped Paris after the Massacre. A little silver cross worn over the heart, or pinned to one's cap, became the universal symbol of orthodoxy. The priests of Rome, wrote Sassetti, were gathering a bountiful harvest. The churches were bursting, and much envied was the person who could squeeze a place for himself at the foot of the altar. The prices of the *Little Office of the Madonna* and the Rosary had soared, so great was the demand. And when the priest raised the Host there was a beating on breasts and a fluttering of lips that was awesome to behold. And all these displays were for ceremonies that many among them had only recently despised.[38]

---

[34] The nuncio Salviati concurred in this opinion. See the recent edition of his correspondence by P. Hurtubise, and the essay by Robert M. Kingdon in this volume. For a sophisticated analysis of the most important contemporary accounts of the Massacre, see N. M. Sutherland, *The Massacre of St Bartholomew*, chap. xvii.

[35] Albèri, *Relazioni*, ser. I, vol. IV, 311–42.

[36] See below, p. 141.

[37] On the non-resistance of Protestants during the Massacre, see N. Z. Davis, "The Rites of Violence," n. 124, and the essay by Donald R. Kelley in this volume.

[38] See below, p. 145.

The "Brieve Raccontamento" and the anonymous "Parere" that follows it are in Castelvetro's hand, unlike the majority of other writings in the collection which were copied by Danish scribes. The first of the two texts contains numerous erasures and changes in word order. Either Castelvetro took liberties and made substitutions arbitrarily, or he possessed another copy (or copies) of Sassetti's narrative from which he occasionally selected variant readings.[39] My textual notes to the "Raccontamento" record many instances of his editorial activity; and wherever they remained legible after his erasures I have attempted to note the cancelled readings. Castelvetro's marginal comments are transcribed at the bottom of each page. In editing the manuscript, I have reproduced the original spelling but have modernized the punctuation and introduced a minimum of apostrophes and accents in order to facilitate comprehension. Phrases underscored in the manuscript are printed in italics. Where I have corrected obvious errors made in the copying, my departures from the text are enclosed within brackets. Interminable passages have been broken up into paragraphs. Elipses indicate words which are illegible owing to the condition of the manuscript.[40]

[39] Castelvetro's marginalia in a few of the writings in the collection indicate that he possessed more than one copy of a given document. See, e.g., Codex 59/2, fol. 167^v where he wrote: "tutte queste parole mancano nell'altro testo."

[40] I am grateful to Dr. Alfred Soman for his assistance in preparing the "Brieve Raccontamento" for publication. His meticulous revision of the text was a labor far beyond his duties as editor of this volume.

BRIEVE RACCONTAMENTO DEL GRAN MACELLO FATTO NELLA CITTÀ DI PARIGI IL VIGGESIMO QUARTO GIORNO D'AGOSTO D'ORDINE DI CARLO NONO RE DI FRANCIA, & DELLA CRUDEL MORTE DI GUASPARRO SCIATTIGLIONE, SIGNORE DI COLIGNI & GRANDE AMMIRAGLIO DI FRANCIA MDLXXII

Dopo il mio ritorno[1] (Molto magnifico S.r mio oss.mo) non ho mancato di porre ogni studio per intendere intieramente come sia passato il fatto della morte del S.re Ammiraglio Sciattiglione, et la gran mortalità degli altri suoi seguaci, seguita in questa città il giorno dedicato a San Bartolomeo; et similmente s'ella sia stata di lungo tempo prima pensata, o pur se a caso sia accaduta come accidente non pensato, o come per vendetta dell'opinione che la casa di Guisa havea concetta ch'egli havesse, già sotto la città d'Orliens, fatto ammazzare da Giovanni Poltrot[2] il prode capitano Mons.r de Guisa, che colà era generale della hoste del Re Christianissimo, come contrario et grave persecutore di chi s'havesse abbracciata la religione evangelica o (come altri dicon) riformata. Intorno a che sono i pareri molto diversi, secondo la diversità degli humori, delle passioni et degl'interessi, come altresì secondo l'accidente et la maniera tenuta nell'ammazzamento et nell'essecuzione di cotanto fatto.

Pertanto vi racconterò, con la maggior brevità che potrò, quel tanto che io ne ho ritratto da persone che[3] si trovarono in sul fatto et d'altri della corte, li quali, quantunque sieno catolici, fan però mestiere di non volere spiacere a questi nè a quelli; onde si puo credere che lo raccontino nella maniera ch'è seguito; non ubligandomi però d'affermare che così per a punto sia passato, non comportando i tempi che l'huomo si possa (come converebbe) certificarsi. Nè meno vo ubligarmi a dirvi l'opinion mia per molti degni rispetti, contentandomi del nome di simplice raccontatore.

---

[1] Sassetti returned to Paris from Lyons on 9 September. See below at conclusion of "Raccontamento."
[2] Jean Poltrot, sieur de Méré, shot the duc de Guise before Orléans (which Guise had under siege) on 18 February 1563. The duke died from his wounds on the 24th.
[3] Cancelled: "vi."

È dunque necessario (perchè 'ntendiate le cagioni c'han mosse tante male sodisfattioni et tante guerre) ch'io comincia da cose lontane, per venirmi poi alle più vicine. Onde dico che i predetti disgusti et le predette guerre hebbero cominciamento dalla pace fatta a Cambresi[a][4] fra il Christianissimo e'l Catolico, con tanto danno di questa Serenissima Corona, dopo la morte della felice memoria d'Arrigo, padre del presente Re,[5] il qual lasciò questo reame cotanto nudo di giustitia, di denari et di capitani, et nell'universale una molta licentiosa vita. Laonde,[b] per cagione della predetta morte, pretendevano i Prencipi del sangue reale la tutela del Re pupillo e'l reggimento del regno, secondo le sue antiche leggi, et ciò non desiderava meno di loro la Reina madre, come similmente faceva la casa Lorena per essere zii della Reina regnante, moglie del Re Francesco secondo. Et per questa ragione havevano eglino il peso del reggimento in mano, il per che ogni cosa passava per le mani del Cardinale di Lorena,[6] sì che non pure governava, ma (secondo il parere di molti) s'arrogava anchora troppa autorità per essere straniero, per la qual cosa era molto odiato da Prencipi del sangue et da quasi tutta la nobiltà.

Dopo la morte d'Arrigo, dunque, si levaron molti de' grandi, chi sotto preteso di torgli il reggimento, et chi per darlo alla Reina madre. Et perchè di già bolliva la causa della religione, il preteso d'alcuni tumulti popolareschi fu da lei pigliato che su quei cominciamenti seguitarono, già principiati nel tempo del predetto Arrigo, da quali poi nacque la guerra che per dieci anni durò. Nel qual tempo molte zuffe, molte battaglie, molti homicidi, molti abbrusciamenti di case et struggimenti di città seguitarono, e'l tutto sotto preteso della religione, accompagnato però da uno smisurato desio di signoreggiare, contrastando la casa di Guisa con quella di Borbone, non ostante che quella sia straniera, et questa non solo antica et naturale, ma etiandio del sangue reale.[c] Il che tutto procedeva per essere caduto il reame

---

[a] Dalla pace di Cambresi cominciaron le cagioni delle guerre civili della Francia.

[b] Per la morte d'Arrigo, i Prencipi del sangue, la Reina madre, et i Guisi (come zii di Maria Stuarda, moglie di Francesco II Re di Francia) pretendono la tutela del Re pupillo e'l reggimento del reame.

[c] Competenza della casa di Guisa straniera, con la Borbona antica, naturale et del sangue reale.

[4] Treaty of Cateau-Cambrésis concluded in April 1559 between the kings of France and Spain.

[5] Henri II, father of Charles IX, the reigning monarch, died as a consequence of injuries received during a tourney in June 1559. See below, at n. 114.

[6] Charles de Guise (1525-1574), cardinal of Lorraine.

nelle mani de' Re pupilli, com'è stato Francesco II et hoggi è Carlo IX. Et per questo la Reina madre desiderava, anzi voleva in sua balìa havere il reggimento di quello, come madre de' predetti Re, giudicando ogni volta ch'ella reggesse che il Re sarebbe servito con maggiore fede et meglio, sì negli affari dello stato et[7] in quelli de' Prencipi stranieri, come similmente in quelli delle 'ntrate regie et della giustitia. Et avegna[8] con destro modo tutti i ministri dipendessero da lei, et così le armi, come tutte le altre cose appartenenti al bene essere di questo reame; et come *prudente Prencipessa*[d][9] andava intrattenendo quando gli uni et quando gli altri in isperanza, secondo i casi et le opportunità, et anchora l'autorità ch'eglino s'attribuivano. Si scopersero per ciò nel medesimo tempo molte congiure et tradimenti, così contra la persona *di lei* come contra quella *del Re*,[e] et contra quella d'altri gravi personaggi che reggevano, et seguitarono molte intraprese memorevoli, così di zuffe come di fatto d'arme, di prese di città, et di rubamenti con assai ruina et danno del popolo. Furono gittati a terra bellissimi edifici, tanto di persone publiche quanto di private, et de' tempii dedicati dagli antichi al culto divino, et quello che montava più, levavano al Clero le 'ntrate, mostrando ch'egli n'usava male; et erano stati commessi dall'una et dall'altra parte molti stupri, molti rubamenti, molti *brutti assassinamenti*,[f] et molte violationi di vergini ch'erano serrate ne' monasteri, chi per elettione volontaria et chi per volere del padre, sì che s'era fatta guerra a ferro et a fuoco, come si dice.

Erano anchora seguitate molte conventioni et molti accordi, ne' quali includevano sempre che il tutto era stato fatto per servigio del Re. Conciò sia cosa che gli aversari del presente governo habbiano sempre guerreggiato sotto pretesto di liberare il Re dalla tirania di chi governava, et tutte le loro speditioni che facevano erano in nome del Re. Et così s'inseriva poi nelle paci, le quali son sempre durate poco, per essere sute violate da diversi accidenti et sospetti che sono a me nascosti. Nè stimo, quando ben gli sapessi, che fossero da con-

---

d Era lo scrittore di questa opera fiorentino et da lei salariato. Però non dice malitiosamente ma prudente.

e Se leggerai il ragionamento sopra questo passo, ch'è a carta [32^r] di questo libretto, vedrai quanto questo autore s'inganna.

f Sì, dal canto de' papeschi, ma non già da quello degli evangelici.

7 "et" substituted for "come."
8 Cancelled: "che."
9 "Prencipessa" substituted for "Reina."

fidare alla carta. Ma ben dirò che ciò sia[10] seguito per giusto giudicio di Dio per castigare i nobili et i plebei insieme.

Gli aversari dunque di S. M.tà, quantunque habbiano il più delle volte perduto nelle giornate campali, et che con onta si sieno levati dall'assedio delle città, son nondimeno stati sempre d'un animo invitto et costante, onde son morti dall'una et dall'altra parte molti prodi capitani, prencipi et gentilhuomini di rinome, li quali sarebbero stati attissimi a conquistar qual si voglia grande et forte reame, se non fossero stati estinti da quella crudelissima guerra civile. Laonde, trovandosi il misero regno esausto di denari, di munitioni, di viveri, i soldati stracchi, i communi affaticati, et l'universal desideroso della quiete; et considerando la Reina madre che la continua guerra haverebbe potuto dare qualche entrata ad alcun prencipe straniero et grande di fomentare[11] et ad abbracciare l'una parte, venirsi ad acquistare tal credito che gli sarebbe venuto fatto d'occupare se non tutto, al men buona parte del regno, tenne mezzi che l'una parte et l'altra mandassero pacificatori.

Et così l'anno 1569[g][12] del mese d'agosto fu conchiuso accordo tra S. M.tà et i protettori di quelli della religione riformata, con grandissimo honore dell'Ammiraglio, et con somma riputatione de' suoi seguaci, de' suoi amici et de' suoi confederati, havendo ottenuto per virtù del detto accordo et per benignità di S. M.tà assoluto perdono per tutti coloro c'havevano pigliate l'armi contro gli suoi esserciti. Anzi fu messo (come s'è detto) nelle conventioni che tutto ciò havessero eglino fatto et esseguito per comandamento[13] et per servigio del Re lor sovrano signore, et furon per ciò restituiti agli honori, alle dignità, alle preminentie, et a gradi, tanto ecclesiastici quanto temporali, con restitution de' loro beni. Et furon cancellati i processi criminali, i giudicii di fellonia, et le altre accuse in crimine di lesa maestà ch'erano stati fatti et publicati contro di loro, et che le sentenze[14] civili si potessero risumere con giudici competenti et non suspetti. Furon levate dalle forche le imagini di molti di loro che v'erano state dal magistrato appese, perchè voi dovete sapere esser

---

[g] La pace del 1569 [corrected from 1599].

[10] "ciò sia" substituted for "siano" (which is not cancelled).
[11] Cancelled: "l'una parte a venire."
[12] The Peace of St. Germain signed in August 1570 (not 1569 as the MS incorrectly states). On the negotiations that preceded it, see N. M. Sutherland, *The Massacre of St Bartholomew and the European Conflict 1559–1572* (London, 1973), chap. vi.
[13] Cancelled: "de."
[14] "sentenze" substituted for "cause."

costume di questa natione[h] quando non possono havere il malfattore
nelle mani, non pur lo bandiscano, ma gli fanno anchora il suo processo; et sopra una tavoletta fanno pingere la colui imagine, o appesa
per la gola, o squartato, o posto su la ruota, secondo il suo misfatto, la
quale poi appendono alla publica forca et in diverse parti della città.
Per la qual cosa, se dopo questo viene il predetto malfattore a dar
nelle mani della giustitia, egli senza altro processo viene giustitiato
conforme a quella tavoletta.

Ritornando hora al tralasciato ragionamento, dico che[15] coloro li
quali[16] si trovarono già dichiarati per colpevoli di morte, furono
rilasciati liberi a loro amici et dichiarati innocenti della data sentenza;
et in quelli ne' quali era stata esseguita, a gli heredi loro renderano
ogni honore per ciò perduto, et ogni havere anchora che fosse loro
stato confiscato veniva restituito; et oltre a ciò erano admessi a
giudici, così civili come militari, et rendosi atti ad ogni grado d'honore.
Laonde, essendo una tal conventione messa in atto, pareva a papeschi
et a coloro c'havevano fatto servigio al Re effettualmente, che fosse
lor di gran pregiudicio, perchè dicevano d'esser sempre stati fedelissimi
sudditi et buoni servitori a S.M., et havere[17] messe le vite loro a
rischio della morte per servigio di questa sacra corona, onde mormo-
ravano. Crebbe lor poi così tanto [?] disgusto la venuta d'alcuni
di quegli riconciliati alla corte alcuni dì dopo l'editto, li quali furono
accettati, carezzati et ben veduti, sì dal Re come dalla Reina madre
et da Mons.r d'Angiù.[18] Et fu lor date delle confiscationi, de' salari
et de' beni, et usata lor di quella liberalità ch'è solita S. M.tà d'usare
a chi serve bene et a chi è benemerito. Et quantunque facessero
predicare in diverse parti del regno secondo le conventioni fatte, et
che nelle case lor vivessero liberamente secondo la religione loro, et
che amministrassero i sacramenti loro senza impedimento alcuno, non
dimeno non bastava loro che ogni cosa stata convenuta per[19] l'editto
di pacificatione fosse adempiuta, che tenessero molte città per lor
sicurezza, et la gran liberalità stata loro usata, che cercavano anchora
d'assicurarsi meglio per tutti que' mezzi migliori che potevano.

Laonde, l'Ammiraglio, come huomo d'ingegno et aveduto molto, ma

---

[h] Uso particolar della Francia in bandire i malfattori.

[15] Cancelled: "a."
[16] Cancelled: "erano in absenza stati giustitiati."
[17] Cancelled: illegible word, perhaps "spesso."
[18] Henri duc d'Anjou, brother of Charles IX, the future Henri III (1574–1589).
[19] "per ... pacificatione" inserted from the margin.

per aventura un poco accompagnato da quella riputatione che honorava se et beneficiava que' della religione, s'imaginò che col credito non picciolo c'havea, se fosse ito a corte, haverebbe potuto con vive dimostrationi ridurre S. M.tà a formare un governo nel quale egli havesse havuta parte et autorità. Sì che, volendosi mostrar buon suddito et fedel servitor di Sua M.tà, le restituì alcuni luoghi che teneva, con patto però che il Re non vi mettesse guarnigione, et che si levassero anche quelli che non erano soliti tenersi avanti la guerra civile. Et consultata la cosa con più intimi favoriti suoi, giudicarono, quando egli fosse stato in corte, c'haverebbe data riputatione et credito alla causa loro, et sarebbe stato d'accrescimento alla religione. Et che con le sue dimostrationi et autorità harebbe mosso il Re a pigliar l'arme et assalire la Francia Contea et la Fiandra, favoreggiando i rubelli del Re di Spagna, et in un medesimo tempo entrare nel regno di Navarra ingiustamente posseduto dal predetto Re, et assalire quel regno con l'armi et con la predicatione[20] dell'evangelio. Et benchè[21] il lor concistoro[1] non approvasse una così fatta deliberatione, nè l'andata dell'Ammiraglio in corte, come quello che pensava che anchora vi fossero di molte male intentioni per le molte ingiurie fatte al Re, et che la molta autorità della Reina madre, di spirito italiano, vendicativa secondo il naturale di tutta la famiglia de' Medici,[j] che non perdonano nè dimenticano giamai i ricevuti torti, et c'hanno la vera arte di signoreggiare in virga ferrea; l'havere app[ress]o di lei il conte di Rets,[22] ancorchè fosse nato in Francia, non dimeno serbare in parte uno spirito fiorentino et esser di razza sottile et diabolica; et l'esser nel governo il cardinale Birago,[23] huomo che

---

[1] Il Concistoro de' Calvinisti in Francia non approva l'andata dell'Ammiraglio in corte.

[j] Que' di casa Medici non perdonano nè si domenticano mai i torti ricevuti.

[20] "predicatione" substituted for "religione."
[21] MS: "Et a benchè."
[22] Albert de Gondi, comte de Retz, born at Lyons in November 1522, the son of a Florentine banker who transferred to that city between 1505 and 1510. Albert became a marshal of France, an intimate adviser to the queen mother and was considered one of the fomentors of the Massacre. See J. de Corbinelli, *Histoire généalogique de la maison de Gondi* (2 vols.; Paris, 1705); M. J. de Pommerol, *Albert de Gondi, maréchal de Retz* (Geneva, 1953).
[23] The Milanese, Renato di Birago (1506–1583), succeeded Jean de Morvilliers as chancellor of France (1571) and was elevated to the cardinalate by Gregory XIII (1578). He, Retz and Luigi Gonzaga, duc de Nevers, were the principal "Machiavellian" Italian counsellors of Catherine de Medici excoriated in the post-Massacre Huguenot pamphlet literature. See S. Mastellone, "Aspetti dell'Antimachiavellismo in Francia," *Il Pensiero Politico*, II (1969), 381ff. On Birago, see now the *voce* by M. François in the *Dizionario biografico degli Italiani*, X, 613–18.

tiene che il mancare i Prencipi della fede loro verso i sudditi sia cosa di poca coscienza, allegando che così porti la ragione di Stato, et che ne venghi assoluti per li canoni pontificali,[k] faceva lor temer molto. Oltre che l'odio si poteva presumere da[24] gli passati portamenti di Mons.r d'Angiù, che apertamente ciò più volte havea dimostrato, ma spetialmente quando fece ammazzare il Prencipe di Condé;[25] dalla conventione dell'accordo fatta con tanta poca riputatione del Re et del governo; da potententi nemici ch'egli havea nella casa di Lorena,[26] sapendo bene quanto i preti sieno poco domentichevoli delle nemicitie, parendo lor di fare a Dio sacrifitio quando collo spargimento del sangue humano posson fare una loro vendetta.

Onde nel predetto Concistoro pareva ch'egli si mettesse a manifesto pericolo, et gli fu pronosticata la sua rovina[l] et di que' della religione, dal gran cancelliere del re di Navarra,[27] huomo di grande sperienza et di molta avedutezza nelle cose del mondo, il con la sua molta industria ha più fiate condotto molta fanteria et cavalleria tedesca senza denari in Francia. Hora dopo molte lettere che andarono attorno di S. M.tà della Reina madre, dell'Ammiraglio, sotto colore di maneggiare il matrimonio del Prencipe di Navarra[m] con Mad.a Margherita sorella del Re, che s'era di lunga mano traficato in vita di Giovanna Reina di Navarra, che lo confortavano a venire in corte, acciochè con la sua presenza havesse levato via ogni scrupulo, et acciochè ognun secondo la sua coscienza fosse venuto sicuro, et che si fossero adempiuti alcuni articoli dell'editto, et abolite et scancellate le memorie ch'erano ne' parlamenti et ne' publici luoghi.

Onde fu più volte mandato dalle lor M.tà all'Ammiraglio il S.r Gio. Galeazzo Fregoso,[n][28] nomato il lupo bigio, huomo di spirito in superfitie, non suspetto all'Ammiraglio nè alla Reina di Navarra, per-

---

[k] I canoni de' pontefici romani assolvono i Prencipi di poter mancar di fede verso i loro sudditi.

[l] Fu pronosticata all'Ammiraglio la sua ruina s'andava a corte.

[m] Guarda questo passo, nel qual credo esserci errore.

[n] Gio. Galeazzo Fregoso (cognominato il lupo bigio) è mandato all'Ammiraglio.

[24] "da" substituted for "per."

[25] Louis de Bourbon, prince de Condé, was taken prisoner at the battle of Jarnac, 13 March 1569, and later killed by an unknown assassin. See Denys d'Aussy, "L'assassin du prince de Condé à Jarnac (1569)," Revue des questions historiques, XLIX (1891), 573–82.

[26] Cancelled: "Lorenza."

[27] Barbier de Francourt, chancellor of Navarre. See N. L. Roelker, Queen of Navarre: Jeanne d'Albret, 1528–1572 (Cambridge, Mass., 1968), pp. 312, 366, 373, 375–77.

[28] See above, p. 108.

ciochè si mostrava d'esser della religione[29] et era stato in Inghilterra come amico di Mons.r di Maligni, Vidame di Ciartes,[30] che in quel reame s'era riparato per cagione di religione, et haveva seco trattato il modo che si poteva havere per congiugnere in matrimonio la Ser.ma Reina d'Inghilterra con l'altezza di Mons.r d'Angiù, nè poco pratico delle cose del mondo, et da saper condurre la sposa al letto con ogni artificio.

Così dunque l'Ammiraglio dalla fede havuta dal suo Re, da conforti di molti, guidato[31] forse da fatal destino, si ridusse in corte, o per meglio dire a precipitare, facendosi a credere che non potesse nascere cosa così repentina che egli non havesse havuto tempo da rimediarvi. Venne adunque alla corte, che si trovava a Bles[o][32] l'anno passato, accompagnato da gran compagnia di gentilhuomini, et fu menato a S. M.tà dal duca di Memoransi,[33] suo cugino, et da Mons.r di Gleovor,[34] marescalco di Francia, li quali in nome del Re l'havevano assicurato che poteva liberamente venire, senza dubitar di cosa alcuna. Fu da S. M.tà con ogni lieta maniera abbracciato,[p] ben veduto et grandemente accarezzato, et così dalla Reina madre. Ma da Mons.r d'Angiù, che si trovava indisposto, od al men ne facea sembianza (a cui dal Re fu condotto a far riverenza) non fu cotanto ben veduto, come quelli che non sapean anchora perfettamente dissimulare la natura sua. In qual cosa, se non fosse l'Ammiraglio stato del tutto abbagliato, gli haverebbe potuto servir d'indizio delle sciagure future, et tanto più che in corte si trovava il legato del papa,[35] che ogni dì era all'orecchio delle loro M.tà et di Mons.r,[36] ch'era frate assai fino et maligno.

Stando dunque l'Ammiraglio in corte ove gli affari si governavano

---

[o] Venuta dell'Ammiraglio a Bles, ove si trovava la corte.
[p] O gran Re del simulare.

[29] E. Palandri (*Les négociations politiques et religieuses entre la Toscane et la France* [Paris, 1908], p. 132) cites a Spanish ambassador's description of Fregoso: "le plus hérétique des hérétiques."
[30] Jean de Ferrières, seigneur de Maligny, vidame de Chartres, Huguenot leader who fled to England in 1569 after having been condemned to death and hanged in effigy. There he participated with Fregoso in the negotiations to marry Elizabeth to the duc d'Anjou. See L. de Bastard, *Vie de Jean de Ferrières* (Auxerre, 1855); Conyers Read, *Mr. Secretary Walsingham and the Policy of Queen Elizabeth* (3 vols.; Cambridge, 1925), I, 101.
[31] "guidato" substituted for "accompa[gnato]."
[32] Blois, where Coligny joined the court in mid-September 1571.
[33] François duc de Montmorency.
[34] *Sic:* Arthus de Cossé, comte de Secondigny, seigneur de Gonnor.
[35] The cardinal of Santa Croce, who arrived in France in June 1571.
[36] *Viz.*, Anjou.

con finta honestà, tanto dall'una parte quanto dall'altra, haveva ogni giorno l'orecchia del Re et della Regina Madre. Gli fu dato grosso salario per lo S.r di Tiligni,[37] suo genero, per Briemor,[38] per La Nua,[39] et per molti altri, con un donativo di cento mila franchi et più, et alla moglie quaranta mila, se fu vero, per ricompensa del danno patito alla casa sua di Sciattiglione. Et per chè era sovente nel *gabinetto*[q] del Re, et forse gonfio de' supremi favori gli venivano fatti dal Re, non poteva star quieto, come huomo di gran sapere et dalli affari, et come ottimo conoscitore della natura di que' popoli armiggeri, et per lo lungo uso della guerra fatti martiali, che gli rendono impa-tienti d'una lunga quiete. Come ottimo francesco, et desideroso che la misera patria godesse di così dolce pace, cominciò a mostrare al Re come S. M.tà (per levare ogni minima cagione[40] di mala volontà degli uni verso gli altri, et ischivare ogni nuovo tumulto che ne potesse nascere[41]) doveva far levare un obelisco con una croce vicino a S.ti Innocenti, il qual nomava in generale et in particolare alcuni casi seguiti, cosa per conturbare ogni forte animo, et ch'era a disprezzo de' Protestanti quivi stata rizzata.[42] Il Re, mosso dalle buone dimostra-tioni dell'Ammiraglio, commise che la predetta memoria con la croce fosse da quel luogo levata, et la piazza sopra la qual era prima stata una gran casa d'un protestante, che fu dal furioso popolo gittata per terra et ivi postovi la predetta memoria, fosse agli heredi restituita,[r] et che il commune di Parigi rifacesse il danno delle case che da suoi eran state gettate a terra.

Fu, dico, tanta l'autorità dell'Ammiraglio, che per le dimostrationi fatte al Re et al consiglio[43] segreto, che fu comandato sotto pena d'indignatione et di maggior pregiudicio al Parlamento et agli altri

---

[q] Gabinetto, chiamano la camera segreta.
[r] Giusta sentenza.

[37] Charles de Téligny, Huguenot military leader and a chief negotiator on the Protestant side of the Peace of St. Germain. He was married to Coligny's daughter Louise (by his first wife, Charlotte de Laval). I have not been able to confirm the stipends that Sassetti declares Téligny and the others named with him received. See J. Delaborde, "Charles de Téligny," *Bulletin de la Société de l'histoire du protestantisme français*, XXIII (1874), 434–51.
[38] François de Beauvais, seigneur de Briquemault, illustrious Huguenot military leader, one of the commissioners appointed to administer the Peace of St. Germain.
[39] François de La Noue, Huguenot leader and a negotiator of the Peace of St. Germain. He was soldiering in Flanders during the summer of 1572 and thus escaped the Massacre. See H. Hauser, *François de La Noue (1531–1591)* (Paris, 1892).
[40] After "cagione" the text is in disorder and several indecipherable words have been cancelled.
[41] "ischivare ogni" and "che ne potesse nascere" inserted from margin.
[42] On the affair of the *Croix de Gastines*, see above, p. 107.
[43] "consiglio" substituted for "parlamento."

ufficiali di Parigi, che la gittassero a terra et abolissero ogni memoria d'un tal fatto. Fu esseguito il comandamento regio, ma non già senza grave scandalo di quel popolo et dell'universale anchora, il qual diceva esser cosa contra il diritto divino et alla sacrosanta religion catolica romana. Nè vi mancò molto che quel popolaccio non tumultuasse, se ben non passò senza offesa l'essecutione, perchè furono svaliggiate alcune case et alcune botteghe, et feriti alcuni di coloro ch'erano sospetti di religione. Nè seguirono maggiori scandali per li buoni ordini della giustitia et da buoni cittadini, et per intercessione dell'Ammiraglio non furon castigati nella vita alcuni del predetto tumulto.

Operò anchora che la Ser.ma Reina di Navarra venisse in corte,[s] et che si concludesse il matrimonio col prencipe suo figliuolo, con articoli (per quello che ne dicono i catolici) dishonoratissimi, et tutto per la temerità et arditezza di quella prencipessa, li quali non vo qui raccontare per non offendere amendue le parti, o per non darne la colpa a suoi ministri, troppo mossi dal proprio interesse. Ma ben dirò ch'erano del tutto contrarii a quello che convenga a seguaci della fede romana, perchè si discostavano dal suo rito, et ogni dì accrescevano gli odii et la mala volontà contro di lui et de' suoi adherenti. Nè s'avedeva che porgevano cagion di machinare per lo sospetto che nasceva dalla grandezza degli altri.

Successe fra poco tempo la rubellione di Flessinghe [t][44] nelle isole del mare occeano, et d'altri luoghi ne' paesi bassi, et così la 'mpresa di Valentiana et di Mons en Enau,[45] terre principalissime, poste lunghe le frontiere et ottimamente munite et fortificate. Et ivi concorse il conte Lodovico di Nausau, fratello del prencipe d'Orange, il S.r della Nua, il S.r di Gianlis,[46] et molti altri gentilhuomini franceschi et borgognoni, vecchi nell'arte militare. Et si giudica che fosse ciò stato ritrovamento del S.r Ammiraglio, il qual veggendo come Mons d'en Enau, Flessinga,

---

[s] Reina di Navarra va a corte.
[t] Rubellione di Flessinga.

[44] Vlissingen (Flushing).
[45] The revolt of the Netherlands from Spanish rule began with some initial successes, notably the capture of Valenciennes and Mons in Hainault by the insurgents led by Louis of Nassau. They were recaptured shortly by superior Spanish forces. There is an abundant literature on the May–July 1572 military campaigns. See N. M. Sutherland, *The Massacre of St Bartholomew*, chaps. xiii-xvi; J. Shimizu, *Conflict of Loyalties: Politics and Religion in the Career of Gaspard de Coligny, Admiral of France, 1519–1572* (Geneva, 1970), chap. xi.
[46] Jean de Hangest, sieur de Genlis, Huguenot military leader. On the French participation in the war, see Kervyn de Lettenhove, *Les Huguenots et les Gueux*, II: (*1567–1572*) (Bruges, 1884).

Encusen, la Briglia, Canfiere[47] et altre piazze erano afforzate, guarnite di munizione, di huomini da guerra, di strumenti bellici, come d'una malvagia volontà verso i ministri spagnuoli, cominciò a mostrare al Re che non era da perdere una tale opportunità d'impatronirsi di tutti i paesi bassi,[u] o al men di parte di loro. Et continouamente protestava al Re di prender l'arme a danno del re di Spagna, suo antico nimico, mostrandogli come questo era il tempo di abbassar l'alterigia et la possanza di casa d'Austria, poi chè la riputatione cominciava a mancargli, et che in Filippo non era quella felicità che fu già in Carlo suo padre, et che il valore spagnuolo era più in opinione che in effetto.[v] Come Don Federigo di Toledo[48] lor colonello haveva adulterata quella militia, n'havea dato buon saggio nelle fazioni della Frigia quando combattì col conte Lodovico di Nausau, nella qual vilmente senza combattere si lasciaron tagliare a pezzi.[w] Et se la 'ntrapresa di Valentiana non havea havuto quel felice fine che s'era desiderato, che la colpa era stato del picciol numero delle genti c'havevano per menare a fine una tanta impresa, et senza il favor d'alcun gran prencipe. Et che il prencipe d'Orange verrebbe in Fiandra con numerosa hoste di fanteria et di cavalleria tedesca; et con una buona banda di soldati vecchi franceschi, et col credito ch'egli havea nella Gheldria, nell'Hollanda, et con la giusta causa di voler rimettere nella primiera antica libertà i paesi bassi, tenuti sotto estrema tirannia et governati in virga ferrea da gli Spagnuoli, volterebbe incontinente que' paesi già dati a rubellarsi, non potendo tolerare il tirannesco governo del duca d'Alva, con le continue gravezze che messe sopra a poveri popoli. Sì che con alcune dolci conditioni et honesti privileggi ritornerebbero sotto l'ubidienza et governo di questa sacra corona, come altre volte erano stati.

Aggiungneva anchora che quando la M.tà S. non si determinasse di fare tale impresa, non poteva tener que' della religione non pigliassero le armi per aiutare i fratelli loro, et diceva che non pigliandosi tal determinatione, non vedeva come la Francia potesse stare lungamente in pace, nè conosceva il miglior modo per conservarla che far la guerra

---

[u] O quanto sano e verace era quel consiglio per la nul sana Francia.
[v] Il valore Spagnuolo esser più in opinione che in effetto.
[w] Viltà de' soldati Spagnuoli.

[47] Brill was captured by the Sea Beggars on 1 April 1572. "Encusen" and "Canfiere" (?) are possibly to be identified with Enkhuizen and Kampen on the Zuider Zee (or perhaps "Canfiere" may stand for Cambrai).
[48] A son of the duke of Alva.

nell'altrui, la qual non puo che ad honore di S. M.tà et utile de' popoli tornare. Onde col suo efficace et più che verace parlare, havea ridotta la cosa a tale che i più pensavano che veramente s'havesse da rompere la pace con la Spagna. Nè si ragionava d'altro che delle speditioni [da] Mons.r d'Aste,[49] Piles[50] et altri prodi conduttieri della lor religione, e'l gran seguito c'haveva il Re di Navarra, e'l veder la corte piena de' lor seguaci, non accresceva poco cotale opinione. Et tanto più che ne' medesimi tempi, venendo la flotta di Spagna in Fiandra, di Spagnuoli, di Portughesi et di Fiaminghi, che per maggior sicurezza erano venuti con l'armata del duca Medina Celi,[51] per suspetto de' pirati inglesi et franceschi, la qual quando fu alla bocca della Schelda, riviera famosa dove sorgono le navi grosse che vanno in Anversa, per tradimento d'alcuni patroni di navi, si rendettero prigioni a que' di Flessinga. Onde rimasero ventidue navi in poter de' nemici del Re Filippo, et tre n'abbrusciarono; et se non fosse stato lo dop[pie]ggiare del governatore di Flessinga et poca sperienza, del certo pigliavano tutta l'armata del predetto Medina Celi, con 1500 bisogni, cioè soldati nuovi, che conduceva in Fiandra per suplimento di quelle terre. Et, per quello che si disse, la preda montava da un million d'oro et più, per la molta spetieria et quantità di reali d'argento ch'era su quelle navi. In qual denaio haverebbe servito (come si diceva) per pagare la cavalleria et la fanteria che il prencipe d'Orange conduceva della Magna,[52] per assoldare un 4 o 5 mila franceschi anchora.

Si diceva similmente, come alli confini della Picardia s'era messi insieme da quattro mila fanti et cinquecento cavalli, sotto sembianza di voler passare in Fiandra per soccorrere i loro ch'erano in Mons en Enaut. Le quali genti facevano a que' confini danni non piccioli, et usavano crudeltà, oltre al vivere a discretione, come se fossero stati in paese nemico.[53] Monsig.r di Gianlis, fratello del vescovo di Noion,[54] uscì con gran suo rischio di Mons et, forse per communicare alcuna impresa, o per altro rispetto, s'abboccò con l'Ammiraglio secretamente, il qual mostrò d'haver timore del Re suo signore. Però conchiusono che si conducesse le predette genti a congiugnersi col prencipe d'Orange, o

---

[49] Antoine d'Aure (known as Grammont), comte d'Aster et de Guiche (d. 1576).
[50] Armand de Clermont, baron de Piles.
[51] Don Juan de la Cerda y Silva, duke of Medinaceli (d. 1575), viceroy of Sicily and short-lived successor to Alva as governor of the Spanish Netherlands (1572). See H. G. Koenigsberger, *The Practice of Empire* (Ithaca, 1969), pp. 179–80.
[52] *Viz.*, Germany.
[53] "nemico" substituted for "straniero."
[54] Jean de Hangest, bishop of Noyon (d. 1577).

al meno condurle salve a Mons, avegna che all'Ammiraglio non paresse ancora tempo di mettere ad essecutione cosa alcuna sino che non haveva più certa la volontà del Re, oltre che non havea opinione che Gianlis fosse atto a condurre tali genti. Ma vinto da prieghi di quello, et da ch'erano in essere, et per levar la cagione del danno che facevano alle frontiere, n'acconsentì.

Haveano pertanto determinato di fare l'impresa di Malines et la tenevano sicura, perchè quella città non haveva voluto accettar la guarnigione spagnuola, et s'intendeva come que' cittadini erano d'animo di rubellarsi. Hora dove il predetto Gianlisi haveva da marciare in un giorno et in una notte,[x] et poscia condurli in tre giorni a Malins, fece poco più di tredici leghe, perch'erano soldati volontari, onde volevano tutti i loro agi. Et così si condusse vicino a Mons un tre leghe in uno alloggiamento assai forte entro un bosco. Ma essendo que' soldati stracchi, nè senza alcuna disensione tra loro per cagion d'ire a combattere, furono in su la notte assaliti da capitani del duca d'Alva, et anchora che facessero alcuna sorte di difesa furon rotti et tagliati a pezzi[y] la maggior parte di loro, sì perchè eran pochi, nè havevano cavalleria et erano nul d'accordo tra loro. Moriron in detta zuffa molti gentilhuomini, et Gianlis rimase prigione (che fu perfidamente da questi Spagnuoli ucciso); et si diede la colpa alla sua poca avertenza, perchè diede tempo a nimici et determinaron di combatterli, et n'ottennero la vittoria confortati in ciò da Chiappin Vitelli,[55] maestro General dell'hoste[56] spagnuola.

L'Ammiraglio cominciò di nuovo a persuadere et a mostrare che bisognava anticipare il tempo col pigliar l'armi, et supplicava il Re che, quando S. M.tà non s'havesse voluto scoprire apert[amen]te nimico del Re di Spagna, che lasciasse fare a lui, et come a capitan di ventura permettesse di soldare huomini, di prender viveri et munitioni del suo denaio. Non posso io lasciar di pormi a considerar la buona mente di questo et gran capitano et veramente buon francesco, il quale con ogni suo studio cercava di tirar la guerra fuori della sua amata patria, et di volgerla addosso all'antico et ver nimico della sua patria et del suo Re, bene merito d'un tanto odio, per li alti et incredi[bi]li torti fatti a questa corona. Onde se a Francesco primo od ad Arrigo suo

---

[x] Error di Gianlisi.
[y] Gianlis rotto, et la sua gente tagliata a pezzi.

[55] Chiappino Vitelli (d. 1576), marquis of Cetona, Italian captain in the service of Spain. He was a close friend of Sassetti. See Read, *Walsingham*, I, 264–65.
[56] "hoste" substituted for an indecipherable word, perhaps "campo."

figliuolo fossero state fatte contro proferte, non in vano sarebbero ite.
Ma ritornando ove lasciai, dico che il prode Ammiraglio prometteva
a S. M.tà che col congiugnersi col prencipe d'Orange sperava di fare
alcun segnalato servigio alla M.tà Sua, la quale da suoi continoui
ricordi, prieghi, consigli, minaccie et spaventamenti era necessitato di
dargli alcune speranze di parole, alcune lettere patenti et chiuder
gl'occhi a molti che si partivano. Onde si teneva che le genti c'haveva
insieme il S.r Filippo Strozzi,[57] colonello generale della 'nfanteria
francesca, dovesse ad un tale effetto servire, ateso che haveva seco
molti capitani della religione.

Vi parrà peraventura strano ch'io non habbia anchora fatto men-
tione della morte della Reina Giovanna di Navarra, per essere suta di
molto danno alle cose dell'Ammiraglio et alla causa universale del[la]
religione sua.[58] Il che ho fatto per non havere ad allungarmi in troppo
lungo trattato, perchè vi sarebbe stata assai materia, ateso ch'ella
era prencipessa d'animo veramente virile et costante. Onde la sua
riputatione, accompagnata con l'ostinatione, dava incredibil credito a
lui, et a tutti que' di quella parte. Dirò solamente che s'è tenuto che
sia stata fatta avelenare con un paio di guanti perfumati; et saprei
anchor dir da chi, ma non è licito.[59] Onde per ritornare all'Ammiraglio, rimaso per la predetta morte sol capo di que' della religione,[60] che
al suo consiglio tutti que' tali si achetaruno come ad un oraculo, tanto
era la riputation sua et la sua auttorità.

Io ho voluto fare (S.r mio) questo lungo et malcompilato ragionamento senza ordine delle cose passate, accompagnato d'accidenti
stranieri eseguiti fuori di questo reame, per due ragioni: l'una perch'eglino hanno alcun conlegamento insieme, et l'altra per poter tanto
più agevolmente venire a considerare se questo grave accidente sia
stato premeditato o no. Perchè pare ad alcuni che si possa creder l'uno
et l'altro secondo le occasioni et gli accidenti.

Et in prima la pace fatta con tanto disavantaggio, per non dir
dishonore di questo Re. Secondariamente, la venuta dell'Ammiraglio

---

[57] Filippo Strozzi (1541–1582), son of the great marshal of France, Piero Strozzi (d. 1558).

[58] "sua" substituted for "loro."

[59] "The belief that Jeanne d'Albret was poisoned is an item of Huguenot mythology developed after the Massacre of St. Bartholomew. It first appears in a libelous attack on Catherine de Medici, *Discours merveilleux sur la vie, actions et déportements de Catherine de Médicis* published in 1574 ..." (Roelker, *Queen of Navarre*, pp. 391–92). The poisoner was thought to have been René Bianchi, perfumer to the queen mother, who sold Jeanne a pair of perfumed gloves.

[60] Cancelled: "era honorato, stimato et."

in corte, cotanto cara et accetta. La terza, quello c'havevano comportato alla morta Reina di Navarra, delle insolenti et ingiuriose parole ch'ella usava, et anchora degli articoli ottenuti del matrimonio del prencipe suo figliuolo con la sorella del Re, Mad.a Margherita, e'l matrimonio del prencipe di Condé con la figliuola di Francesco di Cleves, duca d'Aniversa,[61] senza dispensa o ritto della romana chiesa. Quarto, con compiacere all'Ammiraglio et a suoi tutto ciò che domandavano, od almen dando loro speranza non picciola di compiacer loro; et l'abboccamento fatto più volte col conte Lodovico di Nauso, l'absenza del Guisa[62] dalla corte, la partita d'Humena[63] per Italia, l'havere il Re mandato il cardinale di Lorena a Roma, non esser più quella casa in governo, mostra[va] S. M. d'haver caro seguisse la pace fra la casa di Guisa con l'Ammiraglio, et di già se n'era trattato. Quinto, la confederatione si fece la potentissima Reina d'Inghilterra, tanto offensiva come difensiva, l'andata che fece il duca di Memoransi[64] alla medesima Reina per giurar la lega, come havevano prima fatto la pace in man di quella M.tà et de' prencipi protestanti della Magna, il quale era in sommo favore et admesso al governo, et era cugino dell'Ammiraglio, in grandissimo conto tra la nobiltà per la qualità degli amici che il gran connestabile suo padre s'havea acquistati con benefici fatti loro. Si vedeva il Re dato a suoi piaceri, et che si lasciava governare dal consiglio della madre; ben pensava egli di poterlo da ciò rimore et di guadagnar la Reina madre con prometterle di guadagnare stati per gli altri figliuoli. Sesto, havea grandissima intelligenza co' prencipi tedeschi, come col duca Augusto, duca di Sassonia, col conte Palatino del Reno, con l'Angravio d'Essia, col duca di Vittemberga, et con altri prencipi della casa di Baviera, di Nausau et di Mansfelt. Et era amato in Inghilterra da quella Reina et da primi del regno, che lo stimavano huomo di gran governo et integrità di vita et di sua parola.

In Francia haveva seguito grande di nobiltà, et havea guadagnato la gratia del duca d'Angolemo,[65] secondo fratello del Re, il qual quantunque fosse molto giovanetto, dava non dimeno di lui grande spe-

---

[61] The marriage of Marie de Clèves, daughter of François duc de Nevers, to Henri I de Condé took place on 10 August 1572.

[62] Henri duc de Guise (1550–1588).

[63] Charles de Lorraine, duc de Maine (or Mayenne, 1554–1611), brother of the duc de Guise.

[64] François de Montmorency, son of Anne de Montmorency, constable of France (1493–1567), was one of the signers on the French side of the Anglo-French defensive treaty ratified on 29 April 1572.

[65] Henri de Valois, chevalier d'Angoulême, natural son of Henri II.

ranza. Et perchè il concistoro l'haveva per veramente gran politico et di sovran valore, haveva fatto un commune segreto con molte belle leggi et ordini,[z] taleggiandosi per tanti anni in una somma di denari che ascendeva a due millioni di franchi, o nobili lire tornesi. Perchè davano la quarta parte delle 'ntrate de' loro beni, et di più quello che le loro chiese facevano montava ad otto mila franchi. Et anchor più, accomodavano le querele d'honore, le liti civili per via d'arbitri, di compromessi et di giudici pettorali, dando il gastigo con pena pecuniaria et d'infamia a chi non ubidivano. Havevano un depositario con 18 mila franchi l'anno di salario, il quale havea cura di riscuottere et di condurre il denaio ove facesse di mestieri per servigio del lor commune. Et entrava questo anno in ufficio di depositario Benedetto Calandrini, Lucchese.[a'] [66]

All'Ammiraglio davano di salario l'anno, come a lor protettore et capitano, venticinque mila franchi con altri donativi; al conte della Rocca Focao,[67] dieci mila; a Tiligni, 3500; a Bricamor, alla Nua et ad altri altrettanto; a ministri et a capitani, a chi più et a chi meno, secondo le qualità, i meriti e'l valor loro, il che arrivava alla somma di 100 mila franchi. Il rimanente fino alla somma di 800 mila franchi tenevano per pagare gli allemani c'havevano condotti in Francia. Onde s'erano convenuti col Re di pagare i due terzi, e'l terzo S. M.tà. Et s'è ritrovato che dicevano che il debito ch'havevano con gli allamani ascendeva a 5 millioni di franchi,[68] quantunque si sia poi saputo che non era che d'un millione et mezzo di franchi. Sì che venivano ad avanzare il restante per servirsene col scopo a far qualche grande impresa, come si vedeva nell'animo loro. Un tal modello di reggimento fu trovato tra le scritture dell'Ammiraglio, a cui non mancava la publica nè la segreta audienza quando la voleva da le M.tà loro.

---

[z] L'Ammiraglio con que' della religione haveva fatto una rep[ubblica].
[a'] Benedetto Calandrini, depositario della rep[ubblica] degli Ug[o]notti.

[66] Calandrini (1518–1587), merchant and banker, was a prominent figure among the Lucchese religious émigrés who sought haven first in France and later in Geneva. See A. Pascal, "Da Lucca a Ginevra: Studi sulla emigrazione religiosa lucchese a Ginevra nel secolo XVI," *Rivista storica italiana*, XLIX (1932), 300, 462, 466, 475; L (1933), 232, 234–35, 241–42. Calandrini was received as an *habitant* of Geneva on 8 Nov. 1585, many years after the arrival in that city of the majority of Lucchese exiles. See P.-F. Geisendorf, *Livre des habitants de Genève*, II: *1572–1574 et 1585–1587* (Geneva, 1963), p. 137. There are numerous passing references to the institution of the Consistory in R. Kingdon, *Geneva and the Consolidation of the French Protestant Movement, 1564–1572* (Geneva, 1967), but the financial arrangements described by Sassetti and Calandrini's role as officer of the Consistory are not mentioned.
[67] François III, comte de La Rochefoucauld.
[68] Cancelled: "et nello."

Onde il mondo fermamente credeva che gran capitale si facesse del suo consiglio da quelle M.tà, come esso medesimo se lo dava ad intendere. Onde con simili modi di fare l'assicuravano in guisa che il misero non si dubitava di nulla, li quali erano non dimeno chiaro indizio, perchè non fosse suto del tutto abbagliato degli occhi della mente, che sotto tante carezze et sotto si alti favori vi stesse nascosto alcun lacciuolo, secondo quel vulgar proverbio: "Chi ti fa più carezze che non suole, o che t'ha ingannato, o che ingannar ti vuole."

Delle predette cose, adunque, credo che si potrà tirare argomento assai verisimile che la sua, et degli altri suoi seguaci, morte fosse premeditata, et più d'una volta ben consultata,[b'] sì per l'animo macchiato di S. M.tà et della madre, che ottimamente conosceva di che momento fosse l'haver nel suo reame un suddito di cotanto elevato spirito, atto a menare a fine ogni 'mpresa pur grande et malagevole che si fosse, et come i papeschi dicevano, di spirito maligno, che volesse dar le leggi et fare alle lor M.tà violar la pace, l'amista et la parentella c'havevano con la potentissima casa d'Austria. Et tanto più ne' tempi presenti, et senza evidenti cagioni, nel qual i capitani del Re Cattolico difendevano il Serenissimo commune di Vinegia[c'] contro il potentissimo nimico di tutta la Christianità. Et pareva alle M.tà loro d'esser molto tenuto a Filippo per haver[69] mandate più fiate denari et genti da piedi et da cavallo in lor servigio nelle passate guerre.

Ma[70] fu bontà di Dio, come dicono, che conosceva il bisogno della chiesa Romana, et di coloro che non si son mai dilungati dal suo ritto, et che l'hanno continouamente difesa, inspirato nell'animo di S. M.tà Ser.ma et della Ser.ma Reina madre,[d'] dell'Altezza di Mons.r d'Angiù et di molti altri prencipali fedeli sudditi,[e'] et amorevoli servitori di questa sacra corona, un ardente desio di volerla liberare da una tale et tanta importunità che crudel tirannia nominano, acciochè la Chiesa et il Re sieno servit[i] secondo le divini et humani leggi, et secondo *i sacri canoni[f'] che concedono et approvano ogni crudeltà per pietosa che sia messa*

[b'] Che l'humicidio dell'Ammiraglio et de' suoi seguaci fosse di lungo tempo prima pensato et deliberato.

[c'] Non la 'ntesero giamai così i Venitiani.

[d'] Quale inspiramento divino.

[e'] Intende la casa di Guisa tutta, il Card. Birago, il Conte di Res, et simili tutti stranieri, che per la propria difesa di non essere privati de' non meritati uffici, metton lor bene un cotanto diabolico inscrivamento.

[f'] Nota.

[69] Cancelled: "lui."

[70] "Ma ... Dio" substituted for two indecipherable cancelled words.

in atto per servigio di santa Chiesa, ma sì anchora per alcun sospetto che cominciarono havere dell'Ammiraglio per l'osservanza ch'egli mostrava al duca d'Angolem et d'Alanson,[71] natural nimico degli Spagnuoli. Oltre a ciò, essendo il cardinale di Lorena a Roma *instigato da S. S.tà*[g'] *con promesse che non mancherebbe di porgere al Re ogni favore et aiuto temporale quando S. M.tà volesse rompere così ignominiosa pace data sotto qualche velame o pretesto che havesse color d'honestà; facendo lui conoscere che per regnare i Prencipi son dispensati d'ogni mancamento di fede,*[h'] *et particolarmente verso i sudditi et machinatori della republica ecclesiastica.*

Il Re Cattolico havea egli gran piacere che si facesse cotal guerra in questo regno,[i'] et che si levassino del mondo color tutti che consigliavano di turbar la pace fra il Christianissimo et lui, et d'entrare ne' suoi stati et di dar favore a suoi rubelli. Con ciò sia cosa che gli mettesse conto, avegna che ciò[73] gli dovesse costare qualche migliaia di scudi, da dividere questo reame in partialità, et d'indebolirlo di maniera che, s'egli[74] poteva [?] superare il male che gli soprastava nella Fiandra, gli fosse facile l'assalirlo et impadronirsene;[j'] non che, dico io, ch'egli[75] desiderasse di dividerlo. Aih che di già egli era troppo diviso, non nomandosi più niuno per lo sacro et santo nome di christiano, che porta ciascun nella sua fronte sculpito[76] per lo battesimo ricevuto, ma s'appellavano Papeschi, Ugonotti, gli uni gli altri, Berrettoni et Cappellacci.

[g'] Qual Vicario di Christo sia il Papa romano da questo si potrà conoscere.

[h'] Attribuiscono questa sceleratezza all'honesto Macchiavello, il qual non dice che ciò si convenga al Prencipe naturale et buono, ma sì al nuovo Prencipe et che voglia tiranneggiare, e'l libero huomo, nimico mortal d'ogni tirannesca signoria, come quelli che vedea nel suo libero commun di Firenze sorgere il tiranno di lei.[72] Questo scrisse acciochè il popolo fiorentino conoscesse quanta differenza sia dal viver libero all'esser sottoposti allo 'mperio del Tiranno con magnifica virtù et prodezza, havesse difesa la sua antica et cara libertà. Però il Papa, come trovator d'una così mal opinion, è da biasimare.

[i'] Lo credo bene, perchè guai alla sua camiscia s'una volta la misera Francia acheterà le civili disordie, perchè Manet sub alta mente repostum Ursurpationem tirannicam Reg. Navarrae.

[j'] Ipsam veritatem nunc dicis [from the inner margin with the final letters hidden].

[71] François duc d'Alençon (1554-1584).
[72] *The Prince,* chap. viii: "De his qui per scelera ad principatum pervenere."
[73] Cancelled: "non."
[74] Cancelled: "havesse."
[75] Cancelled: "et altri."
[76] Cancelled: "non di tutta" and one or two other indecipherable words.

Laonde, per tutte le predette cagioni ch'erano accompagnate da una mala dispositione del Re verso ciascuno della religione riformata, venne il Guisa nella città. Et il viggesimo secondo giorno d'Agosto tornando la mattina da corte l'Ammiraglio per andare a desinare al suo alloggiamento, accompagnato da suoi servitori, da suoi seguaci et amici, quando fu fuori del portone che va verso l'albergo di Mons.r d'Angiù, gli fu data una lettera, secondo alcuni a caso, ma secondo altri a studio per dare agio a chi era in aguato per ucciderlo di poterlo fare. Perchè havuta l'Ammiraglio la lettera si fermò per volerla leggere,[k'] et da una fenestra d'una casa colì dirempetto, ch'era, od era suta d'un maestro di casa del Guisa, gli fu tirata un arcobugiata nella mano stanca, che gli passò dentro nel braccio. Era la finestra nella quale s'era nascosto l'humicida tutta turata di panni per non esser veduto, da un picciol pertugio in fuori largo mezza spanna, dal qual potè poi pigliare la mira a suo agio, ne fece. Dicono che per sentirsi fedito, non si sbigotì punto et disse, "Non sono anchor morto, no";[l'] et subito fu da suoi condotto a casa sua, ove concorse gran numero de' suoi amici, et fu da' primi medici di questa città giudicato che perdrebbe il braccio, volendo scampar la vita.

Udendo il Re questa novella, che giocava alle palle, mostrò di *conturbarsene* molto,[m'] et visto che n'havrebbe fatta alta dimostratione contro il tiratore dell'arcobugiata et contro i consapevoli; et perchè il vulgo et altri dicevano che il predetto Guisa gliele havesse fatta sparare per l'antica lor animosità, S. M.tà rivoltatosegli, perchè era quivi presente, gli domandò se ciò che si diceva fosse vero. Il qual negò di non saperne cosa veruna, nè uscì dal palagio regio per degni rispetti, et per non dar cagione con la sua vista a seguaci del ferito di solevarsi. Laonde, gli amici più affettionati all'Ammiraglio, accompagnati da molti di que' della religione, furon subito al Re, a cui gravemente si conpiansero, chiedendo giustitia. I capi de' quali furono i S.ri di Roccafocao, Vidame di Sciartes, Bricamor, Piles, Tiligni et altri gran capitani; ove Tiligni,[n'] come genero dell'Ammiraglio, et come giovane di molto valore, sapere, gratia et eloquenza, parlò altamente, accenando che tale arcobugiata fosse stata sparata di commissione et ordine di Mons.r di Guisa. Et nel suo grave ragionamento usò parole

---

[k'] L'Ammiraglio leggendo una lettera nella strada publica vien fedito in una mano d'un arcobugiata.

[l'] Parole dell'Ammiraglio sentendosi fedito.

[m'] Ciò credo, perchè gli rincresceva che il colpo non l'havesse ucciso.

[n'] Tiligni parla altamente al Re chiedendo del misfatto giustitia.

che toccavano la dignità reale, quasi minacciando, in caso che non fosse da S. M.tà fatta spedita giustitia, che da se medisimi se la farebbero. Dove il Re (tenendo la maestà del grado suo, accompagnato da gran dissimulatione) rispose brevemente che non si mancherebbe loro di farne segnalata dimostratione, come ben tosto vedrebbero, che fur parole di doppio sentimento.

Andò similmente Tiligni dalla reina Madre in compagnia d'alcuni gentilhuomini di suo seguito, supplicandola ch'ella fosse ardente in lor favore, per ritrovare donde venisse un tal misfatto et chi v'haveva tenuta mano. Gli rispose, ella, che ne dessero memoriale al Re et a Mons.r d'Angiù et a lei, che con giustificata et vera informatione non si mancherebbe di tosta giustitia. Della qual risposta si partì egli sdegnato.

Si ragunarono poi insieme tutti i capi Ugonotti che allhora [erano] in questa città, et v'intervenne il Re di Navarra col prencipe di Condé, et consigliaron di levar l'Ammiraglio di quella casa a viva forza,o' quando fosse loro impedito, per condurlo fuori di Parigi. Et incontamente spediron lettere alle chiese et agli amici loro sparsi per lo reame, acciochè stessero in arme per difesa della religione et delle vite loro. Agli amici più vicini mandaron che stessero presti per incaminarsi un tal giorno alla volta di questa città, come dissero i catolici loro aversari haver trovate tali speditioni.

Il Re, la Reina madre, Mons.r d'Angiù, il Duca d'Anivers,[77] et altri personaggi, parte consapevoli del fatto et di quello anchora ch'era per seguire, facendo buon sembianza, andarono a visitar l'Ammiraglio,p' condolendosi del caso accaduto con lor grave dispiacere, et consolandolo, acciochè stesse di buona voglia, che non mancherebbero di fargli sommaria giustitia, mostrandogli che s'havesse sospetto del popolo o d'altro particolar nimico, ch'era bene si facesse portare a Lo[u]vro, dove essendo la persona del Re con la sua guardia, che vi starebbe sicurissimo. Grande furon l'offerte che la Reina madre gli fece, et mostrava (per l'affettione che ella gli portava) di sentirne grave dispiacere. L'Ammiraglio diede (come si dice) passata a tutti, ringratiando le M.tà loro di tanta loro humanità, et hanno detto alcuni

---

o' Ottimo parer se l'havessero subito esseguito.

p' Le M.tà vanno sotto finta sembianza a visitar l'Ammiraglio per adormentarlo, acciochè ritirandosi di Pa[rigi] non fosse loro scappato vivo dalle mani.

77 Louis de Gonzague, duc de Nevers.

che mostrasse animo vendicativo, usando gravi ma imperiose parole, le quali punsero alquanto le loro M.tà, maravigliandosi che un tanto huomo si lasciasse trasportar dall'ira et vincer dalle proprie passioni, et massime essendo in alcun pericolo della vita, non mostrando alcuna humanità d'animo o christiano, nè men[78] di simulato, conoscendolo di sua natura huomo freddo, paziente, non ventoso, nè rotto. Nè mai prima altre disgratie od accidenti aversi l'havevano spaventato. Ma, se pur fu vero che ne dimostrasse alteratione, non è da maravigliarsene; con ciò sia cosa che le cose che concernono lo 'nteresse universale si governino più pesatamente che le proprie offese,[79] sì con gli effetti come con le parole; et per ciò si veggono di molti che son tenuti savi, scapuzzare in somiglianti accidenti.

Il Sabbato poi viggesimo terzo giorno del medesimo mese andaron Mons.r della Roccafocao, Piles et diversi altri gentilhuomini a corte, sì per intendere che movimento si faceva, come per domandar di nuovo giustitia, et sì per dar tempo a potersi apparecchiare per qualunque accidente potesse accadere, et in quel mentre veder se scoprivasse alcuna cosa a beneficio loro o danno. Trovandosi qui al desinare della Reina di Navarra, dicono che Piles parlasse di questo tenore:[q'] "Madama, se il Re vostro fratello non farà una rigorosa dimostratione[80] et severa giustitia contro coloro c'hanno commesso un cotanto vituperoso fatto, o v'hanno tenuto mano, noi saremo sforzati a vendicarsene, non già per violar l'editto della pace et del ben vivere, come hanno fatto di già gli aversari nostri. Et se S. M.tà e'l Re vostro marito non ci s'intrometteranno con prestar lor favore, noi passeremo sopra il ventre degli altri, et che costerà la vita a più di 30 mila gentilhuomini." Et usò somiglianti parole verso la Reina madre, alla cui presenza si trovavano i seguenti sig.ri: Mons.r d'Angiù, il duca di Guisa, il duca d'Anivers, Mons.r de Tavanes,[81] il conte di Rets, e'l cancelliere[82] Birago, et altri ch'egli stimava esser consapevoli del fatto; soggiugnendo di più che, se tosto non vi si rimediava, le strade di Parigi correbbero sangue,[r'] et altre parole impertinenti. Et fu in ciò indovino, il misero, in dire che le strade di questa città correbbero sangue, ma non

---

q' Ragionamento di Pile colla Reina di Navarra.
r' Can che abbaia non morde. Protestò contra di lor medesimi il misero.

78 "nè men" substituted for "o almen."
79 Inserted from margin.
80 "dimostratione" substituted for "giustitia."
81 Gaspard de Saulx, maréchal de Tavannes (1509-1573), intimate counsellor of Catherine de Medici.
82 "cancelliere" substituted for "presidente."

inteso del suo et di quello de' suoi consorti, come poi pur troppo accade. Questi fu quel Piles che si trovò in San Gian d'Angeli quando il Re con grosso essercito n'andò ad assediarlo,[83] che con sommo suo valore et senno lo difese assai lungo tempo.[s'] Fu altresì non men prode sul mare occeano, et pigliò quelle due navi vinetiani cariche di ricchissime merci, le quali non furono di picciolo aiuto a Roscelleschi, sì di viveri, di munitioni et d'artiglieria, come per la mercatantia che passava il valsente di 300 mila scudi.[84]

Havendo il Re udite tali bravate, fece uno stretto consiglio, nel quale non v'intervenne, oltre la Sua M.tà, che la Reina madre, Mons.r d'Angiù, il cancellier Birago, il Guisa, d'Anivers, Tavanes, Rets et alcuni pochi altri; et consultarono, havendo presentito come gli amici dell'Ammiraglio havevano dato ordine di ragunarsi et di levarlo fuori di quella casa a il mercoledì seguente a una ora con le genti c'havevano nella città et nel borgo di San Germano, che potevano esser di 400 buon cavalli, di non esser bene lasciarlo partire; et fu quivi detto che volessero uccidere le M.tà loro. La qual cosa si tenne (da huomini non passionali) che fosse trovata per dar colore all'affare. Onde la Reina madre, Mons.r d'Angolem (fratel bastardo del Re), i Guisi et altri interessati si ristrinsero insieme, et conchiusero che era bene d'ultimarla[t'] et non perder l'occasione, poichè dall'un de' complici era stato scoperta la congiura c'havevano fatta contra la persona del Re et suo governo, di liberarsi d'un altra guerra civile, ch'era d'ammazzare l'Ammiraglio et gli altri suoi seguaci. Sì che la Reina madre ne parlò al Re, dipignendogli la forma, quanto fosse picciolo il rischio che si correva et quanto grande il bene. Prima, perchè Iddio veniva in ciò servito, et la Santa chiesa catolica Romana,[u'] et quanto segnalato beneficio ne ritornerebbe al suo regno, alle sue chiese et alla sua auttorità, soggiugnendo altre manifeste ragioni che non erano da

---

[s'] Fatti nobili di Piles.

[t'] Conchiudono d'ammazzare non pur l'Ammiraglio, ma etiandio tutti i suoi seguaci.

[u'] Come i papeschi stimano che questo spaventoso assassinamento fino a Turchi fosse grato a Dio, et come la lor chiesa l'approvasse.

[83] Charles IX personally besieged Saint-Jean-d'Angély, defended by Piles, in the autumn of 1569.

[84] I have not succeeded in identifying this episode. Not even an echo of it can be found in the *relazioni* read to the Senate of Venice in 1569 and 1572 by Giovanni Correr and Alvise Contarini who had served as Venetian ambassadors in France. The *relazioni* are published in E. Albèri, *Le Relazioni degli ambasciatori veneti al Senato*, ser. I, vol. IV (Florence, 1860), pp. 177-206, 227-73.

sprezzare da chi desidera signoreggiare i popoli secondo il suo bene-placito.

Hora, quantunque il Re fosse desideroso di castigarli per vendi-carsene, non gli pareva nondimeno proprio il tempo, e'l mancar di fede a cotanti prencipi gli dava alcuno scrupolo che lo faceva star dubioso, nè sapeva diterminarvisi. Laonde, vi mandarono a parlare et a confortarvelo Mons.r di Guisa, Mons.r d'An[i]vers, Mons.r d'Hu-mala,[85] il bastardo S.r d'Angolem, Tavanes et altri, che allora per fine guadagnaron la volontà del Re con le dimostracioni gli fecero et con l'acesoria di Mons.r d'Angiù, che si presume che sia stato quelli c'habbia dato il tracollo alla bilancia; temendo egli molto che il suo minor fratello non venisse (col mezzo dell'Ammiraglio et d'altri lor seguaci) a maggior grado di lui nell'arte della guerra, per lo che fosse per guadagnarsi eterna fama et riputatione con gli stati di Fiandra et con buona parte di questi, se la guerra proposta dall'Ammiraglio fosse ita avanti. È bene opinione commune che un così fatto consiglio fosse di Tavanes et del duca d'Anivers,[v'] perch'erano i primi nelle armi da questa parte, et temevano che risurgendo la grandezza dell'Ammi-raglio app[ress]o il Re,[86] non scemasse la lor riputatione. Onde erano non poco invidiosi della virtù et della gloria dell'altro; o pur, come zellanti veramente della religione romana, vedessero che s'egli fosse stato lungo tempo in corte, vedessero che quella sarebbe anichilata et quasi venuta in disprezzo.

Così comandarono a Sig.ri della città di Parigi, al Prevosto de' mercatanti,[87] et ad altri lor confederati che destramente et con silenzio facessero mettere insieme i loro caporioni et conestabili, con impor loro che si tenessero armati per esseguire quanto poi sarebbe loro imposto da S. M.tà, et c'havessero ottima cura alle porte, acciochè chi entrasse lasciasse quivi le armi, nè si lasciasse uscire niuno senza passaporto. Ubidiron i predetti cittadini con alcuna dificultà, temendo che non dovesse ciò produrre qualche ruina sopra i catolici, od altro lor danno, per castigamento dell'arcobugiata tirata all'Ammiraglio. Pure alla fine, come sudditi fedeli et buoni catolici romani ubidirono.[w'] Et così

---

v' Il Duca d'Anivers et Tavanes, trovatori et princi[pali?] d'un così scelerato, anzi diabolico macello.
w' Sì al malfare.

85 Claude de Lorraine, duc d'Aumale (d. 1573), uncle of Henri de Guise.
86 Cancelled: "come invidiosi."
87 Jean Le Charron had recently replaced the goldsmith Claude Marcel as *prévôt des marchands*. Both were summoned.

pigliarono tutte le porte della città, posero buone guardie a capi delle strade, levarono il passare de' fiumi alle barche, misero grossi corpi di guardia a ponti, et diedero tutti que' migliori ordini ad ogni cosa che comportasse la brevità del tempo.

Ordinata dunque la maniera d'uccider l'Ammiraglio et i suoi seguaci, et per ciò fatta una essortatione dal Re a S.ri di Guisa, d'Humala, al cavagliero suo fratello, a Tavane et ad altri, acciochè uccidessero tutti i capitani contenut[i] nella sua proscrittione che fu lor data,[x'] come quelli che ottimamente sapevano dove i proscritti albergavano, essendo loro stato dato gli alloggiamenti dal foriere vicino alla corte. Laonde, il Guisa e'l cavagliere mandaro[no] per Pietropaolo Tosinghi,[89] gentilhuomo fiorentino, il sabbato sera vegnente il viggesimo quarto giorno, giorno dedicato a San Bartolomeo aposto, a cui commisero che facesse passar nella città et al palagio del duca d'Angiù tutti i suoi amici italiani che stantiavano nel borgo di San Germano, per alcuno effetto et servigio del Re, et che venissero armati copertamente. Il Tosinghi mandò loro un suo huomo a chiamarli, il qual fu rattenuto dalla guardia della città, nè men potette passar l'acqua per non havere havuto il motto della sentinella. Havea la Reina madre prima mandati spioni per tutto, et a visitar l'Ammiraglio per intender se vi fossero ragunanze. Et quello si diceva et faceva per esser la sua volontà, accompagnata da non picciola timidità.

Intorno dunque della mezza notte, il Guisa,[y'] d'Humala, il[90] bastardo d'Arrigo et altri personaggi (ciascun de' quali havea in sua compagnia huomi[ni] da menar le mani) andarono alla volta della casa dell'Ammiraglio, col motto delle sentine. Perchè dovete sapere che il Re mandò alquanti soldati Svizzeri[91] della sua guardia a guardar

---

[x'] Proscrittione francesca molto maggiore et cioè più crudele et lagrimevole che quella de' 3 tiranni di Roma.[88]

[y'] Il Guisa con altri va ad assassinar l'Ammiraglio.

[88] See below, n. 147.

[89] Tosinghi had a long record of service to the court of France. He fought with Monluc at Siena and Montalcino in 1557; in 1569 he was at Poitiers leading a detachment of Italian infantry under Guise. After the Massacre he participated in the siege of La Rochelle and later accompanied the duc d'Anjou to Poland where the latter was crowned king. The Venetian ambassador Michiel credited Tosinghi, rather than the Frenchman Maurevert, with having fired at Coligny in the abortive assassination attempt of 22 August. See Albèri, *Relazioni*, ser. I, vol. IV, 295–96; M. J. de Pommerol, *Gondi*, pp. 69, 87, 92, 93, 114, 118, 170, 172, 186; L. Fournier, *Les Florentins en Pologne* (Lyons, 1894), p. 231; E. Picot, "Les Italiens en France au XVIe siècle," *Bulletin italien*, II (1902), 114–15.

[90] Cancelled: "cav.ro."

[91] "Svizzeri" inserted from margin.

la casa sua,[z'] quando esso Ammiraglio fu ferito, per assicurarlo; ma altri stimano che fosse per adomentarlo in guisa, con simili dimostration[i] di zelo della colui salute, ch'el misero non pensasse ad uscir di là, o al meno ad afforzarsi de' suoi più fedeli. Furon dunque da quegli Svizzeri col predetto motto lasciati entrar nella corte della prenomata casa, et era col Guisa il Capitano Tosinghi, cavagliere dell'ordine, con alcuni suoi buoni huomini, tutti buona gente, che furono in tutti di 30. Nè trovando contrasto di persona alcuna che facesse lor resistenza, mandarono cinque o sei alla camera dell'Ammiraglio, il quale havendo non dimeno sentito alcun romore, *ancorchè non havesse con esso seco che due valetti di camera e'l valente cirugico del Re, M.ro Ambrogio Perretto,*[a''][92] coraggiosamente si levò, et con casse et panche fortificò l'uscio della camera per difendersi, et in mano pigliò la spada, non ostante la grave sua ferita et debolezza del male. Fu non dimeno da Guisiani sforzat[o] l'uscio,[93] et subito ammazzaron i valetti dell'Ammiraglio. A lui uno[94] nomato …[95] lo ferì malamente d'una allabarda nella faccia, et un altro su la testa, et d'un altro gli fu sparata un'arcobugiata, et molte altre ferite, tra le quali s'udì che disse, "Ahi, soldati, habbiate compassione alla vecchiaia."[96] Il Guisa, che stava nel cortile con gli altri gentilhuomini, impatiente, gridò che lo gittassero dalle finestre a basso.[b''] Onde lo pigliaron così semivivo per gittarvelo nel cortile, et esso si ritenne mezzo morto con la mano diritta ad un ferro della finestra.[97] Onde di nuovo il Guisa gridò che gli tagliassero la mano in quello ch'egli, non potendosi dalla molta fievolezza più ritener, cade

---

[z'] Guardia degli Svizzeri data all'Ammiraglio per meglio poterlo assassinare.

[a''] Quanto la nation francesca, per altro nobile, sia poco considerata da questo si può chiaramente vedere. Nè mi si scorderò mai quel che già a simil proposito un savio italiano mi disse di lei, cioè: Del passato non si ricorda, al presente non bada, et al futur[o] non pensa.

[b''] Gli ucciditori al comandamento del Guisa gittono l'Ammiraglio.

[92] Ambroise Paré, who survived the Massacre.
[93] "l'uscio" substituted for "la porta."
[94] Cancelled: "diede."
[95] The dots are in the text. The name of the assailant was to be filled in later.
[96] Contemporaries disagreed whether Coligny uttered any words before dying. See the nuncio Salviati's account, dated 22 Sept. 1572: "Che egli [Coligny] non parlasse punto quando entrarono per ammazzarlo, infra gl'altri lo dice Pietro Paolo Tosinghi, il quale havendo al collo la catena che detto Armiraglio soleva portare, si può credere che egli fusse de' primi et conseguentemente che se gli possa aggiustar fede. Molti altri vogliono in tutti i modi che dicesse, 'Giovani soldati habbiate risguardo alla vecchiezza'" (A. Theiner, *Annales Ecclesiastici* [Rome, 1856], I, 331).
[97] The word order of this sentence is garbled in the MS.

giù senza anchora morir; onde subito vi furono addosso con le pugnalate alcuni di coloro[98] che seco erano, a quali il Guisa (veggendolo morto) disse, "Basta, non più al povero huomo."[c'']

Egli[100] era huomo savio, sagace, cauto, patiente nel negotiare, segreto, molto esperto delle cose del mondo, et in generale de' governi di questo regno. Ascoltava volentieri et a pochi manifestava il suo concetto. Gran politico, non lo spaventava la fortuna aversa, sobrio, vigilante, non dato a passar tempi, huomo di sua parola, et negli affari del publico fedelissimo. Rare volte s'adirava, et di complession savissima, sì che non appariva in lui altro vitio che della religione, ch'è stata la sua rovina, perchè se ... nel suo ...

Il misero cirugio (ch'era della religione), veduto una tanta crudeltà, si mise (dicendo egli, "È venuta l'hora mia, S.re") da pie' del letto in ginocchione a fare oratione, et così costantemente porse la gola agli ucciditori. Li quali poscia si diedero a rubare la casa,[101] nella quale (è opinione di molti) che vi fossero gioie di molto valore, appartenenti alla prencipessa di Condé, matrigna del presente Prencipe. Furon levate le scritture tutte, tra le quali trovaron zifre, motti, segni, caratteri et altre cose di gran momento da trafficare fuori et dentro del regno, come instrutioni, avertimenti, minute di governo, rifformationi delle sacre, come delle civi[li] et militari leggi, et altri ammaestramenti, con infinite medaglie antiche.

Partitosi di colà, mandarono alle case degli altri capi della religione. Arrivaron prima a quella dell'honorato vecchio il conte di Roccafocao,[d''] il quale tosto che sentì il romore, si levò a raccomandarsi l'anima sua a Dio; et dicono alcuni che, con le mani alzate al cielo, dicesse, "Amici, non mi fate languir, se in voi è alcuna pietà." Altri dicono che gli ucciditori bussarono all'uscio, et essendo dimandati chi si fossero, risposero venir da parte del Re. Il che udendo il conte, che subito commandasse che fosse loro aperto, et che col porger lor la mano, raffrenasse alquanto la crudeltà di coloro. Onde gli dissero,

---

c'' Pietà di cocodrilo. O giustissimo Iddio, quanto giustamente faceste sopra così crudele Antropofago cader la medesima morte del [vertical and horizontal dashes] a punto nella camera ove egli ordì così scelerata trama.[99]

d'' Costante et religiosa morte del conte di Roccafocao.

98 "coloro" substituted for "quei."
99 A reference to the assassination of Guise at the château of Blois in 1588.
100 This paragraph is inserted from the bottom margin and runs on into the inner margin where a few final words are lost in the binding.
101 "casa" substituted for "camera."

"Habbiam comandamento d'uccidervi, però s'havete che dire, speditevi." "Come" (ripose egli) "è ciò possibile?" Et affermando quelli che così conveniva, gli pregò prima a volerlo condurre al Re, et dinanzi agli occhi suoi, se l'havesser patito, ucciderlo. Il che non volendo quelli fare, si levò in camiscia et pregalli di lasciarlo prima pregare Iddio. Et poi chiusi gli occhi et perto loro il lato, disse, "Fate tosto quel che havete a fare." Era Sig.re d'honorate et rare qualità, et ch'era estremamente dal Re amato, il quale fece ogni suo sforzo perchè dormisse seco (come sovente faceva) quella notte. Ma non volle (per nascosto voler di Dio) fare, con dirgli, "Sire, havete buon tempo. Io son vecchio, et quando non dormo la notte non istò tutto il giorno bene." Et ho udito affermare da gente di credito che S.M. a queste parole fu vicino a dirgli la cosa per farlo restare, ma si ritenne dal timore ch'egli non havesse palesato il fatto. Ammazzaron poi i suoi servitori, et rubaron la camera.

Così amazzaron Subise et Tiligni, l'eloquenza del quale incantò gli ucciditori,[e"] sì che lo lasciaron vestirsi, et si contentaron di menarlo al Re. Et in andarvi sopravenendo un più di loro crudele, et il nome di Dio bestemiando, disse, "Corpo di Dio, state voi ad ascoltare costui"; et e'l dire e'l dargli d'una stoccata nel ventre fu tutto uno, onde cadde quivi morto.[f"] Era bello, gratioso, cortese, valente, et fornito di lettere et di belle maniere, quanto giovane di quella età,[102] et alcuni lo tassano di bugiardo et di vano. Ben dicono[103] che più volte egli si maravigliasse che il Re facesse lor tanti favori et concedesse tutto quel domandassaro, che pareva non dovesse durare per esser contra la dignità del Re. Ma non giovò però a far loro aprir gli occhi da poter fuggir tanta malora.

Dicono che uccidessero anchora i due fratelli Visconti di Turena. Piles s'era fuggito in corte et nella guarda roba del Re di Navarra, quindi lo cavarono per forza, et gli Svizzeri della propria guardia l'ammazzarono,[g"] et insieme il governante del medesimo Re[104] con

---

[e"] Gli ucciditori restano incan[tati] dalla gratia et eloquenza di Tiligni.

[f"] Morte del nobile et virtudioso Tiligni.

[g"] Gli Svizzeri della guardia regia (posposta la lor naturale bontà) divengono ammazzatori di Mons.r de Pile et d'altri.

[102] The remainder of this sentence inserted from the inner margin; the next two sentences from the outer and lower margins.

[103] Cancelled: "alcuni."

[104] Louis de Goulard, seigneur de Beauvais.

altri suoi gentilhuomini, tra quali fu il S.r di San Martin.[105] Et dicono che fra que' gentilhuomini vi fossero molti catolici, a cui non valeva il dire d'esser papeschi.

Fu dato il corpo dell'Ammiraglio al forsenato popolo, che lo strasinò per tutta la città, gli tagliò le mani e'l membro virile. Et quando fu satio, lo mandarono ad impiccar per gli piedi alla publica forca di Monfalcone, dove havevano anchora attacata la sua efiggie. Vicino al qual luogo havea egli coragiosamente pochi anni prima combattuto l'essercito del Re, et costrettolo a vituperosamente riffugirsi in Parigi, nel qual fatto d'arme fu fedito et morto Anna di Memoransi, gran Conestabile di Francia et suo zio.[106] Ma che noi qui? Poichè si trovarono huomini cotanto affettionati al suo corpo, che [con] tutta la calamità grande, et con tutto il grandissimo pericolo di quel tempo, non lasciaron d'andare a trarlo di là, et a portarlo in luogo honorato a seppelirlo. Fu detto che un Piemontese comperasse il capo di lui per dieci scudi da mandarlo a Roma.[h''] Furon in diversi luog[hi] della città messe a ruba molte case, et ammazzati in questa città da 2 mila, tra quali ve n'erano di molti nobili et ricchi, come l'Averdì[107] et altri, che veniano palesati da chi gli havea in casa.

Sì che, data che fu la licenza delle armi al furioso et precipitoso popolo, si commisero sceleratezze non udite, et erano così bene uccisi de' fedeli catolici come degli altri, perchè bastava che alcun gridasse, "Ecco colà un Ugonotto," che senza ascoltarlo era il cativello ucciso. Il che a molti accade per havere piato con altri, et per haver d'haver denari d'alcuni degli ucciditori che se veniva veduto era spedito, come accade ad un ricco canonico di Nostra Donna ch'era consigliere anchora, et al Salsedo, Spagnuolo[108] et salariato del Re. Furono usate crudeltà grandissime contra le donne et i fanciulli, onde erano senza riguardo alcuno uccise, quantunque molte di loro fossero gravide.[1''] Le vergini erano prima stuprate et poi uccise, et rapito il loro

---

h'' Fu comperata la testa dell'Ammiraglio [per] dieci scudi, per mandarla a Roma.

1'' Crudeltà veramente pagana usata contra le donne et i fanciulli.

105 The anon. author of *Le tocsain contre les massacreurs* [1579] lists among those killed in the Louvre, "un jeune gentil-homme de Beausse, nommé Sainct-Martin ou de Brichanteau ..." (reprinted in L. Cimber and F. Danjou, eds., *Archives curieuses de l'histoire de France*, VII [Paris, 1836], 53).

106 Montmorency was killed at the battle of St. Denis on 11 Nov. 1567.

107 Charles de Beaumanoir, marquis de Laverdin.

108 Possibly to be identified with Pedro Salcedo, a personal enemy of the Guises.

havere. Erano molti et molte condotte al ponte de' Mugnai,[109] et
dato loro d'un coltello nel petto, gittate nella riviera, et per la coppia
di simili miseri si vide correr tinta di sangue. Un' orafo[j''] che habitava
alla valle della Miseria,[110] vicino al predetto ponte, si vantò d'haverne
con le sue proprie mani scannati più di 400 d'ogni sesso et qualità. Un
prete[k''] nomato Potri n'uccise più di 500, come mi è stato affermato;
et un altro, che faceva del Giesù,[111] ha detto a me haverne morti nel
suo quartiere 700 con le sue mani, et con quelle d'altri più 400, il quale
stava verso S.to Antonio. Nel borgo di S. Germano ne furono uccisi
alcuni, ma molti più fatti prigioni et posti nelle carceri del commune.
Erano quivi ammazzati dopo haverli prima essaminati et tormentati,
et tutti da predetti macellai d'huomini, perchè il ministro della
giustitia rifiutò di farlo,[l''] essendone stato richiesto, dicendo non
volerlo fare se non glieli davano convinti et giudicati degni di cotal
martirio.

Era il conte di Mongomeri alloggiato nella rua della Senna nel
borgo di S. Germano[112] con molti altri signori et gentilhuomini della
religione,[113] il quale si salvò nella seguente maniera per esser bene
a cavallo.[m''] Ma prima vi dirò come egli è quell[o] ghiostrando disgra-
tiatamente uccise il gran Re Arrigo primo [sic], et fu figliuolo d'un
nobile huomo scozzese, capitano della guardia di S. M.tà.[114] Udito
dunque il romore, si ristrinsero insieme nella predetta rua intorno da
80 cavalli per aspettare, perchè ignoravano la verità[115] a che riuscisse
la cosa. Et così stettero fino il tardi del giorno seguente, che fu la
Domenica, nel quale tempo udirono, come è publica fama, una

[j''] Crudeltà d'un orafo.

[k''] Degno vanzo d'un fedel di Santa Chiesa Romana.

[l''] Il manigoldo, o Boia di Parigi, più pietoso di que' scelerati macellai,
rifiuta di volergli ammazzare.

[m''] Il conte di Mongomeri et il Vidame di Sciartes con molti altri,
fuggendo a cavallo, si salvano in Inghilterra.

[109] Le pont des Meuniers.
[110] Allée d'Isère?
[111] A Jesuit?
[112] "S. Germano" cancelled, but it is needed for the meaning.
[113] Corrected in MS from "signori della religione et gentilhuomini."
[114] Gabriel de Montgommery had killed Henri II at the tourney organized to celebrate
the weddings of the daughter and sister of the king. Montgommery fled to England after the
Massacre, became the principal leader of the Huguenots and tried to organize a fleet for
the relief of Protestant La Rochelle, besieged by Charles IX.
[115] "la verità" substituted for "il fatto."

voce,[n″][116] perchè è voce publica che uscì una voce del Lo[u]vro, che gridò queste parole: "Salvatevi, salvatevi, che si fa macello di que' della religione," et che a noto passò un de' sacri loro ragguagliandoli del tutto. Onde conosceva di non poter giovare a suoi, già uccisi, onde il male era senza rimedio, si determinaron di partirsi. Tra quali v'era il S.r di Comon,[117] gentilhuomo c'haveva 6o mila lire d'entrata, et molti altri di nome, li quali furon seguitati dal Guisa con un buon drapello di cavalli tra Francesi et Italiani. Ma per essersi partiti di gran pezzo prima ch'egli si metesse a seguitargli, et anchora perch'erano bene a cavallo, non gli potette giugnere, salvo alquanti pochi che per colpa de' cavalli non potettero seguitar gli altri, che furono uccisi. Hora si dice che i salvati si siano riparati in Inghilterra,[o″] et che siano stati ben veduti et humanamente raccolti da quella Ser.ma Reina.

S'è detto che chi hebbe la cura d'esseguir sopra lor cotal sentenza non habbia adempiuto il comandamento regio, parendo che fosse troppo crudele et troppo severo, atteso che tra que' della religione ve ne fossero molti che non havevano giamai pigliate l'armi contra S. M.tà. Onde gl'ingegni speculativi argomentano che, se fosse suto caso pensato, che vi sarebbe stato maggiore ordine, et che Mongomeri con gli altri non si sarebbero salvati. Et di più che, dovendosi menare a fine la vigilia di S.to Bartolomeo una cotanta spaventosa sentenza, il Guisa, Mons.r d'Angiù, il cavalier bastardo, d'Humala et gli altri non havevano armi difensive nè offensive, onde bisognò la medesima notte che mandassero agli armaruoli et in altri luoghi a pigliarne. Non è dunque dubbio che, se que' della religione si fossero ristretti insieme, che si sarebbero potuto difendere, o per viva forza salvarsi, od al men non morire invendicati come fecero, havendo eglino armi et cavalli. Et così voglion molti che a ciò sia stato tirato il Re da pura necessità et da timore, et non da diterminata volontà, et che popochl [sic] sapessero la mente sua, da uno in fuori, ch'io lascio in bianco. Egli ha poi usata clemenza a molti che l'hanno dimandata,[p″] come ai

---

[n″] Voce miracolosa uscita dal palagio regio.
[o″] Mongomeri con gli altri si salvano in Inghilterra.
[p″] Il Re perdona la vita ad alcuni Sig.ri.

[116] The remainder of this sentence transported here from above, according to Castelvetro's instructions.
[117] Caumont.

figliuol dello Roccafocao,[118] al S.r d'Agramonte, [119] i due visconti, il
S.r d'Asti, et a molti altri che sono stati salvati dal Guisa, dal bastardo
et d'altri signori, de' quali non mi ricordo il nome. Et così sarebbe
campato il S.r della Roccafocao s'havesse voluto ubidire a S. M.tà,
il quale il Sabbato sera lo volle ritenere in corte seco a dormire, e'l
meschino non volle restarvi, guidato alla morte dal destino.

I capi de' morti[q''] sono 72 persone, tutti di comandamento o
soldati vecchi, i nomi et cognomi de' quali haverò col tempo, che vi
manderò. Ben vi dico che non ce n'è stato tra loro niuno c'habbia fatto
difesa, o si sia messo in atto per farla, dall'Ammiraglio in fuori, come
ho detto, perchè la maggior parte de' loro sono stati trovati nel letto o
dallo spavento presi, nelle gole de' camini nascosti, o chi sotto il
tetto delle case, altri nelle stalle, et altri in luoghi più imondi, per
salvar la vita a ciascun cotanto cara. Bé, c'è stato un huomo di roba
lunga che, sentendo manomettersi la casa sua, si mise gagliardamente
alla difesa, et prodamente sempre menò delle mani fino che fu ucciso;
ma prima vide de' molti ch'egli ammazzò la sua gloriosa vendetta.

Pare a molti che il Re si sia mostrato troppo severo[120] et alquanto
crudele, perchè diceva agli ucciditori, "Ammazzateli tutti, finitela,
acciochè questa peste non ci molesti più."[r''] Et ha fatto grande
instanza per haverne alcuni particolari vivi nelle mani, o per intender
cosa di momento, o pur per satiare gli occhi suoi in vederli morire;
come accade di Bricamore, il qual [si] salvò in una casa d'un povero
huomo, ne quivi tenendosi sicuro, quando il Re, con tutta la corte
dietro, passava quindi per ire al palazzo del parlamento a render conto
di cotal fatto, come commesso per ordine et volontà sua (quantunque
prima havesse negato di voler ciò dire) per liberarsi della congiura
ch'esso havea scoperta che gli uccisi trattavano d'esseguire nella sua
propria persona; et anchor andava colà per farlo passare in parlamento
per editti, con assolver tutti coloro che in simile affare si fossero

---

q'' Settandue sono i capi, et tutti gran capitani, li quali havrebbero
potuto fare ottimo servigio a quel pazzo come malvagio Re.

r'' Crudeltà insatiabile del sanguinoso Re, dicendo parole più convene-
voli per la bocca d'un boia che d'un suo pari.

118 See the anonymous report, dated 27 Aug. 1572, addressed to the Medici secretary
Bartolommeo Concini in Desjardins, *Négociations*, III, 817: "Al capitan Lago, Basco, fu
data carica d'uccidere la Rochefoucauld, il che eseguì subito, e prese il figliuolo di dieci
otto anni ... a cui il Re ha donata la vita e i beni di suo padre."
119 Grammont. See above, n. 49. Sassetti, who mentions "il S.r d'Asti" almost immediately following, seems to have been confused, making two persons out of one.
120 "severo" substituted for "crudele."

insanguinati. Laonde il predetto Bricamore con due castrati sopra le spalle dietro al maestro di casa del S.r Francesco Valsingame, ambasciatore d'Inghilterra, si salvò nel borgo di San Marceo in casa del medesimo ambasciatore.[8''] Et pervenuto alla porta della città cadde in terra, et senza essere riconosciuto gli furon rimessi i due castrati addosso, et salvo pervenne in casa [del]lo 'mbasciatore, il qual lo consigliò et gagliardamente confortò a partirsi di casa sua et andarsene, offerendogli per ciò denari et cavalli, temendo di non poterlo salvare se fosse riconosciuto o saputo che quivi fosse, et così fosse palesato al Re che bramava d'haverlo nelle mani. Ma il misero, o non gli fu da Dio conceduto, o non volle mai partirsi. Anzi non rispondendo a proposito, si gittò in gignocchione domandandogli la vita, et così stette quattro o cinque giorni in una stalla facendo sembiante d'acconciare cavalli;[121] et fu scoperto da un suo servitore ch'egli mandò dentro la città, non già per poca fede de povero servitore, ma sì da troppo timore per essere egli stato riconosciuto; et pigliato confessò, palesando ove il suo padrone si trovava. Imperò il Re subito mandò all'Ambasciatore acciochè volontieri gliel' desse, facendogli dire che quando non gliele havesse dato per amore, che l'haverebbe a tutti i modi volato, et comise che a mira forza gli fosse levato di casa. Fece il buono Ambasciatore quanto potè per non darlo, ma veggendo di non poterlo salvare, lo menarono[122] nel suo cocchio prigione. Era costui huomo di cuore, et tenuto per buon soldato, ma tale sciagura lo fece uscir dal sentimento d'huomo forte, per cagion per aventura de' suoi passati peccati, o pure per haversi veduti amazzare dinanzi gli occhi due figliuoli, o per altra più occulta cagione. Si dice che sia un di coloro che sapevano gli occulti segreti dell'Ammiraglio, et che sia huomo astuto et d'ingegno, ma pien di vitii, et che sia altre volte stato alla strada facendo molti homicidi et ladronezze. Lo condannarono,[123] come altre volte è stato di pena capitale (secondo si dice) condannato.

[8''] Bricamore si salva in casa dello 'mbasciatore Inglese.

[121] See the dispatch of the Venetian ambassador Michiel, dated 5 Sept. 1572, in H. A. Layard, *The Massacre of St. Bartholomew* (London, 1887), p. 57: "... fu preso ... in casa dell'Ambasciator d'Inghilterra in habito di famiglio da stalla un principal capitano et persona confidente d'esso Ammiraglio chiamato Briemero ..." There is no mention of Walsingham's role in shielding Briquemault either in C. Read, *Walsingham*, or in James M. Osborn, *Young Philip Sidney, 1572–1577* (New Haven, 1972), which contains an excellent chapter on the Massacre.
[122] "menarono" substituted for "mandò."
[123] Cancelled: "dicendosi che già."

È stato anchor pigliato Mons.r de Cavagne[124] (che s'era pure [nascosto] in casa del suddetto ambasciatore, et fu trovato[t''] cercando l'altro), il quale è huomo di roba lunga, gran negotiatore, et è stato assai adoperato dall'Ammiraglio. Onde è opinione ch'egli sappia molti particolari di persone con chi l'Ammiraglio, dentro di questo reame et fuori, havesse amicitia, et che fare; che gioverà a S. M.tà non poco. Dovranno essere martoreggiati (per quello si giudica)[125] se non havranno migliore aiuto di quello della ragione.[126]

Il danno che gli Ugonotti hanno da questo fatto ricevuto è grandissimo, et ha potuto più la sfoderata spada con questa pietosa crudeltà,[u''] che quante ammonitioni sono mai state fatte sui pulpiti da francescani, da domenicani, da gesuiti et da molti altri valenti teologi con le dispute loro scolastiche. La Reina madre intendendo come la moglie del S.r di Tiligni, figliuola dell'Ammiraglio, era mal trattata da alcuni de' predetti beccai d'huomini, fece ogni opera acciochè l'honestà le fosse salvata. Et perciò mandò huomini et donne, che la condussero in luogo sicuro.

Dura tuttavia il rubare, il porre taglie, et l'ammazzare in alcuni de' circonvicini villaggi; et chi non vuole essere stimato di quella religione, conviene che porti una crocessina d'argento nel petto o nella berretta, così bene i grandi di questa corte come il popolo et tutto l'universale.[127] Il Re di Navarra,[v''] il Prencipe di Condé et sua moglie, con[128] molte altre dame et personaggi, da tanta rovina et ammazzamenti de' lor più cari amici stavano spaventati in molto timore. Onde fu lor mandato a dire da parte del Re che pensassero di farsi catolici, a che si dice c'habbiano acconsentito, et che alcuni di loro

---

[t''] Mons.r de Cavagne è trovato et pigliato.

[u''] Pietosa crudeltà, chiama l'autore di questo raccontamento, lo sozzo, crudele et brutal macello.

[v''] Il Re di Navarra et il Prencipe di Condé con altri si fan papeschi.

[124] Arnauld seigneur de Cavagnes, member of the Parlement of Toulouse, one of the Huguenot negotiators of the Peace of St. Germain.

[125] "(per ... giudica)" inserted from margin.

[126] Briquemault and Cavagnes were tried on charges of having participated in an alleged Huguenot plot to overthrow the king. They were executed on 27 Oct. 1572. The gruesome details were reported by the Florentine ambassador Petrucci to Francesco de Medici on the following day (Desjardins, *Négociations*, III, 853).

[127] A white cross worn on one's cap was originally intended as a sign by which Catholics were to be identified during the Massacre; and afterwards it was adopted by the surviving Huguenots to mislead their persecutors. See Salviati's dispatches to Rome in Theiner, *Annales*, p. 329; *Il Vero Successo* in H. A. Layard, *The Massacre*, p. 27; and an anonymous writer to the Medici secretary Concini, in Desjardins, *Négociations*, III, 820.

[128] "con ... personaggi" inserted from margin.

v'[hab]biano veramente acconsentito per credere così, et altri per prudenza umana.ʷ" I frati et i preti fanno la vendemia loro vi prometto, i tempii si veggon pieni, et bravo è colui che puo havere il primo luogo alla predella dell'altare. Gli Ufficiuoli della Madonna, et le corone sono incarite, sì che quel che valea uno, ne val dieci. Et si sente, quando il sacerdote leva l'ostia, un darsi delle mani nel petto et nella bocca, che è cosa mirabile.[129] Tanta dimostratione vien fatta di simil cerimonia da coloro che prima la disprezzavano. Ma essendo una divotione sforzata, et mossa da soverchio timore più che da zelo d'essere ridotti alla religione catolica romana, [questa] religione (a mio giuditio) non doverà continouare lungo tempo, et spetialmente non ne' Francesi, che per lo più sono volubili et ventosi. Si ragiona anchora che Navarra et Condé manderanno ambasciatori a Roma, sì per domandare assolutione et dispensa come per dare al papa la dovuta ubidienza. Son, però, cose di cui si parla, ma v'anderà più tempo prima che ciò si faccia.

Come di sopra dissi che se l'Ammiraglio non havesse mutato la religione, et che havesse sempre badato al servigio del Re, che sarebbe stato grande, così torno quì a dire che la religione lo rendè sospetto. Onde molti, hoggi ch'egli è morto et che di lui non hanno paura, lo incolpano che non fosse della persona sua del valor nè dell'ardir francese,ˣ" perch'era troppo pesato et troppo circospetto nelle attioni militari, benchè con gran prudenza le governasse. Ci sono anchora alcuni papeschi che dicono che l'ambition sua fosse tanto grande che non si curava di veder la ruina di questo reame, et che la sua non era religione nè pietà christiana, et era stata la cagion della morte di più d'un millione et mezzo d'huomini, parte morti di ferro, di fuoco et di fame, et parte di peste et di stento. Et haveva comportato[130] che si fossero rovinate tanti be' tempii et rasati molti luoghi per la continua guerra et discordi civili, et che in ciò si sia servito della religione come causa principale a levarsi contro il prencipe, et a mettere l'armi in mano a sudditi et a colloro c'hanno volontà di tumultuare et di

---

ʷ" Crescimento della hippocresia papesca.
ˣ" L'Ammiraglio non era nè del valore nè del ardir francesco.

[129] Confirmation of this phenomenon in Claude Haton's *Mémoires* (Paris, 1857), p. 689: "Les huguenotz qui restèrent après les séditions, tant à Paris que par le reste de la France ... allèrent tous à la messe, sans qu'ilz y fussent contrainctz et qu'on leur commandast d'y aller." Cf. the letter to Francesco de Medici from his ambassador in Paris, Petrucci, dated 8 September: "Molti ugonotti si sono convertiti, e han preso questo santissimo Giubileo; talchè questa resoluzione ha giovato in più modi" (Desjardins, *Négociations*, III, 837).
[130] "comportato" substituted for "permesso."

mettersi in libertà di coscienza, per non ubidire alle leggi papali et spesso a quelle del suo prencipe anchora. Sì che s'egli havesse occupato il suo bello et raro ingegno nel servigio del suo Re et honorata la Reina madre, sarebbe stato un de' rari stormenti che fosse suto di lungo tempo in questo potentissimo regno, ma ch'habbia potuto più in lui il desio di governare assolutamente, mosso cioè più d'ambitione che da regolata ragione, da che è proceduta la totale sua ruina.

Laonde, quando s'avvide che il Re non era d'animo di romper la guerra col Re Filippo,$^{y''}$ et che la Reina madre voleva governare senza volere in ciò compagno alcuno, et voler mantener l'amicitia di Spagna, si dovea ritirare et stare discosto dalla corte et, per mezzo de' confidenti, negotiare. Perchè l'opinione che di lui s'era concetta l'haverebbe mantenuto vivo et in riputatione, et necessitava il Re per mantener la pace nel regno fare la guerra fuori di lui.[131] Hora Dio voglia che cotal sua morte non generi peggior ruina, et se S.M. non è presto ad insignorirsi de' luoghi che i suoi seguaci anchor tengono et c'hanno a lor diretione, è da temere che non sia anchora finita la miseria di questa misera patria. Con ciò sia cosa che si possa temere uno sdegno non picciolo de' prencipi stranieri nelle cui mani havea giurato la pace, et che non s'inchinino a compassione et ad abbracciare que' della religione per la gran distruttione che s'intende essersi fatta di simil gente per tutto questo reame, et che faccino ogni loro sforzo per mantenerli vivi. Perchè si puo credere che alla Ser.ma Reina d'Inghilterra, come a prencipi della Magna, dispiacerà,$^{z''}$ et anchora a molti catolici, come nemici della crudeltà et d'un così fatto spargimento di sangue humano.

Ben' è vero che S. M.tà non potea fare maggior servigio al Re di Spagna che levar dal mondo tanti prodi capitani, et in questo regno si ricominci la guerra, la qual egli favoreggierà, perchè la segua. Il papa ha d'haver molto obligo a questo Re Christianissimo et in particolare alla Reina madre, c'ha saputo così ben dissimulare con la sua sagacità et sembianza, in che ha superata l'astutia dell'Ammiraglio. [Tra] gli

---

$^{y''}$ Che l'Ammiraglio, se fosse stato quell'avveduto che altri predica, dovea abbandonar la corte quando vide il Re non inclinato a rompere la guerra in Spagna.

$^{z''}$ Ben giudicò direttamente in questo, perchè i Prencipi della Magna se ne risentiron molti, et negli stati loro si vide una moneta con la effigie di questo Re, con lettere allo 'ntorno che dicevano, "Questa è l'effigie del gran traditor Carlo IX, re di Francia."

[131] "lui" substituted for "quello."

ucciditori del quale fu un valente soldato tedesco,[132] già paggio di Mons.r di Guisa, padre di questo, che in compagnia di cinque altri che gli tirò l'arcobugiata. Et vogliono che fusse il medesimo che pochi mesi prima uccidesse il S.r di Muy,[133] ma altri vogliono che sia stato un arcier del Re.[134] Ma basta che portò pericolo di portar la pena del delitto commesso.

La notte che fu ammazzato l'Ammiraglio la Reina madre mandò il S.r Gio. Galeazzo Fregoso all'Ammiraglio, sotto pretesto di invitarlo, et seco stette più di quattro hore trattenendolo et confortandolo, con dirgli che il Re et la Reina darebbero ordine a tutto, et la Reina si serviva di lui per intendere i propositi che andavano attorno, per essere egli molto famigliare dell'Ammiraglio. Et per quanto ho potuto intendere di cotal maneggio, egli servì ottimamente con la sua doppiezza S. M.tà, quantunque il Guisa l'havesse in sospetto et in mala consideratione, et per ciò fu per lasciarvi la vita, come del certo ve l'haverebbe lasciata, se dall'Ammiraglio l'havessero trovato quando l'andarono ad uccidere.

Nè sarà per aventura mal fatto ch'io vi narri qua parte dell' humor del predetto Fregoso.[a'''] Onde primieramente dico che non era nato di leggittimo matrimonio, havea spirito capricioso et alcuni affari in apparenza grandi et di momento, onde si ficava per tutto senza verun rispetto. Era di gran fatica et arischiato, onde più vol[t]e queste M.tà l'hanno mandato in Germania, in Fiandra, in diverse parti di questo regno, et in Italia lo mandarono al gran duca, et alcune volte ha portato perico[lo], essendo stato per lasciarvi la vita ignominiosamente. I fiorentini fuorusciti non l'hanno in buona opinione,[b'''] anchora che si mostri amico di tutti. È gran simulatore, doppio, vano, et che si dà ad intendere d'esser persona di gran maneggio, et ci sono alcuni fiorentini che l'honorano et lo tengono per valenthuomo, et sovente sono in sua compagnia, et la Reina Madre mostra di vederlo volontieri. Ma il S.r Valsingame, di sopra mentionato, m'ha più volte detto d'haverlo in cattiva opinione, come un' altro amico che dipende

---

[a'''] Chi si fosse Gio. Galeazzo Fregoso.
[b'''] Non è dunque da maravigliare se s'immisca [?] in cotanto male.

[132] Yan Yanovitz, known as Besme, a Czech (d. 1575).
[133] Arthus de Vaudrey, sieur de Mouy, was assassinated by Charles de Louviers, sieur de Maurevert.
[134] A number of individuals were taking credit for the assassination. See P. Hurtubise, "Comment Rome apprit la nouvelle du massacre de la Saint-Barthélemy," *Archivum Historiae Pontificiae*, X (1972), 206.

di Savoia, et che n'ha ammonito l'Ammiraglio acciochè non si fidi di lui, et pronostica cattiva fine all'uno et all'altro. Et dopo che son qua ritornato, perchè prima in Inghilterra et poi qua lo conobbi, un giorno che in lui m'incontrai, così gli dissi: "S.r Fregoso, io non dubito punto che voi non sappiate ogni particolare come questo fatto si sia passato, essendo voi più volte stato dalla Reina all'Ammiraglio mandato, et s'è detto che siete corso gran rischio." A che rispose ch'egli era fedel servitore delle M.tà loro, et mentre ch'egli vide l'Ammiraglio caminare per istrada honorevole et in servigio del Re, gli fu amico et servitore. Ma poi che da quella lo vide storcersi, et procurava contro il Re male cose, egli tenne tutti que' modi che convengono ad un gentilhuomo suo pari per servigio di suo Signore; et che se l'Ammiraglio si fosse governato da fedel suddito, come a lui più volte havea promesso di voler fare, non gli sarebbe accaduto quello che non ha guari gli è intervenuto. Et ch'egli vide et iscoperse cose ch'erano per diametro diritte contro le M.tà loro, onde più volte le havea ammonite et detto come l'Ammiraglio havea app[ress]o se huomini di valore et di fatti, come Piles, La Trappa et altri. Le quali cose havea dopo la ferita d'esso Ammiraglio replicate loro. Et che l'ultima sera fece lor sapere come le M.tà loro non doveano temere de' predetti valenthuomini, le quali havea trovati nella camera dell'Ammiraglio, et quando egli v'andò ch'eglino se ne partirono. Et soggiunse che quanto al rischio suo particolare, che il Guisa havea ordine di non offenderlo. Onde si crede che per costui rispetti le M.tà loro lo carezzino et gli diano il modo da vivere, perch'egli è largo spenditore, et del suo non ha gran cosa. Mi disse di più come egli havea grande inventione per trovar denari per servigio del Re.

S'intende anchora che la Regina madre ha gran piacer[c'''] di veder d'havere ella sola condotto tal affare al desiato fine, et che il tutto sia proceduto dal suo giudicio et dal suo consiglio, et c'habbia rimesso il Re nella sua autorità, liberata la chiesa da tanti nimici, et per ciò aspetta dalla Santità del papa molti ringratiamenti et infinite gratie spirituali; quantunque con tutti coloro che ne le hanno parlato, commendandolo per fatto egregio et degno d'un animo reale, non ostante sia stato accompagnato[135] d'alcuna crudeltà et danno di molti, ella se

---

[c'''] Allegrezza della Reina madre d'essere stata ritrovatrice et consegliatrice del macello.

[135] "stato accompagnato" substituted for "seguito."

ne scusa con dire che sia seguitato senza volontà del Re nè di lei, nè erano d'animo che il publico ne patisse. Ma la non picciola mortalità commessa in Lione fu pura volontà[136] degli stampatori et de' testori che s'insanguinassero le mani in molti di que' miseri, a che con difficultà il Governatore[137] poteva rimediare, et che mostrerebbe in effetto quanto li dispiacessero le cose mal fatte. Affermò anchora che l'editto di pacificatione si manterrà, et che non sarà ricercata la coscienza d'alcuno, nè confischeranno i beni, se non a coloro che haveranno machinato contra la persona del Re. Degli allemani, degli inglesi et altri forestieri non n'è stato ammazzato niuno, o ben pochi, perchè così fu ordinato dalle Sue M.tà. Et se pure è toccato ad alcuno sgratiato italiano, è accaduto per errore.

Io v'ho scritto una lunga diceria di tutto quello ho udito dire, senza passion veruna, rimettendomi del tutto alla verità, et a coloro che sono più esperti di me et consumati negli affari del mondo, come anchora per non essermi vi trovato, perchè ero andato a Lione in compagnia del S.r Lodovico da Diaceto; a cui per lo camino dissi che l'Ammiraglio et gli altri suoi seguaci[d'''] non haveva[no] ben estudiato il Macchiavello, per chè haverebbero appresi come le 'ngiurie che si fanno a grandi non debbeno esser domenticate da coloro c'hanno minore autorità et possanza. Et avegna che i prencipi et gran monarchi mostrino di non se ne ricordare, hanno sempre delle persone che quelle riducon loro a memoria, et tanto più quanto si presenta loro opportunità di vendicarsene, le quali fanno bene sovente altresì nascere sotto altro colore; et che la Reina Madre era di grande spirito, et che allo 'ntorno di se havea delle persone che a ciò la spingevano, et che la sua autorità vi farebbe condescendere il Re. Il S.r Lodovico mi rispose che ciò trattava dello 'mpossibile per ch'erano gli Ugonotti troppo forti, et che la cosa era malagevole d'esseguirsi.

Io mi partetti per ritornar qui a punto da Lione quel giorno che seguì la grande uccisione che, s'io non sono errato, fu il primo di Settembre;[e'''] et non è dubbio che seguì con volontà, permissione et commandamento del Governatore Mons.r di Mandelot, a cui Mons.r

---

[d'''] Che l'Ammiraglio et i seguaci suoi non havevano bene studiato il savio Machiavello, che dice che l'huomo non si debba giamai fidar del Tirano offeso una sol vol[t]a.

[e'''] Il macello di Lione sul Rodono fu il primo di Settembre.

[136] Cancelled: "delle loro M.tà."
[137] François de Mandelot.

d'Ubertat portò la commissione, per lo che fece pigliar tutti que' della religione et imprigionare. Et la mattina per tempo io vidi certi segnali, per li quali si poteva far sicur giudicio che dovesse una simil cosa seguire. Nondimeno gli uccisi, se ben furon molti, furon però quasi tutti plebei, poveri et di poco conto, dal S.r della *Bessea*[138] et due altri in fuori, perchè quivi chi hebbe denari et amici si salvarono dal medesimo Governatore, dal Castellano et d'altri.

Io son giunto qui a nove di questo, che ho consumati quasi tutti fra visite d'amici et complimenti. Et tra predetti amici, due ne ho trovati che hanno corso non picciol pericolo. L'uno è il capitan Masino del Bene,[140] et l'altro il capitan Nicolo Franciotti, lucchese.[141] Quello fu

---

[*] Io non vo lasciar di raccontar l'atto virile et forte commesso dalla nobil consorte del S.r della Becea, la quale restata vedova del caro et amato marito con due bambolini, l'uno di 6 anni, et l'altro di tre, et udendosi dal maggior figlio (mentre il meschino vedea la madre senza dir nulla starsi a guardare gli ucciditori del marito che la rubavano la casa) dire, "Aih, madre, costoro ti furano il nostro havere," dissegli, levatasi su da quel fanciullesco parlare, quasi desta da profondo sonno, col più picciolo in braccio, "Prende il lembo di questa mia gonella, et seguitemi." Et uscitasi di casa quanto più tosto puote, si ridusse (con somma maraviglia di chiunque la vide) alla presenza del Governatore, al quale, veggendolo ella in atto di [?] ricevere, così dicono che favellasse: "Io non vengo alla presenza sua, crudele et spietato Tiranno, per trovar pietà, perchè so che nel suo cuore non albergò giamai, nè men per desio di vita, la qual sola mai fu cara per colui che un [?] scelerato contro ogni diritto ha fatto uccidere. Ma sol ci vengo per dare a te le innocenti gole di questi due agnoletti, et insieme quella della loro afflitta madre, acciochè satiandovi del sangue humano, accresci Empio la misura de' tuoi misfatti, come sono io certa di vederti pagare nell'ultimo et a te sommamente tremendo giudicio." Et (veggendolo tacere) soggiunse, "Che tardi? Che non satii le tue umicidiali mani di queste misere creature, poichè loro hai tolto il lor padre et tuttor [?], et hora fai lor rapire que' beni che Iddio misericordioso havea lor dati per lo mantenimento di questi miseri corpi." O gran potenza della verità. Dicono che quel crudele a queste minacciose parole tremò sempre come fosse dal fuoco sbattuto, et disse, "Signora, havete torto ad haver di me così rea opinione, perchè non fui colpevole della morte del ....[139]

[138] Probably Julian de La Bessée, who was slain in prison on the pretext that he had helped to arrange for the purchase of arquebuses from Geneva. He carried the honorific title of *valet de chambre du roy*. See A. Puyroche, "La Saint-Barthélemy à Lyon et le gouverneur Mandelot," *Bulletin de la Société de l'histoire du protestantisme français*, XVIII (1869), 409ff.

[139] Passage ends abruptly at this point.

[140] Early evidence of Del Bene's Protestant sympathies is provided by a dispatch from the Venetian ambassador Suriano, 14 May 1561. He described recent disturbances in Paris following the discovery of clandestine evangelical conventicles. The names of certain

salvato dal bastardo del Re, et questo dal S.r Gio. Battista Gondi.[142]
Il qual Franciotto trovai alle mani col reverendo padre Panigarola,[143]
che mi disse come havea sperato di ridurlo alla fede della Romana
chiesa. Et in tanti finimondi ho però trovati molti che si sono salvati,
chi per un modo et chi per un'altro, ma[144] specialmente da S.r Valsingame, che più di 200 ne salvò, la Reina regnante anchora, et molti
da catolici ne salvarono,[145] li quali[146] non trovavano buono l'usare
cotanta crudeltà.

Anzi per lo camino qua venendo, trovai un prete, a cui domandando
s'havesse udito un tal fatto: "Come s'io l'ho udito, così non l'havessi,"
mi disse. Et io chiedendogli la ragion di ciò, mi disse, "Perchè temo
di vedere sopra a consiglieri et agli essecutori d'un tanto misfatto
grave et volubile gastigo." "Come," dissi io, "anzi si crede da ogniun
buon catolico che siano per esser qua giù lodati, et nel cielo giudi-
donati." A che così replicò: "Io so d'esser catolico, nè mai fui d'altra
religione. Ma ben dico che se non ne vedrò tardi o tosto giusta vendetta, che non crederò che in cielo vi sia Dio nè giustitia alcuna." Et
così mi lasciò seguire il mio camino.

Si son però scoperti effetti et atti simili, et anchor più spietati che si
fossero que' del macello commesso in Roma per comandamento de'

Italians who had participated in these meetings were now known: "They were a son of
the late Signor Pietro Strozzi, and two captains – Nicolò Francisto of Lucca, and Massimo
del Bene – who had for many years been in the service of the French Crown" (H. A. Layard,
*Despatches of Michele Suriano and Marc'Antonio Barbaro, Venetian Ambassadors at the Court of
France, 1560–1563* [Lymington, 1891], p. 25). After the Massacre, Del Bene "retired into
Germany," while the English ambassador in Paris, Walsingham, wrote to the earl of Leicester
(8 Oct. 1572) volunteering the Italian's services to Queen Elizabeth. The letter is published
in Dudley Digges, *The Compleat Ambassador* (London, 1655), p. 270.

141 For the earliest evidence of Franciotti's Protestant leanings, see the preceding note.
Clearly, he is to be identified with the Nicolò Francisto named in Suriano's letter. He is
probably also to be identified with that "Franchiotto the Italian" who was serving Walsingham as an agent in 1568. Conyers Read describes Franciotti (for whom he uses the name
Tommaso rather than Nicolò) as being of Lucca, "an Italian Protestant of long experience
in diplomatic secret service, who had for the past forty years been in the pay of the French
crown" (*Walsingham*, I, 55–57, 231).

142 Jean-Baptiste de Gondi (1501–1580), banker of Lyons, "écuyer tranchant" to
Catherine de Medici, married the widow of Luigi Alamanni. See Pommerol, *Albert de Gondi*,
pp. 8, 18, 27, 167; Catherine de Medici, *Lettres, ad indicem*.

143 Francesco Panigarola (1548–1594), Franciscan controversialist, preacher and author,
created bishop of Asti in 1587. Sermon 28 in Panigarola's collected *Prediche* (Venice, 1599)
was preached by him in Paris in the presence of Charles IX and the queen mother one
month after the Massacre.

144 "ma ... catolici" inserted from margin.

145 "salvarono" substituted for "furono salvati."

146 Cancelled: "non ostante questo."

3 tiranni del mondo.[147] Con ciò sia cosa che molti figliuoli habbiano palesati i padri, molti fratelli il fratello, i nipoti i zii et gli avi loro hanno scoperti; et infiniti servitori i lor padroni hanno accusati, chi per haver l'heredità et chi per premio commetter tanta malvagità. Per tutto si trovavano i persecutori et gl'ucciditori, sì che tutta la città era sosopra per la troppa libera licenza che (col porre inconsideratamente le armi in mano al popolazzo) ognuno havea di far quello che più gli piacea, senza temer di gastigo alcuno. Maestro Rinieri[148] melanese vostro è divenuto capo del popolo et ha fatto pigliare et ammazzare molti.

Hor questo è quanto io ho potuto in questi pochi giorni ritrarre di questa lagrimosa tragicomedia, che a voi sol mando, acciochè ridotta a migliore ordine, ch'io[149] mi conosco atto a saper fare, ve la godiete in segno del desiderio che ho di far per voi cosa di maggior momento. Iddio vi guardi dal furor del popolo et dall'ira de' prencipi et vi bascio la mano. Di Parigi a XIII di Settembre 1572.

Finisce il Raccontamento del Cap.no Tomasso
Sassetti, gentilhuomo catolico fiorentino,
donato a G.C.,[150] l'essempio di cui egli
riscrisse già in Londra a 20 di Giugno
1583.

Seguita sopra ciò il parere d'un amico,
non del tutto delle cose del mondo
ignorante.

---

[147] Sassetti may have had in mind the persecution which befell Christians early in the fourth century A.D., in which case the "Three Tyrants" might be a reference to Diocletian, Maximian and Galerius. (See K. S. Latourette, *A History of Christianity* [New York, 1953], pp. 90–91.) Cf. marginalia to text *apud* n. 88 above.

[148] Two lines stricken and, with minor changes, retranscribed below beginning with "Hor questo." Noteworthy, however, is the substitution of "lagrimosa tragicomedia" for the deleted "pietosa tragedia."

[149] "ch'io ... fare" inserted from margin.

[150] "G.C." substituted for "me."

PARER DI N SOPRA IL RACCONTAMENTO DEL[151] GRANDE ET CRUDELE ET BIASIMEVOL MACELLO DI PARIGI, ET DI TUTTA LA MISERA FRANCIA

Quanto gravemente et quanto lungamente sia sparsa l'ira di Dio sopra questo, come nobile et grande[152] così infelice et miserevol, reame, è, senza ch'io lo dica, assai palese. Però venendo alla consideratione di questo ultimo come crudel suo accidente, dico che si puo assai buona fede prestare a questo ragionamento del Capitan Tomasso Sassetti, ottimamente da me in diversi et lunghi temp[i] cognosciuto. Il quale, quantunque sia veramente catolico papesco, è non dimeno huomo molto humano et non appassionato. Sì che è da credere ch'egli l'habbia raccontato come (più volte) dice d'haverlo udito d'altri narrare. Onde considerando prima quella parte nella qual dice[g'''] che, per la morte del Re Arrigo primo [sic], pretendevano i Prencipi del sangue la tutela del Re pupillo, et che altresì la pretendeva la casa di Lorena,[h'''] io dico che i Prencipi havevano ottima ragione di pretendere la tutela, et che la casa di Lorena non ve ne potea havere alcuna, perchè l'antica legge di Francia non concede niuna sorte di reggimento alle femine, nè a chi da lor discende, nè meno a forestieri. Onde in buona ragione non poteva ciò toccare alla predetta casa di Lorena, et che veramente et bene dice il Sassetto che da questo nascesse ogni principio delle guerre civili di questo miserissimo reame. Et è cosa sicura che se il Re di Navarra e'l Prencipe di Condé, suo fratello, non fossero suti della religione evangelica, che haverebbero senza contrasto alcuno ottenuta la tutela; perchè la Reina madre, che voleva governare, non haverebbe havuto, come hebbe, tanti prencipi, signori et

---

[g'''] A carta [2r].
[h'''] Che la casa di Lorena non poteva di ragione pretendere la tutella di Francesco II et di Carlo IX.

[151] Cancelled: "Macello."
[152] Cancelled: "reame."

capitani dalla sua contra i predetti prencipi, li quali la seguitarono
per coscienza, et non perchè non conoscessino far a Prencipi torto, nè
per amor portassero a Lorenaschi.

Dice il nostro Sassetto[1'''] che dall'haversi i Lorenaschi arrogata
autorità grande, si scopersero molti tradimenti, così contra la persona
del Re come contra colloro che governavano. Che credo intenda la
impresa d'Amboisa, che fu la prima, s'io non sono errato, nella quale,
quanto sia falso che contra la persona del Re non havessero machinato,
lo mostrò apertamente l'atto di que' capi et soldati, che alle false et
bugiarde promesse del duca di Nemurs[153] si resero, senza molta contesa
nè necessità. Ai quali, essendo loro stato mancato della data promessa,
fu tagliata la testa; et nel patir costantemente, chiamando il nome del
vivente Iddio in testimonio della 'nocenza loro, apertamente mostra-
rono che non già contra il lor Re et prencipe naturale, di cui erano fedel
sudditi, s'erano armati, ma sì per levargli d'attorno quelli a quali in
tal luogo non apparteneva, anzi che per comandamento de' Prencipi
del sangue le havevano giustamente pigliate, perchè a loro de iure
regni apparteneva la tutela del pupillo, et conseguentemente il gover-
namento del reame.[154] Et qui si vede come que' governatori, essendo
tutti stranieri, non amavano la salute del reame, anzi la ruina sua,
privandolo subito di tanti prodi soldati.

1''' A c. [2ᵛ].

153 Jacques de Savoie, duc de Nemours. His role in the suppression of the Conspiracy of
Amboise is described in a contemporary recital of the affair published in H. Naef, *La
conjuration d'Amboise et Genève* (Geneva and Paris, 1922), p. 259.

154 Modern scholarship agrees with this estimate that the conspirators of Amboise had
considered themselves to be acting in the service of the king. Their intention had been to
end the tyranny of the Guises. See N. M. Sutherland, "Calvinism and the Conspiracy of
Amboise," *History*, XLVII (1962), 111–38.

THE DISCOURSE DEDICATED TO COUNT GUIDO SAN GIORGIO ALDOBRANDINI

by

ALAIN DUFOUR

Those who catalogue the sources of the history of the Massacre of Saint Bartholomew – as did Henri Hauser in his *Sources de l'histoire de France*[1] – distinguish not only those which are Catholic from those which are Protestant, but also draw a distinction between sources which manifest democratic tendencies, and those sources which incline towards absolutism. Obviously, the former category is more appealing to study. The origins of the momentous debate on the right of political resistance is one of the chief elements of "modernism" of the sixteenth century. Protestant and pro-democratic sources, moreover, are more in keeping with the feeling of profound horror which permeates the modern historiography of the Massacre, and, more generally, our sense of morality.

Nevertheless, we must not be forgetful of the opposing strain of opinion, the current of ideas which is tied to the Counter Reformation and emerging absolutism – even if we find such ideas antipathetic – for they too are an important aspect of the history of the sixteenth century. The sixteenth century, after all, did not merely prefigure the twentieth, but also (naturally enough) the seventeenth. The document I am about to discuss is a specimen of this "antipathetic" tendency. It is to be hoped that our analysis will make a modest contribution to the broader discussion of the Massacre of Saint Bartholomew.

The document to which I refer is a manuscript volume in folio, bound in parchment, and containing 107 sheets of paper. On its spine we read: "Discorsi delle cose di Francia." Written in the hand of a professional scribe, corrected here and there in another hand, it is a "Discourse on the affairs of France" in the style of many such composed by the diplomats of those days, reviewing the history of the wars

---

[1] H. Hauser, *Sources de l'histoire de France: XVIe siècle*, vol. III: *Les guerres de religion* (Paris, 1912), p. 233ff.

of religion, including of course the story of the Massacre of Saint Bartholomew. The manuscript was purchased from a Milanese dealer in 1958 by the Musée historique de la Réformation in Geneva.

Our "Discourse" is anonymous. There is no clue as to the identity of the author. One feature, however, is significant: it is dedicated to Count Guido San Giorgio Aldobrandini. Guido San Giorgio belonged to an ancient family of Casale Monferrato, a small town in Piedmont. Occasionally, certain members of this family – and other patricians of Casale – left the service of their natural lords, the Gonzagas (dukes of Mantua and marquis of Monferrat), and entered the service of Savoy. Thus it was that Guido San Giorgio Aldobrandini supported Charles Emmanuel I of Savoy in 1613, and was subsequently banished from Casale. Later, when war broke out between Savoy and Monferrato, San Giorgio led Savoyard troops against his previous lords. And in 1623 he served as the ambassador of Savoy in Rome.[2]

But our "Discourse," written in 1574, long antedates those events. What was Guido San Giorgio Aldobrandini doing in 1574? He was probably a mere boy, or perhaps not even born. We know that he was raised at the court of Rome and educated by his uncle, Giovanni Francesco di San Giorgio, bishop of Acqui, who became a cardinal in 1596. The young man apparently showed great promise and pleased Pope Clement VIII, who granted him the right to take the name Aldobrandini and bear the arms of the family. It is unlikely that this took place before 1596; for although Clement VIII (Ippolito Aldobrandini) ascended the papal throne in 1592, he probably did not give his name to the young Guido San Giorgio before he had raised the uncle to the cardinalate.[3]

Thus we are confronted with an enigma. Our manuscript postdates by a good quarter of a century the composition of the text. (The watermark of the paper – a lily in a circle – can be identified; it is No. 7017 in Briquet's catalogue, and was used in Ferrara in 1586). The most probable hypothesis is that, sometime around 1596–1600, an old cleric of the court of Rome took from his papers a text at least twenty-five years old, and had it copied and dedicated to a young nobleman in the pope's graces.

---

[2] Roberto Bergadani, *Carlo Emanuele I, 1562–1630* (Turin, 1932), pp. 99, 118, 125, 151, 219. An uncle, Count Guido San Giorgio, who was living at Vienna in the service of the duke of Savoy, Emmanuel-Philibert, at the time of the Massacre of Saint Bartholomew, cannot be the person in question since he was never called Aldobrandini.

[3] Vittorio Angius, *Sulle famiglie nobili del Piemonte* (Turin, 1841–1857), IV, 1292–95; Antonio Manno, *Il patriziato subalpino*, vol. II: *Dizionario genealogico* (Florence, 1906), pp. 288–89.

Although it is, and alas! must remain anonymous, the "Discourse" can be dated with considerable precision. The author speaks of the new king, Henri III, who was returning from Poland to take possession of his kingdom of France. At the moment when the "Discourse" was written, he had not yet arrived there; and, in the second of the two extracts published below, we find mention of the fact that the duke of Savoy intended to accompany the new king as far as Lyons with 800 horses and 4000 footsoldiers. These circumstances place the composition of the "Discourse" in August 1574; for Henri III was still in Turin on 28 August, and he had already arrived in Lyons on 1 September.[4]

Anything that we can learn about the author of this anonymous discourse must be deduced from the text itself – from its ideas, and from the predilections it reveals. In the first place, the author, and probably the recipient of the dedication, were of the court of Rome. In the conclusion, where we read the enthusiastic wishes of the author for the prosperity of Count San Giorgio, whom the author declares himself "extremely desirous of serving," we read: "prego Nostro Signore che la faccia tanto felice quanto ella merita, et quanto desidera *questa corte*, cioè infinitamente." Now the words, *questa corte*, where both the author and the recipient of the dedication are obviously trying to establish their careers, must be the court of Rome. For, in another passage which concerns the need for naming learned and wise prelates to benefices in France, the text reads: "Sopra questo si debbe *di qua* scrivere continuamente in Francia, al Re et a la Regina, et fargliene parlar da i Nontii apostolici et da altri devoti religiosi." *Di qua*, which means "from here," clearly indicates Rome. From where else would one be writing to the king of France about nominations to benefices? Furthermore, the language he uses in referring to the pope leaves no room for doubt. The author belonged to the papal court.

Was he an eyewitness of the events he reports? He himself said at the end of the "Discourse" that he wrote "what he knows to be true, and what he heard from many people, and what he found in books." Thus he used both written and oral sources, and from these he distilled "what I know." It can be assumed, therefore, that he had first-hand experience of the affairs of France, and that he had spent some time there. In several places he speaks highly of Paris – its population so Catholic, the College of the Sorbonne so zealous for the faith. Here and there he specifies that the population of the capital was 300,000

---

[4] Michel François, ed., *Lettres de Henri III roi de France* (Paris, 1959 etc.), I, 377, and II, 3.

to 400,000 (fol. 51). These details suggest that he had lived in Paris. But to tell the truth, our "Discourse" contains few picturesque details, and I think it unlikely that it contains much that is not more fully described in the contemporary chronicles.

It is, rather, the interpretation of the events which merits our attention. First of all, it should be noted that our author maintains a certain sobriety, and he is critical enough to avoid repeating gossip and tales of the miraculous with which most contemporary accounts abound. For example, on the subject of the Massacre of Saint Bartholomew, he recounts no miracles, no stories of hawthorn bushes suddenly bursting into bloom – such as one finds even in Camillo Capilupi.[5] He does not believe that the Massacre was premeditated by the queen mother, the king and the Guises – only the abortive attempt to murder the admiral de Coligny on 22 August. To be sure, he mentions that on the 23rd of August, a Protestant conspiracy was discovered, and that this incited the king and the queen mother to employ violent methods; but all this is preceded by a cautious "it is said." In this particular case, moreover, he was merely relating the official version, the one which Charles IX publicized by his letters patent of 28 August.[6] The account given by our author is thus as restrained as those we find in modern historians, e.g., Mariéjol (in the Lavisse series) or von Pastor,[7] who are convinced that the assassination of Coligny was premeditated (plotted as early as 11 August if not before), but think that the massacre of 24 August was more or less a spur-of-the-moment decision, a step dictated by fear.

Our author is clearly an Italian of the Counter Reformation, influenced by the first theoreticians of politics, the pupils of Machiavelli. On the one hand he expresses with many a rhetorical flourish his horror of heresy: the child of Luther, himself begotten of the Devil (fol. 17). And on the other hand, we see him analyze with great care, and no little admiration, the policies of Catherine de Medici – her carefully laid plans to pit her adversaries one against the other, to weaken the house of Lorraine by means of the house of Montmorency, and vice versa, the better to preserve royal power and rebuild the authority of the state. All this is reminiscent of the Florentines and their deliberate development of theories of balance-of-power politics in the course of the fifteenth and sixteenth centuries. Such praise of

[5] "Le stratagème ou la ruse de Charles IX contre les huguenots ... escrit par le seigneur Camille Capilupi," in L. Cimber and F. Danjou, eds., *Archives curieuses de l'histoire de France*, VII (Paris, 1836), p. 470.

[6] Cimber and Danjou, *Archives curieuses*, VII, 162.

[7] L. von Pastor, *Geschichte der Päpste* ..., IX (Freiburg i.Br., 1923), *passim*.

the queen mother even leads us to wonder whether the author might
have been one of her suite, one of the numerous Italians who followed
her to France. There is a passage in the text, however, which makes
this supposition unlikely. Writing of the beginning of the first war of
religion in 1562, our author does not hesitate to mention the four
famous letters written by Catherine to the prince de Condé to ask for
his help. These letters were immediately published by the Huguenots
as an official proof that they took up arms only to rescue the royal
family which was being held prisoner by the Guises.[8] Later, Catherine
bitterly regretted those letters, and her true servants (for example,
Davila, her godson and protégé) pass them over in silence.[9]

Our author, then, is an admirer of the queen mother and her
policies, but not to the extent of being her spokesman. It is as a con-
noisseur that he relishes the intrigues of the châtelaine of the Tuileries.
He also mentions proudly the many Italians who held important
positions in France; reminds us that the duc de Nevers was also a
prince of Italy, that many of the great merchants and even the
chancellor, Birague, were also Italians; and that Gondi de Retz, a
Florentine, was the only marshal of France who remained loyal to the
crown. He considers these Italians the most trustworthy – if not the
only trustworthy – servants of the royal family of France. For the
French themselves were too divided between the two religions and the
two factions.

Which aspect of the wars of religion most interests our author?
The hostility of the two factions, the house of Guise against the house
of Montmorency-Châtillon, or the struggle between heresy and
orthodoxy? To be sure he concedes primacy to the religious aspect.
He declares that the poison of heresy was spread by Satan and because
of the negligence of the clergy at the beginning of the century (and
throughout the long tradition of Catholic historiography this has
always been cited as the chief cause of the Reformation), and that the
situation would be remedied by good preachers and good parish
priests. (The Council of Trent had ordered the establishment of
seminaries for just this purpose.) But our author, I think, is even more
interested in analyzing royal policies and the ambitions of the great
nobles. He is truly a technician of politics, a devotee of reason of state,
as only an Italian could be at that epoch. Carried away by his subject,
he forgets the religious zeal which inspires him elsewhere. Typical in

[8] See L. Romier, *Catholiques et huguenots à la cour de Charles IX* (Paris, 1924), p. 332.
[9] Henrico Caterino Davila, *Historia delle guerre civili di Francia* (Venice, 1676), pp. 71–72.

this regard is his treatment of Coligny. For the most part he employs pejorative epithets: "accursed," "wicked," and even calls him an upstart noble out of the backwoods of Savoy (the Châtillons are from Bresse), risen to prominence through excessive ambition aided by the influence and favoritism of his uncle, the constable de Montmorency (fol. 75). And then, suddenly, we find two whole pages filled with unabashed admiration for the admiral, when he recounts how, in 1569, he succeeded in maintaining his army at full strength, including a host of German mercenaries, in good discipline throughout an entire winter, although he had not a *sou* to pay them: "Thus Coligny was no less glorious than Hannibal" (fol. 78). In the age of humanism such praise cannot be dismissed as void of meaning. Our author was aware that he had contradicted himself, and he reconciled these divergent themes when he came to his eulogy upon the death of the admiral: so much talent should have been employed in the service of a better cause.

There is a fundamental discrepancy between Catholic and Counter-Reformation sentiments on the one hand, and a predilection for autonomous politics – politics free of the restraints of morality, such as Machiavelli had bequeathed to his pupils – on the other hand. One is tempted to regard this discrepancy as characteristic of all the Italians who wrote on reason of state at the end of the sixteenth century. In any case, such feeling for reason of state dominates our author's interpretation of the Massacre of Saint Bartholomew. His account is laconic. He mentions the decision of the king, the king's brother, the queen, of Tavannes, Aumale, Guise, and the murder of the admiral and his suite; then the spontaneous outbreak of the fury of the Parisian populace; and he reminds us on almost every page of the "Discourse" that the people of Paris have always detested the Huguenots. The death toll he gives is 5,000 to 6,000 in Paris. He makes his point without mincing words. It was truly a fine piece of states-manship, a great success. "Fatto il colpo così bello et quietato il tumulto, il Re andato il 26 del mese a la capella regia con gl'ornamenti regali, et quivi udita la messa solenna ..."

A fine piece of statesmanship. The young king of Navarre and the prince of Condé both converted and kept under close surveillance. Later, after the affair of La Molle and Coconas, two more marshals of dubious loyalty were in prison – Montmorency and Cossé. What remained was to take full advantage of the situation, now so aston-ishingly improved, to re-establish order, secure complete obedience to the king, and restore the kingdom of France to its ancient splendor. This is the opinion of our author at the moment when he wrote the "Discourse," and it is the harshness of his program that I wish to emphasize.

The Huguenots were slaughtered. The nobility, which had been "so badly infected with heresy," was largely destroyed, thanks to the Massacre of Saint Bartholomew. The king could easily replenish its ranks by ennobling foreigners – there was no lack of Italians ready to accept such honor – or by ennobling Frenchmen of the Third Estate. Thus he would assure himself of a new *faithful* nobility. (I cannot overstress this word which I have italicized – *faithful*.) As for the malcontents still to be found here and there in the kingdom, the cause of their disaffection lay more in their hatred for the cardinal of Lorraine and his family than it did in "the new religion." What was needed was a strong, even ruthless policy of repression against the rebels, making it clear that they were being punished *qua* rebels and not *qua* Huguenots. In this manner, the Huguenots of the lower classes, who were not rebels, would no longer have any reason to take part in uprisings. Above all, it was necessary to be rid of the maréchal de Montmorency. If the young king of Navarre could also be dispatched, that too would facilitate the program. His sister could be married to the duc d'Alençon, and by this means the duchy of Albret and the kingdom of Navarre would escheat to the crown of France. Under no circumstances must the new king, Henri III, make peace. He should hasten into Languedoc to force Damville to show his true colors, and to defeat him in case he did not submit. Next, the king should exterminate the rebels from his other provinces, by arming the people and giving them permission to massacre all who were disloyal. Finally, there was the difficult task of reducing the fortress of La Rochelle. But once order was restored to the kingdom, the king could reform both State and Church, following the provisions of the Council of Trent.

In a word, this was a "harsh" program, envisaging the vigorous re-establishment of absolute royal power by a ruthless repression of rebels and a few judicial murders on the side. It was a program worthy of a Richelieu.

Need we say that, at the time, it was impossible to implement such a program? First of all, so energetic a plan was incompatible with the character of Henri III, whose head was full of dreams of festivities, his coronation, and his triumphal entry into Paris. He had not the slightest inclination to set out on a military campaign. And then the actual situation of France made such a project chimerical. Our author deliberately omits mention of the way the entire south of France organized spontaneously in the aftermath of the Massacre of Saint Bartholomew, the Catholic *politiques* allying themselves with the Huguenots. The Assembly of Montauban in August 1573 was bold enough to lay down terms to the king, and Charles IX did not know how to reply. For it was now clear that the "Huguenot party" was so well structured that it could no longer be overthrown merely by chopping off the heads of its leaders.

The illusion of the Massacre of Saint Bartholomew persisted – the old idea that had been broached so many times by Catholic advisors, that Protestantism would completely vanish if only the Huguenot leaders were executed. Even two years later, a good Italian technician of politics like our author could still believe that this drastic method would work. We historians know that it was an illusion, that it would take most of the seventeenth century to convince the nobility to abandon Protestantism – mainly by withholding honorific positions from those who refused to convert to Catholicism. We know that only a Richelieu would dare to execute a Montmorency. And we know today that the only practicable method of government was that of Henri IV, who depended far more on national sentiment, rallying the French against the Spanish enemy, than he did on reason of state or on terror.

Nonetheless, to broaden our historical perspective, we might recall that the illusion of a policy of fear and order was widespread in the wake of the Massacre of Saint Bartholomew. For I consider our unpublished "Discourse" not as an isolated example, but representative of a broad current of opinion – the "Italogalles," for instance, whom Hotman denounced so violently in his pamphlets. There was also the *France-Turquie* of the chevalier Poncet, upholding Turkey as the example of the only country where the sovereign was obeyed.[10] And it is sobering to remember that this dream of law and order is still abroad in the world today.

The "Discorso" is obviously too long to be published in its entirety here. I have therefore selected two portions which seem to me to be most relevant for the purposes of this volume – the relation of the Massacre itself, and the conclusion, where the author comments on

[10] Hauser, p. 274.

the political situation in France in the aftermath of the Massacre and proposes the harsh policy he hoped would be adopted by the new king. My editorial principles have been to reproduce the original orthography, except for the modernization of the punctuation and the addition of a few accents where necessary. The lacunae in the second extract indicate gaps left by the copyist of the original manuscript.

TWO EXTRACTS FROM THE "DISCORSO"

1. THE ACCOUNT OF THE MASSACRE OF
ST. BARTHOLOMEW (FOLS. 86–90)

... [Coligny] non conoscendo il misero accecato da la sua molta arroganza d'esser con tutti i suoi in una città populatissima [Parigi], nemica capital di lui et di tutta la sua setta, ne le mani di quel Re ch'egli haveva tanto altamente offeso et procurato di torgli la corona et la vita. In queste allegrezze, il Re, o che così havesse già longo tempo deliberato aspettando l'occasione, o che havesse, come si publicò, scoperti nuovi disegni degli ugonotti contro se et la casa sua, deliberato [i.e., deliberò] non tardar più a vendicarsi di tante ingiurie et danni a ricoverare l'onor de la Maestà sua oscuratogli da suoi sudditi et assicurarsi nel regno et ne la vita con dare a suoi perpetui nemici et ribelli quel castigo che havevano già tanto tempo meritato. Ma perchè pareva che, mentre viveva l'Amiraglio, non si potesse tentare cosa che egli con la sagacità et astutia sua non havesse prevertite, [il Re avendo] consultato tutto con la Regina madre, Mons.r suo fratello, il duca di Ghisa, quel d'Aumala, e'l sig. Tavanes,[1] il dì 22 agosto, ritornando l'Ammiraglio da Palazzo accarezzato infinitamente, gli fece da un gentilhuomo franzese,[2] per quanto si dice servitore del duca di Ghisa, tirar un'archibugiata, la quale andando alla volta de la testa, avenne che l'Ammiraglio alzò il brazzo destro per cavarsi la beretta a non so chi, et così lo colse nel gombito del braccio, rompendoli l'osso in due luoghi. De la qual botta sbigottito et dubitando di qualche tramma maggiore, si fece subito portare a casa, dove mentre attese a curarsi, mandò Teligni e'l conte de La Rocca-

---

[1] Henri duc de Guise (1550–1588); Claude II de Lorraine, duc d'Aumale (d. 1573), his uncle; Gaspard de Saulx-Tavannes (1509–1573).
[2] Maurevert.

focaut[3] a dolersi a lui et a la Regina di tanto assassinamento, i quali ne mostrorono un dolore incredibile, dicendo di volerne in ogni modo pigliare vendetta contro quel che fusse che l'havesse commesso. Ritornati a l'Ammiraglio, cominciarono a restringersi tutti insieme et a pensare di vendicarsi con l'arme, togliendoli senza dubio Iddio l'intelletto di conoscer il pericolo di stare in quella città, et che uscendo fuor di Parigi in così grossa banda, com' erano di più di mille cavalli tutti armati, non solo non gli harebbe il Re potuti offendere, ma harebbono posto lui in nuovo travaglio. Il 23, ritornati coloro a dolersi et ad accusare il duca di Ghisa come autor del misfatto, dimandandone insolentemente vendetta, minacciando il Re per più stimolarlo contro di loro, il Re et la Regina, licentiatili con buone parole, fatta una asprissima bravata contro il duca di castigarlo se si trovava mai colpevole, andarono a visitare l'Ammiraglio consolandolo et promettendogli di dar' severissimo castigo a chi l'havesse offeso. L'Ammiraglio mostrandosi contento de l'animo del Re, lo pregò volesse concedergli che i suoi potessero tirarsi a star' intorno alla sua casa con l'armi per la sicurtà sua; il Re gli offerì la sua guardia, la quale da lui accettata fu posta alla porta. Al capo della quale Mons.r[4] diede l'ordine di ritirarsi sentendo rumore. Partitosi il Re et veduto che gli ugonotti tuttavia si radunavano insieme et preparavano l'arme, volendo finirla et prevenirli, la notte molto al tardi, ridottosi con quelli nominati di sopra, armatisi et avisati i principali cattolici parigini che stesser' pronti, restando il Re in camera con la madre, la moglie, Mons.r d'Anvilla,[5] che haveva chiamato all'improviso a quella consulta, ne lo lasciò uscir sotto giusto colore, fatti chiamare in fretta il Re di Navarra, il P. di Condé da le loro stanze, gl'altri andati a casa de l'Ammiraglio, gettata la porta a terra et uciselo, con quanti erano in casa, levato il rumore, fecero il medesimo a gl'altri suoi seguaci, che niente meno aspettavano; et in un tratto il popolo parigino prese l'armi sino al tardi del giorno seguente, diede per la testa a quanti si conoscevano essere ugonotti, o erano tenuti. Dicesi che fussero ammazzati da 5. in 6 m. huomini, tra i quali tutti quei nobili principali che havevano portato l'arme contro il Re loro; solo di tutti coloro che vennero a Parigi di qualità, si salvò Mons.r Mongomiero,[6] il quale

---

[3] Charles de Téligny, son-in-law of Coligny; François comte de La Rochefoucauld, prince de Marcillac.
[4] "Monsieur," Henri duc d'Anjou, brother of Charles IX, whom he succeeded on the throne as Henri III.
[5] Henri de Montmorency-Damville, governor of Languedoc.
[6] Gabriel de Montgomery, who had accidentally killed Henri II in a tourney in 1559.

stava fuori de la terra, ne' borghi, forsi non si assicurando così di
venire ne le mani de la Regina et del Re, a quali haveva ammazzato il
marito e'l padre; il corpo dell'Ammiraglio strascinato per tutto Parigi
fu impiccato in quel luogo dove già fu impiccato in statua. Questo fu
il fine di Guaspar da Colligni, huomo che di mediocre casa et di
razza savoiarda, cresciuto con la fortuna del Contestabile suo zio a
pare de tutti gli altri grandi di Francia; se havesse adoprato quel
valore et quella prudenza che era in lui in vero servitio di Dio et del
suo Re naturale, sarebbe altretanto perpetuamente glorioso, quanto
sarà sempre infame il nome suo per esser stato causa de le tante ruine
del nobilissimo regno di Francia. Fatto il colpo così bello et quietato
il tumulto, il Re, andato a li 26 del mese a la capella regia con gl'ornamenti regali, et quivi udita la messa solenne, di poi entrato nel suo
Conseglio publico, diede ad ogn'uno particolar conto de la giustissima
causa che l'haveva mosso a far quell'essecutione, approvando la
morte dell'Ammiraglio et de suoi seguaci come fatta d'ordine suo.
Mandò poi commandamenti per tutto il regno che non ardisse alcuno
pigliare l'arme o amazzare gl'ugonotti, perche già i popoli s'erano
sollevati, et in Lione et altri luoghi n'havevano uccisi molti, et il Re
dubitava di non condurli in tanta disperatione che non accendessero
un'altra guerra, non essendo massime egli armato et forse perseverava
ne' vecchi disegni di cercare di disgiunger le cause et mostrare che non
havesse fatto quell'essecutione per conto de la Religione, ma per
haver l'Ammiraglio conspirato contro la sua persona; acciochè alcuni
fussero di parere che si doveva lasciar scorrere alquanti giorni la
licenza de populi, che ne havessero ammazzati molti di quelli che
hoggidi hanno preso l'arme di nuovo, et ridotto gl'altri quasi a niente,
et poi fare l'ordine; attese poi il Re a far ritornare il Re di Navarra et il
P. di Condé a la fede cattolica. I quali doppo molto travaglio, forse
più per paura, da quel che s'è veduto, et per trovarsi soli che per altro,
abiurarono publicamente gl'errori ugonotti; era[no] però alcuni di
parere che si facessero morire, non dovendo credersi che dovessero mai
star quieti sempre che havessero occasione di tumultuare, havendo
inanzi gli essempi paterni, et essendo educati nell'eresie, et nodriti
nell'arme contro l'Re, et sempre sarebbono stati refugio di mal
contenti et disperati. A l'incontro, la morte loro havrebbe, oltre il
remediar tanti inconvenienti, in maniera spaventati (e) tutti gl'altri
con veder non perdonarsi nè anco al sangue regale, che non havrebbe
alcuno havuto ardire di pensare più cose nuove; ma pare non meno
orenda cosa in Francia il metter mano ne' principi del sangue che

sarebbe a noi di far guerra con li santi del paradiso, oltro che forse il Re temeva d'irritare tutta la casa di Borbone et gl'aderenti, et sperava che questi giovani che havevano errato per inganno d'altri et per la poca età loro si dovessero riconoscere, et con li molti beneficii diventargli buoni parenti et servitori. Voleva similmente alcun levarsi subito dinanti, in quel empito et terrore, i marescialli di Momoransi et d'Anvilla, et estinguer' quella casa, prima origine di tanti mali; ma, o ch'l Re non potesse, o che temesse far peggio, o sperasse col mezo loro acquetar gl'altri che rimaneano, o pur che sia vero quello che si dice che gl'huomini non sanno venire a questi fatti per elettione, ma per necessità, non diede segno alcuno di pensarci. Li restava la recuperatione di quelle terre che tenevano gl'ugonotti, ne le quali s'erano ridotte quasi tutte le reliquie, et certo fu molto lento il Re a fare questa impresa, la quale si doveva far subito morto l'Ammiraglio, mentre che gl'altri erano tutti atterriti et più morti che vivi, se ben si dice che non puotè metter prima in ordine l'essercito, per che quando fece la botta dell'Ammiraglio, era disarmato, nè poteva prepararsi per non dargli sospetto, overo sperò d'haverli per concordia, come si trattò un pezzo; fatto l'essercito, si dubitò se se dovesse prima attender ad espugnar quelle terre che erano per la Francia, et estinguer' dentro del Regno tutte le reliquie, poi andare a La Rocchiella, posta negl'ultimi contorni del Regno, che si sarebbe senza altro sospetto potuta assediare et combattere, o vero andare prima quivi dov'era Mons.r de La Nua[7] con la maggior parte de le reliquie, et vi s'aspettava Mongomeri con soccorso d'Inghilterra, et dandogli tempo havrebbe potuto quella terra con la commodità del mare Oceano tirar in Francia un essercito di forastieri et accendere una nuova guerra col seguito, massime che havevano gl'ugonotti in quei paesi di Guascogna; finalmente si deliberò di andare a La Rochiella, lasciato Mons.r d'Anvilla in Lenguadoc con un altro essercito, che serrasse Montalbano[8] et trattenesse i ribelli che non potessero far male sichè non si finisse l'altra impresa, dove intorno al mese di marzo del '73 s'inviò Mons.r, [che] assediò et cominciò a batter la terra; et andando l'impresa a longo, per accelerarla vi venne il Re con la madre, conducendo seco il Re di Navarra, il P. di Condé . . .

---

[7] François de La Noue, known as "Bras-de-Fer," author of the *Discours politiques et militaires* (1587).
[8] Montauban.

2. CONCLUSION OF THE "DISCORSO" (FOLS. 95–107)

Ho narrato diffusamente le cagioni et i successi di tanti mali et guerre civili di Francia sino a la morte di Carlo IX, di gloriosa memoria,[9] da la quale narratione se ben si possa conoscere in quale stato hoggi si trovi il regno, niente di meno per esserse il terzo capo da me proposto nel principio di questo discorso, non voglio mancare di ragionare alquanto a la guerra, quali forze habbia il Re, quali inimici et quel che si possa cavare per conjetture che ne debba seguire, massime pervenuto che sia in Francia Enrico III, hoggi Re felicissimo, il quale v'è già così vicino che possiamo aspettare di giorno in giorno la nova che egli ci sia gionto.

Morto il Re, essendo il successore absente, cadeva per gl'ordini del regno il governo in mano al più prossimo P. del sangue, il quale era il Duca d'Alanzone suo fratello. A lui si poteva opporre l'età, perchè, come habbiam detto ragionando di Francesco II, è stato longamente disputtato se s'intendeva maggiore uno di XX anni per governare il regno, et ancorchè il Parlamento di Parigi dichiarasse di sì, pur vi sono esempi contrarii. Doppo l'Duca, il Re di Navarra, et poi il P. di Condé, primi de la casa di Borbone; ma in questi si sarebbe potuto anco fare il medesimo ostaculo de l'età, il quale vedendo che'l cardinale di Borbone era, come prete, escluso, restava primo il Duca di Monpensieri, et poi il suo figliuolo chiamato il P. Delfino.[10] Ma troncò tutte queste difficultà la volontà del Re, il quale inanti a la morte dichiarò reggente la Madre sino a la venuta del fratello. Questa dichiaratione si sarebbe potuta ridurre in dubbio se ci fussero stati capi d'importanza contrarii a la Regina, massime i Prencipi del sangue. Perchè s'è più volte conteso che, morendo, il Re non potesse alterar gl'ordini publici in lasciar l'autorità a chi per le leggi non l'haveva, come, oltre a gl'essempi allegati di sopra, seguì a la morte di Luigi XI, che havendo lasciato reggente di Carlo suo figliuolo et del regno la figliuola, il duca d'Orlians, che fu poi Luigi XII, pretendendo che toccasse a lui come principe del sangue più prossimo, suscitò una guerra civile, et bisognò far confermare quella ordinatione del Re Luigi da i tre Stati. In questa morte di Carlo IX, tutto l'forte si riduceva nel duca d'Alanzone et nel Re di Navarra, se havessero voluto, o volendo havessero potuto uscir da le mani de la Regina; ma

---

[9] Charles IX died on 30 May 1574.
[10] Louis de Bourbon, duc de Montpensier, and his son, François de Bourbon, prince-dauphin d'Auvergne.

più nel Duca, che essendo primo P. fratello del Re, et pari a gl'altri d'età, sarebbe sempre stato da tutti preferito, per che il cardinale di Borbone, oltre all'esser prete, è principe di buona et quieta mente, a lui simile è il duca di Monpensieri molto da bene signore, nè il suo figliuolo è differente dal padre, ancorchè la gioventù lo faccia un poco più vivace, et essendo ora con l'essercito in mano adoperato possa far qualche miglior riuscita, poichè l'essercitatione può mutare le nature et megliorarle o deteriorarle; la Regina, donna che quanto maggiori sono stati i pericoli tanto s'è mostrata di maggior animo et sapere, conoscendo tutto questo, et potendo temer' assai del Re di Navarra, et non poco del figliuolo, sì per la mala sodisfattione de le cose seguite come per quello che potesse l'ambitione mettere in capo a giovani portati dal calore del sangue, subito morto il Re, senza dar tempo di pensare o fare cosa alcuna, entrata in un cocchio con loro, havendo apresso tutte le guardie, se n'andò a Parigi, città fedelissima et molto devota al nome suo. Quivi havendo, come si dice, assai bene disposto il duca d'Alanzone a le sue voglie, cessando in lui per aventura il timor de la disgratia del Re, non havendo mai offeso il presente, anzi sperando acquistarci la gratia con mostrarsi pronto a conservarle il regno quieto, et trovandosi anco unico fratello del Re tanto vicino a la corona, fu dal Parlamento Parigino publicato Re Enrico III et confermata Regente la Regina madre, et il medesimo havendo fatto il Conseglio privato, del quale la Madre fece capo Mons.r d'Alanzone per tenerlo contento, seguì a far il simile il Parlamento di Tolosa,[11] non meno di quel di Parigi fedelissimo al Re et a la Regina, et nemico capitale a gl'ugonotti, et poi gl'altri cinque che vanno appresso [a] l'ordinario a le deliberationi del Parigino. Si sarebbe potuta metter' in dubbio questa confirmatione de la Reggente, se fussero state arme in compagnia sotto capi potenti d'autorità et di seguito, come toccante a i Tre Stati; ma non volendo nè potendo il Duca d'Alanzone innovare cosa alcuna et nei medesimi termini essendo il Re di Navarra, preso Mongomeri il quale fu decapitato in Parigi, non restando de nemici capo di qualità, restò la Regina quieta al governo, impadronitasi de l'arme del Re morto, seguendo il nome suo il Duca di Monpensieri et il figliuolo, che havevano gl'esserciti di Normandia et Delfinato, et il Duca di Ghisa, che haveva i Svizzeri, et poi tutti i cattolici fedeli, che sono i tre quarti del popolo, et la città et fortezze principali che si tenevano per lo Re et havevano governatori fedeli et a sua devotione. Preso in mano il governo, la Regina ha subito proveduto a due pericoli

---

[11] Toulouse.

di maggior importanza: l'un d'impedir il P. di Condé che non entrasse
in Francia, il quale s'intendeva che, havendo abiurato publicamente
in Argentina[12] la religion cattolica, aiutato dal conte Palatino et da
alcuni altri principi protestanti, faceva 4 m. reistri[13] et 6 m. fanti
tedeschi; l'altro, di prevenire il Marescial d'Anvilla che non potesse
far danno alcuno di momento in Linguadoc, col'essercito che ci
haveva dei dependenti de la casa sua et con l'autorità tra li popoli et i
soldati d'esser stato tanti anni governator di quella provincia; al
pericolo del P. di Condé, ha rimediato col mandar subito ai confini di
Campagna,[14] per dove può verisimilmente entrare, il Duca di Ghisa,
giovane signor di molto valore, cattolico et fedele per gl'interessi
publici et privati di casa sua, con 6 m. Svizzeri, da 4 in 5 m. fanti
francesi, et intorno a 2 m. cavalli; in Linguadoc, havendo levato il
governo ad Anvilla, l'ha dato al Conte del Vilars, Ammiraglio,[15]
acciò, essendo cognato del fu Contestabile, potesse divertire molti
parenti et affettionati a la casa di Momoransi, et prudentemente ha
sempre atteso la Regina a separar gl'interessi l'un dal altro, opponendo
quanto poteva ad uno che havesse forze per un rispetto, un altro che
l'havesse per lo medesimo; et havendo il Marescial d'Anvilla mandato
a dimandare licenza a la Regina, forse per intender l'animo suo, di
poter andare in un luogo confidente a lui et a lei, sin a tanto che
potesse far conoscere l'innocentia et la fideltà sua, raccomandandogli
insieme il fratello Momoransi, ella con amorevoli parole gli ha risposto
che quanto al fratello, riserva la sua causa intiera al Re, il quale può
credere che non mancherà favorirlo quanto si potrà onestamente,
quanto a lui, che gli dà licenza o di ritirarsi appresso al Duca di
Savoia, o d'andare ad incontrare il Re verso Polonia, et che ha fatto
governatore di Linguadoc l'Ammiraglio suo zio, et [che] sarà contento, sino alla venuta del Re, ubedire et partirsi. Ma egli non ne ha
però fatto altro, et ha più tosto accresciuto il sospetto contro di lui,
come diremo. Non ha nel resto del governo innovato la Regina cosa
altra, et i medesimi ufficiali sono hoggidi che erano vivente Carlo IX.
Nè voglio mancare, per non lasciare indietro cosa alcuna di momento,
di parlare un poco de' principali.

Habbiam' detto a bastanza de' principi del sangue che sono i primi
membri del regno. Tra gl'ufficii, il primo è quello del Contestabile,
che hoggidi da la morte di Momoransi in qua è vacante, et difficil-

---

12 Strasbourg.
13 Cavalrymen (from the French, "reîtres").
14 Champagne.
15 Honorat de Savoie-Villars, admiral of France.

mente discenderà il Re a farne alcuno, havendo nociuto tanto a la Francia la troppa potenza del passato. Da i quattro Marescialli, due sono prigioni, Momoransi et Cossé,[16] il terzo è ritirato, et più sospetto che fidele, l'ultimo è il Conte di Retz, di casa Gondi,[17] Fiorentino, il quale per se non è di molto valore, ma è venuto a questo grado portato da la Regina et dal estraordinaria gratia che s'haveva acquistato col Re Carlo per essersi allevato seco. Questo sarà sempre fedele dipendente da la Regina; se'l Re deliberasse cosa alcuna contro i marescialli prigioni, o contro Anvilla, o se per altro modo vacasse uno di questi luoghi, è opinione che lo darebbe a Mons.r di Bellagarda,[18] gentilhuomo di nobilissima casa, di molto valore, di gran sapere, et di longa esperienza nele cose de la guerra, amator de virtuosi et assai de' Italiani, de' quali è stato sempre prottettore, et servitore particolare di molti anni a questo Re, quando egli era in minor fortuna. Ammiraglio di Francia è il Conte di Vilars, de la casa di Savoia per linea bastarda, buon signore cattolico et che nel resto sarà fedele et quieto. Gran Cancelliero è il Birago,[19] cresciuto con li longhi servitii fatti da lui et da la casa sua a la casa [et] a la corona di Francia, huomo che vale assai, prudente et pratico de le cose di quel regno, et cattolico, dipendente da la Regina, et sarà sempre da lei portato et per ciò caro al nuovo Re. De' Parlamenti, il Parigino e'l Tolosano, che sono i primi, sono tutti cattolici fedeli et pieni d'huomini di valore. Gl'altri sono per la maggior parte cattolici, e qualche eretico, ma coperto, però dependono, come habbiamo più volte detto, da i primi. Il Consiglio privato ha qualche mistura d'humori, perchè la qualità de i tempi ha necessitato il Re a pigliar di tutti per non parere di dipendere da parte alcuna, et per altri varii disegni. Però il novo Re doverà secondo il solito tutto mutarlo et rinovarlo. In tanto questo dipende per la maggior parte de la Regina, la quale ne la somma de le cose si ristringe con il gran Cancelliero, et con lui si dice che assolutamente si consigli, et anco in molte cose col cardinale di Lorena,[20] ma tanto quanto è il bisogno, et non più, tra che per essere egli odiato da molti non vuol dare mala sodisfattione a coloro, [e] tra che ella non si lascia volontieri governare da lui, che ne vuole spesso più de la sua parte. De i Tre Stati, il clero, levatine certi pochi, de' quali alcuni sono

---

[16] François duc de Montmorency, brother of Montmorency-Damville; Arthus de Cossé-Brissac.
[17] Albert de Gondi, maréchal de Retz (1522–1602).
[18] Roger de Saint-Lary de Bellegarde, who was shortly to become a marshal, at the end of 1574.
[19] René de Birague (1507–1583).
[20] Charles cardinal de Lorraine (1525–1574).

prigioni o fugiti, è hoggi assai tutto cattolico, et per li proprii interessi contrario a gli ugonotti, e fedele al Re. Una cosa sola lo tiene ancora alquanto diviso, che ve ne sono molti nemici al Cardinale di Lorena, che spesse volte hanno novi pensieri. Ma la Regina ha saputo sino a qui con molti modi tenerli in fede, et sarà facile al Re guadagnarli et conservarli tutti adoprando la sua solita prudenza nel negotiare. De i nobili ne sono già tanti morti in queste guerre che tolti ancor via questi fratelli di Momoransi con alcuni adherenti, la nobiltà sarà quasi tutta rinovata di forastieri o di francesi novamente da la Regina, dal Re Carlo et da questo [nuovo Re] retirati inanti; et ogni dì più, massime in questa entrata del novo Re, se ne faranno; tutti questi saranno fedeli. I nemici, o sospetti, sono di quei nobili primi et dependenti la maggior parte de la casa Momoransi; ma levati i prigioni potrà il sapere del Re provedere a questo a le passioni, che fussero contro la casa di Ghisa, et altri simili diffetti. Il popolo, come habbiam detto, è i tre quarti cattolico et massime quello de la città principale fidelissimo al Re et inimicissimo a gl'ugonotti, ma le guerre l'han fatto un poco insolente, et bisognarà al Re, persino a tanto che le cose siano meglio accomodate, alquanto de la destrezza per facilmente maneggiarlo. D'huomini di gran valore, che si possano chiamare perfetti da dargli il carico degli esserciti, ne ha la Francia carestia, et [dei] duoi Marescialli che sariano tenuti buoni, Momoransi et Anvilla, uno è prigione, l'altro quasi nemico al Re; gli altri si ristringono in due, il Duca di Nivers,[21] Italiano, et v'è a molti vecchi capitani di gran fama, [et] se il Re tira inanzi Mons.r di Bellagarda, come si tiene, egli sarà per molte sue rare parti tra i Francesi quasi il primo ne le cose de la militia; vi sono molti capitani arditi et prudenti, ma non so se n'è fatto ancor tanta prova di dargli essercito in mano. Così sta brevemente il governo di Francia. Quello che debba seguire in questo nuovo regno si può non più pensare che dire.

Ci resta a trattare de l'arme del Re et de' suoi ribelli, et di quello che possa farsi d'ogni parte chiamar reliquie, se bene in Provenza, in Perigort et in altre parti fanno scorrerie et guerreggiano più da fuorusciti che da soldati. Il lor forte è in Delfinato, in Linguadoc et a La Rocchiella. In Delfinato è un gentilhuomo particolare di non molto nome[22] con assai buona banda di gente, ma dipende da le forze di Linguadoc, dove è Mombruno,[23] soldato vecchio, il quale ha

---

[21] Louis de Gonzague (of the ducal family of Mantua), duc de Nevers.
[22] François de Bonne de Lesdiguières, future duke, marshal and constable.
[23] Charles Dupuy de Montbrun (1530–1575).

il maggiore et il migliore numero di tutti, perche tiene molte terre et
non ha mai havuto molto ostaculo da Mons.r d'Anvilla, che era
governatore, anzi come si tiene n'era aiutato. Scorre assai, et hoggidì
molto più che per la ritirata d'Anvilla resta questa provincia in
confusione, et fa qualche progresso di pigliar luoghi, ma non forsi di
molta importanza. La Normandia, dove sotto Mongomieri era una
gran banda di ribelli, per la rotta, presa et morte del capo, resta
tutta netta; a La Rocchiella è Mons.r de La Nua; è il primo, fra tutti
coloro che hoggidì portano l'arme, di casa, di nome et seguito, ma
gentilhuomo privato, che non ha mai havuto carico d'importanza.
Non ha gran forze da potersi distendere molto. Tutti coloro che
hoggidì portano l'armi, si dice che messe insieme non fariano 1500
cavalli et 12 m. fanti, dove già solevano haver tre o quattro esserciti
grandi; hanno alquante terre, de le quali sono ancor quelle prime La
Rochiella, Montalbano, Cognac et La Chiaritè, di più Nimes, Sanserra
et altre, ma tutte de La Rochiella in poi saranno facilmente del Re,
sempre che egli sia padrone assoluto de la campagna; La Rocchiella
per la fortezza del sito, et per la speranza veramente dei ribelli, come
dei malcontenti, debbe essere di tenersi tanto che possano cavare
qualche pace; per hora gli assicuri con voler forsi qualche terra
d'avantaggio, et riducendosi tutti ne le loro piazze andarsi preparando
con procacciarsi aiuto d'Inghilterra, di Germania et massime di
Fiandra, di dove se'l P. di Oranges prosperasse, possono aspettarne, et
quando anco fusse cacciato un'altra volta di là, non mancherà, come
disperato, tornare un'altra volta in Francia. Talchè la Fiandra potria
nuocere molto, se'l Re non si spedisse presto, ma la maggior speranza
di costoro è di vedere qualche novità del Duca d'Alanzone, s'egli ha
questi pensieri, et nel Re di Navarra, o che'l P. di Condé entri in
Francia con gente, et si congiunga con qualchedun di loro, o che'l
marescial d'Anvilla, se ciò prendesse apertamente, uscisse fuori con
quelle genti che ha et che potria far maggiori, et con'l seguito de la
casa Momoransi, et con l'autorità sua in Linguadoc et paesi circonvicini, facendosi capo de l'impresa, renovasse la guerra et la memoria
del'Ammiraglio. Ma del Duca d'Alanzone possono essere chiariti che
non haverano altro, così del Re di Navarra, che la diligenza de la
Regina provede ad ogni cosa, et certo quando un di questi principi
fugisse, ma molto più Alanzone, il quale non si crede che habbia
più queste fantasie, potria suscitar gran foco. Il P. di Condé s'è detto
che faceva 4 m. Reistri et 6 m. fanti, ma si sa che non ha dinari da
pagarli, et certi pochi, che gli erano venuti, si dice che siano stati

ritenuti da alcuni colonelli d'Reistri che pretendono essere creditori di
lui et del P. suo padre per le paghe de le guerre passate; si disse che'l
Conte Palatino con li collegati instava a i capi de i Reistri et fanti che
facessero le genti che li prometteva, sariano pagati a l'arrivar in Francia, dando certezza il Principe che quivi havrebbe denari et, o col
felice successo acquistarebbe molta preda, o con la pace li farebbe
pagare dal Re come l'altre volte s'è poi inteso per altra banda; che
tra queste difficultà, et tra la presta et inaspettata venuta del Re, egli
si sia pentito o smarito, et habbia levato l'ordine di far le genti. Ma
quando le facesse, 6 m. fanti et 4 m. Reistri non sono tanto forze da
entrar in Franza, da passare tanti passi, tanti luoghi forti, superar'
gl'esserciti Regii, et unirsi con gli altri, se a i Regii non succede quasi
che gran disordine, o non fanno qualche segnalato errore. Nè [Condé]
a gli capitani di tanto valore, è giovane d'anni, nè ha altro di meglio
che l'esser del sangue reale, nè seco ha tan poco huomini di grande
stima et reputatione. Il marescial d'Anvilla, par certo strano a molti
come, a la morte del Re chr.mo, non sia saltato in campagna,
havendo così giusta causa de la presa del fratello et de la persecutione
che è fatta a lui, et si tiene che harebbe potuto far gran danno, mentre
[havrebbe] astretto la Regina, et forsi necessitarla, a liberare il fratello
et a fare qualche accordo. Ma s'ha da credere che essendo egli accorto,
habbia ben conosciuto l'esser suo et quello della Regina et del Re, et
sperato d'accomodar meglio le cose sue con lo starsi quieto a vedere,
che con l'arme, massime non havendo mancato la Regina di dargli
sempre qualche buona speranza; ma più il Duca di Savoia, che subito
morto il Re Carlo, gli scrisse et l'essortò a perseverare ne la fedeltà del
Re nuovo, offerendosi a pigliarsi carico d'accomodare egli le cose.
Dipoi fa professione d'innocente et che quando il fratello Momoransi
havesse errato in qualche cosa, egli non ne sarà mai trovato consape-
vole; s'egli ha havuto o ha pensiero a l'armi, debbe stare aspettando
quel che succeda de la mossa del P. di Condé, dove sta l'importanza,
et quello che farà il novo Re, la cui presta venuta debbe senza dubbio
havere rotto molti disegni; intanto egli si sta in una terra forte, dove
quando il Re voglia offenderlo debba sperare di fare diffesa, poter
uscir fuori, unirsi con gli altri ribelli et fare una guerra gagliarda, et
che questa paura et l'opera di molti, et massime del Duca di Savoia,
che s'intende vi s'interponga caldamente, debba disporre il Re ad
accordarsi et liberar Momoransi; ha però preso alcune castilla, se ben
di poca importanza, che, se gli sono mandate a dare et messovi la
guardia a nome del Re ma di gente sua, forsi [sarà] per far più facile

l'accordo. Ma non ha mancato questo procedere d'accrescere il sospetto contro di lui. Queste sono le forze et le speranze de' ribelli, che si sanno.

All'incontro, il Re superiore d'ogni parte, ha Iddio in suo favore et la giusta causa, ha l'auttorità regia, che importa molto, tanti popoli fedeli; tutte le terre et fortezze principali sono per lui con gl'esserciti, e d'ogni parte più potente; ha, contro il P. di Condé in Campagna, il Duca di Ghisa con l'essercito; che habbiamo detto s'è di più ordinato in Germania a i suoi [i.e., di Condé] soliti colonelli, che, movendosi il Principe, facciano 4 m. Reistri et gli vengano dietro. Talchè da quella parte si può stare sicurissimo. In Delfinato [il Re] ha l'P. Delfino con forze superiori a' nemici, et con tutte le terre et piazze principali in Normandia ha il Duca di Monpensieri con un altro campo, del quale essendo quivi finita la guerra con la morte di Mongomeri, se ne puote servire altrove. In Linguadoc, de l'essercito che haveva Mons.r d'Anvilla, gran parte è per lui; tutti i governatori de la provincia et delle terre sono armati. Di più sono in esser 6 m. Svizzeri fatti d'ordine del Re morto, che non sono ancor mossi, ma havendone il Re bisogno gli potria haver' in pochi giorni; haverà il resto de le sue compagnie d'ordinanza, che sogliono essere tutte secondo gl'ordini di Francia 4 m. huomini d'arme, 6 m. arcieri, cioè cavalli leggieri, che'l Duca di Savoia l'accompagna sino a Lione con 800 cavalli et 4 m. fanti, dove, volendosene servire insieme con le sue guardie, con la nobiltà che concorrerà tutta a trovarlo, farà un altro campo. Ma varrà quanto un essercito la persona sua, tanto amata, tanto stimata da i suoi populi et tanto temuta dai ribelli che gli potrà metter tutti in terrore et in confusione. Nè può S. M.tà sentir danno di cosa alcuna, eccetto che se la strettezza del danaro per non poter durare, massime in questo primo del suo regno, non la necessita a far la pace, la qual cosa terrei per pessima, perciò che non se potria sperare che facesse in questa pace quello che s'è fatto nell'altra contro i rebelli,[24] conciò sia che gl'ugonotti non si fidarano per le cose successe mai più di parole o promesse sue. Ma peggio saria che con la pace sarà constretto liberare quei Marescialli prigioni, i quali una volta offesi, mai più non pensarano ad altro che a vendicarsi et ad assicurarsi, et questo non sarebbe se non dare capi gagliardi a i ribelli dispersi, tanto peggiori d'animo dell'Ammiraglio, quando a lui erano state fatte minore offese, e a questi maggiori, non essendo a lui stati amazzati tanti parenti, non lui posto prigione, nè trovatosi così vicino al perdere la

---

[24] *Viz.*, the Peace of St. Germain in 1570.

vitta sotto il carnefice, non fattogli vedere una festa di Parigi, che li dovesse mantenere in perpetua diffidenza; et se ben pare che sia morto il Re Carlo, dal quale venne tutto questo, et contro cui furono fatte le congiure, questo è quel medesimo Mons.r d'Angio che tagliò a pezzi l'Ammiraglio con tutti i suoi,[25] che sempre ha fatto guerra a gl'ugonotti, et gli ha mostrato mal animo adosso ... [*lacuna*] ... Sì che'l fare adesso la pace non fusse altro, se non dare l'utile del tempo a i [ribelli] ... [*lacuna*] ... marescialli, che senza dubbio uscendo sarano capi, et al P. di Condé ... [*lacuna*] ... la guerra, o far qualche gran congiura con pericolo di tirarsi a dosso a la Francia quella furia di Fiandra. Ma se'l Re sostiene la guerra et ha danari et n'è aiutato da i principi cattolici amici de la salute di quella coronna, senza dubbio si vedrà finito ogni tumulto di Francia. Quello che debba fare il Re seguendo l'impresa contro i ribelli, si può discorrere, ma malamente sapere. Dicono questi Francesi ch'egli se n'andrà da Lione dritto a Reins per farsi sacrare secondo l'antico rito dei Re francesi et di là forsi farà l'entrata solenne in Parigi per confirmarsi nel Regno prima che far altro. Questo potrebbe essere un perder molto tempo et far grossa spesa, quando meno bisogna et l'uno et l'altro, et per aventura saria più utile con tutte quelle forze che potesse metter presto insieme andar dritto in Linguadoc, necessitar il Marescial d'Anvilla a scoprirsi da dovero, che con la prestezza del Re, il quale gli havrebbe [tolta] ogni autorità ne la provincia, et ogni poter di far male, non potrebbe far altro, se prima non cercasse di fugirsi di là, che venir a la mercè sua con speranza di haver dal Re ogni gratia et benigna dimostratione, ne la qual speranza non saria male trattenerlo con molti mezi; sin che gli arivassi adosso o ridotto a l'ubedienza, o preso, o scacciato, Anvilla, gli altri ribelli sariano fugati dal solo apparire del Re, come le nuvole dal sole, non havendo arme da resisterli, nè terre tanto forti da far longa diffesa con poca speranza di soccorso. Finita questa impresa, che è la più importante, si finirebbe presto la guerra in Delfinato, in Provenza et negl'altri contorni, facendo armare i popoli, et dando per publico bando licenza d'ammazzare i ribelli; sarebbe bene che'l Re medesimo attendesse all'espugnatione de le terre di Linguadoc et altri più importanti, con ogni diligenza et prestezza, che essendo venuto così risoluto a l'impresa d'ogni parte del regno, concorrerà gente in suo favore, et i ribelli si mettriano in maggior fuga, timore et disordine. Nè potrebbe, fatto questo, temer più

---

[25] The reference is to the battles of Jarnac and Moncontour, in which Anjou (the future Henri III) defeated the Huguenots.

l'entrata del P. di Condé o d'altri, i quali, non havendo un essercito così potente che superasse tutti quelli del Re, il che non si vede come possa seguire, non venirebbono su la speranza de i compagni così mal condotti. Restarebbe l'ultima impresa de La Rocchiella, la quale se l'altra volta fu vicina ad essere espugnata, molto più lo sarebbe ora, mancando Mongomieri con tanti altri, essendo il Re superior di forze, più assoluto padron di Francia, senza stimolo d'altra parte del suo regno, con haver prigioni quei Marescialli, i quali all'hora impedivano occultamente i buoni successi di S. M.tà, la quale impresa finita, come si può sperare felicemente, dovrà di ragione il Re spegner' quei pochi prigioni, acciò quasi nove teste d'Idra non rinascano, et levi a i tristi ogni speranza di novi tumulti. Di che non è anco tempo di parlar se non finita la guerra, anzi in tanto darne buona speranza per non mettere gl'altri in disperatione et estrema necessità di diffendersi. Del Re di Navarra non parlo, ma dico bene che se piacesse a Dio chiamarlo a se, si potrebbe dare la sua sorella,[26] che restarebbe erede, per moglie al Duca d'Alanzone, con dargli quel che si tiene de la Navarra, il ducato d'Albret et i contadi di Fois et di Bigorre con altri stati suoi paterni, che così si contentarebbe ben questo giovine, et si terebbe più unito col Re, et più nemico a gl'ugonotti per suoi proprii interessi; non restando più capo alcuno di momento, nè arme nemiche, potrebbe cominciare S. M.tà con prudenza a fare i suoi editti intorno a la riforma del regno et de la religione, di che non sarebbe similmente bene parlare, se non finita la guerra, per non necessitar tutti gli erettici ad unirsi con li ribelli; ma divenuto il Re padrone senza contrasto potrebbe rimediarsi con quei modi che gl'insegnasse l'occasione et il tempo, tra quali non ne volendo pigliare dei più gagliardi, sicurissimi saranno il prohibire tutte le assemblee et congregationi di coloro de le nove religioni, lasciando per le conscienze, acciò non vedendosi nè conoscendosi, così facilmente dispersi, s'anichilassero col tempo; similmente il non dare ad alcuno ugonotto o sospetto d'eresia ufficio o dignità di sorte alcuna, acciò non possano far male et sostentare gl'altri, et anco acciò quei nobili che per ambitione si sono fatti eretici, per la medesima ambitione diventino cattolici. Ma ottimo mezo sarà a ridure quelle genti minute spogliate di capi d'aiuto di nobili et d'ufficiali, oltre all'esempio del Re così pio et devoto a la vera religione, la diligenza che si dovria porre alquanto migliore, che non s'è fatto sino a qui, nell'ellettione de' prelati et pastori, et massime de' vescovi, pigliando coloro che per bontà di vita

[26] Catherine de Bourbon-Albret (d. 1604).

et per dottrina son veramente degni d'esser preposti a la cura dell'anime et del grege di Christo; et sopra questo si debbe di qua scriver continuamente in Francia al Re et a la Regina, et fargliene parlare da i Nontii Apostolici et da altri devoti religiosi, acciò le cose spirituali si dieno per cagion spirituale et non per rispetto temporale, come s'è fatto da quel maledetto concordato[27] in qua a beneplacito d'ogni sorte di gente; et acciò finalmente, sì come per questa porta de mali prelati sono entrati in gran parte in Francia tante eresie, per questa medesima da buoni custodita se ne tornino ad uscire, et così in breve tempo potremo con la gratia di Dio sperare di rivedere il regno di Francia ridotto ne la sua antica religione et devotione et nel suo pristino splendore; et essendo armato di tanti valorosi et esperti soldati di tante artiglierie et municioni con un Re bravo, savio et fortunato et giocondo, quelle arme così gloriose contro gli eretici, con quelle del Re cattolico, del Duca di Savoia et de gl'altri prencipi Italiani, si potrebbe tentare l'impresa de l'empia città di Ginevra, et sradicare quella pestifera pianta, da cui sono nati tanti velenosi frutti, otturare quel fonte infernale, i cui turbidi et apestati rivi hanno macchiato et amorbato il mondo. Il che, piacesse alla bontà divina che potessimo veder a i giorni nostri sotto questo felice Pontificato del S.mo S.r N. Gregorio XIII.

Questa è, Illustrissimo Signor mio, quella relatione che io ho saputo fare de le cose di Francia, ne la quale se fusse stato troppo lungo, dovrà il soggetto di tanti anni, che rechiederebbe un grosso volume, essere in mia diffesa; se havessi detto molte cose o non vere e imperfette, mi scuso d'haver detto quello che so, et che ho inteso da molti, et cavato di diverse scritture, rimettendomi sempre al vero; se finalmente havessi mancato o nel ordine, o nel modo di dire, o in altro, mi diffendo con quello estremo desiderio ch'è in me di servirla, il quale m'ha dato una grande spinta a farmi saltare il fosso, et me la darà sempre gagliarda in ogni cosa dove io conosca di poter mostrare a V.S. Illustrissima l'animo mio, ne la cui buona gratia raccomandandomi, prego Nostro Signore che La faccia tanto felice, quanto Ella merita, et quanto desidera questa corte, cioè infinitamente.

---

[27] The Concordat of 1516 between François I and pope Leo X.

PART III

MARTYRS, RIOTERS AND POLEMICISTS

MARTYRS, MYTHS, AND THE MASSACRE: THE BACKGROUND OF ST. BARTHOLOMEW*

by

DONALD R. KELLEY

How, from a distance of four hundred years, can we obtain a clear view of the Massacre of St. Bartholomew? The refractory powers of time always present difficulties, but in this case our vision is further distorted by a screen of false and conflicting evidence and by an endless stream of partisan debate. Perhaps the answer is that we should discard altogether the idea of describing some objective set of circumstances independent of ideological presuppositions and the passions aroused in witnesses and interpreters. Perhaps we should try rather to restore the event to its various contexts, conceptual as well as historical, and from a point of view that accommodates political and religious consciousness as well as social reality, that recognizes the mythical as well as the historical dimension. For it is upon some such symbolic level that the historical significance of events is to be found.

Over the past four centuries the Massacre of St. Bartholomew has presented many faces. It has been seen as a sensational explosion of violence fired by a half-century of mounting religious hatred; as a tragedy so shocking, according to one contemporary witness, that posterity would never believe it; as a turning point in a great world conflict; as a storm center of religious polemic and a seedbed of political theories; as a legend of gigantic proportions promoted by publicists and sanctioned by men of letters; as a puzzle and topic of debate for generations of historians; as an occasion for Catholic masses, Protestant lamentations, and historical conferences.[1] It was all these and more.

* Copyright Donald R. Kelley. This paper, originally published in *The American Historical Review*, is an offshoot of two projects: a biography, *François Hotman, A Revolutionary's Ordeal* (Princeton, 1973), and a study in progress of sixteenth-century propaganda.
    [1] The most important source material is the anonymous pamphlet literature, which is fairly exhaustively listed in the following publications: Robert Lindsay and John Neu, *French Political Pamphlets, 1547–1648* (Madison, 1969); the *Catalogue de l'histoire de France*, I (Paris, 1845), which is a listing by shelf mark of the Bibliothèque Nationale (BN), principally the range Lb.33 to Lb.35; the catalog of the Bibliothèque de l'Arsenal, unfortunately

It was also an archetypal occurrence that transcended its historical context – transcended it not only in the direction of the future (by endless debates over premeditation, guilt, and consequences) but also in the direction of the past (by seeming to symbolize, summarize, and confirm long-standing fears and anticipations and indeed to repeat earlier misfortunes on a grander scale). It was, in other words, an almost generic human experience that came as no surprise in the event, that followed a familiar pattern in its course, and that would be relived in various ways afterwards.

In order to suggest the basis and dimensions of this historical epiphe-nomenon, we must look beyond the conventional narrative and diplo-matic sources that help to show (in Ranke's view) "what really happened." One of the most convenient as well as fashionable proce-dures is to choose some analyzable model. This seems to be all the more appropriate since the model in this instance does not have to be imported from any of the more structured social disciplines. On the contrary, it is suggested, indeed imposed upon us, by the historical context of the sixteenth-century wars of religion. Here is a clear case of history repeating itself, or at least of men seeing it as a repetition. For the witnesses, participants, and interpreters of the events of late summer 1572 knew what the phenomenon was practically before it happened: it was not a "tumult" or a "disorder" or the suppression of a "conspiracy" as various observers supposed; it was a massacre, by no means unexpected and not even the first in that generation. And they knew what part they might ultimately have to play: it was that highly stylized and stereotyped role called "martyrdom," the most exalted and yet in some ways the simplest form of sainthood. The fundamental psychological model for this phenomenon, then (again with a nominal bow to intellectual fashion), was what can only be called the martyr complex.[2]

The remaining problem is where to find reflections of this model, or in other words, how to gain access to this aspect of the Protestant conscience. The most obvious and direct source would seem to be that

unpublished, in nine MS vols. (8ºH. 12868); and F.-A. Isambert et al., eds., Recueil général des anciennes lois françaises (29 vols.; Paris, 1821–1833), vol. XII.

[2] A convenient bibliography on the question of martyrdom may be found in W. H. C. Frend, Martyrdom and Persecution in the Early Church (New York, 1967). In all the massive literature I find no useful studies from a psychohistorical or sociohistorical point of view. General Catholic treatments – of which the best is perhaps Henri Leclercq's in Fernand Cabrol and Henri Leclercq, eds., Dictionnaire d'archéologie chrétienne et de liturgie (Paris, 1924–1953), vol. X, Pt. 2 – tend to be so rigidly legalistic and orthodox that Protestant experiences do not even come into the discussion.

most human and down-to-earth variety of Protestant historiography, the martyrology. The tradition of latter-day martyrs was inherent in Protestant self-consciousness from the beginning – Luther's stand at Worms in 1521, so reminiscent of Hus's a century before, was potentially that of a martyr – but not for another generation did this tradition take a consciously literary form. The first fruits came within a few years and showed a pronounced family resemblance. Most significant were Jean Crespin's *The History of the Martyrs* and the first Latin version of John Foxe's *Acts and Monuments*, both appearing in 1554, in Geneva and Strasbourg respectively. Ludwig Rabe's *Stories of God's Chosen Witnesses and Martyrs*, published in Strasbourg in 1552, antedated these two but was limited to martyrs in antiquity until later, derivative editions. Also related were Heinrich Pantaleone's *History of the Martyrs*, Johann Sleidan's great history of the Reformation, published in Strasbourg in 1555 and soon translated into German, French, and English, and Matthias Flaccius Illyricus' *Catalog of the Witnesses of Truth*, published in Basel in 1556.[3]

Though independently conceived, these works were all products of the international Protestant community and had a collective, to some extent coöperative, character. The links between Geneva and Strasbourg, the two leading Calvinist centers, were particularly strong and were strengthened by the presence of the exiles from Marian England. Crespin was in close touch with Calvin's friend Sleidan, drew upon Sleidan's book, and in 1556 published a French translation of it in Geneva. For later versions of his own *History* Crespin drew also upon Foxe's concomitantly growing *Book of Martyrs*. Foxe himself had gone to Strasbourg in 1555 and then settled in Basel to continue his work, but he continued to receive materials from his friend Edmund Grindal, and no doubt indirectly from Sleidan. Foxe also made use of Flaccius Illyricus' *Catalog*, which was printed in 1556 by Foxe's own publisher, Johann Oporinus. In addition Foxe's work was continued by Pantaleone, who was also Sleidan's German translator. The relation of Rabe, a leading theologian in Strasbourg's Lutheran congregation, is not known, but in any case it seems clear that the first generation of martyrologists constituted something approaching a literary circle, a kind

3 Ludwig Rabe, *Der heiligen aus erwohlten Gottes Zeugen Bekennen und Martyren* (Strasbourg, 1552), with a treatment of the modern period in the expanded edition (Strasbourg, 1571); Jean Crespin, *Le livre des martyrs* ([Geneva], 1554); John Foxe, *Commentarii Rerum in Ecclesia Gestarum* (Strasbourg, 1554), dedicated to Christoph von Württemberg, 31 Aug. 1554; Heinrich Pantaleone, *Martyrum Historia* (Basel, 1563); Johann Sleidan, *De Statu Religionis et Reipublicae, Carolo Quinto, Caesare, Commentarii* (Strasbourg, Sept. 1556); Matthias Flaccius Illyricus, *Catalogus Testium Veritatis* (Basel, 1556).

of Protestant pleiade of the exile circuit, which drew upon a common fund of experience, a common ideological commitment, a common historical perspective, and a common reliance upon what Foxe called the "miracle" of printing.[4]

In many respects the groundbreaking work was Crespin's, and for France, certainly, it provided the model. Crespin was himself an exile from the Netherlands and, along with his friend François Baudouin, had barely escaped from his native Artois with his skin. That was in 1545. Afterwards Crespin settled in Geneva, set up his printing press, and launched into his life's work. The *History of Martyrs* was based on a wide range of printed and unprinted sources and on several other independent works, including those of Foxe, Antoine de La Roche Chandieu, and François Hotman, the first historian of the Massacre of St. Bartholomew. Crespin also drew on the *Ecclesiastical History of the Reformed Churches of France*, long attributed to Theodore Beza. The *History of Martyrs* appeared in successively augmented and altered editions between 1554 and 1570 (the last published by Crespin) and thereafter was continued by Simon Goulart, the prolific polemicist who issued the most comprehensive edition in 1619, when he had succeeded Beza as head of the Genevan church. This book is the centerpiece, as far as France is concerned, of the modern martyrological canon.[5]

Perhaps the most fundamental theme of this whole genre was, in

---

[4] For some of these complex interrelations, see G. Moreau, "Contribution à l'histoire du livre des martyrs," *Bulletin de la Société de l'histoire du protestantisme français*, CIII (1957), 173–99.

[5] Besides the invaluable edition by Daniel Benoît of Crespin and Simon Goulart, *Histoire des martyrs* (Toulouse, 1885–1889), see Arthur Piaget and Gabriel Berthoud, *Notes sur le livre des martyrs de Jean Crespin* (Neuchâtel, 1930); C.-L. Frossard, *Le Livre des martyrs de Jean Crespin* (Paris, 1880); and more generally, Ferdinand Vander Haeghen et al., *Bibliographie des martyrologies protestants néerlandais*, II (The Hague, 1890); also the article on Crespin in Eugène Haag and Émile Haag, eds., *La France protestante* (2d ed.; Paris, 1877–1888); the notes to Calvin's correspondence in Calvin, *Opera Quae Supersunt Omnia*, ed. J. W. Baum, Eduard Cunitz, et al. (Strasbourg, 1863–1900), vols. XXXVIII and XXXIX; and J.-F. Gilmont, "Une édition inconnue du martyrologie de Jean Crespin," *Bibliothèque d'Humanisme et Renaissance*, XXX (1969), 363–71. The latter article and that by Moreau ("Contribution à l'histoire du livre des martyrs," p. 174) refer to the work of E. E. Halkin and his students, which is important though devoted mostly to the martyrs of Belgium and the Netherlands. On Rabe's book, see Robert Foncke, *Duitse Vlugschriften van de Tijd over het Proces en de Terechtstelling van de Protestanten Frans en Nikolaas Thys te Mechelen* (Antwerp, 1937), pp. 60–65; William Haller, *Foxe's Book of Martyrs and the Elect Nation* (London, 1963), pp. 55–73. The other related works are Antoine de La Roche Chandieu, *Histoire des persecutions et martyrs de l'eglise de Paris depuis l'an 1557* (Lyons, 1563), BN, Rés. Ln.25. 91; J. W. Baum and Eduard Cunitz, eds., *Histoire ecclésiastique des églises réformées au royaume de France* (Paris, 1883); [François Hotman], *De Furoribus Gallicis* ("Edinburgh" [probably Basel], 1573); and [Hotman], *Gasparis Colinii Castelonii, Magni Quondam Franciae Amiralii Vita* (hereafter *Vita Colinii*) (n.p., 1575).

Crespin's words, "the conformity of the modern history of the martyrs with that of antiquity." This parallel was perhaps what Lefèvre d'Étaples had in mind when he began to compile his *Agonies of the Martyrs*, as did Rabe, who referred explicitly to the "proto-martyrs" of antiquity. "The memory of the first persecutions," as Chandieu put it, "is a school that teaches how to remain true to one's calling." Indeed the purpose of collecting these biographical accounts included all of the basic ingredients of the humanist prescription for history. They offered "consolation," as Crespin wrote in his first preface; they constituted a treasury of *exempla* for imitation and a kind of moral and anagogical "mirror" for Christians; and they were commemorative, preserving for posterity the "deeds and writings" of exemplary men of faith.[6]

Yet there is no doubt that these humanist commonplaces were transformed by their conscription into the service of militant Protestantism. The biographical form of martyrology resembled less the *de viris illustribus* of classical tradition than the *vitae sanctorum* of the medieval Church. In each biography Crespin wrote, it was his intention to describe the doctrine as well as the life of the martyr and above all his "happy ending"; and to suit this purpose Crespin did not hesitate to stretch the already flexible standards of sixteenth-century editorship, improving in various ways upon the texts even of original documents. Chandieu took pride in declaring his "fidelity" to truth and especially to his sources, but his partisanship was still more flagrant. The purpose of his book was both to afford "profit" to his brothers and to demonstrate the justice of his "Cause" to the "poor ignorant ones" outside of it. The book was quite literally a call to arms. "We are not in this world to rest," he declared, "but rather to fight."[7]

The most direct source of inspiration for these martyrologies was clearly the Protestant view of ecclesiastical history, as variously expressed by Luther, Melanchthon, and Calvin. "From all authors and histories," declared Flaccius Illyricus, "it is evident that our church ... is truly ancient and takes its origin from the time of Christ and the apostles."[8] In the subsequent life of this true church the persecutions of the faithful constituted a major source of continuity, which according

---

[6] Crespin, *Histoire des martyrs*, I, prefaces of 1570 and 1554, *passim;* [Lefèvre d'Étaples], *Agones Martyrium Mensi Ianuarii. Libro Primo* (Paris, 1529; no more published); Rabe, *Heiligen aus erwohlten Gottes Zeugen Bekennen und Martyren* (1571), II; Chandieu, *Histoire des persecutions*, p. xiii.

[7] Chandieu, *Histoire des persecutions*, p. xxviii.

[8] Flaccius Illyricus, *Catalogus Testium Veritatis*, preface.

to Crespin paralleled the progress of Grace on earth and indeed represented its carnal counterpart. "The blood of martyrs is the seed of the church" was the invariably quoted motto of Tertullian, and its life-giving force was continuous over the centuries. Moreover, like Christian tradition in general and in sharp contrast to the national orientation of pagan historiography, the history of martyrs was truly universal in scope and included, as Crespin remarked, "all conditions, ages, sexes, and nations."[9] It differed from medieval historiography, too, especially from the saints' lives with which it had undeniable resemblances, in that it was concerned not with the idolatrous relics but with the spiritual legacy of the faithful – with their "words and deeds." Like the view of eccleasiastical tradition held by Melanchthon and Flaccius Illyricus, the view of the Crespin-Goulart martyrology was not merely "human" but doctrinal or confessional.

Between the first, archetypal age of Christian martyrs and the moderns came a time that seemed darker to Crespin than it did to many of the most critical of humanists (which may serve as a reminder, though surely not a revelation, that the myth of the "Dark Ages" was as much a creation of the Reformation as it was of the Renaissance). After the primitive church came the papal monarchy – "la monarchie papistique" is Crespin's phrase – and then, at a still lower level, a third age ridden with Scholasticism, canon law, relic worship, and other forms of idolatry.[10] Throughout this period there was a tradition of "pure religion," but it was tenuous and took the form only of scattered "witnesses to the truth" – "precursors" is the word modern historians prefer for this still no less mythical phenomenon. Finally came the revival of true doctrine begun by Luther, which brought with it, according to Crespin, a renaissance of martyrdom as well.

So much for martyrology as a model. The original, martyrdom itself, is more difficult to define. A legal concept, a value judgment, a psychological condition, a social role, a weapon of propaganda – again it was all these, and more. The idea, if not the terminology, long antedated Christianity. As early as the fifth century, for example, Athenians killed in war were assured of deification; and this notion of dying in battle for a just cause has always been associated with that of martyr-

---

[9] Crespin, *Histoire des martyrs*, I, 1; Chandieu, *Histoire des persecutions*, p. lxii. See also Hans Campenhausen, *Die Idee der Martyrium in der alten Kirche* (Göttingen, 1964), and the references there to Augustine, Luther and Calvin.

[10] Crespin, *Histoire des martyrs*, I, 41; see also Heinrich Bullinger, *Origines Errorum* (Zurich, 1549).

dom.[11] But it was Christianity that adopted the Greek term *martys* to this general behavior pattern. Although the original signification was lost in the Latin West, Protestant martyrologists quite consciously, in the spirit of Biblical humanism, restored it and identified the martyrly condition with one "testifying" to the faith.[12] It was not the fact of death, in other words, but the inner attitude that admitted one to the pantheon of martyrs and so, though theologically this could not be explicit, to the certainty of salvation as well as earthly immortality. The vital importance of the act of testifying in early Protestantism is further highlighted by the counterconcept – "Nicodemitism" was the term coined by Calvin in 1543 – referring to the concealment of one's faith, one of the most heinous of all sins.

Martyrdom was a highly conventional as well as highly painful process: it was a form of mimesis – *imitatio Christi* with a vengeance. And to follow Christ, "captain of the martyrs," as Crespin put it, entailed a heavy weight of ritual, rhetoric, etiquette, and symbolism, as reflected in interrogations, confessions of faith, execution scenes, crowd reactions, and contemporary graphic representations. The stereotyped character of the role is clearly evident in the martyrologies – not only in the "ten marks of the martyr," which Crespin established for purposes of identification and as the Protestant equivalent of canonization, but also in the unarticulated categories, including the status of the accused and the types of punishment, which modern scholars have extracted and applied in an almost quantitative fashion.[13] These categories were confirmed, and in some cases created, by the more or less predictable reactions of established authority, which in France was determined to uproot all heresy. The result was to intensify the impression of Protestants that they were recapitulating the experiences of early Christians – confronting the same style of interrogation, the same inseparable charges of blasphemy and sedition, and the same sorts of repression and punishments. It may be added that they also

[11] Ernst H. Kantorowicz, "*Pro Patria, Mori* in Medieval Political Thought," *American Historical Review*, LVI (1950–1951), 472; included also in his *Selected Studies* (New York, 1965), p. 308.

[12] See H. A. M. Hoppenbrouwers, *Recherches sur la terminologie du martyre de Tertullien à Lactance* (Nijmegen, 1961); Carlo Ginzburg, *Il Nicodemitismo* (Turin, 1970).

[13] Crespin, *Histoire des martyrs*, preface of 1570. A modern example is Piaget and Berthoud, *Notes sur le livre des martyrs*, drawing upon Vander Haeghen, *Bibliographie des martyrologies*. Such attempts deserve to be followed up by more statistically grounded studies, not only along the lines suggested by Geoffrey Nuttall ("The English Martyrs, 1535–1680," *Journal of Ecclesiastical History*, XXII [1971], 191–97), but also, and indeed at the same time, along those of Lacey Baldwin Smith ("English Treason Trials and Confessions in the Sixteenth Century," *Journal of the History of Ideas*, XV [1954], 471–98).

anticipated the same kind of vengeance, that is, the decline and fall of the persecuting state; for such was the judgment often expressed by Protestants about the fate of France in the later sixteenth century.[14]

It is not going too far to suggest that the coherence of the modern tradition of martyrs was created as much by external pressures as by the sharing of a common ideology and a common "Cause."[15] Catholic attempts to discredit individual martyrs only provided further publicity. Stories about last-minute recantations were always being circulated, remarked Erasmus, rejecting one such rumor about Louis Berquin, the first notable French martyr (who indeed, against Erasmus' advice, had chosen to stand upon his conscience).[16] Catholics were always as ready to attribute a "Virgin, intercede for me" to a man about to be killed as Protestants were to find a martyrly defiance; what counted most, however, was the fact of execution. The Catholic solution was to create a kind of countermythology about heretics and, ultimately, an "antimartyrological" tradition to undo the work of Crespin and his fellow authors.[17] In ideological wars, it seems, demonology has often been the response to hagiography.

This dialogue was also pursued on the official level. From the mid-1520s Protestants were plagued by a wide range of repressive legislation that constituted a kind of mirror image of their own propaganda and was an almost continuous effort to regulate their behavior on every level. The legislation was not always consistent (alternating between prescribing banishment and forbidding emigration, for example, and between controlling the printing press and abolishing it altogether), but its tone was unmistakable. Except for intermittent periods of crisis or compromise, it reflected an almost totalitarian, off-with-their-heads attitude toward heresy and disobedience that was hardly less intense than the fanaticism of the Huguenots themselves. The royal ordinances are filled with repetitive orders banning weapons, expelling vagabonds and such dangerous elements, forbidding Protestants the right to inheritance, officeholding, and burial, and prescribing death for the printing, selling, or even possession of heretical or seditious literature and for the convening of "illicit assemblies." Again and

---

14 See, e.g., Chandieu, *Histoire des persecutions*, p. lxv.
15 "La cause," i.e. of the Huguenots, became a central theme of debate between Protestants and Catholics immediately following St. Bartholomew. See esp. Pierre Charpentier, *Epistola ad Franciscum Portum* (n.p., 1572); Franciscus Portus, *Responsio* (n.p., 1573); Jean de Montluc, *Oratio* ... (Paris, 1573).
16 Erasmus, *Opus Epistolarum Des. Erasmi Roterdami*, ed. P. S. Allen and H. M. Allen, VIII (Oxford, 1934), No. 2188.
17 Jacques Severt, *L'Anti-Martyrologie* ... (Lyons, 1622).

again government policy was declared to be "the extirpation and extermination" of heresy.[18] The most spectacular expression of official disfavor, of course, was the unending series of executions staged as public exhibits at strategic spots, especially market places like the Place de Grève and the Place Maubert.[19] It was this campaign, more than anything else, that gave French Protestantism its persecution complex and Protestant propaganda its paranoid style.

From the time that the winds of Lutheran doctrine first reached France, bracing to some, to others bringing an odor of heresy and sedition, the production of martyrs became a familiar feature of religious opposition. In many cases, of course, the pattern of early Christianity was consciously and pridefully followed. From the execution of the self-styled hermit Jean Vallière on 8 August 1523, the honor roll of this special echelon of the elect grew and was carefully preserved by religious chroniclers and martyrologists. From 1534 – the notorious "year of the placards," when heretical posters were distributed in the streets of Paris and even affixed to the king's chamber door in the castle of Amboise – the official reaction became more intense, and within a few months the list of martyrs increased considerably. It was at this time, Crespin reported, that the practice of cutting off the tongues of heretics before execution was initiated, although this symbolic act was notably unsuccessful in silencing French Protestantism in general.[20]

It was the "miracle" of printing that gave Protestantism its voice, but this same miracle also produced one most unattractive offshoot – the institution of preventive censorship. Book burning was by no means a Catholic monopoly, as Luther's sensational act of throwing the corpus of canon law into the fire demonstrates, but it was specifically Protestant literature that furnished most of the fuel at the beginning. Bearing witness in the embarrassingly public form of print often entailed equally drastic retaliation by established authority; and condemning and destroying books may well be regarded as one of the preliminaries of martyrdom itself, since more than one printer and propagandist followed his books into the flames. So it was with Berquin, so it would be with Étienne Dolet (that unwilling "martyr

---

[18] Isambert, *Recueil*, XII, No. 128 (10 June 1525), No. 211 (29 Jan. 1534), No. 367 (23 July 1543), No. 382 (24 July 1557).
[19] See John Viénot, *Promenades à travers le Paris des martyrs, 1523–59* (Paris, 1913).
[20] Crespin, *Histoire des martyrs*, I, 297.

of the Renaissance" who did in fact recant),[21] and so it would have been with Calvin and Beza if they had returned to France.

One crucial factor in the ideological polarization of society was the alienation of the younger generation. A year before the affair of the placards there was an indication of this alienation in an edict that sought to bring greater discipline into the University of Paris. Specifically the order banned "the impudent books of the heretics" and called for interrogation of younger students if such books were found in their possession. The edict also frowned upon long whiskers (*prolixa barba*) worn by masters, and it was later derided by Beza, a student in these years, as the "edict of the beards."[22] In the course of the reaction to the placards (in which university persons were deeply implicated), François I issued a special warning to the university community about the danger of heresy. "I pray that you ... be especially solicitous of the youth," he told the faculty in the spring of 1535, "and see that they are well instructed and indoctrinated [*indoctriner*] so that they do not fall into the evil and forbidden opinions."[23]

This incipient conflict of generations affected the family as well as education. One striking but not unusual example is that of François Hotman, who was converted to the "new opinions" at precisely the time that his father was taking his place on that special tribunal of the Parlement of Paris, the *Chambre ardente*, which took over the official campaign of suppression in 1547. The conflict was so intense that the next spring the younger Hotman made his decision – after a crisis very much like that of his friend Beza a few months later – to break ties with his home and go into exile; and he made quite clear the significance of the martyr complex in his choice. "My father ended his career by oppressing more than a thousand martyrs," he later told Melanchthon. "As long as I was with him he tried to keep me forcibly from impiety, but God kept me for His church, and here I intend to spend the rest of my life." He denounced the way of the Nicodemite and chose Calvin, quite literally, as his new "father." "He [Hotman] abandoned the hope of a fine inheritance," Calvin later told Heinrich Bullinger, "in order to fight for Christ."[24] A contemporary scholar

---

[21] R. C. Christie, *Etienne Dolet, The Martyr of the Renaissance: 1508–1546* (London, 1899).

[22] Beza to Maclou Popon, 7 May 1542, in Beza, *Correspondance*, ed. Fernand Aubert and Henri Meylan (Paris, 1960—), I, 43.

[23] François I, qtd. in C. E. Bulaeus, *Historia Universitatis Parisiensis* (Paris, 1673), VI, 252–53.

[24] François Hotman to Melanchthon, 24 May 1556, BN, MS Dupuy 797, fol. 212ᵛ. The record of the elder Hotman's activities has been published by Nathaniel Weiss, *La Chambre ardente* (Paris, 1889); the son's conversion and flight may be followed through his corre-

has suggested that the martyr is a kind of religious adventurer,[25] and it was in some such spirit that Hotman, like many another young man in these years, committed this act of rebellion.

In the spring of 1549 Hotman left Geneva (in the company of Beza, who had just decided not to go into the printing business with Crespin) to take a position in the Calvinist academy of Lausanne. Even here Hotman was not out of reach of the royal campaign of persecution. Less than four years later five students from Lausanne, on their way to join congregations in southern France, were imprisoned by the Catholic authorities of Lyons and became a *cause* more *célèbre* than that of the placards. Despite Calvin's efforts and despite pleas from various Swiss cities these young men were condemned in 1553 and, one by one, were burned at the same stake. Crespin publicized the fate of these latter-day "martyrs of Lyons" by printing their prison correspondence with Calvin in the first edition of his *History*, which appeared the following year (and which provided Sleidan with his account).[26] Whether these letters were authentic or assembled in some way by Crespin himself, they provided most effective Protestant propaganda and took their place in the martyrological tradition.

The creation of martyrs seriatim was alarming enough, especially when it was the result of institutional persecution, but far worse was the creation of martyrs en masse. According to a famous distinction of the Huguenot historian Agrippa d'Aubigné, massacre victims, though their names often went unrecorded, constituted a second type of martyr, and these were still more disturbing to the Protestant conscience.[27] The first sensational episode was the notorious persecution of the Waldensians in Mérindol, which Crespin called "as memorable as anything within the memory of man" and in fact thought worthy of a separate volume.[28] In 1545 a veritable campaign of extermination was waged in which twenty-two villages were destroyed and hundreds of persons killed; others were put to flight, and many went to Geneva, as was becoming increasingly common. This episode, together with

spondence with Calvin, published in the *Opera*. See Calvin to Bullinger, 25 Nov. 1549 (*Opera*, vol. XLIV, No. 1324).

[25] Michael Walzer, *The Revolution of the Saints* (London, 1965), p. 9. This study contains many interesting suggestions concerning the psychology of martyrdom.

[26] Crespin, *Histoire des martyrs*, II, 595.

[27] Agrippa d'Aubigné, *Histoire universelle* (Paris, 1616–1620), ed. Alphonse de Ruble (Paris, 1886–1909), I, 227.

[28] Crespin, *Histoire des martyrs*, II, 381; Crespin, *Histoire memorable de la persecution et saccagement du peuple de Merindole et Cabrieres* ... ([Geneva], 1556). See also Isambert, *Recueil*, XII, No. 316 (8 Nov. 1540).

the work of the *Chambre ardente*, haunted Protestants with the prospect of martyrdom or exile, which represented a kind of political martyrdom. Further incidents and the repressive legislation of the 1550s served to magnify such fears among the Huguenots, as they were beginning to be called, as well as to bring civil war closer.

Such fears played a part, too, in that complex set of uprisings referred to as the Conspiracy of Amboise, which such Protestants as Hotman, Beza, and Crespin looked upon as in effect the opening phase of the wars of religion. The conspiracy, brewing already in the fall of 1559 after the death of King Henri II, aimed at breaking the power of the Guise family by gaining possession of the young King François II. It was further stirred up by the famous trial of Anne du Bourg, who was executed at the end of that year.[29] In his responses to interrogators and in his last words, widely publicized by Crespin and others, du Bourg provided a *locus classicus* not only for Huguenot political propaganda but also for the tradition of martyrs.

The conspiracy itself was a fiasco. Hotman, one of the conspirators as well as the historian of this attempt to overthrow the Guise "tyranny," described the terrible fate of the captured "rebels." Some of them were hanged from the parapets of the castle of Amboise and others decapitated, and Hotman quoted in particular the words of his old friend the Sieur de Villemongis: "Having dipped his hands in the blood of his headless companions, he lifted them as high as possible to the heavens and cried, 'Here is the blood of your children, O Lord; for this you shall be avenged.'"[30] This scene, depicted in an often-reproduced contemporary engraving,[30a] was another to treasure in that martyrological canon that Hotman and Crespin were in the process of compiling.

The villain of this piece, of course, was the cardinal of Lorraine. He was denounced a few weeks later by Hotman as the "Tiger of France" in a pamphlet that was in effect the *J'accuse* of the religious wars. The cardinal, supported by his brother, the duc de Guise, was the true conspirator, Hotman charged, the one responsible for spilling the blood of so many innocents. "If Caesar was killed trying to gain the sceptre justly," he asked, "can we permit you to live, who pretend

---

[29] Crespin, *Histoire des martyrs*, II, 675.

[30] [Hotman], *L'histoire du tumulte d'Amboyse* (Strasbourg, 1560), BN, Lb.[32]. 15; see also [Hotman], *Vita Colinii*, p. 33.

[30a] [Editor's note: when published in *The American Historical Review* (LXXVII, 1333), this article included a reproduction of "The Execution of Conspirators at Amboise, 1560," also to be found in Jean Héritier, *Catherine de Medici*, tr. Charlotte Haldane (New York, 1963), facing p. 208.]

to it unjustly?" It must be added that Hotman himself was responsible for the creation of at least one more martyr, for during the summer the printer of his *Tiger* was seized by the police, who were apparently chasing a murderer at the time. The printer, a certain Martin Lhommet, was executed a month later in the Place Maubert near the university. Only three copies of Hotman's book seem to have survived: one in Strasbourg, one in Switzerland, and the other in Paris, which was to be discovered in the nineteenth century, reprinted, and made the center of an extensive controversy over the "freedom of the press."[31]

The next two years were a time of indecision, wavering duplicity, and futile attempts at compromise. Persecutions continued, especially against the Waldensians, and a recent historian has spoken with justice of "the impossible toleration of the Colloquy of Poissy" in the fall of 1561.[32] Few hoped to prevent war; it was only a question of time, and the time came the following spring. The spark was provided by the tragic confrontation at Vassy between a force led by the duc de Guise and a Huguenot congregation – the "Sarajevo of the religious wars," as it has been called.[33] As Guise and his men approached, perhaps looking for trouble, they heard singing from the Protestant church – "I am afflicted and ready to die" is one of the verses from the psalm – and were outraged at this violation. Whichever side cast the first stone, the result was seventy-four Huguenots dead or dying and a political situation out of control. "If you will forgive a snap judgment," wrote one observer, "this is the beginning of a tragedy that we shall all be playing."[34] No Protestant hesitated to regard the affair as a full-fledged massacre. So within a few weeks Hotman and other observers represented it, and so later it would be interpreted by Huguenot historians, again including Hotman as well as Crespin.

The blood of these martyrs rapidly nourished the seeds of civil war. Barely a month later Huguenot forces gathered at Orléans and prepared for a major conflict. Hotman was among them and made the connection most explicitly. "In this event," he remarked of the affair

---

[31] [Hotman], *Epistre envoiée au tigre de la France* (Strasbourg, 1560), ed. Charles Reade, *Le Tigre de 1560* (Paris, 1875), and the offprints among Reade's papers located in Paris, Bibliothèque de la Société de l'histoire du protestantisme français, MS 816, vol. IV. See also *Calendar of State Papers, Venetian*, VIII, 234.
[32] Alain Dufour, "L'impossible tolérance au Colloque de Poissy," *Musées de Genève*, n.s., IV (1963), 8–11.
[33] H. O. Evennett, *The Cardinal of Lorraine and the Council of Trent* (Cambridge, 1930), p. 21.
[34] Étienne Pasquier, *Les Lettres* (Paris, 1617), Bk. iv, No. 15. Other accounts of the massacre are in Crespin and Goulart, *Histoire des martyrs*, II, 209; and *Mémoires de Condé* (London, 1743–1745), III, 111.

of Vassy, "our leaders see the signal for a general massacre being prepared by our enemies in all parts of the kingdom."[35] Underlying this view one may see not only a kind of conspiracy theory of history, which was to become increasingly common, but also a doctrine of political expediency, which was to become a central feature of Huguenot propaganda and self-justification.[36] In either case the Massacre of Vassy was transformed into a myth – not a "nonevent" but a kind of "hyper-event," which served at once as an excuse for resistance, as a means of shifting all guilt to the Guise party, and as a most satisfactory explanation for the coming of the wars of religion.

There were other "massacres" over the next decade, of course, but Vassy remained the archetype; and for the rest of the century Huguenots operated upon the assumptions generated – or rather confirmed – by this tragedy. The Massacre at Vassy fitted in perfectly with the belief, based upon countless statements of official policy, that the government was literally intent upon the "extermination" of those of the religion. The theme recurred again and again over the next decade. The most famous illustration is the meeting in 1565 between Catherine de Medici and the duke of Alva. Although their conversations were generally inconclusive, they immediately provoked suspicions among Huguenots about a universal Catholic conspiracy, turning upon a Paris-Madrid axis linked in turn with the Council of Trent, whose canons and decrees had been published only the year before. This meeting between Catherine and the duke of Alva has always been associated with St. Bartholomew seven years later, but it should be understood that the legend surrounding it came earlier and was in fact part of the general fear of that Florentine woman, Catherine de Medici. Hotman later published a letter by her, supposedly written in 1569 and intercepted; and although it is undoubtedly spurious, it sounded quite convincing to her Protestant critics. "To restore the crown of France," she is supposed to have written, "there is no better way than to kill all the Huguenots."[37]

---

[35] Hotman to Bonifacius Amerbach, 12 Apr. 1562, Basel, Universitätsbibliothek, MS G. II. 19, fol. 148r.

[36] See, e.g., *Advertissement sur la falseté de plusieurs mensonges semez par les rebelles* (Paris, 1562) (Lindsay and Neu, *French Political Pamphlets*, No. 258), which is a Catholic response to the *Histoire comprenant en brief ce qui est advenu depuis le partement des sieurs de Guise* ... (Orléans, 1562), BN, Lb.33. 48; see also *Bref discours et veritable des principales coniurations de ceux de la maison de Guyse* ... (Paris, 1565) (Lindsay and Neu, No. 407), one of the many pamphlets carrying on the attack inaugurated by Hotman's *Tigre*.

[37] Qtd. in [Hotman], *Vita Colinii*, p. 57. On "le desseing de Bayonne," see, e.g., the Huguenot pamphlets collected as *Les requests, protestations, remonstrances et advertissements, faits par monseigneur le prince de Condé* ... (Orléans, 1567), BN, Lb.33. 206; and *Discours au vray des*

It was at this same time, that is, during the third war, that Admiral Gaspard de Coligny emerged as the leader of the Huguenots and as a figure of international influence. Protestants began looking to him as their savior, and indeed a number of cities and congregations placed themselves under his protection. In September he was officially condemned by the Parlement and deprived of his offices. According to this *arrêt*, which was printed in eight languages and widely distributed, Coligny was "giltie of traison, distourber and breaker of peace, ennemy of repos, and tranquillitie of the commonwealth: the Captain, author, and ringleder of the rebellion, conspiracie, and faction that hath bin made against the King and his State." It is very interesting to note that when Coligny perished in the Massacre of St. Bartholomew three years later, this same charge was resurrected and in fact the *arrêt* itself republished.[38]

In these same years there was a growing tendency among Protestants to attach these fears and threats to malicious foreign, especially Italian, influence. Among other suspected imports during the early stages of the religious wars came "Papemania" and the practice of assassination – murder "Italian style," as Hotman's friend Henri Estienne called it – which was another source of martyrs.[39] Nor was the overall apprehension in any way allayed by specific pacification agreements, which on the contrary were suspected of being duplicitous arrangements made to trick Huguenots into letting down their guard. This was especially the case with the "limping and uneasy peace" of Saint-Germain of 1570, which Huguenots would later condemn as an evil trick and, according to one of Hotman's imaginative friends, as the diseased offspring of Catherine and her alleged consort, that devil of a cardinal (of Lorraine), who was accumulating his own share of "legends."[40]

All of these proliferating and intertwining anti-Catholic legends

---

conseils et moyens qu'on a tenus pour exterminer la pure doctrine . . . (Heidelberg, 1568), BN, Lb.[33]. 195.

[38] *Arrest de la Court de Parlement contre Gaspart de Colligny, qui fut admiral de France, mis en huict langues, à sçavoir, François, Latin, Italien, Espagnol, Allemant, Flament, Anglois et Escoçois* (Paris, 1569; republished Paris, 1574) (Lindsay and Neu, *French Political Pamphlets*, Nos. 652, 653, 754).

[39] Henri Estienne, *Apologie pour Hérodote*, ed. Paul Ristelhuber (Paris, 1879), I, 353; *La Papemanie de France* (n.p., 1567), Arsenal, 8oH. 12774, vol. I. See also Rabelais, *Pantagruel*, Bk. iv, chap. xlviii.

[40] Anonymous poem, "La Paix Valois," in *Le reveille-matin des François* ("Edinburgh" [Basel?], 1574). See also *Legende de Charles cardinal de Lorraine* in *Memoires de Condé*, vol. VI. In general, see my "Murd'rous Machiavel in France," *Political Science Quarterly*, LXXXV (1970), 545–59; and Salvo Mastellone, *Venalità e Machiavellismo in Francia (1572–1610)* (Florence, 1972).

tended, as legends will do, to group themselves together around a more visible and concrete symbol that could serve as the center of a grander construct. The symbol that finally emerged to take this sovereign position was the figure, or at least the public image, of Catherine's countryman Machiavelli, who came to represent a kind of devilish counterpart to the Protestant martyr ideal. Machiavelli could not assume this posthumous role, however, until there was a crime worthy of his evil genius; and such a "crime" was indeed provided on 24 August 1572. Taken together, this massacre, the Protestant conspiracy theory, and the patterns of martyrdom created a mythology of monumental proportions.

It is in such a conceptual and emotional context, it seems to me, that the events surrounding and succeeding St. Bartholomew's Day 1572 must be understood; and so must the leading actors in the drama. The Huguenot chief Coligny was the very prototype of the Protestant saint, as represented in the official, and indeed hagiographical, account written by Hotman.[41] Coligny's days, even his meals, were filled with prayers, sermons, and psalm singing, and he was most solicitous about spreading the word through education and missionary work as well as by personal example. Yet he never ceased being a fighter, and in the name of these very ideals he had been playing a most dangerous political game, purportedly at the expense of that Tridentine "conspiracy," which by now had taken on the appearance of a Madrid-Rome axis. Indeed he was doing a bit of conspiring himself, though apparently not without royal permission, and had committed himself to supporting William of Orange's projected invasion of the Netherlands. But in July Coligny's credit had fallen off sharply when a force of Huguenot troops, sent to Mons to relieve William's lieutenant Louis of Nassau, was ambushed and slaughtered by the Spanish.

Meanwhile in Paris tensions were mounting. The scheduled wedding of Henri de Navarre and Catherine's daughter Marguerite, a kind of nuptial prefiguring of the conciliatory policy later adopted by the *politiques*, was a hopeful sign; but it had to be postponed because of the death of Henri's mother, Jeanne d'Albret, in June. Stories immediately began to circulate, and to be believed by Huguenots such as Hotman, that she had been poisoned by the enemy. In such a heated atmosphere the wedding was set for 18 August. Alarming rumors

---

[41] [Hotman], *Vita Colinii*, p. 130. See also Crespin and Goulart, *Histoire des martyrs*, III, 663.

continued to fly, and in July Charles IX issued another in a long line of ordinances banning weapons and expelling vagabonds, and *mauvais garçons* within twenty-four hours. Just before the wedding, it seems, Jean de Montluc, a moderate Catholic friend of the Huguenots and a diplomatic agent for Catherine, warned one of Coligny's men to get out of the city. This Coligny himself could not do, and he took up residence in a house belonging, ominously enough, to the family of Anne du Bourg. "I would rather be with you than at court," he wrote to his young and pregnant wife a few hours after the ceremony, "but I must set public advantage above private pleasure."[42]

The first act of the tragedy came on Friday of the same week. On that morning of 22 August, as he was returning from court, Coligny was shot and seriously wounded by a certain Maurevert, called the "king's killer" because of a more successful attempt made against one of Coligny's lieutenants a few years before. The next two days Coligny spent in his quarters, attended by friends and his physician, Ambrose Paré, and visited by embarrassed members of the royal family. Coligny spoke at length and in saintly tones, providing political advice for the king, a confession of faith for his followers, and forgiveness for his would-be assassin, if not for the duc de Guise, whom he held responsible. Already, according to Hotman's secondhand account, Coligny was beginning to sound like a martyr. A royal guard was given to him but was placed under the command of an old enemy. The ban on arms was still in effect, but it did not apply to the king's men, who were rattling their weapons ostentatiously in the streets. So, as Huguenots looked back on the situation, the trap had been set; indeed the events of that weekend all seemed to fall into one terrible pattern.

The second and successful attempt on the admiral early in the morning of 24 August set off the mythopoeic process. "I am ready for death," the admiral had said before the assassin struck, and soon the "Matins of Paris" began. "Away with him, cut of his head and handes,/ And send them as a present to the Pope," the duc de Guise has been represented as saying. The words are Christopher Marlowe's,[43] but

---

[42] Qtd. in [Hotman], *Vita Colinii*, p. 105, but differing significantly from the extant original (which has been published in the *Bulletin de la Société de l'histoire du protestantisme français*, I [1852], 369) by adding a statement to the effect that the admiral would take care not to offend his enemies (presumably to offset the charges of hostility and militancy). See also *Ordonnance du Roy portant injonction à tous ses subjects de vivre en amitié les uns avec les autres* (Paris, 1572), Arsenal, 8°H. 12778, vol. III.

[43] Christopher Marlowe, *The Massacre at Paris*, based on Hotman's well-known *De Furoribus Gallicis*. See Paul Kocher, "François Hotman and Marlowe's *The Massacre at Paris*," *Publications of the Modern Language Association*, LVI (1941), 349–68.

the deed itself has been documented and has taken its place alongside
many other atrocity stories; babies dropped from windows, bodies
stripped and thrown into the Seine, some to be seen for days afterwards, a few as far as Rouen, according to a Huguenot song. As
usual Paris set the fashion for the provinces, and the attacks signaled by
Coligny's murder, carried out by laborers as well as by gentlemen,
spread to a dozen or so towns throughout France. Many Protestants
fled into the countryside. "I am sure that the wild beasts are kinder
than those in human form," Hotman remarked to a friend. Later he
reported that "Huguenot-hunting" – la chasse des huguenots – was becoming a popular sport.[44]

In the international Protestant community the reactions included
shock and outrage but little real surprise. The inhabitants of La
Rochelle had been warning Coligny of some such plot for two months,
Hotman had heard, and throughout France men had been saying
that Coligny was deceived at court.[45] "What an atrocity!" was Beza's
reaction to the admiral's death. "How many times have I predicted
this! How many times did I warn him about it!"[46] Streams of refugees
carried the news in greater detail, but there seems to be little doubt
about the underlying cause of the massacres. The plot was "undoubtedly general and the work of the Council of Trent," declared the
Council of Geneva, which indeed feared that it would extend into
their own territory.[47] During the fall one French agent confessed under
torture that the invasion would be launched from Savoy, and though
the attack did not materialize, the fear continued for the rest of the
century. Hotman, then exiled in Geneva, shared and broadcast this
apprehension about what he called "the Tridentine web and popish
alliance called the Holy League."[48]

One conspicuous sign of the meta-historical impact of the Massacre
was the extremism of the reactions to it from all quarters. The Huguenots, of course, screamed bloody murder. The leaders were all "assassins," Hotman proclaimed, "the likes of whom no age has tolerated."[49]

[44] Hotman to Rodolphe Gualter, 5 Nov. 1573, Zurich, Zentralbibliothek, MS F. 39, fol.
214v. The same phrase is used by Nicolas Pithou, Histoire ecclesiastique de l'eglise pretendue
reformée de la ville de Troyes (published by Charles Recordon as Le Protestantisme en Champagne
[Paris, 1863]), p. 144.
[45] Hotman to William of Hesse, 6 Oct. 1572, published in Ludwig Ehinger, Franz Hot-
mann ("Beiträge zur vaterländischen Geschichte," XIV; Basel, 1896), No. 24.
[46] Beza to Thomas Tilius, 10 Sept. 1572, published in Bulletin de la Société de l'histoire du
protestantisme français, VI (1858), 16.
[47] Registres du Conseil, 4 Sept. 1572, Geneva, Archives d'État, vol. LXVII, fol. 201r.
[48] Hotman to Bullinger, 25 Oct. 1572, Zurich, Zentralbibliothek, MS S. 127, fol. 95r.
[49] Hotman to Abraham Sulzer, 3 Oct. 1572, ibid., fol. 47r. See also Declaration du roy de la

And this specifically included the king, by whose "express command" the deed was admittedly done. On the other side Catholics, arguing that the attacks were designed to crush a Huguenot "conspiracy" arising from the "Theodor-Bezian infection," concluded that it was simply retribution. "There is no gallows, cross, or torture severe enough to punish the crime of a traitor or rebel," one royalist wrote.[50] Others celebrated the event as providential. So François de Belleforest, later one of Hotman's chief critics, declared it to be no less than a miracle; and he found this judgment to be confirmed by the appearance of the great nova (the first in modern history) of November 1572. "I know the heretics will laugh and tax me with superstition," he added.[51] In fact the "heretics" were not laughing and had an explanation of the phenomenon hardly less "superstitious": to them it was the Star of Bethlehem returned, and it signified the salvation to come.

Quantitative estimates were likewise inflated. The massacre was so enormous, said one commentator, "that I doubt if posterity will ever believe it."[52] And in fact posterity has not believed the figures given by contemporary critics. At first Beza himself cried that over 300,000 of his brothers had been killed.[53] Later estimates were commonly placed at 100,000 deaths and revised downwards to 50,000. A decade later a certain "N. Froumenteau" published what purported to be a statistical survey of the costs, social as well as economic, of the religious wars, and his figures offer evidence of the depth of contemporary feeling if not of exact totals. By that date, 1583, Froumenteau estimated that about 765,000 persons had perished in the wars; 76,010 were civilian casualties, and of these 36,000 could be classified as "massacred"; 4,500 bodies had passed Paris on the Seine, while 6,000 had been carried by the Loire. In addition he estimated that 12,000 women and girls had been raped, and he went on to remark that, since this sort of thing so often went unreported, the total was probably

cause et occasion de la mort de l'admiral (Paris, 1572) (Lindsay and Neu, *French Political Pamphlets*, No. 729).

50 Artus Desiré, *La singerie des Huguenots* ... (Paris, 1574), p. 22; *Discours de la mort et execution de Gabriel comte de Montgomery* (Paris, 1574), fol. 2ᵛ (Lindsay and Neu, *French Political Pamphlets*, No. 790).

51 François de Belleforest, *Discours sur l'heur des presages advenus de nostre temps significantz la felicité de regne de nostre roy Charles* (Paris, 18 Nov. 1572), fol. 10ʳ.

52 *Resolution claire et facile sur la question ... de la prise d'armes par les inférieurs* (Rheims, 1577), p. 97, in BN, Lb.³⁴. 103.

53 Beza to Bullinger, 1 Sept. 1572, Zurich, Zentralbibliothek, MS A. 44, p. 679, cited by P. F. Geisendorf, *Théodore de Bèze* (Geneva, 1949), p. 306.

twice as great. If the war continued, he remarked, the total would indeed be 100,000 instead of only 36,000.[54]

Whoever he was, Froumenteau was a Huguenot and had nothing but contempt for the "Machiavellistes" who had so ravaged France. Yet, though his statistics are inflated by partisanship, it should be added that he did make some effort to indicate his sources (*preuves*) and often omitted provincial figures for lack of evidence, so that his conclusions are relatively far closer to reality than those of most chroniclers.[55] While it would be an error to take his figures at face value (as certain nineteenth-century scholars have done), it would be equally mistaken to deny this pioneering work a significant place in the history of statistics, which like other social sciences emerged at least in part from (and has never quite disassociated itself from) ideological conflict. In any case a great effort went into the making of the book, and it testifies again to the enormous intellectual impact of the wars of religion and of St. Bartholomew in particular.

In the field of political thought, of course, the impact of St. Bartholomew was even more spectacular. The Massacre immediately took its place as the pivotal event in the martyrological tradition and became a central force in the flood of propaganda that poured from Protestant presses at a greater than average rate in succeeding years. It was at this point that the enlarged community of martyrs began to take on a more special political significance because of its association with the opposition party led by Henri de Navarre, who succeeded Coligny as the leader of the Huguenots. The point was made best by Beza in his *Right of Magistrates*, a tract so radical that he was refused permission to publish it in Geneva. "And this I conclude," he wrote,

---

[54] The book in question is the fascinating *Secret des finances de France* (n.p., 1581), dedicated to Henri III, by N. Froumenteau (no doubt a pseudonym), a friend of Hotman and author also of the anonymous *Miroir des François* ... (Paris, 1581), *Le cabinet du roy* ... (Paris, 1581), and, if only in part, of the *Reveille-matin*, which is one work that estimates the massacred of St. Bartholomew as 100,000 (p. 78). The first book includes a dialogue between "Provence" and "Le Politique" (who figures also in the *Reveille-matin* and the *Miroir des François*) and a listing, province by province, of the taxes, charges, and expenditures, especially military, over the previous 31 years. The second book discusses the social costs, again province by province (pp. 378–79). The categories of the dead are ecclesiastics, nobles (Catholics and Huguenots distinguished), soldiers (again Catholics and Huguenots), those executed (many for lese majesty), Huguenots "massacred," foreigners, houses destroyed, villages burned and razed, and *filles violées*. Froumenteau's *Preuves* (pp. 401–09) include records of the Chambre des Comptes and *controlles de la gendarmerie* as well as "chronicles and memoirs," but he adds that no "proof" is needed to describe the horror of the massacres.

[55] Froumenteau, *Le secret des finances*, p. 418. The work has not received its due in the history either of economic thought or of statistics; the judgment of Fernand Faure ("France," in John Koren, ed., *The History of Statistics* [New York, 1918], pp. 236–37), contradicting such credulous 19th-century opinions as that of Henri Baudrillart, is probably excessively severe and certainly unhistorical.

"that we must honor as martyrs not only those who have conquered without resistance, and by patience only, against tyrants who have persecuted the truth, but those also who, authorized by law and by competent authorities, devoted their strength to the defense of the true religion."[56] Here is expressed the complete politicization not only of the Calvinist cause but also of the tradition of martyrs – an unmistakable shift from passive to active resistance.

Another conspicious by-product of St. Bartholomew was the mythology, or demonology, associated with Machiavelli, whose ideas of political behavior were widely regarded as the cause both of the Massacre itself and of the political and social degeneration of France in general over the previous ten years and more. Much of this material, especially the *Reveille-Matin* and Hotman's *French Fury*, consisted of highly colored accounts of the event itself or of extravagant elegies of the "hero-martyr" Coligny,[57] but there was also a growing quantity of polemic and theorizing about the problem of war guilt (which has always played so fundamental a role in historical thinking) and about ideas of political resistance, constitutional government, sovereignty, and the structure of society in general. Not only the work of the monarchomachs but also Jean Bodin's *Republic*, which may be taken as a response to the work of the monarchomachs, grappled quite directly with the problems that the Massacre of St. Bartholomew defined in a way that made them impossible any longer to ignore.[58]

---

[56] Beza, *Du droit des magistrats* (Geneva, 1574), critical ed. by R. M. Kingdon (Geneva, 1970), p. 67, and translated in Julian Franklin, ed., *Constitutionalism and Resistance in the Sixteenth Century* (New York, 1969), p. 135.

[57] See, e.g., *Epicedia Illustri Heroi Caspari Colignio ... Beato Christi Martyri, Variis Linguis a Doctis Piisq. Poetis Decantata* (n.p., 1572) (Lindsay and Neu, *French Political Pamphlets*, No. 725), of which Beza's own presentation copy is in the possession of Yale University Library. Professor Samuel Kinser of Northern Illinois University points out a most interesting example of the hero-martyr dichotomy in d'Aubigné's account of Coligny's death. Following the accounts of Jacques-Auguste de Thou (*Historiarum Sui Temporis Opera* [Frankfurt, 1614–1621], I, 993) and of Hotman (*Vita Colinii* and, with some modifications, *De Furoribus Gallicis*), d'Aubigné first represented the admiral, on the point of death, as adopting a hero's stance and lamenting the fact that he was about to be killed at the hands not of a "cavalier" but only of a common servant. But a few years later, in the second edition (1626) d'Aubigné changed the picture so that Coligny appeared as a passive victim, "on his knees beside his bed" and making only the martyrly comment, "My friends, save yourselves." See *Histoire universelle*, III, 313.

[58] For discussions of this large subject, see Ralph Giesey, "The Monarchomach Triumvirs: Hotman, Beza and Mornay," *Bibliothèque d'Humanisme et Renaissance*, XXXII (1970), 41–56; and J. H. M. Salmon, "Bodin and the Monarchomachs," in Horst Denzer, ed., *Jean Bodin. Verhandlungen der internationalen Bodin Tagung in München* (Munich, 1973), pp. 359–78. It has recently been argued that the monarchomach author of the *Vindiciae contra Tyrannos* (n.p., 1578) was not Philippe Du Plessis-Mornay, but rather Johan Junius de Jonge. See Derk Visser, "Junius: The Author of the *Vindiciae contra Tyrannos?*" *Tijdschrift voor Geschiedenis*, LXXXIV (1971), 510–25.

In more concretely historical terms the effect of the Massacre was traumatic. Anticipated for a decade, after its coming it haunted an entire generation of Protestants, who suspected that it might be revived at any time and who were prepared, ideologically if not emotionally, to take their place among the future martyrs. Hotman, for example, having been sent into permanent exile, lived out his remaining eighteen years in almost perpetual fear that the fate he had just barely missed in 1572, and that had claimed so many of his friends, including Petrus Ramus, would overtake him. The tone of his correspondence is consistently that of a victim and even martyr. At one point he was convinced that the pope had hired a man to assassinate him, and in his last years he became obsessed with the idea of dying in battle for his Cause – one of the established "marks of martyrdom." Only the thought of his children, he said, restrained him.[59] In many ways his attitude was typical of the French exile community of his generation, whose politics, perspective, and very lives had been shaped by the Massacre.

Situated as it was at the center of such swirling emotions, revolutionary implications, festering resentments, and indeterminate intellectual repercussions, the Massacre of St. Bartholomew became a legend almost before it happened, and it grew with the telling and with the passage of time. As it furnished a target and motive for endless polemic, so it furnished a target and motive for scholarly debate – a classic "problem" for historians, though ultimately insoluble, at least in the guild-oriented, legend-prone, history-transcending terms of sixteenth-century propaganda, from which we have hardly yet escaped.[60] "The blood of martyrs is the seed of the church": it has also been fuel for the labors of generations of historians, and by now more ink than blood has flowed as a result of the events of that weekend in Paris four hundred years ago. Catholic masses have ceased, Protestant lamentations have been muted, but the historical discussion continues: such is one of the forms, it seems, that myths take in our time.[61]

[59] Hotman to Simon Grynaeus, 27 Nov. 1586, in B. F. Hummel, ed., *Celebrium Virorum ... Epistolae Ineditae* (Nuremberg, 1777), p. 81; and Hotman to Daniel Tossanus, 26 Feb. 1588, in *Hotomanorum Epistolae* (Amsterdam, 1700), No. 162, citing *Aeneid*, Bk. ii, line 353.

[60] Herbert Butterfield, "Lord Acton and the Massacre of St. Bartholomew," in his *Man on His Past* (Cambridge, 1955), pp. 171–201, is a useful survey.

[61] [Editor's note: In his comments on this paper at the Newberry Library Conference, Professor Ralph E. Giesey called attention to two important factors which distinguished the Huguenot martyrs from their early-Christian models – *viz.*, the absence of chiliasm and the frequent recourse to violent resistance in the 16th century. Giesey concluded that "the Protestant use of the term, 'martyr,' therefore, is an episode in the legitimation of their religious ideology or of the politics of language."]

THE RITES OF VIOLENCE: RELIGIOUS
RIOT IN SIXTEENTH-CENTURY FRANCE*

by

NATALIE ZEMON DAVIS

These are the statutes and judgments, which ye shall observe to do in the land, which the Lord God of thy fathers giveth thee . . . . Ye shall utterly destroy all the places wherein the nations which ye shall possess served their gods, upon the high mountains, and upon the hills, and under every green tree:

And ye shall overthrow their altars, and break their pillars and burn their groves with fire; and ye shall hew down the graven images of their gods, and destroy the names of them out of that place [Deuteronomy xii. 1–3].

Thus a Calvinist pastor to his flock in 1562.[1]

If thy brother, the son of thy mother, or thy son, or thy daughter, or the wife of thy bosom, or thy friend, which is as thine own soul, entice thee secretly, saying Let us go serve other gods, which thou hast not known, thou, nor thy fathers . . . Thou shalt not consent unto him, nor hearken unto him . . . But thou shalt surely kill him; thine hand shall be first upon him to put him to death, and afterwards the hand of all the people . . . .

If thou shalt hear say in one of thy cities, which the Lord thy God hath given thee to dwell there, saying, Certain men, the children of Belial are gone out from among you, and have withdrawn the inhabitants of their city, saying Let us go and serve other gods, which ye have not known . . . Thou shalt surely smite the inhabitants of that city with the edge of the sword, destroying it utterly and all that is therein [Deuteronomy xiii. 6, 8–9, 12–13, 15].

And [Jehu] lifted up his face to the window and said, Who is on my side? Who? And there looked out to him two or three eunuchs. And he said, Throw her down. So they threw [Jezebel] down: and some of her blood was sprinkled on the wall, and on the horses: and he trode her under foot . . . . And they went to bury her: but they found no more of her than the skull and the feet and the palms of her hands . . . . And [Jehu] said, This is the

* Copyright The Past and Present Society. The research for this paper has been aided by grants-in-aid from the American Philosophical Society, the American Council of Learned Societies and the University of California, Berkeley.

[1] *Histoire ecclésiastique des églises réformées au royaume de France* (hereafter *Hist. eccl.*), ed. J. G. Baum and E. Cunitz (3 vols.; Paris, 1883–1889), I, 537.

word of the Lord, which he spake by his servant Elijah ... saying, In the portion of Jezreel shall dogs eat the flesh of Jezebel: And the carcase of Jezebel shall be as dung upon the face of the field [II Kings ix. 32–33, 35–37].

Thus in 1568 Parisian preachers held up to their Catholic parishioners the end of a wicked idolater.[2] Whatever the intentions of pastors and priests, such words were among the many spurs to religious riot in sixteenth-century France. By religious riot I mean, as a preliminary definition, any violent action, with words or weapons, undertaken against religious targets by people who are not acting *officially and formally* as agents of political and ecclesiastical authority. As food rioters bring their moral indignation to bear upon the state of the grain market, so religious rioters bring their zeal to bear upon the state of men's relations to the sacred. The violence of the religious riot is distinguished, at least in principle, from the action of political authorities, who can legally silence, humiliate, demolish, punish, torture and execute; and also from the action of soldiers, who at certain times and places can legally kill and destroy. In mid-sixteenth-century France, all these sources of violence were busily producing, and it is sometimes hard to tell a militia officer from a murderer and a soldier from a statue-smasher. Nevertheless, there are occasions when we can separate out for examination a violent crowd set on religious goals.

The sixteenth century itself had its own generalizations about crowd violence. Once in a while it was seen as having a kind of system or sense. In Corpus Christi Day drama, the violence against Christ is represented as a series of formal competitive "games," which hide from His tormentors the full knowledge of what they do.[3] In Dürer's *Martyrdom of the Ten Thousand*, the Persian torturers of the Christians are spaced apart, doing their terrible business in an orderly, methodical way.[4] Most of the time, however, as in Breugel's flaming *Dulle Griet* and *The Triumph of Death*, the image of the crowd was one of chaos.

---

[2] Claude Haton, *Mémoires de Claude Haton contenant le récit des événements accomplis de 1553 à 1592, principalement dans la Champagne et la Brie*, ed. Félix Bourquelot ("Collection de documents inédits sur l'histoire de France," 2 vols. paginated continuously; Paris, 1857), pp. 527–28.

[3] V. A. Kolve, *The Play Called Corpus Christi* (Stanford, 1966), chap. viii. See also L. Petit de Julleville, *Histoire du théâtre en France. Les mystères* (2 vols.; Paris, 1880), II, 391, 408, 444–45. Breugel's *Procession to Calvary* has some of this same gamelike, "orderly" quality.

[4] Philipp Fehl, "Mass Murder, or Humanity in Death," *Theology Today*, XXVIII (1971), 67–68; E. Panofsky, *The Life and Art of Albrecht Dürer* (Princeton, 1955), pp. 121–22. For the range of 16th-century explanations of human violence, see J. R. Hale, "Sixteenth-Century Explanations of War and Violence," *Past and Present*, No. 51 (May 1971), pp. 3–26.

Learned writers talk of grain rioters in Lyons as "the dregs of the populace, with no order, no rein, no leader ... a beast of many heads ... an insane rabble" and of the Paris mob as "an ignorant multitude, collected from all nations ... governed by the appetite of those who stir them up [to] extreme rage, just looking for the chance to carry out any kind of cruelty."[5]

Nowadays this hydra monster has taken on a more orderly shape, as a result of the work of George Rudé, Eric Hobsbawm, E. P. Thompson, Charles Tilly, Emmanuel Le Roy Ladurie and others.[6] We may see these crowds as prompted by political and moral traditions which legitimize and even prescribe their violence. We may see urban rioters not as miserable, uprooted, unstable masses, but as men and women who often have some stake in their community; who may be craftsmen or better; and who, even when poor and unskilled, may appear respectable to their everyday neighbors. Finally, we may see their violence, however cruel, not as random and limitless, but as aimed at defined targets and selected from a repertory of traditional punishments and forms of destruction.

This picture of pre-industrial crowd violence has been drawn primarily from the study of grain and bread riots, tax riots, craft violence, and certain kinds of peasant revolts. The broad spectrum of religious riot, however, has not received analytical attention, except in the case of the anti-Semitic pogrom and the millenarian movement,[7] both of which have evident contemporary significance and

---

[5] Guillaume Paradin, *Memoires de l'histoire de Lyon* (Lyons, 1573), p. 238; *Hist. eccl.*, I, 192–93. See also Christopher Hill, "The Many-Headed Monster in Late Tudor and Early Stuart Political Thinking," in C. H. Carter, ed., *From the Renaissance to the Counter-Reformation. Essays in Honour of Garrett Mattingly* (London, 1966), pp. 296–324.

[6] The literature on crowds and violence is vast. I list here only those works which have especially assisted the preparation of this paper: George Rudé, *The Crowd in History. A Study of Popular Disturbances in France and England, 1730–1848* (New York, 1964); E. J. Hobsbawm, *Primitive Rebels. Studies in Archaic Forms of Social Movement in the 19th and 20th Centuries* (Manchester, 1959); E. P. Thompson, "The Moral Economy of the English Crowd in the Eighteenth Century," *Past and Present*, No. 50 (Feb. 1971), pp. 76–136; Charles Tilly, "Collective Violence in Nineteenth-Century French Cities" (Public Lecture, Reed College, Feb. 1968); "The Chaos of the Living City," forthcoming in Charles Tilly, ed., *The Building of an Urban World;* Charles Tilly and James Rule, *Measuring Political Upheaval* (Princeton, 1965) – I am also grateful to Charles Tilly for his comments on this paper; Emmanuel Le Roy Ladurie, *Les paysans de Languedoc* (2 vols.; Paris, 1966), I, 391–414, 495–508, 607–29; Roland Mousnier, *Fureurs paysannes* (Paris, 1967); M. Mollat and Philippe Wolff, *Ongles bleus, Jacques et Ciompi. Les révolutions populaires en Europe aux XIVe et XVe siècles* (Paris, 1970); J. R. Hale, "Violence in the Late Middle Ages: A Background," in Lauro Martines, ed., *Violence and Civil Disorder in Italian Cities, 1200–1500* (Berkeley, 1972), pp. 19–37; Neil J. Smelser, *Theory of Collective Behavior* (New York: Free Press Paperback, 1971). There are also some helpful classifications of crowds in Elias Canetti, *Crowds and Power* (1960), tr. Carol Stewart (New York, 1966), pp. 48–73.

[7] As in, for instance, Philippe Wolff, "The 1391 Pogrom in Spain. Social Crisis or Not?"

non-religious features. To present-day church historians, especially in an age of ecumenicalism, the popular violence of their Calvinist and Catholic ancestors may have been an embarrassment (as is Belfast). To social historians it is the seeming "irrationality" of most sixteenth-century religious riot that has been puzzling. To bear the sword in the name of a millennial dream might make some sense, but why get so excited about the Eucharist or saints' relics? It is hard to decipher the social meaning of such an event.

Not surprisingly, the pioneering remarks of C. Verlinden and his colleagues on popular iconoclasm, and of Janine Estèbe on popular Catholic violence, insist upon a strong linkage between religious conflict and economic issues. It is argued that a rise in grain prices triggers these disturbances, and that the Saint Bartholomew's massacres are also a "class-crime," "rich Huguenots being attacked and pillaged by preference." Beyond this, Estèbe accounts for the crowd action in the massacres as an expression of the primitive soul of the people, pushed by events into pathological hatred. Similarly, in Philippe Wolff's study of anti-Semitic pogroms in Valencia and Barcelona in 1391 and in George Rudé's analysis of anti-Catholic riots in eighteenth-century London, there is a tendency to identify the "real" elements in the disturbance as the social ones, social being defined only in terms of a conflict of poor against rich, artisans against wealthy burghers or craftsmen, and wage-earners against manufacturers and merchants.[8] There is no doubt that some religious violence has this character – Wolff's evidence for Barcelona is very good indeed – but is this the only kind of social meaning inherent in a religious riot? What does one make of popular religious violence where class conflict of this type is not present?

I will try to answer these questions in regard to sixteenth-century France in the course of this paper. My first purpose is to describe the shape and structure of the religious riot in French cities and towns,

---

Past and Present, No. 50 (Feb. 1971), pp. 4–18; Norman Cohn, *The Pursuit of the Millennium* (2d ed., New York, 1961); Sylvia L. Thrupp, ed., *Millennial Dreams in Action. Studies in Revolutionary Religious Movements* (New York, 1970).

[8] C. Verlinden, J. Craeybeckx, E. Scholliers, "Mouvements des prix et des salaires en Belgique au XVIe siècle," *Annales. E.S.C.*, X (1955), 185–87; Janine Estèbe, *Tocsin pour un massacre. La saison des Saint-Barthélemy* (Paris, 1968), pp. 97–98, 196, 135-36, 189–98. Though I will take issue at several points in this paper with Estèbe's interpretation of the massacres, her valuable book is surely the most imaginative study we have had of the social psychology of those events. Wolff, "Pogrom," p. 16; Rudé, *Crowd in History*, pp. 62, 138. Wolff characterizes the pogrom at Valencia, where "violence directed against the Jews predominates, committed moreover by persons from the most diverse social backgrounds," as "pseudo-religious."

especially in the 1560s and early 1570s. We will look at the goals, legitimation and occasions for riots; at the kinds of action undertaken by the crowds and the targets for their violence; and briefly at the participants in the riots and their organization. We will consider differences between Protestant and Catholic styles of crowd behavior, but will also indicate the many ways in which they are alike. Our sources will be contemporary Catholic and Protestant accounts of religious disturbance, from which we will do our best to sort out utter fabrication from likely fact.[9] I hope this inquiry will put the massacres of Saint Bartholomew's day in a new perspective, and also deepen our understanding of the religious riot as a type of collective disturbance.

I

What then can we learn of the goals of popular religious violence? What were the crowds intending to do and why did they think they must do it? Their behavior suggests, first of all, a goal akin to preaching: the defense of true doctrine and the refutation of false doctrine through dramatic challenges and tests. "You blaspheme," shouts a woman to a Catholic preacher in Montpellier in 1558 and, having broken the decorum of the service, leads part of the congregation out of the church. "You lie," shouts a sheathmaker in the midst of the Franciscan's Easter sermon in Lyons, and his words are underscored by the gunshots of Huguenots waiting in the square.[10] "Look," cries

---

[9] Where possible, I have tried to use both Catholic and Protestant accounts of the same episode. For instance, for events in Toulouse in 1562, I have used among others the account of the Catholic G. Bosquet (*Histoire de M. G. Bosquet sur les troubles advenus en la ville de Tolose l'an 1562* [Toulouse, 1595]) and that of the Reformed *Histoire ecclésiastique*. I have taken especially seriously descriptions of Catholic violence coming from Catholic writers (as in the *Mémoires* of the priest Claude Haton) and descriptions of Protestant violence coming from the *Histoire ecclésiastique*. These sources are not necessarily telling the *whole* truth about their party's violence, but at least we can assume that what they positively describe did occur. I have also taken especially seriously the *omission* of certain kinds of violence in accusations made by one party about the opposing party (e.g., that Catholic accounts say very little about the desecration of corpses by Protestant crowds), since these writers show so little willingness to put their opponents in a favorable light. If certain kinds of violence are regularly *not* attributed to the enemy, then I think we can assume that they did not in fact occur very often.

In regard to accepting evidence about acts of desecration of corpses, torture and acts of filth, where there is no way of getting "impartial" eyewitness accounts, I have used my judgment, based on a general understanding of the range of possibilities in 16th-century behavior. My guides here have been French legal practice and penalty, Rabelais, descriptions by Pierre de l'Estoile of behavior in Paris in the late 16th century, and the comments of Montaigne on tortures in his time ("On Cruelty," "Of Cannibals").

[10] *Hist. eccl.*, I, 248; Jean Guéraud, *La chronique lyonnaise de Jean Guéraud*, ed. Jean Tricou (Lyons, 1929), p. 151. Other examples: Geneva, Advent 1533, a young man interrupts a sermon of the Catholic theologian Guy Furbity, "Messieurs, listen . . . I will put myself in

a weaver in Tournai, as he seizes the elevated host from the priest, "deceived people, do you believe this is the King, Jesus Christ, the true God and Saviour? Look!" And he crumbles the wafer and escapes. "Look," says a crowd of image-breakers to the people of Albiac in 1561, showing them the relics they have seized from the Carmelite monastery, "look, they are only animal bones."[11] And the slogan of the Reformed crowds as they rush through the streets of Paris, of Toulouse, of La Rochelle, of Angoulême is "The Gospel! The Gospel! Long live the Gospel!"[12]

Catholic crowds answer this kind of claim to truth in Angers by taking a French Bible, well-bound and gilded, seized in the home of a rich merchant, and parading it through the streets on the end of a halberd. "There's the truth hung. There's the truth of the Huguenots, the truth of all the devils." Then, throwing it into the river, "There's the truth of all the devils drowned." And if the Huguenot doctrine was true, why didn't the Lord come and save them from their killers? So a crowd of Orléans Catholics taunted its victims in 1572: "Where is your God? Where are your prayers and Psalms? Let him save you if he can." Even the dead were made to speak in Normandy and Provence, where leaves of the Protestant Bible were stuffed into the mouths and wounds of corpses. "They preached the truth of their God. Let them call him to their aid."[13]

The same refutation was, of course, open to Protestants. A Protestant crowd corners a baker guarding the holy-wafer box in Saint Médard's Church in Paris in 1561. "Messieurs," he pleads, "do not touch it for the honor of Him who dwells here." "Does your God of paste protect you now from the pains of death?" was the Protestant answer

the fire to maintain that all he has said are lies and words of the Antichrist;" "Into the fire," shout some of the congregation (Jeanne de Jussie, *Le levain du calvinisme ou commencement de l'hérésie de Genève* [Geneva, 1865], p. 74). Rouen: a barber's journeyman denies at the end of a Franciscan's sermon that there are seven sacraments, insisting that there are only two (*Hist. eccl.*, I, 355). Rouen, March 1562 in *Hist. eccl.*, III, 713 n. 1. Toulouse, 4 May 1562 in Bosquet, *Histoire*, p. 38. Provins, 1560, Protestants disturb a Catholic sermon (Haton, *Mémoires*, pp. 136–37).

[11] Jean Crespin, *Histoire des martyrs persecutez et mis à mort pour la verité de l'Evangile, depuis le temps des Apostres jusques à present (1619)*, ed. D. Benoît (3 vols.; Toulouse, 1885–1889), II, 307–08. For a similar episode in Flanders, *ibid.*, III, 515. See also *Hist. eccl.*, I, 931.

[12] Haton, *Mémoires*, p. 182; "Relations de l'émeute arrivée à Toulouse en 1562," in L. Cimber and F. Danjou, eds., *Archives curieuses de l'histoire de France* (hereafter *Arch. cur.*) (Paris and Beauvais, 1834–1840), IV, 347; *Hist. eccl.*, III, 989; [Richard Verstegen], *Théâtre des cruautés des hérétiques au seizième siècle, contenant les cruautés des schismatiques d'Angleterre ... les cruautés des Huguenots en France, et les barbaries cruelles des Calvinistes Gueux aux Pays-Bas. Reproduction du texte ... de 1588* (Lille, 1883), p. 38.

[13] *Hist. eccl.*, II, 650–51; "Massacres de ceux de la Religion à Orléans," *Arch. cur.*, VII, 295; *Hist. eccl.*, II, 839 (Valognes); *ibid.*, III, 315 (Orange).

before they killed him.[14] True doctrine can be defended in sermon or speech, backed up by the magistrate's sword against the heretic. Here it is defended by dramatic demonstration, backed up by the violence of the crowd.

A more frequent goal of these riots, however, is that of ridding the community of dreaded pollution. The word "pollution" is often on the lips of the violent, and the concept serves well to sum up the dangers which rioters saw in the dirty and diabolic enemy. A priest brings ornaments and objects for singing the Mass into a Bordeaux jail. The Protestant prisoner smashes them all. "Do you want to blaspheme the Lord's name everywhere? Isn't it enough that the temples are defiled? Must you also profane prisons so nothing is unpolluted?"[15] "The Calvinists have polluted their hands with every kind of sacrilege men can think of," writes a doctor of theology in 1562. Not long after at the Sainte Chapelle, a man seizes the elevated host with his "polluted hands" and crushes it under foot. The worshippers beat him up and deliver him to the agents of Parlement.[16] The extent to which Protestants could be viewed as vessels of pollution is suggested by a popular belief about the origin of the nickname "Huguenots." In the city of Tours, le roi Huguet ("King Huguet") was the generic name for ghosts who, instead of spending their time in Purgatory, came back to rattle doors and haunt and harm people at night. Protestants went out at night to their lascivious conventicles, and so the priests and the people began to call them Huguenots in Tours and then elsewhere. Protestants were, thus, as sinister as the spirits of the dead, whom one hoped to settle in their tombs on All Souls' Day.[17]

One does not have to listen very long to sixteenth-century voices to hear the evidence for the uncleanliness and profanation of either side. As for the Protestants, Catholics knew that, in the style of earlier heretics, they snuffed out the candles and had sexual intercourse after the voluptuous Psalmsinging of their nocturnal conventicles. When their services became public, it was no better, for their Holy Supper was perceived (in the words of a merchant-draper of Lyons) as disor-

---

[14] From the memoirs of Canon Bruslart of Paris, qtd. in *Arch. cur.*, IV, 57 n. 1.

[15] Crespin, *Martyrs*, II, 470.

[16] Claude de Sainctes, *Discours sur le saccagement des églises catholiques, par les hérétiques anciens et nouveaux Calvinistes en l'an 1562* (1563) in *Arch. cur.*, IV, 368; Haton, *Mémoires*, p. 375.

[17] *Hist. eccl.*, I, 308. On popular attitudes toward ghosts and the souls of the dead, see Arnold Van Gennep, *Manuel de folklore français* (4 vols.; Paris, 1943–1958), II, 791–803; André Varagnac, *Civilisation traditionnelle et genres de vie* (Paris, 1948), chap. vii; Roger Vaultier, *Le folklore pendant la guerre de Cent Ans d'après des lettres de rémission du Trésor des chartes* (Paris, 1965), p. 80; Keith Thomas, *Religion and the Decline of Magic* (London, 1971), pp. 587–606.

dered and drunken, "a bacchanalia."[18] But it was not just the fleshly license with which they lived which was unclean, but the things they said in their "pestilential" books and the things they did in hatred of the Mass, the sacraments and whole Catholic religion. As the representative of the clergy said at the Estates of Orléans, the heretics intended to leave "no place in the kingdom which was dedicated, holy and sacred to the Lord, but would only profane churches, demolish altars and break images."[19]

The Protestants' sense of Catholic pollution also stemmed to some extent from their sexual uncleanness, here specifically of the clergy. Protestant polemic never tired of pointing to the lewdness of the clergy with their "concubines." It was rumored that the Church of Lyons had an organization of hundreds of women, sort of temple prostitutes, at the disposition of priests and canons; and an observer pointed out with disgust how, after the first religious war, the Mass and the brothel re-entered Rouen together. One minister even claimed that the clergy were for the most part sodomites.[20] But more serious than the sexual abominations of the clergy was the defilement of the sacred by Catholic ritual life, from the diabolic magic of the Mass to the idolatrous worship of images. The Mass is "vile filth"; "no people pollute the House of the Lord in every way more than the clergy." Protestant converts talked of their own past lives as a time of befoul-

---

[18] Haton, *Mémoires*, pp. 49–50, and p. 511 on "incest" among Huguenots, spurred on by reading the Bible in French; Crespin, *Martyrs*, II, 546; Gabriel de Saconay, *Genealogie et la fin des Huguenaux, et descouverte du Calvinisme* (Lyons, 1573), fol. 68ᵛ, citing a work by Antoine Mochi, alias De Mochares, *Apologie contre la Cene calvinique*, printed in Paris in 1558; Guéraud, *Chronique*, p. 147. Also, note the reaction of the Catholics Florimond de Raemond and Claude de Rubys to male and female voices joining together in the Psalms: Raemond, *L'histoire de la naissance, progrez et decadence de l'hérésie de ce siècle* (Rouen, 1623), p. 1010; Rubys, *Histoire veritable de la ville de Lyon* (Lyons, 1604), pp. 390–91 ("Leurs chansons androgynes," etc.).

[19] Gentian Hervet, *Discours sur ce que les pilleurs, voleurs et brusleurs d'eglises disent qu'ils n'en veulent qu'aux prestres. Au peuple de Rheims, et des environs* (Paris, 1563): "The execrable words of diabolic ministers," "pestilential little books full of poison"; Haton, *Mémoires*, p. 150; harangue of Canon Jean Quintin at Orléans, Dec. 1560, in *Hist. eccl.*, I, 476. Another Catholic quotation expressing these attitudes and fears is: "Nothing remains in the churches. The impious takes away everything. He destroys, he overturns, he pollutes all holy places" (from the MS "De Tristibus Francorum," illustrated with pictures of the iconoclastic Protestants of Lyons with animal heads). See also Léopold Niepce, *Monuments d'art de la Primatiale de Lyon, détruits ou aliénés pendant l'occupation protestante en 1562* (Lyons, 1881), pp. 16–17.

[20] *Le Cabinet du roi de France*, described in Jean-Jacques Servais and Jean-Pierre Laurend, *Histoire et dossier de la prostitution* (Paris, 1965), p. 170; Crespin, *Martyrs*, I, 385–90; III, 324; [Pierre Viret], *Le manuel ou instruction des curez et vicaires de l'église romaine* (Lyons, 1564), p. 137 (for the identification of the author of this work see R. Linder, *The Political Ideas of Pierre Viret* ["Travaux d'Humanisme et Renaissance," LXIV; Geneva, 1964], p. 189).

ment and dreaded present "contamination" from Catholic churches and rites.[21]

Pollution was a dangerous thing to suffer in a community, from either a Protestant or a Catholic point of view, for it would surely provoke the wrath of God. Terrible wind storms and floods were sometimes taken as signs of His impatience on this count.[22] Catholics, moreover, had also to worry about offending Mary and the saints; and though the anxious, expiatory processions organized in the wake of Protestant sacrilege might temporarily appease them, the heretics were sure to strike again.[23] It is not surprising, then, that so many of the acts of violence performed by Catholic and Protestant crowds have (as we shall see more fully later on) the character either of rites of purification or of a paradoxical desecration, intended to cut down on uncleanness by placing profane things, like chrism, back in the profane world where they belonged.

This concern of Catholic and Protestant crowds to destroy polluting elements is reminiscent of the insistence of revolutionary millenarian movements that the wicked be exterminated that the godly may rule. The resemblance is real, but is limited. Our Catholic and Protestant rioters have a conviction not so much of their immanent godliness as of the rightness of their judgment, envisage not so much a society of saints as a holier society of sinners. For Catholic zealots, the extermination of the heretical "vermin" promised the restoration of unity to the body social and the guarantee of its traditional boundaries:

---

[21] *Hist. eccl.*, I, 486; "Récit de l'oeuvre du Seigneur en la ville de Lyon pour action de grâce" and "Epigramme du Dieu des papistes" in Anatole de Montaiglon, ed., *Recueil de poésies françoises des XVe et XVIe siècles* (Paris, 1867), VII, 36–39, 42–45. On the loathsome and magical aspects of the Mass, see Antoine de Marcourt, *Declaration de la messe* (Neuchâtel, 1534); *Les cauteles, canon et ceremonies de la messe* (Lyons, 1564) (see below, n. 82); Thomas, *Religion*, pp. 33–35; Calvin, *Institution de la religion chrétienne*, Bk. IV, xviii, in *Ioannis Calvini Opera Quae Supersunt Omnia*, ed. J. G. Baum, E. Cunitz and E. Reuss (57 vols.; Brunswick, 1863–1896), IV, col. 1077 ("ces vilaines ordures"). Calvin comments on the "mire" of his earlier life in the Preface to his *Commentaire sur le livre des Pseaumes* in *Opera Omnia*, XXXI, col. 22. On the danger of "pollution" and "contamination" from Catholic religious life, see Crespin, *Martyrs*, I, 563; Haton, *Mémoires*, pp. 407–08.

[22] Haton, *Mémoires*, pp. 427–28; [Jean Ricaud], *Discours du massacre de ceux de la religion reformée, fait à Lyon par les catholiques romains, le vingthuictieme de mois de août et jours ensuivant de l'an 1572* (1574) (Lyons, 1847), pp. 110–11; *De l'effroyable et merveilleux desbord de la rivière du Rhosne en 1570* (1576) (Lyons, 1848), p. 6.

[23] There were expiatory processions in Paris in the wake of "execrable crimes" against religious statues in 1528, 1547, 1550, 1551, 1554 and 1562, described in *Le journal d'un bourgeois de Paris sous le règne de François Ier (1515–1536)*, ed. V. L. Bourrilly (Paris, 1910), pp. 290–94; M. Félibien and G. A. Lobineau, *Histoire de la ville de Paris* (Paris, 1725), IV, 676–79, 728, 748, 755, 765, 804–05; *Arch. cur.*, IV, 99–102. Note also the expiatory procession in Lyons after an iconoclastic outrage in 1553 (Guéraud, *Chronique*, pp. 65–66).

And let us all say in unison:
Long live the Catholic religion
Long live the King and good parishioners,
Long live faithful Parisians,
And may it always come to pass
That every person goes to Mass,
One God, one Faith, one King.[24]

For Protestant zealots, the purging of the priestly "vermin" promised the creation of a new kind of unity within the body social, all the tighter because false gods and monkish sects would no longer divide it. Relations within the social order would be purer, too, for lewdness and love of gain would be limited. As was said of Lyons after its "deliverance" in 1562:

Lyons has changed indeed . . .
The profit of Mercury, the dance of Venus
And presumption, too, each man has left aside.

And again:

When this town so vain
Was filled
With idolatry and dealings
Of usury and lewdness,
It had clerics and merchants aplenty.

But once it was purged
And changed
By the Word of God,
That brood of vipers
Could hope no more
To live in so holy a place.[25]

24 "Et dirons tous d'une bonne unyon:/ Vive la catholicque religion/ Vive le Roy et les bons parroyssiens,/ Vive fidelles Parisiens,/ Et jusques à tant n'ayons cesse/ Que chascun aille à la messe/ Un Dieu, une Foy, un Roy" ("Déluge des Huguenotz faict à Paris" in *Arch. cur.*, VII, 259). On Protestants as "vermin," see Guéraud, *Chronique*, p. 141; Saconay, *Genealogie*, p. 64a; Claude de Rubys, *Histoire veritable*, p. 404.

I have tried in this paragraph to generalize Estèbe's important insight in regard to the popular aspect of the St. Bartholomew's Day massacres, that the Protestants appeared as "profaners" (pp. 194–95). There seems to me very little evidence, however, that the Catholic killers wished to exterminate "a foreign race" (p. 197). This exaggerates and misreads the evidence in regard to the killing of pregnant women and the castration of males (see below at nn. 87, 100). Heretics were hated for polluting and disorderly actions, not as a "race"; and the crowds sometimes forced them back to the Mass rather than killing them.

25 "Lyon est bien changé . . ./ De Mercure le gain, & de Venus la dance/ Tout homme a

Crowds might defend truth, and crowds might purify, but there was also a third aspect to the religious riot – a political one. E. P. Thompson has shown how in the eighteenth-century English food-riot, the crowd's behavior was legitimated by a widely held belief that it was acting in place of the government. If the justices of the peace failed to do their legal duty in guaranteeing the food supply, then the crowd would carry out the provisions of the Assize for them.[26] I have found the same thing to be true, at least as far as the *menu peuple* ("the little people") are concerned, in the great grain-riot, or *Grande Rebeine*, of Lyons in 1529. Under the slogan, "The commune is rising against the hoarders of grain," the crowd met on the grounds where municipal assemblies were ordinarily held and then went about opening the municipal granary and seizing grain from wealthy people with ample supplies, actions which the city council had undertaken in the past, but had failed to do promptly during the current crisis. In the grain-riot of Provins in 1573, the artisans seized grain that had been sold at a high price to non-residents of the city because the civic authorities had failed to provision the town at an honest price.[27]

Now we can deduce some of the same assumptions from the actions of the religious crowds of the mid-sixteenth century. When the magistrate had not used his sword to defend the faith and the true church and to punish the idolators, then the crowd would do it for him. Thus, many religious disturbances begin with the ringing of the tocsin, as in a time of civic assembly or emergency. Some riots end with the marching of the religious "wrongdoers" on the other side to jail. In 1561, for instance, Parisian Calvinists, fearing that the priests

delaissé, & toute outrecuidance" (*Eglogue de deux bergers, demonstrant comme la ville de Lyon a esté reduite à la religion vrayement chrestienne par la pure predication de l'Evangile* [Lyons, 1564], fol. A 4ʳ. "Quand ceste ville tant vaine/ Estoit pleine/ D'idolatrie et procès/ D'usure et de paillardise/ Clercs et marchans eut assès./ Mais si tost qu'en fut purgée/ Et changée/ Par la Parolle de Dieu:/ Cette engence de vipere/ Plus n'espere/ D'habiter en si sainct lieu" (Antoine Du Plain, "De l'assistance que Dieu a faite à son Eglise de Lyon," in H. L. Bordier, ed., *Le chansonnier huguenot au XVIe siècle* [Paris, 1870], p. 221). On Catholic clergy as "vermin," see *Discours de la vermine et prestraille de Lyon, dechassé par le bras fort du Seigneur, avec la retraicte des moines ... par E.P.C.* (1562) in Montaiglon, *Recueil*, VIII, 24–45.

For the theory in this paragraph, I have found helpful Mary Douglas' remarks on the relation between pollution fears and concern for social boundaries (*Purity and Danger: An Analysis of Concepts of Pollution and Taboo* [London, 1966], chap. vii) and the definitions by Neil J. Smelser of "value-oriented movements" (*Theory of Collective Behavior*, pp. 120–29 and chap. x).

[26] Thompson, "Moral Economy," pp. 91–115.

[27] The essential documents on the *Rebeine* are reprinted in M. C. and G. Guigue, *Bibliothèque historique du Lyonnais* (Lyons, 1886); and on the Provins riot in Haton, *Mémoires*, pp. 714–25. For the relation of the food-riot to governmental action in France in the late 17th and 18th centuries, see Louise Tilly, "The Food Riot as a Form of Political Conflict in France," *Journal of Interdisciplinary History*, II (1971), 23–57.

and worshippers in Saint Médard's Church were organizing an assault on their services in the Patriarche garden next door, first rioted in Saint Médard and then seized some fifteen Catholics as "mutinous" and led them off, "bound like galley-slaves," to the Châtelet prison.[28]

If the Catholic killing of Huguenots has in some ways the form of a rite of purification, it also sometimes has the form of imitating the magistrate. The mass executions of Protestants at Mérindol and Cabrières in Provence and at Meaux in the 1540s, duly ordered by the Parlements of Aix and of Paris as punishment for heresy and high treason, anticipate crowd massacres of later decades. The Protestants themselves sensed this: the devil, unable to extinguish the light of the Gospel through the sentences of judges, now tried to obscure it through furious war and a murderous populace. Whereas before they were made martyrs by one executioner, now it is at the hands of "infinite numbers of them, and the swords of private persons have become the litigants, witnesses, judges, decrees and executors of the strangest cruelties."[29]

Similarly, *official* acts of torture and *official* acts of desecration of the corpses of certain criminals anticipate some of the acts performed by riotous crowds. The public execution was, of course, a dramatic and well-attended event in the sixteenth century, and the woodcut and engraving documented the scene far and wide. There the crowd might see the offending tongue of the blasphemer pierced or slit, the offending hands of the desecrator cut off. There the crowd could watch the traitor decapitated and disemboweled, his corpse quartered and the parts borne off for public display in different sections of the town. The body of an especially heinous criminal was dragged through the streets, attached to a horse's tail. The image of exemplary royal punishment lived on for weeks, even years, as the corpses of murderers were exposed on gallows or wheels and the heads of rebels on posts.[30] We are not surprised to learn, then, that the body of

---

[28] *Histoire veritable de la mutinerie, tumulte et sedition faite par les prestres Sainct Medard contre les fideles le samedy XXVII iour de decembre 1562* [*sic* for 1561] in *Arch. cur.*, IV, 55; memoirs of Canon Bruslart, *ibid.*, p. 57 n. 1; Haton, *Mémoires*, p. 181. On Toulouse Catholic crowds leading Protestants to prison, see *Hist. eccl.*, III, 17–18.

[29] Crespin, *Martyrs*, I, 381–418, 494–500; III, 639.

[30] Samuel Y. Edgerton, Jr., "*Maniera* and the *Mannaia*: Decorum and Decapitation in the Sixteenth Century," in F. W. Robinson and S. G. Nichols, Jr., eds., *The Meaning of Mannerism* (Hanover, N.H., 1972), pp. 67–103; *Journal d'un bourgeois*, pp. 229, 373, 384–85; Claude Bellièvre, *Souvenirs de voyages en Italie et en Orient. Notes historiques*, ed. C. Perrat (Geneva, 1956), p. 26 n. 27; Haton, *Mémoires*, p. 375; Guéraud, *Chronique*, pp. 28–29; Pierre de l'Estoile, *Mémoires-journaux*, ed. Brunet *et al.* (12 vols.; Paris, 1888–1896), II, 323–24; F. A. Isambert *et al.*, eds., *Recueil général des anciennes lois françaises* (29 vols.; Paris, 1821–

Admiral Coligny had already been thrown out of the window by the king's men and stoned by the duc de Guise hours before the popular attacks on it began in 1572. Furthermore, crowds often took their victims to places of official execution, as in Paris in 1562, when the Protestant printer, Roc Le Frere, was dragged for burning to the Marché aux Pourceaux, and in Toulouse the same year, when a merchant, slain in front of a church, was dragged for burning to the town hall. "The king salutes you," said a Catholic crowd in Orléans to a Protestant trader, then put a cord around his neck as official agents might do, and led him off to be killed.[31]

Riots also occurred in connection with judicial cases, either to hurry the judgment along, or when verdicts in religious cases were considered too severe or too lenient by "the voice of the people."[32] Thus in 1569 in Montpellier, a Catholic crowd forced the judge to condemn an important Huguenot prisoner to death in a hasty "trial," then seized him and hanged him in front of his house. In 1551 a masked Protestant group kidnapped and released a goldsmith's journeyman, who had been condemned in Lyons for heresy and was being removed to Paris. And in 1561 in Marsillargues, when prisoners for heresy were released by royal decree, a Catholic crowd "rearrested" them, and executed and burned them in the streets.[33] The most fascinating example of the assumption of the magistrate's role by a crowd, however, is the mock trial by the boys of Provins in Champagne in October 1572. A Huguenot had been hanged for thefts and killings committed during the religious troubles. Groups of boys put ropes around his neck and his feet, but a tug-of-war could not resolve which way the corpse was to be dragged. The boys then elected lawyers and judges from among their midst for a trial. Before the

---

1833), XII, Nos. 115, 210; XIII, Nos. 18, 90; Edmé de La Poix de Freminville, *Dictionnaire ou traité de la police générale des villes, bourgs, paroisses et seigneuries de la campagne* (Paris, 1758), pp. 56, 171; Le Roy Ladurie, *Paysans*, p. 506; Roland Mousnier, *L'assassinat d'Henri IV* (Paris, 1964), pp. 32–34; A. Allard, *Histoire de la justice criminelle au seizième siècle* (Ghent, 1868), pp. 333–34.

[31] *Hist. eccl.*, II, 175; Bosquet, *Histoire*, p. 38. For the Marché aux Pourceaux as a place of execution for heretics, see *Journal d'un bourgeois*, pp. 384–85.

[32] L'Estoile, *Mémoires-journaux*, II, 85 (describing here the freeing by a Parisian crowd of a man condemned to death for impregnating a young woman).

[33] Jean Philippi, *Mémoires*, ed. Michaud and Poujoulat ("Nouvelle collection des mémoires pour servir à l'histoire de France," VIII; Paris, 1838), p. 634; Crespin, *Martyrs*, II, 37; *Hist. eccl.*, I, 983. In Rouen, a Catholic crowd of 1563 pressured the Parlement to condemn Protestants to death; a Catholic crowd of 1571, having had some of its members arrested for killing Protestants, broke into the prison and freed them (*Hist. eccl.*, II, 792 n. 1; Crespin, *Martyrs*, III, 662–63). For two examples of Catholic crowds seizing from the gallows female heretics who had been condemned merely to be hanged, and burning them instead, see *Hist. eccl.*, III, 43–44, and L'Estoile, *Mémoires-journaux*, III, 166.

eyes of a hundred spectators, they argued the penalty, appealing from the decision of the real judge that the Huguenot be only hanged and not burned alive. After the boys' decision, the corpse was dragged through the streets by the feet and burned.[34]

The seizure of religious buildings and the destruction of images by Calvinist crowds were also accomplished with the conviction that they were taking on the role of the authorities. When Protestants in Montpellier occupied a church in 1561, they argued that the building belonged to them already, since its clergy had been wholly supported by merchants and burghers in the past and the property belonged to the town. In Agen the same year, with Reformed ministers preaching that it was the office of the magistrate alone to eradicate the marks of idolatry, Protestant artisans decided one night that "if one tarried for the Consistory, it would never be done" and proceeded to break into the churches and destroy all the altars and images.[35]

To be sure, the relation of a French Calvinist crowd to the magisterial model is different from that of a French Catholic crowd. The king had not yet chastised the clergy and "put all ydolatry to ruyne and confusyon," as Protestants had been urging him since the early 1530s.[36] Calvinist crowds were using his sword as the king *ought* to have been using it and as some princes and city councils outside of France had already used it. Within the kingdom before 1560 city councils had only *indicated* the right path, as they set up municipal schools, lay-controlled welfare systems or otherwise limited the sphere of action of the clergy.[37] During the next years, as revolution and conversion created Reformed city councils and governors (such as the queen of Navarre) within France, Calvinist crowds finally had local magistrates whose actions they could prompt or imitate.

In general, then, the crowds in religious riots in sixteenth-century France can be seen as sometimes acting out clerical roles – defending

[34] Haton, *Mémoires*, pp. 704–06. The boys were aged twelve or younger, according to Haton.

[35] *Hist. eccl.*, I, 970, 889.

[36] Antoine de Marcourt, *The Booke of Marchauntes* (London, 1547), fols. C iᵛ–iiʳ. (The *Livre des marchands* was first published in Neuchâtel in 1533.) See also A. de Marcourt, *A Declaration of the Masse, the Fruyte Thereof, the Cause and the Meane, Wherefore and Howe It Ought to Be Maynteyned* ("Wittenberg: Hans Luft" [actually London: John Day], 1547), fol. D ivᵛ, conclusion written by Pierre Viret. (Marcourt's work first appeared in French at Neuchâtel in 1534).

[37] There were municipal schools in Toulouse, Lyons and Nîmes among other places, and urban welfare systems in Paris, Rouen, Lyons, Troyes, Toulouse and other cities. See N. Z. Davis, "Poor Relief, Humanism and Heresy: The Case of Lyon," *Studies in Medieval and Renaissance History*, V (1968), 216–75.

true doctrine or ridding the community of defilement in a violent version of priest or prophet – and as sometimes acting out magisterial roles. Clearly some riotous behavior, such as the extensive pillaging done by both Protestants and Catholics, cannot be subsumed under these heads; but just as the prevalence of pillaging in a war does not prevent us from typing it as a holy war, so the prevalence of pillaging in a riot should not prevent us from seeing it as essentially religious.

II

What ever made the people think they could rightfully assume the roles of priest, pastor and magistrate? Like other Catholic writers, when the Jesuit Emond Auger composed his *Pedagogue d'armes* in 1568 to urge a holy war to exterminate the heretics, he addressed his instruction only to Charles IX.[38] Like other Reformed preachers, Pastor Pierre Viret told his flock that private individuals should never take it upon themselves to stop public scandals under cover of having some "extraordinary vocation." There was no way that one could get certain evidence from a Scripture to show that a particular private individual had such a calling, and everything was best left to those who held political power.[39] When Protestant resistance theory was fully developed it too never conceded a clear right of violent disobedience to private persons.[40] Nor were secular authorities in sixteenth-century cities in the habit of telling the "little people" that they had a right to riot when they felt like it.

Yet the crowds did riot, and there are remarkably few instances reported of remorse on the part of participants in religious disturbances. Of the many Catholic murderers mentioned in Crespin's *Book of Martyrs*, only three were said to have fallen ill in the wake of their deeds, to have become mad and died invoking devils or denying God. Leading killers in the Lyons Vespers of 1572 exhibited their bloody pourpoints in the streets and bragged of the numbers they had slain; their subsequent absolution by a papal legate appears a formal,

---

[38] Emond Auger, *Le pedagogue d'armes. Pour instruire un prince chrestien à bien entreprendre et heureusement achever une bonne guerre, pour estre victorieux de tous les ennemis de son Estat et de l'Eglise catholique. Dedié au Roy, par M. Emond, de la Compagnie de Iesus* (Paris, 1568), esp. fols. 18ᵛ–24ᵛ.

[39] Pierre Viret, letter to the Colloquy of Montpellier, 15 Jan. 1562, in *Hist. eccl.*, I, 975–77; Viret, *L'interim, fait par dialogues* (Lyons, 1565), pp. 396–97; Linder, *Political Ideas*, pp. 137–38; Robert M. Kingdon, *Geneva and the Consolidation of the French Protestant Movement* (Madison, Wis., 1967), pp. 153–55.

[40] See, e.g., the *Vindiciae contra Tyrannos* on this subject, in J. H. Franklin, tr. and ed., *Constitutionalism and Resistance in the Sixteenth Century* (New York, 1969), pp. 154–56. [Editor's note: see above, the essay by R. M. Kingdon.]

political affair. In cases where Protestants returned to Mother Church, there may well have been some regret for smashing statues or assaulting priests, but here only as part of a whole pattern of "heretical" behavior. So long as rioters maintained a given religious commitment, they rarely displayed guilt or shame for their violence. By every sign, the crowds believed their actions legitimate.[41]

One reason for this conviction is that in some, though by no means all religious riots, clerics and political officers were active members of the crowd, though not precisely in their official capacity. In Lyons in 1562, Pastor Jean Ruffy took part in the sack of the Cathedral of Saint Jean with a sword in his hand.[42] Catholic priests seem to have been in quite a few disturbances, as in Rouen in 1560, when priests and parishioners in a Corpus Christi parade broke into the houses of Protestants who had refused to do the procession honor.[43] (In other cases, the clergy was said to have been busy behind the scenes organizing the crowds.[44]) At Aix a band of Catholic rioters was headed by the first consul of that city, while at Lyons in 1562 the merchant-publisher and consul, Jean de La Porte, led a Protestant group to an assault on the cloister of Saint Just.[45] The fighting crowd of Protestants which "arrested" Catholics at Saint Médard's Church in 1561 had in its midst the chief officer of the "royal watch" in Paris. And among the image-smashers of Agen the same year was the town executioner. "It is my office to set fire," he said as he put the statues to the flames.[46]

[41] Crespin, *Martyrs*, III, 694, 701, 711–12, 717. The infrequency of these tales of remorse is all the more significant because they could be used so readily by Protestants to show the just punishment of God (cf. *Hist. eccl.*, I, 357). Pastor Jean Ruffy, formally rebuked by Calvin for his role in an iconoclastic riot in Lyons in 1562 (Robert M. Kingdon, *Geneva and the Coming of the Wars of Religion in France, 1555–1563* [Geneva, 1956], p. 110), led a Protestant crowd against dancing Catholics in 1565 (de Rubys, *Histoire*, p. 406). On ambivalence about disobedience and violent behavior that might be embedded deep in the feelings of rioters, I have no evidence one way or the other.

[42] Guéraud, *Chronique*, p. 155; Charles Du Moulin, *Omnia ... Opera* (5 vols.; Paris, 1681), V, 618; Kingdon, *Geneva and the Coming*, p. 110.

[43] *Hist. eccl.*, I, 352. For other allegations that priests took part in Catholic riots: in Toulouse, 1562 (*ibid.*, III, 4–5); in Lavaur, 1561 (*ibid.*, I, 938–39); in Clermont in Auvergne, 1568 (Crespin, *Martyrs*, III, 651). Also see the comments of the priest Claude Haton about brawling priests with swords in their hands (*Mémoires*, pp. 17–18).

[44] E.g., priests at Nemours were said to have helped plan an attack on Protestants there in 1561, and Dominicans at Revel are alleged to have organized an attack on Psalm-singers the same year (*Hist. eccl.*, I, 833–34, 959). The bishop of Autun was accused of organizing groups of artisans to exterminate Protestants in that city in 1562, and Cardinal Strozzi, the bishop of Albi, was supposed to have helped to organize a massacre in Gaillac in May 1562 (*ibid.*, III, 487–88, 80–81).

[45] Crespin, *Martyrs*, III, 390–91; Léopold Niepce, "Les trésors des églises de Lyon," *Revue lyonnaise*, VIII (1884), 40 n. 1.

[46] Haton, *Mémoires*, p. 182; *Histoire veritable de la mutinerie ... faite par les prestres Sainct Medard*, in *Arch. cur.*, IV, 56; *Hist. eccl.*, I, 889. On the position of the *chevalier du guet*, or chief officer of the watch, in Paris, see Isambert, *Recueil*, XII, No. 296.

Finally, there is the well-known participation of some of the militia officers in the Saint Bartholomew's Day massacres in Paris and in the Lyons Vespers. Their murdering and sacking, as Janine Estèbe has pointed out for Paris, went beyond any informal encouragement that they had from the king and clearly beyond the official orders given them by the *Bureau de la Ville*.[47]

On the other hand, not all religious riots could boast of officers or clergy in the crowd, and other sources of legitimation must be sought. Here we must recognize what mixed cues were given out by priests and pastors in their sermons on heresy or idolatry. If we do not know whether to believe the Catholic priest, Claude Haton, in his claim that a Huguenot preacher at Sens told his congregation that "to exterminate papal vermin would be a great sacrifice to God," it is surely significant that iconoclastic riots in Gien and Rouen both occurred on 3 May 1562 after sermons on the text from Deuteronomy xii with which I opened this study.[48] However much Calvin and other pastors opposed such disturbances (preferring that all images and altars be removed soberly by the authorities), they nevertheless were always more ready to understand and excuse this violence than, say, that of a peasant revolt or of a journeymen's march. Perhaps, after all, the popular idol-smashing was due to "an extraordinary power (*vertu*) from God." How else was it possible, says Jean Crespin about iconoclasm in the Netherlands in 1566, for a small number of men, women and children, badly equipped and of modest condition, to demolish in four days what it would have taken many masons twice as long to do? How else to explain the fact that artisans, women and children had been able to clean out fifty churches in Rouen in only twenty-four hours?[49] Pastor Pierre Viret may have similarly wondered about God's role in a crowd seizure of Nîmes cathedral in December 1561. Though he had opposed such actions, he was nevertheless willing to preach to the Calvinists in the church three days later.[50]

[47] Estèbe, *Tocsin*, pp. 137–40. The orders given to the militia officers of Paris from 22 Aug. to 30 Aug. 1572 are printed in *Histoire générale de Paris. Régistres des déliberations du Bureau de la ville de Paris*, ed. F. Bonnardot (19 vols.; Paris, 1883–1958), VII, 9–20. Also see the leadership of doctors of theology and militia captains in an unofficial burning of Protestant books by a Catholic crowd in Paris in 1568 (Félibien and Lobineau, *Histoire*, IV, 828; I am grateful to Alfred Soman for this reference).

[48] Haton, *Mémoires*, p. 191; *Hist. eccl.*, II, 537–38, 719–20.

[49] Crespin, *Martyrs*, III, 519–22; *Hist. eccl.*, II, 719–20. Also, see Condé's letter to the king of May 1562, in which he argues that though "le peuple" was at fault for destroying images without waiting for an order from the magistrate, nevertheless their action could be imputed to "a secret movement of God, inciting the people to detest and abhor idolatry, and not to any disobedience or rebellion" (*Hist. eccl.*, II, 74).

[50] Ann Guggenheim, "Calvinism and the Political Elite of Sixteenth-Century Nîmes"

The role of Catholic preachers in legitimating popular violence was even more direct. If we don't know whether to believe the Protestant claim that Catholic preachers at Paris were telling their congregations in 1557 that Protestants ate babies, it is surely significant that, in the year of the attack on the rue St. Jacques conventicle, Catholic preachers did blame the loss of the battle of Saint Quentin on God's wrath at the presence of heretics in France.[51] In the next years, they held up Ahab and his wife Jezebel, and Belshazar and others as examples of the terrible end that would come to those who tolerated idolatry. Before a Catholic riot at the Cimitière des Innocents, Brother Jean de Han told his listeners in the church that they could not count on royal judges to punish Lutherans and would have to take matters into their own hands.[52] On St. Michael's Day 1572 at Bordeaux, a few days before the massacres there, the Jesuit Emond Auger preached on how the Angel of the Lord had already executed God's judgment in Paris, Orléans and elsewhere, and would also do so in Bordeaux.[53] And if Protestant pastors could timidly wonder if divine power were not behind the extraordinary force of the iconoclasts, priests had no doubts that certain miraculous occurrences in the wake of Catholic riots were a sign of divine approval, such as a copper cross in Troyes that began to change color and cure people in 1561, the year of a riot in which Catholics bested Protestants, and the long-barren hawthorn tree at the Cimitière des Innocents, which began to bloom from the beginning of the Saint Bartholomew's massacres.[54]

In all likelihood, however, there are sources for the legitimation of popular religious riot that come directly out of the experience of the local groups which often formed the nucleus of a crowd – the men and women who had worshipped together in the dangerous days of the night conventicles, the men in confraternities, in festive groups, in youth gangs and militia units. It should be remembered how often

---

(unpublished Ph. D. dissertation, New York University, 1968), chap. vi, p. 214.

[51] Crespin, Martyrs, II, 538, 546; Hist. eccl., I, 268–69.

[52] Haton, Mémoires, pp. 527–29; Hist. eccl., I, 192–93, 481.

[53] Crespin, Martyrs, III, 727; Henri Hauser, "Le père Emond Auger et le massacre de Bordeaux, 1572," Bulletin de la Société de l'histoire du protestantisme français, LX (1911), 289–306.

[54] Haton, Mémoires, pp. 195–97, 681–82. Protestant writers also stress divine intervention to show God's disapproval of Catholic rioters and violence. E.g., in Draguignan two Protestants killed by a crowd were found three months later with no sign of corruption in their bodies and with their wounds still fresh in appearance. A Catholic who had been guarding the bodies was killed by Protestant soldiers and his body instantly became rotten, and was eaten by crows and dogs (Hist. eccl., I, 428). In Marennes (Charente-Maritime), a rich burgher who tried to prevent a Protestant service being held and beat up one of the Protestants died shortly after from apoplexy. This was viewed as the "Hand of God" and led to the conversion of his children to the new religion (ibid., I, 357).

conditions in sixteenth-century cities required groups of "little people" to take the law into their own hands. Royal edicts themselves enjoined any person who saw a murder, theft or other misdeed to ring the tocsin and chase after the criminal.[55] Canon law allowed certain priestly roles to laymen in times of emergency, such as the midwife's responsibility to baptize a baby in danger of dying,[56] while the role of preaching the Gospel was often assumed by Protestant laymen in the decades before the Reformed Church was set up. Talking about the Bible among themselves, some Calvinist city-dwellers decided that private persons might be obliged to act independently of the magistrate in defense of religion, and even published a tract – *The Civil and Military Defense of the Innocents and of the Church of Christ* – in support of this view with Old Testament precedents.[57]

Finally, the very experience of singing the Psalms together in French in a large armed group intent on challenging the religious practices of the world around it; the very experience of being part of a Corpus Christi Day procession at a time when danger threatened the sanctity of the host – these processional experiences in themselves would feed a popular certitude that the group did indeed have the right on occasion to move into the realm of violence for the sake of religion.

III

What then of the occasions for religious riot? By "occasions" I don't mean here the specific events, such as the Saint Bartholomew's rumor of conspiracy to kill the king, which have triggered particular instances of religious riot. Nor do I here mean anything as grand as theories of structural strain, relative deprivation among the people or crises among the elite, which might account for the timing of all riots. In fact, I am considering the chronological question of timing very

[55] Fréminville, *Dictionnaire*, p. 400, citing edicts of 1536 and 1550. Isambert, *Recueil*, XII, No. 115 (edict of Sept. 1523), p. 531 (edict of 25 Jan. 1536), pp. 557–58 (edict of 9 May 1539).

[56] Jacques Toussaert, *Le sentiment religieux en Flandres à la fin du Moyen Age* (Paris, 1963), p. 90; T. J. Schmitt, *L'organisation ecclésiastique et la pratique religieuse dans le diocèse d'Autun de 1650 à 1750* (Autun, 1957), p. 166. Until the Council of Trent, canon law allowed that a marriage promised between two persons privately, without the presence of a priest, and consummated was a sacrament. Even after Trent, it took some time for the 1564 legislation requiring a priest's presence to be widely known and followed.

[57] *La deffense civile et militaire des innocens et de l'Eglise de Christ* was published in Lyons in 1563, and burned on 12 June 1563 after a condemnation by the pastors of Lyons and Governor Soubise (Du Moulin, *Opera*, V, 17–22). On Old Testament precedents for private individuals killing tyrants, see Mousnier, *Assassinat*, p. 28.

little in this paper ... that is, I am not asking why there are a cluster of religious disturbances in Lyons, say, in the early '50s,[58] a cluster of religious disturbances throughout France in the early '60s, and so on. I don't have the extensive data upon which to base such an analysis. Working from the crowd behavior itself, I have merely stressed the fact that religious riot is likely to occur when it is believed that religious and/or political authorities are failing in their duties or need help in fulfilling them.

All I would add in regard to the timing and triggers of religious riot is that a rise in grain prices does not seem to be a significant variable. For instance, the religious disturbances in Toulouse in the first five months of 1562 correspond to a period of grain prices which were the same as, or lower than, those of the preceding two years. The supply was surely more abundant there than during the hard times in the spring and early summer of 1557, when there was no religious disturbance.[59] The Catholic attack on the conventicle on the rue Saint Jacques in September 1557 occurred at a time when grain had dropped to a good low price in Paris and was plentiful. The Saint Médard riot at the end of 1561 took place when prices were rising, but were far from what contemporaries would have thought a famine level.[60] As for the 1572 massacres, they occurred at a time of slowly rising grain prices, but not yet of serious dearth, with August-September prices in Paris being a little lower than those of October 1571, and in Toulouse lower than in the immediately preceding summer months.[61] In short, grain prices are relevant to religious riot in France only in the general and indirect sense that the inflation of the last forty years of the sixteenth century had an effect on many aspects of life, as did the

---

[58] These disturbances included armed marches of hundreds of Psalm-singing Protestant artisans and their wives in the spring of 1551; "assemblies and sedition" in the wake of heretical preaching by a Florentine at the St. Lawrence Hospital in August 1551; the theft of all the ornament and the Sacrament from the Church of Fourvières in October 1551; the desecration of a crucifix and an image of Saint Anne in January 1553, etc. (Guéraud, *Chronique*, pp. 54–55, 58, 65–66; Archives départementales du Rhône, B, Sénéchaussée, Sentences, 1551–1552, Dec. 1551).

[59] Georges and Geneviève Frêche, *Les prix des grains, des vins et des légumes à Toulouse (1485–1868)* (Paris, 1967), pp. 44–45. The famine and plague of 1557 were interpreted in Toulouse as the Hand of God falling on the city for its iniquities. The local government then tried to purge the town of the "idle vagabonds," to feed the starving in Toulouse and from nearby villages, and to get rid of "infecting vapors" and other filth in the streets (Antoine Noguier, *Histoire tolosaine* [Toulouse, n.d. (royal privilege, 1559)], pp. 126–33).

[60] Micheline Baulant and Jean Meuvret, *Prix des céréales extraits de la Mercuriale de Paris (1520–1698)* (2 vols.; Paris, 1960), I, 47, 49, 152–53. Maximum prices for wheat in December 1561 were something over 5 *livres tournois* per *setier*, but a famine price would be thought of in Paris as something like the 9½ *l.t.* per *setier*, to which wheat rose in the summer of 1546.

[61] Frêche, *Prix*, p. 46; Baulant and Meuvret, *Prix*, I, 56–57.

religious wars themselves. Perhaps it is only in this broad sense that they are part of the background to the Flemish iconoclastic movement of 1566 (I am here raising a query about the interpretation of Verlinden and his colleagues), the specific trigger for the riots being more likely, as Crespin claimed, the sudden upsurge in public Protestant preaching.[62] What are *specific* rises in grain prices correlated with in France? Why, with grain riots and penitential white processions to beg for rain.[63]

Questions of chronological timing apart, then, the occasion for most religious violence was during the time of religious worship or ritual and in the space which one or both groups were using for sacred purposes. There were exceptions, of course. Profanation of religious statues and paintings might occur at night, especially in the early years when it was a question of a small number of Protestants sneaking into a church.[64] Widespread murder, as in the 1572 massacres, might occur anywhere – in the streets, in bedrooms. But much of the religious riot is timed to ritual, and the violence seems often a curious continuation of the rite.

Almost every type of public religious event has a disturbance associated with it. The sight of a statue of the Virgin at a crossroad or in a wall-niche provokes a Protestant group to mockery of those who

[62] See above at n. 8; Crespin, *Martyrs*, III, 518–19. A recent study of 15th-century Spain has shown how complex the relation was between a rise in food prices and anti-Semitic pogroms. Its author suggests that a prolonged rise in food prices is part of the *general* background for a variety of popular risings. The sharper the price rise, the more likely the disturbance was *not* to be "exclusively anti-Semitic in character" (Angus MacKay, "Popular Movements and Pogroms in Fifteenth-Century Castile," *Past and Present*, No. 55 (May 1972), pp. 58–59.

[63] As in the white processions in Lyons in the spring of 1504 and in the great grain riot, or *Grande Rebeine*, of Lyons in 1529 (Paradin, *Mémoires*, p. 281; Davis, "Poor Relief," pp. 227–30). The assertion of the physician Symphorien Champier, whose granary was sacked in the *Grande Rebeine*, that the crowd also smashed religious statues in his house is surely false and was not taken seriously by contemporaries (*ibid.*, n. 43; H. Hours, "Procès d'hérésie contre Aimé Meigret," *Bibliothèque d'Humanisme et Renaissance*, XIX [1957], 20–21). During the drought of spring 1556 in the Lyonnais, there were both penitential white processions of rural parishioners to Lyons and a crowd attack on boats removing grain from the city for the Order of Malta (Paradin, *Mémoires*, p. 357; Guéraud, *Chronique*, p. 95).
For famine prices and grain riots in Provins in 1573, see Haton, *Mémoires*, p. 714ff; famine prices and a penitential procession in Paris in June 1521, Baulant and Meuvret, *Prix*, I, 94, and *Journal d'un bourgeois*, pp. 82–83; and for extraordinary prices and a bread riot in Paris in July 1587, Baulant and Meuvret, *Prix*, I, 223, and L'Estoile, *Mémoires-journaux*, III, 58.
[64] As in Paris on the day after Pentecost 1528, when some heretics cut off the head of a Virgin in a wall-niche at night (*Journal d'un bourgeois*, p. 291). Iconoclastic episodes in Lyons in January 1553 probably occurred at night (Guéraud, *Chronique*, p. 65). For iconoclastic riots in Annonay at night in 1561, see Achille Gamon, *Mémoires*, ed. Michaud and Poujoulat ("Nouvelle collection des mémoires pour servir à l'histoire de la France," VIII; Paris, 1838), p. 611. For an inconoclastic riot by sailors of Dieppe at night in 1562, see *Hist. eccl.*, II, 796.

reverence her. A fight ensues. Catholics hide in a house to entrap Huguenots who refuse to doff their hats to a Virgin nearby, and then rush out and beat the heretics up.[65] Baptism: in Nemours, a Protestant family has its baby baptized on All Souls' Day according to the new Reformed rite. With the help of an aunt, a group of Catholics steals it away for rebaptism. A drunkard sees the father and the godfather and other Protestants discussing the event in the streets, claps his sabots and shouts, "Here are the Huguenots who have come to massacre us." A crowd assembles, the tocsin is rung, and a three-hour battle takes place.[66] Funeral: in Toulouse, at Easter-time, a Protestant carpenter tries to bury his Catholic wife by the new Reformed rite. A Catholic crowd seizes the corpse and buries it. The Protestants dig it up and try to rebury her. The bells are rung, and with a great noise a Catholic crowd assembles with stones and sticks. Fighting and sacking ensue.[67]

Religious services: a Catholic Mass is the occasion for an attack on the Host or the interruption of a sermon, which then leads to a riot.[68] Protestant preaching in a home attracts large Catholic crowds at the door, who stone the house or otherwise threaten the worshippers.[69] In the years when the Reformed services are public, the rivalry of the rites becomes graphic. Side by side at Saint Médard, the vesper bells are rung to drown out the pastor's sermon; side by side at Provins, the Huguenots sing their Psalms to drown out the Mass.[70]

[65] Haton, *Mémoires*, pp. 340–41; *Hist. eccl.*, I, 284.

[66] *Ibid.*, I, 833–34; Crespin, *Martyrs*, III, 210.

[67] *Hist. eccl.*, III, 4–5; Bosquet, *Histoire*, pp. 67–69. For an episode concerning a Reformed burial at Bordeaux on All Souls' Day 1561, see *Hist. eccl.*, I, 870–71.

[68] E.g., at the vespers service on 18 Mar. 1562 in Rouen (*Hist. eccl.*, II, 713 n. 1); at Paris at the Sainte Chapelle in 1563 (Haton, *Mémoires*, p. 375); at Toulouse at the Eglise Saint Sernin while the inquisitor Della Lana was preaching, 4 May 1561 (Bosquet, *Histoire*, pp. 38–39). Bosquet claimed that an heretical merchant was killed by the zealous *menu peuple* after he shouted, "You lie, hypocritical monk" and other blasphemous remarks. A Protestant account claims that the merchant was actually a Catholic, dissatisfied with the seditious remarks made by the preacher (*Hist. eccl.*, I, 905). Protestant sources report other episodes in which jumpy Catholic worshippers killed persons as heretics who were in fact Catholics. The victims had been merely asking for more room or had laughed at a neighbor's remark – e.g., Angers in 1561 (*ibid.*, p. 837); Paris, Church of Saint Eustache, 1558, and at the Cimitière des Innocents, 1559 (*ibid.*, pp. 193–94).

[69] In addition to the well known attack on the conventicle on the rue St. Jacques in Paris in 1557, there were four attacks on conventicles in Paris in April–May 1561 (Félibien and Lobineau, *Histoire*, IV, 797–98; R. N. Sauvage, "Lettre de Jean Fernaga, procureur syndic de la ville de Caen, touchant les troubles survenus à Paris en avril 1561," *Bulletin de la Société de l'histoire du protestantisme français*, LX [1911], 809–12). Crowds in Lyons in Sept. 1561 were out to sack all houses in which "people were having certain assemblies" and threatened the house of the Protestant merchant Jérôme Pellissari (Archives départementales du Rhône, B, Sénéchaussée, Audience, Sept.–Dec. 1561). For an attack on a conventicle in Auxerre on 9 Oct. 1561, see *Hist. eccl.*, I, 852; and on one in Cahors on 16 Nov. 1561, see Crespin, *Martyrs*, III, 211.

[70] *Histoire veritable*, in *Arch. cur.*, IV, 52; Haton, *Mémoires*, pp. 179–82, 147, 177–78;

But these encounters are as nothing compared to the disturbances that cluster around processional life. Corpus Christi Day, with its crowds, colored banners and great crosses, was the chance for Protestants *not* to put rugs in front of their doors; for Protestant women to sit ostentatiously in their windows spinning; for heroic individuals, like the painter Denis de Vallois in Lyons, to throw themselves on the "God of paste" so as "to destroy him in every parish in the world." Corpus Christi Day was the chance for a procession to turn into an assault on and slaughter of those who had so offended the Catholic faith, its participants shouting, as in Lyons in 1561, "For the flesh of God, we must kill all the Huguenots."[71] A Protestant procession was a parade of armed men and women in their dark clothes, going off to services at their temple or outside the city gates, singing Psalms and spiritual songs that to Catholic ears sounded like insults against the Church and her sacraments. It was an occasion for children to throw stones, for an exchange of scandalous words – "idolaters," "devils from the Pope's purgatory," "Huguenot heretics, living like dogs" – and then finally, for fighting.[72] Sometimes the two processions encountered each other, as in Sens in 1562. The Calvinists would not give way and insisted upon passing through the center of the Catholic procession. The groups confronted each other again after services, and the Catholics, aided by processions from peasant villages, prevailed in a bloody battle.[73]

The occasions which express most concisely the contrast between the two religious groups, however, are those in which a popular festive Catholicism took over the streets with dancing, masks, banners, costumes and music – "lascivious abomination," according to the Protestants. In Lyons, when Catholics did their traditional summer dancing on St. Peter's Day 1565, the Huguenots attacked them in a

Félibien and Lobineau, *Histoire*, IV, 800. Also see the conflict between a Protestant service at a pastel mill at Castelnaudary and a Catholic procession for *Pâques fleuries* in 1562 (*Hist. eccl.*, III, 157).

[71] E.g., at Geneva at the *Fête-Dieu*, see Jeanne de Jussie, *Le levain du calvinisme*, p. 94; at Le Croisic in Brittany in 1558, and at Rouen in 1560 (*Hist. eccl.*, I, 179–80, 352); the Lyons episode on Corpus Christi Day, 1560 (Guéraud, *Chronique*, pp. 133–34, and Archives départementales du Rhône, B, Sénéchaussée, Sentences, 1561–1562, sentence of 12 Sept. 1561); at Clermont-Ferrand in 1568 (Crespin, *Martyrs*, III, 651).

[72] The first big Psalm-singing parades seem to have occurred in 1551 in Lyons, with artisans, esp. printers' journeymen, taking the initiative in organizing them (Guéraud, *Chronique*, pp. 54–55; letters of Claude Baduel to Calvin in 1551 in Calvin, *Opera ... Omnia*, XIV, 16ff.) On an episode in Lyons in Dec. 1561, see Guéraud, *Chronique*, p. 145. On Toulouse in 1562, see Haton, *Mémoires*, pp. 177–78, 190; Bosquet, *Histoire*, p. 60; *Hist. eccl.*, III, 2. On the stoning of "Huguenot troops" returning from services into Paris in Sept. 1576, followed by a violent melee, see L'Estoile, *Mémoires-journaux*, I, 157.

[73] Haton, *Mémoires*, pp. 189–94.

riot that led eventually to the exile of Pierre Viret and another pastor from the city. In Montpellier, in the summer of 1561, the confraternities organized Sunday processions of hundreds of men, women and children with *pains bénits* ("blessed loaves of bread") – dancing, jumping, and crying, "In spite of the Huguenots we dance."[74]

But festivities led to more than spite and intimidation. For Mardi Gras at Issoudun in 1562, a Catholic group organized a dramatic costumed dance for thirteen pilgrims, thirteen reapers, thirteen wine-harvesters and thirteen tithe-collectors, each armed with large macabre tools. The Protestants got hold of the scenario for this grisly carnival and were able to get the players arrested.[75] In Pamiers in 1566, however, the festive youth society, with its popes, emperors, bishops and abbots, was able to dance its Pentecostal dance to the end. The Calvinists, who had stoned earlier dances, tried to prevent the affair, but the Catholic group insisted. "If [the heretics] can preach secretly, then we can dance – or it will cost five hundred heads." After a procession with relics and a silver statue of St. Anthony, the dancing began, three by three, with tambourines and minstrels. When they got to the quarter where Pastor Du Moulin was preaching, the song turned into "kill, kill," and serious fighting began which was to divide the town for three days. "It's a long time since I was up to my elbows in Huguenot blood," one of the dancers said. He was to be disappointed, for this time it was the Huguenots who won.[76]

These occasions for religious riot show us how characteristic was the scenario for the Paris St. Bartholomew's massacres. A marriage – one of the great rites of passage, but here, as with the baptism of Nemours and the burial at Toulouse, conflict over whether its form should be Catholic or Protestant – and then wedding masques of all kinds. In one, later seen as an allegory of coming events, the king and his brothers prevent wandering knights from entering Paradise and are pulled down to Hell by demons.[77] Soon after, as in Pamiers, the festivity turned into a rite of violence.

[74] De Rubys, *Histoire*, p. 406; *Hist. eccl.*, I, 969–70 and 970 n. 1. In Rouen in 1562, Protestant *menu peuple* stoned the members of the festive Abbey of Conards as they were about to begin their Mardi Gras activities (*ibid.*, II, 713).

[75] *Hist. eccl.*, I, 844.

[76] *Discours des troubles advenus en la ville de Pamiés le 5 iuin 1566. Avec un brief recit des calamitez souffertes l'année precedente* (1567), in *Arch. cur.*, VI, 309–43. On the relation between carnival and masked festivities, and various kinds of disturbance, see Le Roy Ladurie, *Paysans*, I, 395–99; N. Z. Davis, "The Reasons of Misrule: Youth Groups and Charivaris in Sixteenth-Century France," *Past and Present*, No. 50 (Feb. 1971), pp. 68–70; A. W. Smith, "Some Folklore Elements in Movements of Social Protest," *Folklore*, LXXVII (1966), 241–51.

[77] *Relation du massacre de la Saint-Barthélemy* in *Arch. cur.*, VII, 88–89; Frances Yates, *The*

IV

As with liturgical rites, there were some differences between the rites of violence of Catholic and Protestant crowds. The good Calvinist authors of the *Histoire ecclésiastique* went so far as to claim that outside of the murder of a certain seigneur de Fumel, killed in the Agenois "not for religion but for his tyrannies," "those of the Reformed religion made war only on images and altars, which do not bleed, while those of the Roman religion spilled blood with every kind of cruelty."[78] Though there is some truth in this distinction, Protestant rioters did in fact kill and injure people, and not merely in self-defense; and Catholic rioters did destroy religious property. At the Patriarche garden in Paris, at Vassy, at Senlis, Catholics smashed the pulpits and benches used in Reformed worship; at Amiens they went on to burn them.[79] As houses which had been used for Protestant worship in Meaux and Paris were ordered to be razed by Parlementary decree, so in Lyons in 1568 a Catholic crowd razed the Protestant *Temple du Paradis*, which hundreds of Psalm-singing men, women and children had built only a few years before.[80] *Both* Protestant and Catholic crowds destroyed books. The Catholic target was especially the French Bibles which they had so often seen burned publicly by the authorities in the 1540s and 1550s.[81] The Calvinist targets were especially the priests' manuals, the missals and the breviaries which Protestant writers like Viret had already desecrated in gross and comic satire.[82]

French Academies of the Sixteenth Century (London, 1947), pp. 254–59. Marriage as a possible occasion for slaughter remained in the mind of Henri de Navarre. In 1588 he feared that the festivities which an Armagnac nobleman was giving for his daughter's wedding were an occasion for a plot on his life. To prevent this, one of Navarre's supporters, a neighbor of the nobleman, entered the house with a band of men during the festivities and slaughtered about 35 gentlemen (L'Estoile, *Mémoires-journaux*, III, 121).

[78] *Hist. eccl.*, I, 887.

[79] *Histoire veritable de la mutinerie . . . faite par les prestres Sainct Medard*, p. 62; Crespin, *Martyrs*, III, 205; *Hist. eccl.*, II, 425, 433–35.

[80] Crespin, *Martyrs*, I, 495–98; *Discours de ce qui avint touchant la Croix de Gastines l'an 1571, vers Noel*, extracted from *Mémoires . . . de Charles IX*, in *Arch. cur.*, VI, 475–78; de Rubys, *Histoire veritable*, pp. 402, 412; [Jean Ricaud], *Discours du massacre . . . l'an 1572*, pp. 9–13.

[81] Crespin, *Martyrs*, III, 204; *Hist. eccl.*, II, 650–51, 839, 883, 932–33; III, 15, 315; Félibien and Lobineau, *Histoire*, IV, 828.

[82] Bosquet, *Histoire*, pp. 22, 143–44; Haton, *Mémoires*, p. 181; de Sainctes, *Discours sur le saccagement . . .*, in *Arch. cur.*, IV, 384; *Hist. eccl.*, I, 935; II, 720 n. 1, 925; III, 515. A Catholic polemical piece from Toulouse describes the opening Protestant "crime" in that city as the sale by Protestant *libraires* of the *Canon de la Messe*, which the Calvinists had depraved. This is in all probability a Protestant edition of the missal, with mocking and satirical footnotes throughout, which had various editions, including one in Lyons in 1564: *Les cauteles, canon et ceremonies de la messe. Ensemble la messe intitulé, Du corps de Iesuchrist. Le tout en Latin et en François: Le Latin fidelement extraict du Messel à l'usage de Rome imprimé à Lyon par Iean de Cambray l'an mil cinq cens vingt* (Lyons: Claude Ravot, 1564). In the comic tradition of Marcourt's

Nevertheless, when all this is said, the iconoclastic Calvinist crowds still come out as the champions in the destruction of religious property ("with more than Turkish cruelty," said a priest). This was not only because the Catholics had more physical accessories to their rite, but also because the Protestants sensed much more danger and defilement in the *wrongful use of material objects*. In Pamiers, the Catholic vicar might drop his Black Virgin of Foix when she failed to bring good weather; but then he tenderly repaired her broken neck with an iron pin. When the Protestants found her, they promptly burned the head in Pamiers and the body in Foix.[83]

In bloodshed, the Catholics are the champions (remember we are talking of the actions of Catholic and Protestant crowds, not of their armies). I think this is due not only to their being in the long run the strongest party numerically in most cities, but also to their stronger sense of *the persons of heretics* as sources of danger and defilement. Thus, injury and murder were a preferred mode of purifying the body social.

Furthermore, the preferred targets for physical attack differ in the Protestant and Catholic cases. As befitting a movement intending to overthrow a thousand years of clerical "tyranny" and "pollution," the Protestants' targets were primarily priests, monks and friars. That their ecclesiastical victims were usually unarmed (as Catholic critics hastened to point out) did not make them any less harmful in Protestant eyes, or any more immune from the wrath of God.[84] Lay people were sometimes attacked by Protestant crowds, too, such as the festive dancers who were stoned at Pamiers and Lyons, and the worshippers who were killed at Saint Médard's Church.[85] But there

---

Livre des marchands, the work resembles in organization Pierre Viret's satirical *Manuel, ou instruction des curez et vicaires* (Lyons: Claude Ravot, 1564).

As with statue-smashing, Protestant pastors much preferred that ecclesiastical libraries be confiscated and catalogued by the authorities (as in the Archives départementales du Rhône, 3E566, inventory of 10 May 1562) and not destroyed by the crowds. The *Histoire ecclésiastique* (III, 515) expressed regret at the insolence of Huguenot soldiers who destroyed an enormous quantity of books at the Abbey of Cluny under the impression that they were all missals.

[83] Hervet, *Discours sur . . . les pilleurs; Hist. eccl.*, I, 957. On the complexity of Catholic attitudes towards their statues, see Richard C. Trexler, "Florentine Religious Experience: The Sacred Image," *Studies in the Renaissance*, XIX (1972), 25–29.

[84] That priests and religious were the preferred (though not the exclusive) target for Protestant crowds is a fact emerging not only from an analysis of many crowd actions, but also from Catholic literature. The *Théâtre des cruautés des hérétiques* gives few examples of lay persons murdered, but many of priests and religious. Claude de Sainctes (*Discours sur le saccagement*, 1563) also stresses Protestant attacks on priests. Gentian Hervet's *Discours sur . . . les pilleurs* talks with horror of the Protestant war against unarmed priests, and the Protestant claim that their grudge is against the priests only. He warns that once all the churches are destroyed, the Protestants will start on the common people.

[85] *Discours des troubles advenus en la ville de Pamiés*, p. 318; de Rubys, *Histoire veritable*, p. 406; Haton, *Mémoires*, p. 181.

is nothing that quite resembles the style and extent of the slaughter of the 1572 massacres. The Catholic crowds were, of course, happy to catch a pastor when they could,[86] but the death of any heretic would help in the cause of cleansing France of these perfidious sowers of disorder and disunion. Indeed, while the number of women killed by Protestant crowds seems to have been very small, observers' reports show about one out of ten people killed by Catholic crowds in the provinces in 1572 was a woman, and the ratio was higher in Paris.[87]

Clearly, crowds that attacked unarmed priests and unarmed women were not trying to destroy only the physically powerful. But is Janine Estèbe right in suggesting that the 1572 massacres were also an expression of class hatred, by which she means a rising of the people against the rich Huguenots?[88] We can even broaden her question and ask whether it's true of other Catholic disturbances and of Protestant riots as well. As Charles Tilly and James Rule have asked in *Measuring Political Upheaval*, is the "isomorphy" of these disturbances high or low, by which they mean is there a high or low "degree of correspondence between the divisions separating the antagonists in a ... disturbance

---

[86] Among the pastors killed or assaulted by Catholic crowds were Leonard Morel at Vassy, 1561; Pastors Richer and Marcil at Poitiers, 1562; Pastor Giscart at Castelnaudary, 1562; a pastor at Gaillac, 1562; and Pastor Bonnet at Mâcon, 1562. Martin Tachard, formerly pastor at Val d'Angrogne and Montauban, was led in mockery through Foix in 1567. Among the pastors killed in the 1572 massacres were Bugnette, Le More and Des Gorris at Paris; Jacques Langlois and N. Dives at Lyons; Pierre Loiseleur dit de Villiers and Louis Le Coq at Rouen; and a minister at Bordeaux.

[87] Estimates in Crespin of persons killed in the 1572 massacres give, for Rouen, about 550 men and about 50 women; for Orléans, 1800 adult men and 150 adult women. No female deaths were reported from the Lyons Vespers. So many women were victims at Paris that word went out on 28 or 29 Aug. 1572 that no more women were to be killed, especially pregnant women. Even here, the listings show many fewer female deaths than male. The same is true for earlier crowd actions by Catholics, as in Provence in 1562 (Crespin, *Martyrs*, III, 695, 721, 710ff., 678, 371–88). It is clear from these estimates that pregnant women could not have been *preferred* targets, though they obviously were not spared. Whether they were the "choice victims" (*victimes de choix*) of Catholic crowds, as Estèbe claims (*Tocsin*, p. 197), I do not know. She associates this, as well as the castration of male corpses, with an attempt to extinguish "a foreign race, a hated and cursed race." As suggested above (n. 24), I find no evidence of the perception of the Huguenots as a "race." By their heresy, they appeared outsiders and finally non-human to their killers, but this is not a *racial* distinction. On the castration of corpses and the killing of unborn infants as ultimate efforts to humiliate and weaken the dangerous enemy, see below at n. 98.

As for Protestant killing of women, Catholic sources report women killed by the Huguenots in the Saint Médard massacre at Paris, in the May events at Toulouse in 1562, and in the diocese of Angoulême (Haton, *Mémoires*, p. 181; *Relations de l'émeute de Toulouse*, p. 351; *Théâtre des cruautés*, p. 44). Bosquet reports nuns raped at Montauban in 1562 (*Histoire*, chap. ii). On the whole, accounts of Protestant crowd action say little about assaults on females; with *statues* of the Virgin and female saints, it is another matter.

[88] Estèbe, *Tocsin*, p. 196.

and those prevailing in the social system within which the disturbance occurs"?[89]

Though only extensive quantitative research could establish the point, it seems to me that Estèbe's view does not hold for these *urban* disturbances. To be sure, pillaging played its role in all riots. To be sure, the Catholic crowds who threw slime and shouted "putains" ("whores") at the Protestant noblewomen being led from the rue Saint Jacques conventicle to prison in 1557 were savoring social resentment as well as religious hatred. So probably were the embroiderer's journeyman who slew a notable jewel merchant in 1572 at Paris and the cutler who slew a lawyer in Orléans.[90] For Protestants at Valence in 1562 who killed the sire de La Motte Gondrin, lieutenant-governor of the Dauphiné, there were political grievances to reinforce religious and social complaint.[91]

Nevertheless, despite such individual cases of "high isomorphy," the overall picture in these urban religious riots is not one of the "people" slaying the rich.[92] Protestant crowds expressed no preference for killing or assaulting powerful prelates over simple priests. As for Catholic crowds, contemporary listings of their victims in the 1572 massacres show that artisans, the "little people," are represented in significant numbers. In Lyons, for instance, in a list of 141 males killed in the Vespers, eighty-eight were artisans, thirty-four were merchants and six were lawyers.[93] Reports from other cities give a similar spread,

---

[89] Tilly and Rule, *Political Upheaval*, pp. 59–60.

[90] Crespin, *Martyrs*, II, 545; III, 676, 696.

[91] *Hist. eccl.*, III, 301–05. So also in Troyes, where a stockingmaker killed the merchant-provost of the town, who had formerly been a member of the Reformed Church, one expects that political grievances reinforced religious hatred (Crespin, *Martyrs*, III, 685). At Meaux, Crespin reports that one Gilles Le Conte was killed in the 1572 massacres, less because of his Reformed religion than because he was a tax-farmer for Catherine de Medici and was sometimes hard on Catholics (*ibid.*, p. 682).

[92] Though numerous other examples of "high isomorphy" can be found, the pages of Crespin are full of examples where artisans and merchants slew people in their trade (*ibid.*, p. 675) and where relative slew relatives (*ibid.*, pp. 676, 697). There are also individual cases of "high isomorphy" where the killing occurred "downward," i.e., the wealthy Catholic killed a poor Protestant. Indeed, the author of the *Tocsain contre les massacreurs* (in *Arch. cur.*, VII, 58–59) asked the following question: as for the little people who professed the Reformed religion, what humanity could they expect after the illustrious families had been treated in such a fashion?

[93] Figures compiled from *Première liste des Chrétiens mis à mort et égorgés à Lyon par les Catholiques romains à l'époque de la S. Barthélemi août 1572*, ed. P. M. Gonon (Lyons, 1847) and Crespin, *Martyrs*, III, 707–18. Letters from Lyons to Paris in early September reported that 600 to 700 persons were killed in all (A. Puyroche, "La Saint-Barthélemy à Lyon et le gouverneur Mandelot," *Bulletin de la Société de l'histoire du protestantisme français*, XVIII [1869], 365; Jacques Pannier, *L'Église réformée de Paris sous Henri IV* [Paris, 1911], p. 369 n. 1). These estimates seem high on the basis of all the available evidence from wills and burials.

as can be seen in the following table. Only in Orléans were more merchants reported to have been killed than artisans, while in Rouen and Meaux the "little people" outnumber the wealthier merchants among the victims many times over. The distributions are all the more significant because the prominent and rich who were slain were especially likely to be remarked. If we had fuller evidence about the massacres, it would doubtless multiply the names of victims of modest background.

TABLE

SOCIAL-OCCUPATIONAL DISTRIBUTION OF MALE VICTIMS
IN CONTEMPORARY LISTINGS OF THE 1572 MASSACRES*

City	Nobles †	Lawyers, Officers	Merchants	Teachers, Pastors	Artisans	Unskilled, Servants	Occupation unknown	Total
Bourges	0	7	6	0	8	0	2	23
Meaux	0	5	13	0	10 (+200) ‡	1	0	229
Troyes	0	1	11	0	22	2	0	36
Orléans	2	15	50	2	47	11	15	142
Rouen	3	9	18	3	119	3	31	186
Lyons	0	6	34	3	88	5	5	141
Paris	36	14	13	5	40	2	11	121

* Sources for Lyons are given in n. 93. Other lists are from Crespin, *Martyrs*, III.

† Nobles are here defined as persons listed with the title "sieur de" in Crespin. Some of the lawyers and high officers killed may also have been ennobled.

‡ The names of ten artisans are listed for Meaux, after which the author says and "other artisans to the number of 200 or more." This figure has been added, not because it is believed to be accurate, but because it reflects the impression of contemporaries as to what level of the population was hit by the massacres.

As I show in detail in my forthcoming book *Strikes and Salvation at Lyons*, Catholic and Protestant movements in French cities up to 1572 cut vertically through the social structure, but had each a distinctive occupational distribution. On the basis of limited evidence, that distribution seems to be fairly well reflected in the victims of crowd action,[94] and (as we will see more fully in a moment) in the make-up

[94] In my forthcoming book, *Strikes and Salvation at Lyons*, an analysis of the social and vocational distribution of several thousand male Protestants in Lyons in the period up to 1572 shows them to be drawn from the Consular elite, notables and *menu peuple* in numbers roughly proportional to their distribution in the population at large, but to be selected especially from the newer or more skilled occupations, occupations where the literacy rate was higher, or occupations (such as tavernkeeping) which had been transformed by the urban developments of the early 16th century. At the top of urban society, it is the new elite

of the crowds. Only the most vulnerable of the urban poor – the *gagnedeniers*, that is, the unskilled, the day laborers and the jobless – are not among the killers or the killed. Neither committed to the Calvinist cause nor well integrated into the Catholic city parish, these *bélîtres* ("rascals") appear only after the violence is over, stolidly robbing clothing from the corpses.[95]

Is popular religious violence in sixteenth-century France never then correlated in a *systematic* way with socio-economic conflict? Not when it is among the city-folk, who account for most of the disturbances; but when peasants raise their arms for the faith, the relationship is more likely to exist. How else to explain the dispatch with which peasant pilgrims fell upon the Huguenot burghers of Sens, surprising even the urban Catholics by their initiative? And when Protestant peasants in the Agenois pursued their persecuting lord, the seigneur of Fumel, they were shouting, "Murderer! Tyrant!" Even Catholic peasants joined in the siege of his chateau.[96]

Before turning to the composition of the urban crowds, let us look a little further at what I have called their rites of violence. Is there any way we can order the terrible, concrete details of filth, shame and torture that are reported from both Protestant and Catholic riots? I would suggest that they can be reduced to a repertory of actions, derived from the Bible, from the liturgy, from the action of political authority, or from the traditions of popular folk justice, intended to purify the religious community and humiliate the enemy and thus make him less harmful.

The religious significance of destruction by water or fire is clear

rather than the more established elite that tends to produce Protestants (in Lyons, therefore, among the Consular families it is the wealthy merchants rather than the lawyers who tend to become Protestant). This vocational distribution is, of course, not perfectly expressed in the victims of the massacres, since so many factors operated in the choice of any one person as a victim. E.g., very few persons from the publishing trade were killed in the Vespers at Lyons (the *libraires* Jean Honoré, Mathieu Penin and Jean Vassin, the bookbinder Mathurin Le Cler, and the proofreader Jean de Saint-Clément), though a very large percentage of the industry had been Protestant in the 1560s, and many masters and publishers still were so in 1572. It is my impression that in other cities, members of the publishing trade, though certainly found among the victims, were under-represented relative to their presence in the Reformed Church. This can probably be explained by the special relations among the men in the trade or by their absence from France.

[95] *Rélation du massacre de la Saint-Barthélemy*, reprinted from *Mémoires de ... Charles IX* in *Arch. cur.*, VII, 151; Crespin, *Martyrs*, III, 703.

[96] Haton, *Mémoires*, pp. 190–93; *Hist. eccl.*, I, 885–86. See also a religious riot with "high isomorphy" in Beaune, a small town with a very high percentage of winegrowers – i.e., a large *rural* element – within its walls. In 1561 the winegrowers and others of the "little people," supported from above by one of the city councilors, attacked Protestants returning from services. The latter group included some of the wealthier families in Beaune (*ibid.*, pp. 864–65).

enough. The rivers which receive so many Protestant corpses are not merely convenient mass graves, they are temporarily a kind of holy water, an essential feature of Catholic rites of exorcism. The fire which razes the house of a Protestant apothecary in Montpellier leaves behind it not the smell of death, of the heretic whom the crowd had hanged, but of spices, lingering in the air for days, like incense. If Protestants have rejected holy water and incense, they still follow Deuteronomy in accepting fire as a sacred means of purification.[97]

Let us take a more difficult case, the troubling case of the dese- cration of corpses. This is primarily an action of Catholic crowds in the sixteenth century. Protestant crowds could be very cruel indeed in torturing living priests, but paid little attention to them when they were dead.[98] (Perhaps this is related to the Protestant rejection of Purgatory and prayers for the dead; the souls of the dead experience immediately Christ's presence or the torments of the damned, and thus the dead body is no longer so dangerous or important an object to the living.) What interested Protestants was digging up bones that were being treated as sacred objects by Catholics and perhaps burning them, after the fashion of Josiah in I Kings.[99] The Catholics, however, were not content with burning or drowning heretical corpses. That was not cleansing enough. The bodies had to be weakened and humiliated further. To an eerie chorus of "strange whistles and hoots," they were thrown to the dogs like Jezebel, they were dragged through the streets, they had their genitalia and internal organs cut away, which were then hawked through the city in a ghoulish commerce.[100]

[97] On Catholic rites of exorcism, see Thomas, *Religion and the Decline of Magic*, chaps. ii and xv. For the Montpellier episode, see Philippi, *Mémoires*, p. 634. Cf. the somewhat different treatment by Estèbe of the St. Bartholomew's Day Massacre as a "ritual crime" and purification rite (*Tocsin*, p. 197).

[98] Though Catholic writers such as the priest Claude Haton (*Mémoires*, pp. 704–06) admit to various acts of desecration of corpses by *Catholic* crowds, they make remarkably few accusations against *Protestants* for the same kind of acts. Haton gives only one example – the dismemberment of a doctor of theology killed in the Saint Médard massacre (p. 181) – though he accuses the Huguenots of many other kinds of vicious actions. Bosquet's book on Toulouse gives one example (at Montauban) of Protestants disemboweling a priest and displaying his entrails (*Histoire*, pp. 9–10), but stresses much more the Protestant humiliation and torture of living persons. The *Théâtre des cruautés des hérétiques*, which would surely have mentioned the Protestant acts of desecration of corpses if they had been common, talks only of the torture of living priests. In contrast, Protestant writings are full of descriptions of Catholic desecration of corpses, and Catholic sources describe these as well.

[99] For Calvin on Purgatory and the whereabouts of the soul between death and the Last Judgment, see *Institutes*, Bk. III, chap. v, secs. 6–10, and chap. xxv, sec. 6. See also Keith Thomas' discussion of Protestant attitudes towards the dead in *Religion*, pp. 588–95, 602–06; C. de Sainctes, *Discours sur le saccagement*, p. 381 (burning of "holy bones" at Orléans). For the digging up and throwing around of saints' bones at Lyons, see Guéraud, *Chronique*, p. 156; Niepce, *Monuments*, pp. 42–43.

[100] On strange sounds in Paris at the St. Bartholomew's Day massacres, see Crespin,

Let us also take the embarrassing case of the desecration of religious objects by filthy and disgusting means. It is the Protestants, as we have seen, who are concerned about objects, who are trying to show that Catholic objects of worship have no magical power. It is not enough to cleanse by swift and energetic demolition, not enough to purify by a great public burning of the images, as in Albiac, with the children of the town ceremonially reciting the Ten Commandments around the fire.[101] The line between the sacred and the profane was also re-drawn by throwing the sacred host to the dogs, by roasting the crucifix upon a spit, by using holy oil to grease one's boots, and by leaving human excrement on holy-water basins and other religious objects.[102]

And what of the living victims? Catholics and Protestants humiliated them by techniques borrowed from the repertory of folk justice. Catholic crowds lead Protestant women through the streets with muzzles on – a popular punishment for the shrew – or with a crown of thorns.[103] A form of charivari is used, where the noisy throng humiliates its victim by making him ride backward on an ass. In Blois in 1562, the Catholics did this to a Protestant saddler, poking him with a pike and shouting, "Oh, don't touch him, he belongs to the queen mother." In Montauban, a priest was ridden backward on an ass, his chalice in one hand, his host in the other, and his missal at an end of a halberd. At the end of his ride, he must crush his host and burn his own vestments. And, as in the festive parade on an ass of henpecked husbands it was sometimes necessary to get a neighbor to

Martyrs, III, 681. Bodies were thrown to the dogs in Draguignan and in Fréjus in 1560 (Hist. eccl., I, 421, 429) and in Orléans (Crespin, Martyrs, III, 693). Parts of corpses were sold at Villeneuve d'Avignon in 1561 ("Five pence for a Huguenot's liver!"); at Vire in 1562 ("who wants to buy the tripe of Huguenots?"); at Paris in 1572; at Lyons in 1572, where an apothecary rendered fat from Protestant corpses and sold it at 3 blancs the pound (Hist. eccl., I, 978; II, 846; Le tocsain contre les massacreurs in Arch. cur., VII, 51; Crespin, Martyrs, III, 713).

There are also a few reports of cannibalism by Catholics in the wake of crowd murder ("not for hunger," as Montaigne says of "Cannibals" in his Essais, "but to represent an extreme vengeance"): at Carcassone in 1561, Troyes in 1562, and Sens in 1562 (Hist. eccl., I, 94; II, 478; III, 419–20). Le Roy Ladurie reports a curious story of cannibalism among Protestants at Lodève in 1573. The body of St. Fulcran, miraculously conserved, was shot and then eaten by order of the Huguenots in the wake of an uprising there (Paysans, I, 398 n. 5).

[101] Hist. eccl., I, 931.

[102] Haton, Mémoires, pp. 181–82; Guéraud, Chronique, p. 156; Bosquet, Histoire, p. 148; de Sainctes, Discours, p. 372. See above at n. 21.

[103] For the muzzle at Toulouse in 1562, and the crowns of thorns at St. Martin de Castillan and Brignolles in 1562, see Hist. eccl., III, 43; Crespin, Martyrs, III, 386–87. On punishments for the shrew, see Davis, "Reasons of Misrule," pp. 52, 56 n. 48. Prisoners were sometimes muzzled on the way to execution (L'Estoile, Mémoires-journaux, III, 166).

replace the husband, so sometimes a Protestant had to replace the priest. Dressed in holy vestments, he would be led through the streets pretending to say mass, while the crowd with him sang in derision *Te Deum Laudamus* or a requiem.[104]

With such actions, the crowds seem to be moving back and forth between the rites of violence and the realm of comedy. Are we at a Mardi Gras game, with its parodies and topsy-turvy mockery? At Lyons, a Protestant, in the midst of sacking the Church of Saint Irénée, dresses up as the saint with his episcopal ring around his neck. At Rouen, the host is paraded at the end of a Rogation's Day lance with a dragon on it: "The dragon has eaten the host"![105] At Mâcon in 1562, the familiar blessing from Numbers vi. 24–26 is parodied as Protestants are slain: "The lord God of Huguenots keep you, the great Devil bless you, the Lord make his face to shine upon you who play the dead." Murder finally began to be called a "farce" in Mâcon, the "farce of Saint-Point," the lieutenant-governor. The game was to go with some women after a party and get one or two Protestant prisoners from jail, have the ladies chat pleasantly with them, as they walked to the Saône bridge, and then drown them.[106]

These episodes disclose to us the underlying function of the rites of violence. As with the "games" of Christ's tormentors, which hide from them the full knowledge of what they do, so these charades and ceremonies hide from sixteenth-century rioters a full knowledge of what they are doing. Like the legitimation for religious riot examined earlier in this paper, they are part of the "conditions for guilt-free massacre," to use a phrase from a recent study of violence in our own

---

[104] Crespin, *Martyrs*, III, 311–12; *Hist. eccl.*, I, 935; Bosquet, *Histoire*, pp. 9–10; de Sainctes, *Discours*, p. 384. There were other charivari-like actions in religious riots. At Tours in 1562 Protestant women were taken back to mass on horseback "in derision" (probably facing backward on the horse) (*Hist. eccl.*, II, 695). At Mâcon in 1562 Pastor Bonnet was promenaded through the town with "mockery, a thousand punches and raps on the nose," the crowd crying, "Whoever wants to hear this pious and holy person preach, come to the Place de l'Escorcherie" (*ibid.*, III, 522). In 1567 Pastor Martin Tachart was led through Foix in triumph, in a "white bonnet, with a rosary around his neck" (*Discours des troubles advenus en la ville de Pamiés*, p. 342). On charivaris, see Davis, "Reasons of Misrule."

[105] Claude de Rubys, *Oraison prononcée à Lyon à la creation des conseillers et eschevins ... le iour de la feste S. Thomas ... 1567* (Lyons, 1568), fol. Bb 2ᵛ; the journal of Canon Bruslart of Rouen, qtd. in *Hist. eccl.*, II, 720 n. 1.

[106] *Hist. eccl.*, III, 518, 524. Other examples of the renaming of objects or actions of violence: Protestants in Béziers and Montpellier called the clubs with which they hit priests and religious and other Catholic enemies *époussettes* or "whiskbrooms"; Catholics in Mont-de-Marsan and its region used the same term for the clubs with which they hit Protestants (*Hist. eccl.*, III, 158–59; II, 963–65; Philippi, *Mémoires*, p. 624). At Agen the gibbet on which Protestants were hanged was called the "Consistory" (*Hist. eccl.*, II, 941–42). At Rouen, Catholic crowds referred to killing Huguenots as "accommodating" them (Crespin, *Martyrs*, III, 721).

day.[107] The crucial fact that the killers must forget is that their victims are human beings. These harmful people in the community – the evil priest or hateful heretic – have already been transformed for the crowd into "vermin" or "devils." The rites of religious violence complete the process of dehumanization. So in Meaux, where Protestants were being slaughtered with butchers' cleavers, a living victim was trundled to his death in a wheelbarrow, while the crowd cried "vinegar, mustard." And the vicar of the parish of Fouquebrune in the Angoumois was attached with the oxen to a plough and died from Protestant blows as he pulled.[108]

V

What kinds of people made up the crowds that performed the range of acts we have examined in this paper? First, they were not by and large the alienated rootless poor that people the pages of Norman Cohn's *Pursuit of the Millennium*.[109] A large percentage of men in Protestant iconoclastic riots and in the crowds of Catholic killers in 1572 were characterized as artisans. Sometimes the crowds included other men from the lower orders, as in 1562 in Gaillac, where Catholic boatmen from Montauban participated in the May massacres, and in Dieppe, where Protestant sailors entered the churches at night to smash statues. More often, the social composition of the crowds extended upward to encompass merchants, notaries and lawyers, as well as the clerics whose role has already been mentioned.[110] De-

[107] Troy Duster, "Conditions for Guilt-Free Massacre," in Nevitt Sanford and Craig Comstock, eds., *Sanctions for Evil* (San Francisco, 1971), chap. iii. Duster especially stresses the dehumanization of victims, and this volume contains several interesting essays on this matter.

[108] Crespin, *Martyrs*, III, 684; *Théâtre des cruautés des hérétiques*, p. 44. There are several examples of Catholics associating Protestants not only with animals but also with excrement. Excrement is thrown at them by crowds (Crespin, *Martyrs*, II, 545; III, 203–04, 672), and in an extraordinary episode in Toulouse Protestants hiding in the sewers along the river are flushed out, covered with excrement, by great streams of water poured into the *cloacas* by Catholics, and are drowned (*Hist. eccl.*, III, 19).

[109] Cohn, *Pursuit*, pp. 32, 137, 281.

[110] On artisans in iconoclastic riots, see *Hist. eccl.*, I, 889; II, 702, 719. For analysis of Catholic crowds, see Crespin, *Martyrs*, III, 663–733. On Catholic boatmen at Gaillac, see *ibid.*, p. 82; on Protestant sailors at Dieppe, *ibid.*, II, 796. Catholics were arrested in the wake of the Corpus Christi Day riot at Lyons in 1561, during which Barthélemy Aneau, rector of the Collège de la Trinité, and others were killed – a boatman, a miller, a tavern-keeper, a shearer, a silkthrower (Archives départementales du Rhône, B, Sénéchaussée, Sentences, 1561–1562, sentence of 14 Aug. 1561). Councilors from the Parlement of Toulouse were present in a violent Catholic crowd of May 1562 (*Hist. eccl.*, III, 15).

Near the conclusion of his "Brieve Raccontamento" (edited by John Tedeschi elsewhere in this volume), Tomasso Sassetti reports that printers were active among the Lyons killers; but his assertion is not borne out by any other accounts by residents of Lyons, nor by the

pending on the size, extent and occasion of the disturbance, the leaders of the crowd were sometimes artisans themselves, but frequently a mixed group. Iconoclastic disturbances, other than those carried out by Protestant noblemen and their soldiers, were ordinarily led by the "little people," but notable personages led the Protestant rioters into Saint Médard's church in 1561. Of twenty leaders of the 1572 massacres at Orléans, three were lawyers, eight were merchants, and others were various kinds of craftsmen – tanners, butchers and candlemakers.[111]

In addition, there was significant participation by two other groups of people who, though not rootless and alienated, had a more marginal relationship to political power than did lawyers, merchants or even male artisans – namely, city women and teenaged boys. As the wives of craftsmen marched with their husbands in the great Psalm-singing parades, so they were always busy in the iconoclastic riots of the Protestants. Sometimes they are active in other ways, as in Pamiers, where a bookseller's wife set fire to the house of the leading enemy of the Huguenots there, and in Toulouse, where La Broquiere, a solicitor's wife, fought Catholics with firearms.[112] As the wives of Catholic tradesmen march with their husbands in Corpus Christi Day processions, so they participate in Catholic religious disturbances. They shout insults at a Protestant funeral in Montauban and throw mire at a minister in Vassy, screaming, "Kill him, kill the evil-doer who has caused so many deaths"; but their most extreme violence seems directed against other women. At Aix-en-Provence in 1572, a group of butcher women torment a Protestant woman, the wife of a bookseller, finally hanging her from a pine tree, which had been used as a meeting place for Protestant worship.[113]

Adolescent males and even boys aged ten to twelve played a strikingly important role in both Catholic and Protestant crowds. In

patterns of deaths (see n. 94 above). Only two merchant-publishers are known to have had a connection with the massacres – Guillaume Rouillé, who was a consul at the time and thus bears some responsibility for what happened, and Alexandre Marsigli, a Luccan exile who killed a merchant, Paolo Minutoli, in the hope that he would be pardoned in Lucca and allowed to return. Sassetti had just arrived in Lyons when the Vespers occurred.

[111] Crespin, *Martyrs*, III, 692.

[112] *Hist. eccl.*, I, 227, 719; Crespin, *Martyrs*, III, 522; *Discours des troubles advenus en la ville de Pamiés*, p. 325; Bosquet, *Histoire*, pp. 148–50. I have also treated this subject in "City Women and Religious Change in Sixteenth-Century France," in Dorothy McGuigan, ed., *A Sampler of Women's Studies* (Ann Arbor, Mich., 1973), pp. 17–45.

[113] *Hist. eccl.*, I, 913; Crespin, *Martyrs*, III, 203–04, 392. At Lyons a woman was among those arrested for her actions in the Corpus Christi Day riot of 1561 (Archives départementales du Rhône, B, Sénéchaussée, Sentences, 1561–1562, sentence of 14 Aug. 1561). Catholic women stoned a Protestant mercer at Vire in Normandy (*Hist. eccl.*, II, 846).

Lyons and Castelnaudary in 1562 *enfants* stoned Protestant worshippers on their way to services. In several towns in Provence – Marseille, Toulon and elsewhere – Catholic youths stoned Protestants to death and burned them. The reputation of the adolescents in Sens and Provins was so frightening that a member of a well-known Huguenot family was afraid to walk through the streets, lest the children of Provins (*enfants de Provins*) massacre him.[114] In Toulouse, Catholic students take part in the massacres of 1572, and a decade earlier Protestant students had had the university in an uproar, whistling and banging in lectures when the canon law or the "old religion" was mentioned. In Poitiers in 1559 and again in 1562, Protestant youngsters from ten to twelve and students take the initiative in smashing statues and overturning altars. Indeed, youths are mentioned as part of almost all the great iconoclastic disturbances – in the Netherlands, in Rouen and elsewhere.[115]

I am struck here by the similarity between the license allowed youth to do violence in religious riot and the festive license allowed adolescents in the youth-abbeys in villages and small towns to act as the conscience of the community in matters of domestic discord. As young teenagers and children participated in the processional life of, say, Rouen ("their prayers are of great merit before God, especially because they are pure and clean in their conscience and without malice," noted a Rouennais priest) and led some of the great League penitential processions in Paris in 1589, so Catholic adolescents moved into religious violence without much criticism from their elders.[116]

---

[114] For Lyons, see Guéraud, *Chronique*, p. 145; for Castelnaudary, see *Hist. eccl.*, III, 157; for Marseille, Toulon, Poignans and Forcalquier, see *ibid.*, pp. 412–15; for Provins and Sens, see Haton, *Mémoires*, pp. 194, 315. In addition the *petits enfans* ("children") of Auxerre start stoning the doors of a conventicle in 1561, and the *petits enfans* of Draguignan, egged on by priests and councilors of the Parlement of Aix, kill the important Protestant, Antoine de Richier, sieur de Mouvans, in 1560 (*Hist. eccl.*, I, 852, 421). The tug-of-war over a corpse by the boys, ten to twelve years old, in Provins has already been described, as has the riot in Pamiers, provoked by the *jeunes hommes* ("young men") of the festive youth group (above at nn. 34, 76). Already in Geneva in 1533 we see Catholic *enfants*, twelve to fifteen years old, joining their mothers in Catholic crowds which stoned the heretical women (Jeanne de Jussie, *Levain*, p. 47).

[115] For Toulouse, see Crespin, *Martyrs*, III, 726; Bosquet, *Histoire*, p. 46. For Poitiers, see *Hist. eccl.*, I, 227–28; II, 703. For Rouen, see *ibid.*, p. 719. For Flanders, see Crespin, *Martyrs*, III, 519 n. 1, 522. Students also participated in the 1572 massacres at Orléans (*ibid.*, p. 695).

[116] F. N. Taillepied, *Recueil des antiquitez et singularitez de la ville de Rouen* (Rouen, 1587), pp. 195–97; L'Estoile, *Mémoires-journaux*, III, 243–44, 247. Peter Ascoli also describes the role of children in the League procession of 1589 in "The Sixteen and the Paris League, 1589–1591" (unpublished Ph. D. dissertation, University of California at Berkeley, 1971). In a recent article on 15th-century Florence, Richard Trexler has emphasized the role of male adolescents first in the processional life of the city and then as zealous and active

In the Protestant case, where sons might sometimes disagree about religion with their fathers and where the revolt is in part against the paternal authority of the clergy, youthful violence seems to have more of the character of generational conflict. But ultimately Calvinism, too, was a movement cutting across generational lines, within which adolescents or artisans sometimes took the early initiative in open militant action. Thus in Lyons in 1551, the first public Psalm-singing marches were organized by printers' journeymen, while in Montpellier in 1560–61 it was the "young people" (*jeunes gens*) who first invited a minister to the city and began public Psalm singing in French in front of the city hall.[117]

Finally, as this study has already suggested, the crowds of Catholics and Protestants, including those bent on deadly tasks, were not an inchoate mass, but showed many signs of organization. Even with riots that had little or no planning behind them, the event was given some structure by the situation of worship or the procession that was the occasion for many disturbances. In other cases, planning in advance led to lists of targets, and ways of identifying friends or fellow rioters (white crosses on Catholic doors in Mâcon in 1562; red bonnets worn by the killers in the *Bande Cardinale* in Bordeaux in 1572; passwords and slogans – "Long live the Cross," "The Wolf," "Long live the Gospel").[118] Existing organizations could provide the basis for subsequent religious disturbance, such as confraternities and festive youth societies for Catholics; and for both Protestants and Catholics, units of the militia and craft groupings.[119]

Zeal for violent purification also led to new organizations. Sometimes the model was a military one, as in the companies of Catholic artisans in Autun, Auxerre and Le Mans raised by the lifting of an ensign; the "marching bands" organized in Béziers by both Protestants and Catholics; and the *dizaines* set up by the Reformed church of Montauban in 1561.[120] Sometimes the model was a youth group, as in the

supporters of Savonarola's war on the vanities ("Ritual in Florence: Adolescence and Salvation in the Renaissance," in C. Trinkaus and H. Oberman, eds., *The Pursuit of Holiness* [Leiden, 1974], pp. 200–64).

[117] N. Z. Davis, "Strikes and Salvation at Lyons," *Archiv für Reformationsgeschichte*, LVI (1965), 51–52; Philippi *Mémoires*, p. 623. For youth-groups and their role in 16th-century France, see Davis, "Reasons of Misrule."

[118] For the role of Protestant targets in Nemours, see *Hist. eccl.*, I, 834. For the white crosses in Mâcon, see *ibid.*, III, 518. For the red bonnets in Bordeaux, see Crespin, *Martyrs*, III, 729. For "Vive la Croix" in Toulouse, "Le Loup" (a Catholic password in Vire in Normandy) and "Vive l'Évangile" in La Rochelle, see *Hist. eccl.*, III, 33; II, 845, 989.

[119] *Ibid.*, I, 355, 844; *Discours des troubles advenus en la ville de Pamiés*, pp. 319–20.

[120] *Hist. eccl.*, III, 487; Crespin, *Martyrs*, III, 287, 641; *Hist. eccl.*, III, 158–59; I, 913. Also see the "company" of horsemen of the draper Cosset of Meaux, founded in 1572 right

case of a band of young unmarried lesser nobles in Champagne, who went around terrorizing Catholics.[121] The creation which best expresses the spirit of religious riot, however, is the band of the sieur de Flassans in Aix-en-Provence. This nobleman, first consul of Aix, in 1562 organized a troop of "little people," butchers among them, and monks, to seek out Protestants in the area, stoning their houses, shouting at them, killing, or imprisoning them. They wore rosaries and special feathered hats with white crosses on them; they sang special songs against the Huguenots; carried an ensign with the pope's keys upon it; and went everywhere led by a Franciscan with a great wooden cross.[122]

That such splendor and order should be put to violent uses is a disturbing fact. Disturbing, too, is the whole subject of religious violence. How does an historian talk about a massacre of the magnitude of St. Bartholomew's Day? One approach is to view extreme religious violence as an extraordinary event, the product of frenzy, of the frustrated and paranoic primitive mind of the people. As Estèbe has said, "The procedures used by the killers of Saint Bartholomew's Day came back from the dawn of time; the collective unconscious had buried them within itself, they sprang up again in the month of August 1572."[123] Though there are clearly resemblances between the purification rites of primitive tribes and those used in sixteenth-century religious riots, this paper has suggested that one does not need to look so far as the "collective unconscious" to explain this fact, nor does one need to regard the 1572 massacres as an isolated phenomenon.

A second approach sees such violence as a more usual part of social behavior, but explains it as a somewhat pathological product of

---

after the massacres to round up and kill Huguenots who had escaped to nearby villages (Crespin, *Martyrs*, III, 684), and the image-breaking band formed in 1562 in Mont-de-Marsan (*Hist. eccl.*, II, 963–64).

[121] Haton, *Mémoires*, p. 334. In Annonay in 1573, a young man, formerly head of the *bazoche* (festive society of law clerks) of Vismes, put himself at the head of 80 men "of his type" and lived off the countryside. This was evidently a Protestant band of young men (Achille Gamon, *Mémoires*, p. 615). The most interesting new youth group formed in this period was, however, the Whistlers or *Sifflars* of Poitiers, so called from a whistle the members wore around their necks. Founded among students around 1561, it initially mocked both religions. Initiates had to swear by flesh, belly, death and "the worthy double head, stuffed with relics" and by all the Divinity in this pint of wine, that they would be devoted Whistlers, and that instead of going to Protestant service, mass or vespers, they would go twice a day to a brothel, etc. The group grew to some 64 youths and became especially hostile to the Reformed Church and its services, perhaps because of Reformed hostility to them. Its members began to go around armed (*Hist. eccl.*, I, 844–45).

[122] *Ibid.*, pp. 983–86; Crespin, *Martyrs*, III, 390–91.

[123] Estèbe, *Tocsin*, pp. 194, 197.

certain kinds of child-rearing, economic deprivation or status loss. This paper has assumed that conflict is perennial in social life, though the forms and strength of the accompanying violence vary; and that religious violence is intense because it connects intimately with the fundamental values and self-definition of a community. The violence is explained not in terms of how crazy, hungry or sexually frustrated the violent people are (though they may sometimes have such characteristics), but in terms of the goals of their actions and in terms of the roles and patterns of behavior allowed by their culture. Religious violence is related here less to the pathological than to the normal.

Thus, in sixteenth-century France, we have seen crowds taking on the role of priest, pastor or magistrate to defend doctrine or purify the religious community, either to maintain its Catholic boundaries and structure, or to re-form relations within it. We have seen that popular religious violence could receive legitimation from different features of political and religious life, as well as from the group identity of the people in the crowds. The targets and character of crowd violence differed somewhat between Catholics and Protestants, depending on their perception of the source of danger and on their religious sensibility. But in both cases, religious violence had a connection in time, place and form with the life of worship, and the violent actions themselves were drawn from a store of punitive or purificatory traditions current in sixteenth-century France.

In this context, the cruelty of crowd action in the 1572 massacres was not an exceptional occurrence. St. Bartholomew was certainly a bigger affair than, say, the Saint Médard's riot, it had more explicit sanction from political authority, it had elaborate networks of communication at the top level throughout France, and it took a more terrible toll in deaths. Perhaps its most unusual feature was that the Protestants did not fight back.[124] But on the whole, it still fits into a whole pattern of sixteenth-century religious disturbance.

This inquiry also points to a more general conclusion. Even in the extreme case of religious violence, crowds do not act in a mindless way. They will to some degree have a sense that what they are doing is legitimate, the occasions will relate somehow to the defense of their

---

[124] The non-resistance of the Protestants is an extraordinary fact which emerges from all accounts of the 1572 massacres, and which is in contrast to the militant high morale of the Protestants when they were attacked in, say, 1561–1562. The Protestant martyrs described in Crespin in 1572 either try to run away – the males sometimes dressed in their wives' clothes (*Martyrs*, III, 698) – or die bravely in their faith. When an individual does try to resist (e.g., Maistre Mamert, a schoolteacher and swordmaster in Orléans), it is the occasion of some notice by Crespin (III, 697).

cause, and their violent behavior will have some structure to it – here dramatic and ritual. But the rites of violence are not the rights of violence in any *absolute* sense. They simply remind us that if we try to increase safety and trust within a community, guarantee that the violence it generates will take less destructive and less cruel forms, then we must think less about pacifying "deviants" and more about changing the central values.

THE WARS OF RELIGION IN
SEVENTEENTH-CENTURY HUGUENOT THOUGHT*

by

ELISABETH LABROUSSE

During the seventeenth century the Massacre of Saint Bartholomew received surprisingly little attention. The Machiavellian *libertin* Gabriel Naudé might have praised it, but he was the exception that proves the rule.[1] Much more typical was Richelieu, who in 1617 depicted the Massacre as a shameful and horrible episode, blaming it on the threats of the Protestants.[2] (Conversely, Tilenus in 1622 regarded it as the origin of the monarchomach views held by some of the Huguenots.[3]) The proper tone in which to speak of the event was one of eloquent revulsion, as we find for example in Mézeray, or Louis XIV's tutor Hardouin de Péréfixe, or even Maimbourg on the eve of the Revocation of the Edict of Nantes.[4]

Nor were the Protestant writers prone to mention it. Generally speaking, they were not the first to steer controversy around to recent French and European history; for it was a dangerous subject, fraught with pitfalls. They tackled it only when the Catholics left them no choice but to respond. Of course *la controverse historique récente* was

---

* These remarks are based on an extensive but by no means exhaustive study of the sources. They are merely an impressionistic sketch, and attempt little more than to suggest certain lines of general interpretation. Annotation has been kept to a minimum. The reader desiring more background is referred to books on the subject by Jean Orcibal and Walter Rex, Jr.

[1] *Considérations politiques sur les coups d'Etat* (1639), chap. iii.

[2] *Les principaux points de la foy de l'Eglise Catholique defendus contre l'escrit adressé au Roy par les quatre ministres* ... See beginning of chap. ii.

[3] *Examen d'un escrit intitulé "Discours des vrayes raisons, pour lesquelles ceux de la Religion Pretendue Reformée en France, peuvent en bonne conscience résister par armes, à la persecution ouverte que leur font les ennemis de leur Religion et de l'Estat. Où est respondu à l'advertissement à l'Assemblée de La Rochelle ..."* The author of this anonymous pamphlet was the firebrand Brachet de La Milletière. Tilenus, who had been professor of theology in the Protestant Academy of Sedan, had been deprived of this job because of his leanings toward Arminianism, but there is no correlation between political and theological attitudes. Pierre Du Moulin, for instance, so hostile towards Arminianism, shared the political views of Tilenus.

[4] See F. Mézeray, *Abrégé chronologique de l'histoire de France* (3 vols.; 1667–1668); Hardouin de Beaumont de Péréfixe, *Histoire du roy Henry-le-Grand* (1661); L. Maimbourg, *Histoire du Calvinisme* (1682) – in all cases under the year "1572."

endemic, reaching a fever pitch at the time of the First English Revolution. For a Roman Catholic assailant, it was an excellent tactic to paint the Huguenots as trouble-makers, enemies of monarchy, in a word, "republicans." This argument was revived again in the years preceding the Revocation. If the Protestants could be branded as potential traitors, their close surveillance and even their persecution could be justified to moderate Catholics on the grounds of simple political expediency.

Thus, when it came to *la controverse historique récente*, the Protestants remained on the defensive. They did not avoid debate – although a Daillé, for example, dolefully reminded his adversaries that the edicts of pacification expressly forbade dredging up the past[5] – but they took care not to challenge the enemy on this terrain.

The Edict of Nantes had locked the Huguenots into their position as second-rate citizens. When in 1617 they spoke of "millions" of French Protestants, Richelieu manifested open disdain for their braggadocio.[6] In 1662, far more realistically, Daillé protested that the Huguenots would not be able to violate the Edict, even if they wanted to do so, "in a country where you [*viz.*, the Catholics] are much stronger and numerous than we."[7] (We can find Amyraut writing in this peevish tone as early as 1647.[8]) The Edict had left the Huguenots in possession of the strongholds they had conquered – a situation which was later to turn into a kind of scattered ghetto. Typical of the mentality of the time, the Edict assumed that society was static. Its authors made no allowance for demographic growth (which can be observed here and there) or for migration. And it did in many cases become a strait jacket. As the population grew, the Huguenots built additional temples; and the commissioners appointed in 1661 found – to their no small pleasure – that they had real evidence to justify some of their reports of Protestant infractions of the Edict in the south of France.

One of the consequences of the Edict seems to have been to displace the center of gravity of Huguenot propaganda. What was originally an outburst of religious fervor became a worldly and political campaign against popery. (In this regard it is significant that the Synod of Gap in 1603 attempted to insert into the Confession of Faith an article

---

[5] *Réplique ... aux deux livres que Messieurs Adam et Cottiby ont publiez ...* (Geneva, 1662), II, end of chap. xvii, pp. 107–08.

[6] See above, n. 2.

[7] *Réplique* (see above, n. 5), II, chap. xvi, p. 97.

[8] *Apologie pour ceux de la religion sur les sujets d'aversion que plusieurs pensent avoir contre leurs personnes et leur créance* (Saumur, 1647), *passim*.

declaring the pope to be Antichrist.[9]) Leaving aside technical theological controversy, popular Protestant polemics were cast in the more appealing form of hyper-Gallicanism. Huguenots vied with Catholics to stress the total independence of the king of France and to exalt his royal rights – rights, it should be said, which paradoxically served as one of the ideological justifications of the Revocation! This is the basis of the convincing explanation offered by Meinecke for the changing role of Rohan;[10] and perhaps it also accounts for the behavior of Brachet de La Milletière.

Since the supra-national character of the Roman Catholic Church was obvious, particularly as manifested in the religious orders – above all by the Jesuits – this hyper-Gallicanism of the Huguenots was a well-chosen weapon. It was particularly effective in the case of moderate Catholic opinion. The hatred of the *parti dévot* for the Protestants was, of course, unalterable. But many Catholics in France had little liking for the Jesuits and other regulars. They longed to see the secular clergy, which was dependent upon the crown, gain the upper hand. Even pious Catholics often harbored a great mistrust for the Ultramontanes, and held the pope in low esteem; so this sort of Protestant propaganda found many sympathetic readers in the general public.

To oppose this super-patriotism so noisily proclaimed by the Huguenots, the Catholic writers stood ready to remind their readers of the Huguenot rebellions during the religious wars of the sixteenth century and the Protestant uprisings in the first half of the reign of Louis XIII. In the face of Huguenot pretentions to uncompromising patriotism, they stressed two points: first, the subversive character of an ecclesiastical organization which gave so important a role to elders (who were laymen), which affirmed equality among the ministers, and which therefore stank of "democracy"; second, the potential treachery of the "Calvinist International," the ties which bound the Huguenots to their brethren in England, the Netherlands and Geneva. In sum, the past actions of the Huguenots, their present organization and sympathies, were said to reveal them to be subjects dangerous to the monarchy and potential traitors to their country.

The First English Revolution (1642) offered a particularly fertile field for this sort of incrimination. "Les bons Français" – for whose favor the controversy was waged – could easily be offended by this

[9] The inclusion of such an article had many complex causes and consequences. We simply mention one of its aspects.

[10] F. Meinecke, *Machiavelism, the Doctrine of "Raison d'Etat" and Its Place in Modern History*, tr. D. Scott (New Haven, 1957). A substantial chapter is devoted to Rohan.

picture of Protestantism as the seedbed of disloyalty and rebellion.

In reply to such serious charges, Protestant writers utilized two interrelated arguments, which are confusing (to a modern reader) because they seem mutually contradictory.

The first tactic was to deny emphatically – or at least to minimize – the religious character of the civil wars of the sixteenth century. Are we justified in suspecting that this attitude was the result of a conflation of the wars of religion with the uprisings of the seventeenth century, which had been largely an affair of the nobility and had ended in disaster? (Naturally, our authors did not divide their past into centuries; they viewed their own age as completely continuous with the preceding period.) In any case, the wars of religion were depicted as purely political, caused by the excessive ambitions of the Guise family. The Protestants had been faithful subjects who had rushed to the aid of their prince in danger, and contributed more than any other group to the preservation of the throne for the Bourbon dynasty. And there was many a clumsy reminder how ill they had been repaid for their loyalty by Henri IV and his descendants. To such arguments the Catholics were quick to retort that, if all this were true, then the Protestants had merely done their duty and were not thereby entitled to any special privileges.

At the same time, on the theoretical level, Huguenot authors took their stand on complete divine-right monarchy – a position which presented them with many a good occasion to castigate the Jesuits and the *Ligue*. In so doing, they assumed they were effectively employing the old debating technique of turning an adversary's arguments against himself. But it did not work, because, while the seventeenth-century Huguenots were proud to claim descent from their forefathers, nobody claimed to be descended from the *Ligue* – not even the "Company of the Holy Sacrament" and the "Spanish Party," who might have been viewed as the progeny of that ultra-Catholic organization.

Such was the first line of defense, which was tainted with quite a bit of sophistry. If it failed to convince, there was a second: admit that the motives of the wars were in part religious, but insofar as they were so, to consider them reprehensible (e.g., Amyraut[11]). A fundamental distinction, however, should be made.

To the extent that they were religiously motivated, the wars of the sixteenth century were blameworthy, but excusable – and Daillé

---

[11] *Apologie* (cited above, n. 8), Section II, pp. 38–82.

did his best to emphasize that they were part of a remote past[12] – on the grounds of the frightful persecutions which had so long been endured. True, it would have been better to cleave to the saintly example of non-resistance set by the early Christian martyrs. But, humanly speaking, the guilt involved in the use of force against persecutors was obliterated by their right of self-defense. And if religious motives were at work in granting victory to the house of Bourbon, *fœlix culpa.*

But as for the rebellions in the reign of Louis XIII, they were both criminal and inexcusable. At the same time, the Huguenot writers hasten to point out that only a small fraction of French Protestants took part in them. After all, there were Protestants in the royal army which laid siege to La Rochelle, and even in Languedoc there were people who violently disapproved of the revolts. Still, there was little excuse to be made for those few who had forgotten the rule of passive obedience.

This latter point of view is predominant in the texts which date from the First English Revolution. Huguenot authors did their best to mitigate the responsibility of the Presbyterians, to execrate the "monstrous" Independents, and make a desperate show of sympathy for the Anglican Church – a sympathy which the Anglican refugees, unfortunately, did not reciprocate.[13]

Clearly, these Huguenot answers to the recriminations of the Catholics were not very convincing. Try as they might, how could they allay the fears of the authorities – at first quite real, but later feigned? The "accident," if indeed it was an accident, could easily recur. There were always small disturbances in the Languedoc to ignite the tinder – in Nîmes, in Castres, in Privas, in Montauban. And the fact that Cromwell, without consulting them, had loudly proclaimed his protectorship over the Huguenots did much to hurt their cause. To be sure, for some years things went rather well for them. Mazarin was in such dire need of the English alliance against Spain that he could hardly withhold concessions from Cromwell. But how could the young Louis XIV ever forget the humiliation of such an insolent intervention in his own affairs? The years 1648–1656 were only a sham "golden

---

[12] Daillé, *Réplique,* II, chap. xv, p. 89.

[13] See my reports in *Annuaire de l'Ecole pratique des Hautes études, IVe Section* (1970–1971 *et seq.*). My lectures in Paris since that date have been concerned with the political doctrines of the Huguenots in France and their close interrelations with the vicissitudes, not only of French, but of European politics.

age" for French Protestantism. In fact they were pregnant with future retaliations.

Furthermore, this kind of argument, and in particular their immoderate praise of the Anglican hierarchy, tended to backfire. It induced the authorities to underrate the obstacles that lay in the way of bringing the Huguenot leaders back within the fold of the king's church. The famous conversion of Turenne in 1668, so obviously motivated by a revulsion for the English Revolution, tended to encourage and stimulate these false hopes.

Finally, in the last fifteen years before the Revocation, the Protestant-Catholic controversy was mostly a gallant rear-guard action on the part of the Huguenots. There were, however, some books like Pierre Bayle's *Critique générale* which tried – at last! – to verify the facts of these much debated questions before attempting to interpret them.[14] But more and more the royal government adopted the policy of the party of *dévots*. Ever since Henri IV, the "Grand Design" included the ideal of religious uniformity – an ideal which political theorists held to be of prime importance, and one in which France regretfully saw herself outdistanced by Spain. Now, finally, the conditions of this ideal were to be realized – peace and internal order. The fate of French Protestantism was sealed. The Revocation of the Edict of Nantes was sugar-coated with pious religious propaganda, but in the last analysis it was a political move, dictated by *raison d'Etat*. The exact date of the Revocation is of little importance. For years, both the letter and the spirit of the Edict had been eroded by a long series of judgments handed down by the Council; and by 1685 the Reformed Church of France was in desperate straits indeed.

Long before, the increasing intervals between national synods – 1631, 1637, 1644, 1659, after which they ceased totally – had had a deadening effect on the presbytero-synodal organization of the reformed churches in France. True, they still regarded themselves as "churches," and this is very significant. From a sociologist's point of view, however, their sectarian nature is now obvious. Provincial synods continued to meet, but their decisions were always subject to suspension by appealing them to a future (illusory) national synod. Thus deprived of legal sanction, these decisions of provincial synods were merely advisory, or at most hortatory. Quite early, the govern-

[14] The first edition of Bayle's book was published in July 1682 in Amsterdam, although under a fanciful imprint. It was such a best-seller that a second, enlarged edition appeared in November of the same year.

ment had adopted the deliberate policy of weakening the vital links among the provincial synods, and as these ties disappeared, the individual churches became increasingly isolated, financially as well as politically. Now, one by one, they fell, ideological victims of a century of divine-right kingship. In 1663, *pasteur* Du Bosc referred to Louis XIV as "our sole source of strength, our safeguard, our fortress, and our place of refuge."[15] Clearly, the Huguenots had become wholly enveloped by, and dependent upon his Majesty's pleasure.

In a book published in 1685 (although composed a few years earlier), the exiled *pasteur* Elie Merlat had no solution to offer to his brethren but that of martyrdom.[16] And, in this, we find we have come full circle back to the first half of the sixteenth century.

How can we account for the way in which *la controverse historique récente* was handled? Were our Huguenot authors guilty of blundering? Did they mistakenly attempt the impossible when they tried to minimize the role of religious motives in their sixteenth-century rebellions? Were they wrong to emphasize so strongly their passive obedience to their king?

First of all, we must bear in mind that, although we are the children of our parents, we are even more the children of our century. Our Huguenot authors were men of the seventeenth century! And we cannot emphasize too strongly that they were Frenchmen from north of the Loire. Quite naturally these leaders of French Protestantism tried to persuade their coreligionists to accept the values which they could not conceive as other than eternal, because based on Scripture. To deplore their commitment to divine right is meaningless. And to regard this commitment as the origin of the weakness of the French Huguenot movement is to mistake the effect for the cause. (The example of the English Presbyterians shows clearly the importance of the socio-political context.)

Next it should be remembered that, like everything in *ancien-régime* France, and perhaps even more so in this case, French Protestantism manifested a sharp geographical division. North of the Loire, technology and commerce were relatively advanced. The Languedoc, however, was quite backward and highly particularistic. While the northerners were inclined to theorize and engage in verbal controversy,

---

[15] *Les estoiles du ciel de l'Eglise: ou sermon sur ces paroles ... de l'Apocalypse, Chap. I, v. 16,* "*Et il avoit en sa main droite sept Estoiles,*" *Prononcé à Quevilly* [Rouen] *le dimanche 10 de juin 1663,* p. 64.

[16] *Traité du pouvoir absolu des souverains pour servir d'instruction, de consolation et d'apologie aux eglises reformées de France qui sont affligées* (Cologne [in fact, the Netherlands], 1685).

the southerners were men of action. Deceived by their demographic density in certain areas, ill-informed and incapable of considering the problem on the national level, these Frenchmen from south of the Loire often acted as if they had no idea how small a minority they constituted. On a trip through the Languedoc in 1660, Turenne was shocked to find people nostalgic for the "wars of the duc de Rohan."[17] The southerners did not write books. Instead they engaged in scattered, minor uprisings. Even when these local riots were legally justifiable – and that was not always the case – they did a great deal of harm to the cause of French Protestantism.

It would be misleading to consider the division between North and South as one of moderates versus zealots, or the bourgeoisie versus the peasantry. There was a substantial middle class in the Languedoc, and not all southerners were extremists. The cleavage was one in theologico-political attitudes, not in intensity of religious faith. The flocks of Huguenots who went into exile after 1685 included moderates as well as zealots.

What was catastrophic was that the moderation expressed by the northerners was belied by the riots in the South. As Tilenus wrote to the Assembly at La Rochelle in 1621, "When you have lit the fires of disorder down there, the smoke will travel far, and more than three hundred thousand people *on this side of the river Loire* will weep bitterly for it."[18] (The number, of course, was a gross exaggeration.) On the other hand, whatever tendency the southern revolts might have had as a deterrent against the crown's harsh anti-Protestant policy was nullified by the emphatic protests of the northern writers that the Huguenots were entirely submissive to an absolute king. The northerners disavowed the wars of religion, whereas the southerners kept them fitfully alive by means of small, local riots. The two attitudes canceled each other out.

Lastly, while the government could pursue a long-term policy, the Protestant writers, caught in the web of circumstances, were obliged to adopt a series of short-term expedients. Increasingly, over the course of the seventeenth century, arguments drawn from the wars of religion became deadly weapons in the hands of Catholic writers; and Huguenots found themselves trying to consign to oblivion the memory of events so distasteful to the classical mind. In the short run, this tactic

---

[17] See Turenne's letter to his wife, 6 April 1660, in Turenne, *Collection des lettres et mémoires,* ed. P.-H. de Grimoard (2 vols.; Paris, 1782), I, 329.

[18] *Advertissement à l'Assemblée de La Rochelle par Abraham Elintus, docteur en médecine* [anagram of Tilenus], p. 24.

seemed to work; but in the end the Huguenots were thereby ill-prepared for the Revocation, To be sure, when the test came the Protestants were not found wanting. They always knew that their primary allegiance was to God, not man. Ideologically, however, they were in total confusion.

It was not until the *Refuge* in the years after 1685, when the transition was made from paleo- to neo-Protestantism (to employ the nomenclature of Troeltsch[19]), that a brilliant conception of religious toleration was fully elaborated by Pierre Bayle. Such an idea, if it had been developed earlier, might have lifted the Edict of Nantes out of the realm of political expediency – where it properly belongs – and established it upon the sound doctrinal foundation which too many older historians mistakenly assumed to have been its motivation. And parallel to the development of a theory of religious toleration, the resistance of the Huguenots to forced conversions was demonstrating – once again, too late! – the fallacy of the absolutist political axioms which had dictated the Revocation.

[19] *Die Bedeutung des Protestantismus für die Erstehung der modernen Welt* (1st ed., 1911; also in English translation).

CONCLUSION: ST. BARTHOLOMEW AND HISTORICAL PERSPECTIVE

by

THEODORE K. RABB

At a certain level the Massacre of St. Bartholomew remains unique, *sui generis*. It haunts historical consciousness as the epitome of the cold viciousness of religious excess, the mindless destroyer of Ramus as well as Coligny. But at another level it blends into those agonizingly slow and deliberate processes that are the historian's main concern. The particular process – the establishment of absolutism in France, the Counter Reformation, the change in the forms of violence, the development of Paris – may vary, but each offers the historian the means to achieve the perspective that is his stock in trade, the long view that alone can lessen the horror of St. Bartholomew.

Labrousse's remarkable achievement is to have opened so many perspectives with such effortless erudition. Looking back from the late seventeenth century, she raises a seemingly simple question: why did French Protestants not make better use of the Massacre in their propaganda? In suggesting an answer, or set of answers, to that question, she gives us insights not only into religious polemic but also into the political and social changes brought about by the growth of monarchical power in Bourbon France.

Extending her reach, she also reveals the influence of international affairs on domestic events, and we can see that under Louis XIV the Huguenots gained far less comfort from their English brethren than had the Puritans from the French in earlier decades. Most significant of all, Labrousse indicates the connections between the Massacre and its more genteel descendant of a century later, the Revocation of the Edict of Nantes. For it was not until 1685 that the story finally ended; and if many Europeans were appalled by the almost anachronistic Catholic resurgence of the 1680s, in England as well as in France (though the elector of Brandenburg, as usual, managed to find cause for rejoicing in the misfortunes of others), we ourselves will not understand the phenomenon unless we realize that in these crises, unlike those of the 1570s or 1580s, religion was almost completely engulfed by politics. That is why recollections of the Massacre had so little effect and why the duc de Rohan, leader of the rebels in the reign of Louis XIII, seemed more of a villain than the duc de Guise – a quite amazing turnabout if one thinks for a moment of the pitiful ineffectiveness of Rohan and the devastating power of the Guises.[1]

Even in more recent times the importance of the Massacre itself has taken second place – in this case to the question of causes and culprits. The issue of premeditation thus figures prominently in the present volume – in the essays by Koenigsberger and Sutherland, and in the account by Sassetti. This is, of course, a classic historian's problem, largely because the documents may never allow a definitive answer. Yet logic alone would suggest that Catherine must have prepared contingency plans in case the attempted assassination of Coligny on 22 August failed, and that these were likely to have been much more severe so as to compensate for earlier mistakes. To exonerate her from complicity in the radical measures of 24 August, therefore – the "elimination," to use Sutherland's word – is to defy belief. Yet that is what the centuries-old argument has been about, mainly, so it seems, because it is an easily defined puzzle, not unduly burdened by the subtleties and complexities that bedevil the consequences and implications of the Massacre. It is for that reason that Labrousse's contribution is so original and so welcome.

What she is exploring is that difficult and complex area between image and reality. Using what may seem the driest body of sources in the world, religious polemics, she is able to bring to life the fatal miscalculations of those seventeenth-century Huguenots who held on to the significance of the Edict of Nantes while missing the significance of the fall of La Rochelle in 1628. They did not realize that wars of religion, as they had been known through the 1620s, had been radically transformed by mid-century. Absolutism and its allies, princely and aristocratic power, were sweeping Europe in the 1650s, 1660s and 1670s as the last of those clashes loosely described as the general crisis of the seventeenth century died away. In the new atmosphere the execution of one man, Charles I, could seem as terrible, and probably more threatening, than the murder of thousands of heretics during a

---

[1] The power of the Guises is most brilliantly evoked by Garrett Mattingly in chaps. xviii, xix and xxxii of *The Armada* (Boston, 1959). Contrast the treatment of Rohan's efforts in Steven Lowenstein, "Resistance to Absolutism: Huguenot Organization in Languedoc, 1621–1622" (unpubl. Ph. D. dissertation, Princeton, 1972).

few bloody days in Paris seventy-seven years before. And only five years after that execution a Puritan soldier, Oliver Cromwell, could blithely negotiate a treaty of friendship with a cardinal of the Roman Church, Jules Mazarin.

What had changed? And why did some people see what had happened while others did not? The answers to such questions take us far beyond the confines of this book. But the questions are certainly implicit in many of the papers published here; consequently it might be worth outlining a few tendencies that would have to be explored before justice could be done to these weighty issues.

The decisive decades, in my view, were the 1620s and 1630s. Despite the political conflicts that one can find embedded in the bewildering warfare of these years, warfare that engulfed every Christian state in Europe, whether Protestant, Catholic or Orthodox, and stretched from the Gulf of Finland to Quebec, the essential motive was still religious. Regardless of the complicated ambitions of individual leaders – and nobody will ever reach a definitive assessment of the aims of a Richelieu or an Olivares, a Wallenstein, a Buckingham, or a Gustavus Adolphus – at the time all the upheavals were regarded as variations on the theme of confessional struggle. An international Catholic diplomatic network, centered in Brussels, fought single-mindedly against a parallel Protestant network centered in Amsterdam. The tentacles of the one extended from Portugal to Poland, of the other from Scotland to Hungary. Moreover, as Hapsburg successes mounted, Protestants of all shades genuinely began to fear that they might be swept off the map of Europe. Camerarius' famous "Spanish Chancellery," revealing the perfidy of Catholic diplomacy, had an even more powerful impact than such recent sensations as the Pentagon Papers;[2] and Wallenstein was the proof of the pudding. It is not surprising, therefore, that the incredible avalanche of Gustavus' successes should have been regarded, quite literally, as a miracle for the Protestants. And when the New Model Army destroyed the faithless King Charles a dozen years later, its victories could be described, most seriously, as the judgment of God.

Yet by the 1640s the sense of threat faded. The heroic times had been the 1620s and 1630s. A great peril for Protestantism had arisen (of which the siege of La Rochelle was a part) but divine favor had enabled the godly to survive and indeed to counterattack. Thus gradually the two sides moved toward the stalemate that was finally

---

[2] See F. H. Schubert, *Ludwig Camerarius (1573-1651). Eine Biographie* (Kallmünz, 1955).